PRINCIPLES OF SOCIOLOGY

PRINCIPLES OF
SOCIOLOGY

ALFRED McCLUNG LEE, Editor

INTRODUCTION BY SAMUEL SMITH

CO-AUTHORS

HERBERT BLUMER
University of Chicago

A. B. HOLLINGSHEAD
Yale University

EVERETT C. HUGHES
University of Chicago

NORMAN D. HUMPHREY
Late of Wayne University

ALFRED McCLUNG LEE
Brooklyn College

EDWARD B. REUTER
Late of Fisk University

BARNES & NOBLE, INC. • NEW YORK

PUBLISHERS   ·   BOOKSELLERS   ·   SINCE 1873

To the Memory of

ROBERT EZRA PARK

Great Teacher and Inspiring Stimulator
of Sociological Research

©

SECOND EDITION, 1946, REVISED, 1951
Reprinted with minor revisions, 1957

COPYRIGHT, 1939, 1946, 1951, 1955
BY BARNES & NOBLE, INC.

L. C. Catalogue Card Number: 55–11750

PRINTED IN THE UNITED STATES OF AMERICA

PREFACE

To be helpful to students of sociology in a wide range of colleges and universities, an outline of sociological principles must grow in many hands and in terms of many points of view. Under the editorship of the late Professor Robert E. Park of the University of Chicago, the first edition of this outline had the benefit of such a broad conception in his inspiration and guidance and in the work of the volume's co-authors. It has been the purpose of the present editor and co-authors to carry on this conception in the revised edition. In doing so, each co-author has had sole responsibility for his own section. The first edition of this outline had not included a section on the "Socialization of the Individual," and the editor has therefore contributed one on this subject to the present edition.

The following related titles in the Barnes & Noble College Outline Series and the companion series of Everyday Handbooks will be helpful to the student of sociology: *Readings in Sociology; Man and Society; General Anthropology; Readings in General Psychology; History of Economic Thought; Labor Problems and Trade Unionism; Dictionary of Economics; Political Science; New Dictionary of American Politics.*

The co-authors and Dr. Samuel Smith, Editor of Barnes & Noble, Inc., have generously given of their time and effort, and their co-operation is appreciated. In addition, Dr. Elizabeth Briant Lee has contributed numerous helpful criticisms and necessary encouragement.

A. McC. L.

INTRODUCTION

By SAMUEL SMITH

The Subject Matter of Sociology. Sociology, the scientific study of society, deals with group behavior, the relationships among men, and the factors entering into and ensuing from these relationships. Wherever an individual is in communication with others, wherever direct or indirect contacts occur, such an individual is an interacting member of the social order. The elements, patterns, and consequences of behavior antecedent or subsequent to this interaction among individuals and between groups is the chief subject matter of sociology.

Sociology is concerned with historical events insofar as they shed light upon the continuous process of group life, this is to say upon the forces common to many events in the history of the group. The history of an institution, for example, may be studied to disclose the factors, principles, and types of group relationships involved in the genesis and career of such institutions.

The total environment as well as the nature of man is considered insofar as it influences the experiences shared by human beings and the progress of their group life. During group life, more or less clearly defined forms, ways, standards, mechanisms, problems, and group characteristics develop. All these factors affect the relations among men and constitute major aspects of sociological analysis.

Sociology as a Science. Science is a systematic search for the facts about the world. Sociology reveals many facts about human beings and their social environment. Problems common to many situations are defined. Data related to these problems are assembled, recorded, classified, and organized. Theories to explain observed phenomena are constructed. Observation, experience, analysis, and experimentation are utilized to test the accuracy of theories. In other words, sociology emphasizes the same quest for the truth about the universe and the same scientific method of inquiry that are characteristic of the other sciences. This field of knowledge deals with events from a sociological point of view, just as other sciences do from a biological point of view, a psychological point of view, etc. The fact of scientific validity is established by the scientific procedures and results of sociological research.

The sociologist studies the structures and processes of social life as a whole, and in this respect uses a somewhat different approach from that of the other social sciences. From economics, he takes many principles and facts that help to clarify sociological problems—facts about the mechanisms, production, and distribution of wealth. From psychology, he secures important data concerning human behavior, motives, stimuli, responses, and growth. From biology and related natural sciences, he obtains fundamental contributions such as the laws of heredity, descriptions of the physiological processes of animal life, and the like. In other words, for its purposes and in dealing with its characteristic subject matter, sociology makes liberal use of information supplied by numerous other fields of knowledge.

DIVISIONS OF SOCIOLOGY

Sociology may be divided into certain broad subdivisions such as the following:

Social Problems, or what is sometimes called Social Politics, seeks to diagnose and deal in a practical way with current social problems. It has been accorded first place in the series of divisions of this outline because the ordinary man becomes aware when he considers these problems in collective existence that he must reckon with a society. Social Problems, therefore, constitutes the natural introduction to more detailed and systematic studies of the typical social situations in which such problems arise.

Human Ecology is concerned with man in the physical, as distinguished from the cultural or institutional environment. The ecological order grows up as a result of competition and the coincident co-operation which inevitably arise among individuals and peoples living together in a common habitat. Ecology looks at society from the point of view of population, its growth and decline, its dispersion and settlement. From this point of view society appears primarily as a biological rather than a civic or moral order.

Race and Culture looks at society as the ethnologist sees it, that is as an association of individuals and peoples each having a common language and possessing at the same time, as a result of intermarriage and interbreeding, certain distinguishing racial characteristics. These racial characteristics become important as human association and civilization expand since, under these conditions, they are likely to become the basis for national, class, or caste distinctions, and as such enter into the organization and structure of society.

Collective Behavior is concerned with the rise of new societies and new social units, insofar as they are formed in the efforts of societies and social groups to act collectively. Collective behavior studies social movements and the tentative organizations by which they carry on before they have become fully institutionalized. Most social movements tend in the long run to terminate in institutions.

Social Institutions have been regarded by some as the only proper subject of a sociological science. A sociology so conceived tends to be identified with social anthropology or ethnology. Ethnology seeks to study institutions historically while sociology studies them comparatively.

Socialization of the Individual relates the person to society. It shows what society does to the individual and what the person can do with society. Man is portrayed as the creature, carrier, creator, and manipulator of culture.

It should be noted that the divisions included in this classification of subject matter are not independent of each other, but are interdependent and overlapping.

PRACTICAL VALUES OF SOCIOLOGY

For the Individual. Knowledge improves understanding and increases the power of action. Adequate comprehension of sociological processes is essential for those who wish to adjust their intelligence and abilities most effectively to the world of man and nature. This science should substantially assist the individual to understand himself, his resources and limitations, his potentialities and his role in society.

As Community Resources. Like the individual, the community of individuals has need of a constantly increasing fund of shared knowledge concerning the life-processes of its members and groups. Individuals, singly or in association, are enabled to draw upon this common fund of facts. With accelerated progress,

in recent years, in the scientific contributions of our "science of
society," the facts of sociology provide a storehouse of resources
for the extension of knowledge and the advancement of civilization.

As Applied to Social Problems. Contemporary society is
beset by numerous maladjustments and crucial problems challenging the best powers of scientists and social idealists. Just as
the facts of chemistry and other natural sciences have proved
eminently useful to the art of medicine, so too we look to the
future in the hope and faith that men will use the contributions
of sociology for the solution of their common problems and the
betterment of society. These contributions have been made and
are constantly being augmented. The social scientist discloses
truths; society can use or misuse these truths as it sees fit. As a
scientist, the sociologist is loyal exclusively to the cause of factual
research. As a constituent member of the human community,
his interest and expectation are that the results of research will
be applied to the benefit of mankind.

Table of Contents

PART FIVE: INSTITUTIONS

BY EVERETT CHERRINGTON HUGHES

PART SIX: SOCIALIZATION OF THE INDIVIDUAL

BY ALFRED McCLUNG LEE

Tabulated Bibliography
of Standard Textbooks

This *College Outline* is keyed to standard textbooks in two ways:
1. If you are studying one of the following textbooks, consult the cross references here listed to find which pages of the *Outline* summarize the appropriate chapter of your text. (Large Roman numerals refer to the textbook chapters, small Roman numerals and Arabic figures to the corresponding *Outline* pages.)
2. If you are using the *Outline* as your basis for study and need a fuller treatment of a topic, consult the pages of any of the standard textbooks as indicated in the Quick Reference Table on pp. xviii–xxiii.

Bierstedt, R., *The Social Order: An Introduction to Sociology*, 1957, Mc-Graw-Hill.
I (vii–x); II (55–59, 102–110); III (67–71, 121–166); IV (140–151); V (121–166); VI (221–222, 290–295, 318–326); VII (256–266, 318–326); VIII (167–222, 267–282); IX (225–282); XI (299–317); XII (72–101, 110–118); XIII (42–54, 318–326); XIV (42–48, 127–139); XV (230–266, 337–341); XVI (102–117, 127–164).

Biesanz, J., and Biesanz, M., *Modern Society: An Introduction to Social Science*, 1954, Prentice-Hall.
I (vii–x); III–V (93–110, 140–164); VI (121–164); VII (79–118, 167–222); VIII (67–92); IX (102–118, 241–282); X (42–63, 318–322); XI (42–59, 162–163, 199–220); XII (285–341); XIII–XIV (299–317); XV–XVI (230–266); XVII (79–92); XXV (248–282, 337–341); XXVI (178–198, 256–266); XXVII (178–198).

Bogardus, E. S., *Sociology*, 4th ed., 1954, Macmillan.
I (178–198, 256–266, 285–298, 318–326); II (121–126, 140–151, 230–235); III (21–41, 233–234, 299–317); IV (14–20, 67–101, 248–255); V (49–54); VI (26, 248–255, 299–307); VII (23–26, 185–198); VIII (214–216, 235, 240–243); IX (42–48, 102–118, 127–139, 152–164); X (55–59); XI (60–63, 199–220, 236–247); XII (3–20, 55–63, 327–336); XIII (225–229, 267–281); XIV (333–341); XV (167–198, 221–222); XVI–XVII (vii–x, 337–341).

Broom, Leonard, and Selznick, Philip, *Sociology: A Text with Adapted Readings*, 1955, Row, Peterson & Co.
I (vii–x, 337–341); II (225–266); III (3–13, 121–164, 267–282); IV (285–308, 318–326); V (30–41, 267–282); VI (42–54, 256–266, 318–326); VII (236–266); VIII (167–222); IX (67–118); X (21–29, 299–317); XI (14–20, 79–118, 236–255); XII (42–48, 121–139, 152–164); XIII (49–54, 256–266); XIV (14–20, 55–63, 199–220); XV (21–29, 36–39, 331–333).

Cuber, J. F., *Sociology: A Synopsis of Principles*, 3rd ed., 1955, Appleton-Century-Crofts.
I–III (vii–x); IV (140–151); V (121–126, 152–164); VI (127–139); VII (140–151, 267–282); VIII (256–266, 285–298); IX (6–8, 147–151, 236–247); X–XII (256–266, 285–298); XIII (267–282); XIV (327–336); XV (191–193); XVI (30–41); XVII (318–326); XVIII (167–198, 256–266); XIX (42–48, 121–139); XX (72–78, 102–118); XXI (67–101); XXII (79–101); XXIII (42–54); XXIV (225–266); XXV (299–317); XXVI

(49–59); XXVII (14–20, 55–63); XXVIII (21–29, 256–266); XXIX (214–216, 235, 240–243); XXX (236–255); XXXI (3–13, 170–177, 199–220); XXXII (14–20, 60–63); XXXIII (152–164, 199–222); XXXIV (3–13, 337–341).

Davis, K., *Human Society*, 1949, Macmillan.
I (vii–x, 60–63); II (67–71); III (8–10, 140–151, 225–229, 267–281); IV (318–326); V (337–341); VI (140–151, 199–220); VII (299–307); VIII (285–298); IX (256–266); X (3–13, 30–41, 327–336); XI (167–177); XII (14–20, 67–101, 248–255); XIII (178–198); XIV (42–54, 111–118, 152–164); XV (21–29, 299–317); XVI (127–139, 230–235); XVII (49–54, 234–235); XVIII (202–214, 219, 234); XIX (214–216, 235); XX (67–71, 102–110); XXI (102–126, 152–164); XXII (3–13, 55–59, 109–220).

Freedman, R., and Associates, *Principles of Sociology: A Text with Readings*, rev. ed., 1956, Holt.
I–II (vii–x); III (167–197, 256–266); IV (121–164); V (318–336); VI (60–63, 72–92); VII (42–54, 167–197); VIII (14–20, 140–164, 337–341); IX (55–66, 102–120); X (72–120, 248–255); XI (79–110, 267–282, 299–307); XII (102–110, 167–198, 318–336); XIII (42–54, 102–118, 325); XIV (60–63, 236–281, 337–341).

Gillin, J. L., and Gillin, J. P., *Cultural Sociology: A Revised Edition of an Introduction to Sociology*, 1948, Macmillan.
I (vii–x); II (167–169); III (121–126, 285–298); IV (67–71, 121–126, 285–298); V (72–78, 102–118); VI–VII (140–151); VIII (170–177); IX (256–266, 299–307); X (42–48, 127–139, 152–164); XI (79–101, 167–198); XII (49–54, 127–139, 178–198); XIII (225–235); XIV (308–317); XV (299–307); XVI (49–54, 248–255); XVII (248–266); XVIII (55–59, 202–214, 219, 234); XIX (214–216, 235, 242–243); XX (236–247); XXI (199–220); XXII (236–247); XXIII (199–220); XXIV (236–247); XXV (55–59); XXVI (256–266); XXVII (318–326); XXVIII (267–281); XXIX (3–20, 327–336); XXX–XXXI (21–41); XXXII (60–63, 221–222, 337–341).

Gittler, J. B., *Social Dynamics: Principles and Cases in Introductory Sociology*, 1952, McGraw-Hill.
I (vii–x, 318–326); II (21–41, 256–266, 285–341); III A (167–169); III B 170–177); III C (299–317); III D (170–177); III E (178–198); III F (178–198); IV A (14–20, 248, 255); IV B (72–78); IV C (67–118); IV D 49–54); V (127–139, 152–164, 267–282); VI A (121–126); VI B (127–139); VI C–D (140–164); VI E (49–54); VI F (148–151); VI G (327–336); VI H (199–220); VI I (152–164); VII A (3–41); VII B (42–48, 121–139).

Green, A. W., *Sociology: An Analysis of Life in Modern Society*, 2nd ed., 1956, McGraw-Hill.
I (vii–x); II (67–71); III (221–222, 285–298, 318–326); IV (167–198); V–VI (121–144); VII (21–29, 285–341); VIII (285–298); IX (318–336); X (72–78); XI (42–54); XII (102–118); XIII (42–48); XIV–XV (67–118); XVI–XVII (230–282); XVIII–XIX (299–317); XX (308–317); XXI–XXII (9–10, 214–216, 243); XXV (30–31, 149–151, 236–247); XXVI (199–220).

Haas, F. J., *Man and Society*, 1952, Appleton-Century-Crofts.
I (67–71, 121–139, 152–164); II (285–298, 337–341); III (3–20, 256–282, 337–341); IV (42–48, 225–235, 256–282, 318–326, 337–341); V (60–63, 256–282); VI (225–235, 299–307); VII (308–326); VIII (21–41, 72–92, 199–220, 230–235); IX (49–54, 72–92, 225–229); X (49–54); XI (49–54); XII (49–54, 93–101, 199–220); XIII (49–54, 236–247); XIV (49–54); XV–XVI (18–19, 60–62); XVII (60–63, 248–255); XVIII (55–59); XIX 55–59); XX (55–59).

Landis, P. H., *Man in Environment: An Introduction to Sociology*, 1949, Crowell Co.
I (vii–x); II (286–290); III (290–295); IV (290–297); V (121–126); VI 67–71); VII (167–169); VIII (170–177); IX (72–78); X (49–54); XI (42–48); XII (318–326); XIII (327–336); XIV (299–317); XV (230–233); XVI (55–59, 234); XVII (235); XVIII (49–54, 234–235); XIX (14–41); XX (337–341); XXI (49–54); XXII (55–57, 320–321); XXIII 60–63, 111–118); XXIV–XXV (267–281); XXVI (127–139); XXVII (140–151); XXVIII (102–110); XXIX (152–164, 178–198, 256–266); XXX 79–101); XXXI (199–222, 236–247); XXXII (3–20); XXXIII (60–63).

Lee, A. M., *Readings in Sociology* (College Outline Series), 1951, Barnes & Noble.
Introd. (vii–x); I (vii–x); II (49–54); III (14–20); IV–VII (3–13, 337–341); VIII (285–298); IX (67–71, 178–198); X (170–177); XI (199–220); XII (140–151, 285–298, 318–326); XIII (140–151, 256–266, 299–307, 318–326); XIV (21–29, 140–151, 256–282); XV (30–41, 299–307); XVI (21–41, 327–336); XVII (327–336); XVIII (79–92, 111–118); XIX (102–118); XX (93–110); XXI (72–78); XXII (121–139); XXIII (121–139); XXIV (152–164); XXV–XXVIII (42–48, 152–164); XXIX (49–54, 79–92); XXX (49–54); XXXI (49–54); XXXII (167–169, 221–222); XXXIII (199–220); XXXIV (199–220); XXXV (55–59); XXXVI–XXXVIII (178–198, 267–282); XXXIX (337–341); XL (225–229); XLI (230–235); XLII (236–247); XLIII (49–54); XLIV (248–255); XLV (267–282); XLVI (267–282); XLVII–XLIX (337–341); L (60–63).

Lundberg, G. A., and Associates, *Sociology*, 1954, Harper.
I–III (vii–x, 337–341); IV (72–78, 102–118, 152–164); V (67–71, 79–118); VI (121–126, 140–151, 225–235, 267–282); VII (285–307); VIII (256–266, 318–326); IX (42–54, 121–139); X (30–41, 327–336); XI (170–177); XII (167–222); XIII (185–198, 275–282); XIV (21–41, 299–317); XV (214–216, 235, 240–243); XVI (14–20, 49–54); XVII (14–20, 55–63); XVIII (3–13, 140–151, 236–247, 337–341).

MacIver, R. M., and Page, C. H., *Society: An Introductory Analysis*, 1949, Rinehart.
I–II (140–151); III (140–151, 256–266, 285–298, 318–326); IV (21–29, 67–71, 121–126, 285–298); V (72–78, 285–298); VI (79–92, 285–298); VII (30–41, 140–151, 267–281, 327–336); VIII–IX (140–151); X (167–169, 248–255); XI (21–29, 248–255, 299–317); XII (14–20, 248–255); XIII (93–110); XIV (49–54); XV (42–48, 111–118, 127–139, 152–164); XVI (170–198); XVII (178–198, 225–229); XVIII (55–59, 202–214, 219, 234); XIX (49–54, 234–235); XX (214–216, 235, 242–243); XXI (267–281); XXII (236–247); XXIII (199–220, 236–247); XXIV (72–78); XXV (236–247); XXVI (3–13, 337–341); XXVII (236–247); XXVIII (60–63, 102–110); XXIX (221–222, 337–341).

Martindale, Don, and Monachesi, E. D., *Elements of Sociology*, 1951, Harper.
I (140–151); II (vii–x, 338–341); III (vii–viii, x, 140–141, 145–146, 286, 288, 328, 335, 338); IV (122–125); V (127–139, 152–164); VI (285–307, 318–326); VII (vii–x); VIII (3–13, 67–71, 167–169, 225–229, 285–298); IX (127–139); X (285–307); XI (256–266); XII (256–266, 318–326); XIII–XIV (318–341); XV (199–220, 225–255); XVI (21–41, 299–317); XVII (55–63, 230–235); XVIII (230–235); XIX (49–54, 60–63); XX (42–54, 72–101, 267–281); XXI–XXII (102–118, 167–222, 236–247); XXIII (3–20); XXIV (60–63, 337–341).

Merrill, F. E., and Eldredge, H. W., *Society and Culture: An Introduction to Sociology*, 1957, Prentice-Hall.
I (vii–x); II (256–266, 337–342); III (230–235); IV (170–198, 230–235); V (167–169, 221–222, 327–335); VI (140–151); VIII (285–298, 299–306); IX (318–326); X (327–341); XI (72–78); XII (127–139); XIII (42–48); XIV (49–54); XV (108–109, 112–118); XVI (225–282); XVII (299–307); XVIII (60–63, 267–282); XIX (84–91, 241–242); XX (67–

101); XXI (108–118, 199–202); XXII (167–222); XXIII (72–78, 193–195, 279–280; XXIV (199–222, 256–266); XXV (3–78).

Murray, R. W., *Introductory Sociology*, 2nd ed., 1946, Appelton-Century-Crofts.
I (vii–x); II (337–341); III–IV (285–298); V (121–126); VI (42–48, 111–118, 127–139); VII (140–151, 236–247); VIII–X (152–164); XI (225–235); XII (285–298); XIII (256–266, 318–326); XIV–XV (327–336); XVI (167–169); XVII (55–59, 170–177); XVIII (49–54, 178–220); XIX (60–63, 221–222, 267–281); XX (67–71); XXI (72–78, 102–118); XXII (79–101, 248–255); XXIII (49–54, 234–235); XXIV (55–59, 202–214, 219, 234); XXV (230–235); XXVI (214–216, 235, 242–243); XXVII (209–317); XXVIII (3–20); XXIX (21–41); XXX (30–41).

Murray, R. W., *Sociology for a Democratic Society*, 1950, Appleton-Century-Crofts.
I (299–317); II (285–298); III (121–139); IV (42–54); V (140–151); VI (236–247); VII (152–164); VIII–IX (285–298); X (167–198, 256–266); XI (21–41, 327–336); XII (67–78); XIII (79–92); XIV (93–118); XV (167–198); XVI (111–118); XVII (42–59); XVIII (199–222, 267–281); XIX (225–255); XX (230–235); XXI (3–20, 60–63, 327–336); XXII (337–341).

Ogburn, W. F., and Nimkoff, M. F., *Sociology*, 2nd ed., 1950, Houghton Mifflin.
I (vii–x); II (121–126); III (140–151); IV (127–139, 152–164); V (127–139); VI (167–177); VII (178–198); VIII (49–54); IX (170–177); X (170–177, 221–222); XI (285–298); XII (299–307); XIII (256–266, 299–307, 318–326); XIV (21–41, 327–336); XV (67–71, 79–101); XVI (72–78, 102–118); XVII (72–78); XVIII (225–229); XIX (49–54, 248–255); XX (248–255); XXI (55–59); XXII (214–216, 235, 242–243); XXIII (30–41, 299–317); XXIV (230–235); XXV (140–151, 230–235); XXVI (199–220, 236–247); XXVII (3–48); XXVIII (60–63, 199–220, 267–281, 337–341).

Rose, A. M., *Sociology: The Study of Human Relations*, 1956, Knopf.
I (vii–x); II (256–266, 299–307); III (267–282); IV (67–71, 318–326); V (225–255); VI (285–317); VII (230–235); VIII (42–54, 100–110); IX (170–222); X (140–151, 318–326); XI (102–120, 199–220); XII (72–78, 102–110); XIII (93–101, 140–151); XIV (60–66, 199–220, 248–284); XV (3–54, 327–336); XVI (49–59, 167–198); XVII (55–59, 152–166).

Sutherland, R. L., Woodward, J. L., and Maxwell, M. A., *Introductory Sociology*, 5th ed., 1956, Lippincott.
I (vii–x); II (140–151, 225–235); III (142–144); IV (299–317); V (214–216); VI (285–298); VII (299–307, 318–326); VIII (256–266, 316–326); IX–X (327–336); XI–XII (167–198, 285–341); XIII (178–224); XIV (178–198); XV (42–59, 121–164); XVI (42–48, 121–164); XVII (67–118); XVIII (140–151, 236–255); XIX–XXII (225–255, 299–317); XXIV–XXV (49–59, 102–151); XXVI–XXVII (14–20, 55–63, 102–118); XXVIII (14–20, 199–220, 267–282).

Timasheff, N. S., and Facey, P. W., *Sociology: An Introduction to Sociological Analysis*, 1949, Bruce.
I (vii–x); II (21–29, 299–317); III (256–266, 285–298); IV (14–20, 42–54, 111–139, 248–255); V (225–235); VI (79–101, 225–235); VII (167–177); VIII (285–298, 318–326); IX (170–177); X (55–59, 178–198); XI (3–13, 30–41, 267–281, 327–336); XII (140–164, 221–222); XIII (72–78, 102–110, 236–247); XIV (60–63, 199–220, 337–341).

Weinberg, M., and Shabat, O. E., *Society and Man*, 1956, Prentice-Hall.
I (vii–x); II (170–198, 337–341); III (285–297, 318–336); IV (140–151); V (21–41, 299–306); VI (93–101, 225–255); VII (49–54, 102–118); VIII (102–110, 149–163); XI (42–48, 337–341); XIII (21–41, 299–317); XIV (72–92); XV (21–41, 327–336); XVI (42–48); XVII–XVIII (102–110); XXI (60–63); XXII (60–63; 236–247); XXVII (55–59).

Williams, R. M., Jr., *American Society: A Sociological Interpretation*, 1951, Knopf.
I (vii–x); II (14–20, 67–71); III (3–13, 121–126, 140–151, 337–341); IV (21–29, 299–326); V (42–54, 121–139, 318–326); VI (225–235); VII (55–59, 225–235); VIII (225–235); IX (225–235); X (30–41, 236–247, 256–266); XI (267–298); XII (72–110, 167–169, 248–255); XIII (152–164, 170–198); XIV (199–222, 327–336).

Wilson, L., and Kolb, W. L., *Sociological Analysis: An Introductory Text and Case Book*, 1949, Harcourt, Brace.
I (vii–x); II (140–151); III (236–247); IV (152–164); V (285–298); VI (256–266, 299–317); VII (318–326); VIII (21–41, 327–336); IX (248–255); X (167–198); XI (79–92, 267–281); XII (67–78, 93–110); XIII (49–54); XIV (42–48, 111–139, 152–164); XV (55–59, 202–214, 219, 225–235); XVI (49–54, 248–255); XVII (299–317); XVIII (248–255); XIX (214–216, 235, 242–243); XX (199–220); XXI (42–59, 199–220); XXII (3–20); XXIII (60–63, 121–139, 199–222, 337–341).

Young, K., *Sociology: A Study of Society and Culture*, 2nd ed., 1949, American Book.
I (vii–x); II (127–139, 167–169); III (121–126, 140–151); IV (121–126); V–VI (3–20, 170–177); VII (285–298); VIII (318–326); IX (225–235, 256–266, 318–326); X (67–71); XI (42–48, 111–118, 152–164); XII (72–78); XIII (67–71, 102–110); XIV (79–92); XV (30–41, 79–101); XVI (79–92, 102–110); XVII (308–317); XVIII (21–29, 299–317); XIX (248–255); XX (214–216, 235, 242–243); XXI (230–235); XXII (49–54, 248–255); XXIII (55–59, 202–214, 219, 234); XXIV (55–59); XXV–XXVI (299–326); XXVII (327–336); XXVIII (49–54); XXIX (178–198, 267–281); XXX (199–220); XXXI (60–63); XXXII (60–63, 337–341).

QUICK REFERENCE TABLE TO STANDARD TEXTBOOKS

All numbers refer to chapters.

Chapter in This Book	Topic	(1) Bierstedt	(2) Biesanz & Biesanz	(3) Bogardus	(4) Broom & Selznick	(5) Cuber	(6) Davis	(7) Freedman & Assoc.	(8) Gillin & Gillin	(9) Gittler
Introd.	Subject Matter of Sociology	1	1	16, 17	1	1–3	1, 2	1	1, 2	1
I	The Character of Social Problems	5, 6, 16	4, 11	12	3	31, 34	10, 22	14	29	7A
II	Community Conditioning of Social Problems	15, 16	8, 12, 17	4	11	16, 17	12	5, 11, 14	29	4A, 7A
III	Children and Youth	11	12, 14	3	10	11, 28	15	7, 11	30, 31	2, 7A
III	Adults and the Aged	10	14	3	2, 10, 15	16	10	11	30, 31	2, 7A
V	Caste and Minority Problems	13, 14	10, 11	9	6, 12	19, 23	14	12, 13	10	7B
VI	Social Class Problems	13	10, 21	5	6, 13	23, 26	14	7	12	4D, 6E
VII	War and Revolution	2	32	12	14	27	22		25	
VIII	Social Planning	9, 15, 16	7, 25, 30	11, 12	14	27, 32	1	14	32	
IX	The Ecological Order	2, 3	8	4	9	20, 21	12, 20	4	4	4C
X	Aggregation	3, 12	7, 8	4	9	20	12	10	5	4B, 4C
XI	Ecological Organization	12	8, 9	4, 10	9, 11	21, 22	12	11, 13	11	4C
XII	Dominance		8	4, 10	9, 11	22	12	10	11	4C
XIII	Migration and Mobility	2, 16	9	9	9, 11	20	20, 21	12, 13	5	4C
XIV	Succession	3, 5	4, 9	9	9, 11	20	14, 21	13	5	4C
XV	The Relations vetween Race and Culture	14	2, 11	2	3, 12	5, 6, 19	21	4	3, 4	6A, 7B

		(1)	(2)	(3)	(4)	(5)	(6)	(7)	(8)	(9)
XVI	Races and Culture Groups	13, 14	2, 11	9	3, 12	6, 19	14	4, 5	10, 12	5, 6B, 7B
XVII	Culture	4	3, 4, 5	2	3	4, 7, 9	3, 6	4	6, 7	1, 6C, 6D, 6F
XVIII	Race and Culture Contacts	14	4, 11	9	3, 12	6	14, 21	9	10	5, 6C, 6D, 6I
XIX	The Field of Collective Behavior	6	7, 12	15	8	18	11	5, 14	11	3A
XX	Elementary Collective Behavior	8	25	15	8	18, 31	11	5, 14	8, 11	3B, 3D
XXI	Elementary Collective Groupings	8, 16	26, 27	15	8	15, 18, 27	13	3	11, 12	3E, 3F
XXII	Social Movements	15, 16	7, 16, 21	11	8	31–33	6, 22	14	23	6H
XXIII	Conclusions Concerning Collective Behavior	6, 7	7, 12	15	8	32, 33	22		32	
XXIV	Institutions Defined	9, 15	5	13	2	24	3	5	13	
XXV	Institutions Classified	15	5, 13, 18	1, 3–8	2	24	16–19	3	14–19	
XXVI	Institutions in Process	9, 15, 16	4, 9, 18	11	2, 7, 11	30	19	12	20–25	
XXVII	Institutions and the Community	15	5, 9	4, 6	2, 7, 11	25–29	12	6	16–19	4A
XXVIII	Institutions and the Person	7, 15	12, 30	1, 3–8	2, 7, 13	8	9	5	9, 26, 27	2
XXIX	Social Control	6, 15	5, 12, 25, 26	13	3, 5	7, 13	3	6, 12	28	5
XXX	Individual and Environment	3, 6	12	1	4	8	8	4	3, 4	2
XXXI	Child and Family	11	14	3, 6	10	25	15	7, 11	9	2, 3C
XXXII	Courtship, Marriage, Divorce	10, 11	13, 14	3	10	25	7, 15	12	14	2
XXXIII	Roles	7	5, 7, 10, 12	1	4, 6	17	4	4, 6	26, 27	1C, 2
XXXIV	Deviants	6	12	12	15	14	10	5, 12	29	2, 6G
XXXV	The Person and Social Policy	15, 16	5, 26, 30	14, 17	1	34	5	14	32	2

See pages xiii-xvii for list of complete titles of books.

QUICK REFERENCE TABLE TO STANDARD TEXTBOOKS (continued)

All numbers refer to chapters.

Chapter in This Book	Topic	(10) Green	(11) Haas	(12) Landis	(13) Lee Readings	(14) Lundberg & Assoc.	(15) MacIver & Page	(16) Martindale & Monachesi	(17) Merrill & Eldredge	(18) Murray Introd.
Introd.	Subject Matter of Sociology $	1		1	Int., 1	1–3	Introd.	2, 3, 7	1	1, 2
I	The Character of Social Problems	25	3	32	4–7	18	26	8, 23	25	28
II	Community Conditioning of Social Problems	10, 26	3	19, 32	3	16, 17	12	23	25	28
III	Children and Youth	7	8	19	14, 16	14	4, 11	16	8, 17	14, 15, 29
IV	Adults and the Aged	19, 26	8	19	15, 16	10, 14	7	16	17	14, 15, 29, 30
V	Caste and Minority Problems	11–13	4	11	25–28	9	15	20	12, 13	6
VI	Social Class Problems	11–13	9–14	10, 18, 21	2, 29–31, 43	9	14	19, 20	14	18
VII	War and Revolution	17	18–20	16, 22	35	17	18	17		17
VIII	Social Planning	4, 26	5	23, 33	50	17	28	17, 19, 24	24, 25	19
IX	The Ecological Order	2	1	6	9	5	4	8	20	20
X	Aggregation	10	8, 9	9	21	4	5	20	11	21
XI	Ecological Organization	10, 14	8, 9	30	18, 29	5	6	20	20, 25	22
XII	Dominance	14	12	30	20	5	13	20	21	22
XIII	Migration and Mobility	10, 12, 14		28	19, 20	4	13, 28	21, 22	21	21
XIV	Succession	12		23	18, 19	4	15	21, 22	21, 25	6, 21
XV	The Relations between Race and Culture	6, 13	1	5	22, 23	6, 9	4	4	12	5

		(10)	(11)	(12)	(13)	(14)	(15)	(16)	(17)	(18)
XVI	Races and Culture Groups	11, 13	1	26	22, 23	9	15	5, 9	7, 12	6
XVII	Culture	5		27	12-14	6	1-3, 7-9	1, 3	6	7
XVIII	Race and Culture Contacts	6, 13	1	29	24	4	15	5	6, 7, 12	8-11
XIX	The Field of Collective Behavior	4		7	32	12	10	8, 21	2, 22	16
XX	Elementary Collective Behavior	4		8	10	11, 12	16	21	3, 23	17
XXI	Elementary Collective Groupings	3		29	9, 36-38	12, 13	16, 17	21	4, 23	18
XXII	Social Movements	26	8, 12	31	11, 33, 34	12	23	15, 21	24	18
XXIII	Conclusions Concerning Collective Behavior	25		31	32	12	29	21	22	19
XXIV	Institutions Defined	5, 6	4, 6, 9	PartIV:Int	40	6	17	8, 15	16, 17	11
XXV	Institutions Classified	16-18, 21	4, 6, 9	15-18	41	6, 14-17	18-21	15, 17, 18	16, 17	11, 23-27
XXVI	Institutions in Process	12, 19, 26	13	31	42	18	22-27	15, 21	2-4	7
XXVII	Institutions and the Community	11	17	15-18	44	14-17	10-12	15	18, 19	22
XXVIII	Institutions and the Person	7	3-5	29	13-14	8	3	11, 12	2, 8-10	13
XXIX	Social Control	3, 7	3-5	24, 25	45, 46	6	7	20	5, 22-25	19
XXX	Individual and Environment	2, 7	2	2-4	8, 12	7	3-6	3, 6, 8, 10	2, 5, 20	3, 4, 12
XXXI	Child and Family	7, 18, 19	6	14	13, 14	14	11	6, 10, 16	17	27
XXXII	Courtship, Marriage, Divorce	18, 20	7, 8	14	15	14	11	16	16	27
XXXIII	Roles	3, 7	4, 7	12, 22	12-14	8	3	6, 12-14	8, 9	13
XXXIV	Deviants	9		13	16, 17	10	7	13, 14	4, 5, 10	14, 15
XXXV	The Person and Social Policy	26	2-5	20	39, 47-49	1-3, 18	29	2, 3, 13, 14, 24	2, 8	

See pages xiii-xvii for list of complete titles of books.

QUICK REFERENCE TABLE TO STANDARD TEXTBOOKS (continued)

All numbers refer to chapters.

Chapter in This Book	Topic	(19) Murray Social.	(20) Ogburn & Nimkaff	(21) Rose	(22) Sutherland & Woodward	(23) Timasheff & Facey	(24) Weinberg & Shabat	(25) Williams	(25) Wilson	(27) Young
Introd.	Subject Matter of Sociology	22	1	1	1	1	1	1	1	1
I	The Character of Social Problems	21	27	15	12, 22, 26	11	1, 7, 8	3	3, 22	5, 6
II	Community Conditioning of Social Problems	21	27	2, 7, 14, 15	12, 27	4	12, 14	2	22	5, 6
III	Children and Youth	11	14, 27	3, 6, 15	7, 23	2, 3	5, 15	4	8	18
IV	Adults and the Aged	11	14, 23, 27	12	23	11	3, 5, 13	10	8	15
V	Caste and Minority Problems	4, 17	27	8, 15, 16	15, 16	4	2, 10, 16	5	14, 21	11
VI	Social Class Problems	4, 17	8, 19	8, 15	15, 26	4	7, 10, 11	5	13, 31	22, 28
VII	War and Revolution	16	21		28	10	27	7		24
VIII	Social Planning	21	28	7, 14, 16	22, 27, 28	14	6, 12, 21		23	31, 32
IX	The Ecological Order	12	15	12, 13	17			2	12	10, 13
X	Aggregation	12	16, 17	12	24	13	12, 14	12	12	12
XI	Ecological Organization	13	15	14	17	4, 6	17, 18, 20	12	11	14-16
XII	Dominance	14	15	11, 12, 13	15	4, 6		12	12	15
XIII	Migration and Mobility	14	16	8, 11, 12	24	13	8, 17, 18	12	12	13, 16
XIV	Succession	14, 16	16	11, 13	11, 12, 24, 25	4	8, 12		14	11
XV	The Relations between Race and Culture	3	2	2, 16, 17	4, 5, 16	4	4, 6, 11	3, 5	14, 23	3, 4

	(19)	(20)	(21)	(22)	(23)	(24)	(25)	(26)	(27)
XVI	Races and Culture Groups	3	4, 5	2, 17	4, 5	4	4, 6, 11, 16	5	14, 23	2
XVII	Culture	5	3, 25	2, 11	2, 3	12	4	3	2, 4	3-6
XVIII	Race and Culture Contacts	7	4	11, 17	11	12	6, 9	13	14	11
XIX	The Field of Collective Behavior	10, 15	6	4, 5	13	7	1, 12, 21	12	10	2
XX	Elementary Collective Behavior	10, 15	6, 9, 10	9, 10	11, 14	7, 9	3	13	10	5, 6
XXI	Elementary Collective Groupings	10, 15	7	9	14	10	3, 6	13	10	23, 29
XXII	Social Movements	18	26, 28	11	19, 27, 28	14	2, 9, 12, 20	14	20, 21, 23	30
XXIII	Conclusions Concerning Collective Behavior	18	10	3, 9	28	12	3, 4	14	23	
XXIV	Institutions Defined	19	18	5	19	5, 6	4, 6	6-9		
XXV	Institutions Classified	19, 20	24	6, 7	19-23	5, 6	6, 12, 13	6-9	15-19	17-24
XXVI	Institutions in Process	6, 19	26	5, 11	27, 28	13	4, 6, 8	10	3	30
XXVII	Institutions and the Community	19	19-23	7, 13, 14	18	4	14, 17, 18	12	9	19-23
XXVIII	Institutions and the Person	10	13	2, 3, 4, 17	7, 8, 13	2, 3	3, 5, 6	10	6	9
XXIX	Social Control	18	28	3	13, 28	11	2, 3, 13	11	11	29
XXX	Individual and Environment	2, 8, 9	11	4	6-8	2, 3, 8	3, 5	11	5	7
XXXI	Child and Family	1	12, 13	4, 6	7, 23	2	5, 13, 15	4	6, 17	18, 25, 26
XXXII	Courtship, Marriage, Divorce	1	23	6	23	2	13	4	6, 17	17, 28, 25, 26
XXXIII	Roles	10	13	3, 4	8	8	3, 5	4, 5	7	8, 9, 25, 26
XXXIV	Feviants	11, 21	14	2, 3, 15	10	11	5, 15	14	8	27
XXXV	The Person and Social Policy	22	28	2, 16, 17	8, 27, 28	14	10, 11	3	23	32

See pages xiii-xvii for list of complete titles of books.

Part One

Social Problems

By

NORMAN DAYMOND HUMPHREY
Late of Wayne University

PART ONE

SOCIAL PROBLEMS
By Norman Daymond Humphrey

TOPICS

CHAPTER ONE

THE CHARACTER
OF SOCIAL PROBLEMS

The Problems of a Dynamic Society. In a primitive local group or in a peasant village, perceptible social changes are rare. But in modern Western society, they are the order of the day, and they have been for the past four hundred years. Our moral order and its technological underpinnings have been in a condition of moving disequilibrium. The growth of industry, commerce, transportation, and communication, the changed ways of looking at and explaining the cosmos, have led to a disruption of the agriculturally conditioned moral order of a former day. These changes have also led to a redefinition of welfare and morality, and this redefinition has brought with it a concern for social problems and social planning.

PERSPECTIVES ON SOCIAL PROBLEMS

Frames of Reference. Social problems have been approached from a number of frames of reference and points of view. The man in the street tends to take what Charles H. Cooley called a "particularistic" explanatory viewpoint. The fallacy here is that, in terms of this frame of reference, all social problems are regarded as products of a single cause. The naïve biological determinist, for example, regards the victims of social problems as persons with inadequate heredity. Usually he thinks social problems would be solved by sterilization or by a lowered birthrate for this group. The geographic determinist, on the other hand, may regard climate as "the cause" of such a problem as poverty and, for that matter, of practically every other social problem.

Such particularistic explanations are readily shown to be inadequate when one enumerates the multiplicity of factors operative in producing any particular phenomenon that might be recognized as a social problem. All factors have to be accounted for before judgments of their relative significance can be made. But it would be equally erroneous to regard all factors as equally causal and dynamic in producing social problems. Sociologists have developed several frames of reference for purposes of encompassing and ordering the data of social problems. Historically these classifications have moved their bases more and more from the moral type of judgment over toward the relatively objective and scientific.

Types of Perspective. In general, sociologists and other social scientists believe that many social problems arise from differential rates of social or cultural change. Problems have also been regarded as accruing from a failure of culture to accord with and sanction impulses arising in the person. A group of sociological perspectives or frames of reference concerning social problems are discussed and assessed in this chapter. These are: social pathology; disorganization and reorganization; natural history of social problems; culture lag; and conflicting morals and mores.

SOCIAL PATHOLOGY

An early sociological approach to social problems utilized the analogy of society to an organism, and in this social problems naturally became the diseases of that organism. Society might lack a "central sensorium" according to Herbert Spencer, but it possessed pathologies. Actually the concept of pathology simply denoted that which was regarded as subject to condemnation and public disapproval. It became a name-calling term. As sociology passed beyond the analogic stage in its development, another conception, that of disorganization, arose.

DISORGANIZATION AND REORGANIZATION

The Concept of Disorganization gained acceptance after the publication of W. I. Thomas and Florian Znaniecki's *The Polish Peasant in Europe and America* in 1920. These authors indicated that personal disorganization in Polish immigrants apparently resulted from attitudes (tendencies to act) and values (things possessing meaning) becoming discordant. In a new environment, new impulses to act appeared, and the old definitions of objects and situations underwent change. Since changes occurred differentially, the life organization of the person also changed. Moreover, the old consensus among persons, or agreement in definitions of situations, altered, and sanctions governing their conduct also changed. Hence, social problems both personalized and community-oriented arose.

Uncritical Use of Concept. But as time went on, other sociologists utilized this conception more and more without critical consideration of its adequacy. It often came to be used more as a moral epithet than as a tool of analysis. Hence, prostitutes who might be well-integrated persons in terms of their own (albeit societally "immoral") scheme of values came to be regarded as "disorganized," because they varied in their behavior from accepted middle-class moral standards. Any similar community, avowedly integrated around vice or political collusion or economic crookedness, was given the same label.

Moreover, there was a frequent failure to recognize that disorganization and reorganization were simply the same ongoing process viewed from different positions. Disorganization of person or of culture never leads to complete chaos, but rather to another level of integration. The concept of disorganization as it usually has been employed, since it always points back to a stabilized integration, fails sufficiently to take into account the dynamic aspects of modern society. In an era of rapid change and a broadening division of labor, consensus among persons generally seems possible only in the most superficial areas of living, and among those persons in comparable positions. Hence to regard lack of agreement among all men as "disorganizing" and condemnatory, is to take a morally nostalgic position about modern life, its problems, and their solution.

NATURAL HISTORY OF SOCIAL PROBLEMS

Richard C. Fuller and Richard R. Myers, conscious of the inadequacies of the "disorganization" approach to social problems, developed a schema under which social problems were to be examined in the light of their natural history. Each social problem, from this viewpoint, goes through phases of (1) attention getting, in which people become aware or conscious of the problem, and (2) efforts to define the difficulty, which lead to (3) proposals for reform. These phases are followed by attempts at (4) organizing for reform. Once programs for reform are set in motion they are accompanied by problems of (5) administration of reform.

Such a schema throws analytical light on society's periodic efforts to cope with such problems as slums and prostitution, race tensions and war, but it does not relate social problems to basic social processes.

CULTURE LAG

Culture has long been regarded in the light of Edward Tylor's definition as the sum total of ways of doing things and the objects of human manufacture acquired by man as a member of society and transmitted from generation to generation. The term has often been regarded as synonymous with civilization, custom, the social heritage, and as often as not with society itself. W. G. Sumner, in his *Folkways* (1907), initiated a popular analysis of culture into folkways, mores, and institutions.

These conceptions frequently divide culture into material (concrete, tangible) and nonmaterial (idea, belief) segments. Change in culture and society focused attention on the relative vitality and acceleration of these two segments.

Culture Lag. By and large, sociologists following the publication of W. F. Ogburn's *Social Change* (1922) held that changes in material culture precede and outstrip changes in nonmaterial culture, and that this results in what he called "culture lag." Culture lag—the gap in adjustment between material and nonmaterial culture—persisted until such time as nonmaterial culture was adjusted to changes in material culture. Social problems, from this viewpoint, marked the hiatus of integration between correlated parts of culture. Institutional lag, a conception derived by Charles H. Cooley and his students, is an early variant of general culture lag, for the adaptation of one institution in either conception fails to keep pace with that of others and with changed human needs.

Difficulties in Application. Despite the immediate appeal of the concept of culture lag and its frequent explanatory application, its rigorous application has been found difficult. Questions such as the following have been asked: Is such a phenomenon as science material or nonmaterial? Does material culture always change before nonmaterial culture? Many mechanical inventions, for example, are obviously tangible and material, yet is it not true that the ideas which precede invention are immaterial? On a more generic scale questions have been asked as to the relative vitality of larger, systematic aspects of culture. Which, for example, came first and laid the grounds for the other, Protestantism or capitalism? Did capitalism develop out of a changing technology which required an ethico-religious sanction such as Protestantism, or did the Protestant ethic give rise to a type of economic behavior? Such questions receive perspective if culture is re-examined and reclassified.

Reconsideration of Culture. Adapting the position of Robert Redfield, culture may be defined as a body of shared symbols to which conventionalized understandings are accorded. Such a conception of culture aids in resolving the problem presented by the fact that one has difficulty placing science, for example, in the material-nonmaterial dichotomy. The shared symbols of culture each stand for objects, concepts, ideas, images—all of varying degrees of concreteness and abstractness, of simplicity and clarity. And value is determined through judgments based upon subjecting these symbols and their referents to several criteria of truth and worth-whileness. But all elements of culture are variants or combinations of four types of symbol-referent-criterion combinations, and these are important in understanding culture changes, culture integration, and what we have called social problems and their resolution.

Material Culture consists of at least two types of shared symbols. The first involves a symbol or concept which accords with its object or referent. Such a symbol-referent combination is illustrated by the concept "automobile" and the tangible object. Here the adequacy or "fit" of concept and referent is determined by how it works, i.e., by its degree of corroboration in the experience of others. A second type of material culture consists of an ill-defined, nebulous conception represented by a tangible object. This type is illustrated by a "good luck" piece, which is useful only so long as one believes in it.

Nonmaterial Culture is also made up of at least two types of concept-referent combinations. The concept of the gene and that of the ghost illustrate these types. Genes are subject to empiric corroboration, and ghosts, in most societies, are not.

Reconsideration of Culture Lag. Culture lag is thus seen not to be a twofold matter but a manifold one. In addition to these possible aspects of culture are its variations among the groups, classes, and castes of a society, a matter taken up below. Even in general, however, "material" culture change does not always precede "nonmaterial" changes. Nor is the "lag" eliminated simply by allowing the backward elements to "catch up." Reintegration may mean the injection of largely fresh elements at points in the ongoing process. These are evidenced by the French, American, and Russian revolutions, by the overthrow of "instinct" psychology, by the development of private and public health programs following the discovery of the microbe theory of disease.

Culture lag makes social problems understandable, then, if the lag is regarded as existing between (1) technological development (material culture) and the growth of empirically grounded ideas, scientifically verifiable by others (nonmaterial culture), and (2) ideas, objects, and practices (material and nonmaterial culture) which persist and are maintained only by faith in their worth-whileness. Dogmas or faiths which have virtue simply because they are old, often do not fit changed material conditions of living and their very persistence provides the framework for social problems.

CONFLICTING MORALS AND MORES [1]

Morals are ethical ideas for conduct regarded as conducive to societal welfare. They are the symbols and concepts of important values shared, more or less superficially, by the members of a society. They are societal typifications of what the man-as-he-should-be in a society presumably should do.

Mores are those standardized group, class, and caste practices or ways of behaving which have developed in a culture and to which a judgment of group welfare and necessity has become attached. Where mores have been long established and are subject to little or only gradual change, as they are in primitive or peasant communities, any inconsistencies between the mores of various groups and between mores and morals have been rationalized, justified, or obscured by social distance. Under such circumstances, too, the person has few sanctioned alternatives for behavior and thus largely conforms to his group's mores without any complications or anxieties of choice.

1 See A. M. Lee, "Levels of Culture as Levels of Social Generalization," *American Sociological Review* (1945), 10:485–495; also his chaps. 30, 33, 34 in part 6 of this outline below.

Morals and Mores in a Changing Society. With the differential rates of change one finds in any culture adjusting to new life-conditions, however, group mores arise that differ from societal morals. Conflicts also develop between mores governing different situations, when efforts are made to carry mores from one group to another. Thus mores applicable to business conduct may bring censure when they are carried over into church affairs.

Social Problems in the Resulting Conflict. Social problems, then, can issue from an actual, although rarely recognized and readily rationalized, conflict between societal precepts (morals) and "right" group conduct (mores) or between the mores of two or more groups. And a morals-mores conflict is accentuated by the fact that moral precepts are often reinforced by legal statutes and adjudications as well as religious dogmas.

Moral Deviation and Statistical Deviation. Moral deviation has no necessary relationship to statistical deviation. Practices which are widespread, such as masturbation, may be condemned as immoral in a society and hence regarded as social problems, or they may be ignored entirely. Murder, on the other hand, a much rarer event, is of universal concern. Thus, many practices which from a statistical standpoint are sufficiently prevalent to be called "normal," are regarded from a moral viewpoint as "abnormal." Premarital and extramarital sexual activities, dissatisfaction in marriage, occupational maladjustment, psychoneurotic personality traits, insecurity in employment, ill-health, poverty, and many other phenomena are probably much more within the statistical range of "normality" than is commonly supposed.

The Dominant Moral Group. In every society, one or more groups, classes, or castes take a greater interest in upholding the societal moral order than do the others. In our society, for example, the most widespread, articulate, and persistent group in terms of upholding societal morals consists of middle-class persons, and as a result their mores and special aspirations tend to color the morals of our whole society. Middle-class preachers, teachers, journalists, and governmental spokesmen advocate the values commonly prescribed in the Protestant version of the Judeo-Christian tradition, centered about private property rights and with vague conceptions of humanitarianism, personal liberties, and human betterment. As W. Lloyd Warner and Leo

Srole note, in *The Social Systems of American Ethnic Groups* (1945), the middle class and other significant segments of the American people "cling to the virtues of the 'protestant ethic,' despite the fact that many are members of other religions."

Because of the dominating position of owners, financiers, managers, and political enterprisers in our economy and especially with respect to the employment of the middle class, these upper-class persons are assured that the morals advocated by the middle class will be interpreted as being protective of upper-class mores, statuses, and interests. In effect, such upper-class persons exercise a degree of permissiveness with respect to society's moral precepts.

Middle-Class Conscience and Social Problems. The content of the moral conscience of the middle class varies from section to section in the United States and from time to time, but there is enough uniformity and agreement among its membership concerning "right" and "wrong," "good" and "bad," that its ideology serves as the chief frame of reference for the identification of social problems. The intellectually dominant middle class, dominated in turn but less directly and understandingly by upper-class persons, identifies what it regards as a social problem from its own moral viewpoint.

Social Problems and the Social Scientist. Once identified as a social problem, it is the social scientist who describes it, indicates its extent, and analyzes the correlations and causes and effects of the problem. The social scientist can also indicate the instrumentalities through which a problem may be alleviated or solved, granted that an actual solution is regarded as desirable by the dominant societal moral groups. Problem solutions (e.g., prohibition as a solution for the liquor problem), however, are frequently experimental and often bring unlooked-for consequences which unbalance other institutional arrangements regarded as desirable by a dominant group. There is considerable controversy among sociologists as to whether it is incumbent upon the social scientist, any more than upon the natural scientist, to work as scientist for the solution of a group's or a class's social problems. Regardless of this discussion, or of the controversy as to whether sociology should be a normative (value judgmental) or an objective (nonvaluative) science, it is generally agreed by sociologists that it is within the province of sociology to study social values and the actions men take with reference to them.

The Nature of Social Problems. Social problems, as the foregoing indicates, are predicated upon the existence of a dominant moral order (set forth in moral precepts) and of subordinate moral orders (formulated in terms of the mores of groups, classes, and castes). When a dominant or subordinate moral order is thought to be threatened or is in actual process of disruption, sufficient numbers of persons become aware of it to identify and define the chief problems, and they then usually organize action programs to prevent or ease the processes of change of which the problems are symptomatic. Because persons may take on contradictory membership roles in dissimilar groups, they may uphold contradictory values simultaneously without conscious conflict. That which constitutes the common denominator of social problems is the actual or anticipated disruption of a set of values shared by a group. The victims of social problems and persons who have internalized social problems find themselves in situations and act in terms of values (morals, mores) decried by other groups and especially by the one or more which are dominant in a moral order.

Interrelatedness of Social Problems. One social problem merges into another. The interrelatedness of social problems is illustrated by the slums of great cities. Slums are characterized by overcrowded housing, poverty, high delinquency and criminality rates, prostitution, broken homes, and the like. Overcrowding in housing is correlated with high infectious disease rates. Thus the existence of one problem makes probable the presence of others. This does not mean, however, that one problem may not exist without another. It simply means that situations make for greater or less probabilities of incidence of problems. The gaps or distances between mores and morals, between human needs, practices, and their morally sanctioned forms of satisfaction occur more in some areas and among some classes than they do among others.

SOCIOLOGY, SOCIAL WORK, AND PUBLIC RELATIONS

Sociology and Social Problems. Social problems are studied by virtually all of the social sciences. Thus economists and psychiatrists are interested, as are sociologists, in phases of unemployment, mental abnormality, dissatisfaction in marriage, and the like. But historically sociology has fallen heir to the study of social problems as such, and sociology is often regarded as the discipline which is peculiarly adapted to this study.

Actually sociology is aimed at the relatively objective description and analysis of the recurrent uniformities in social reality, much as physics, chemistry, and astronomy are concerned with the uniformities of physical reality. It is in the areas of discord and disharmony of function, however, that the processes and problems of social reality are brought to conscious attention, in much the same fashion that human physiological and anatomical processes are brought to awareness in instances of ill-health.

Two fields of study and practice attempt to alleviate or solve social problems. These are social work and public relations management.

Social Work stresses the individual (case work) and the group (group work) approaches to social problems, with some increasing emphasis upon the institutional or social organizational approach. It shares its area with medicine, psychiatry, public health, public administration, and a number of other not very clearly distinguishable efforts at social amelioration. Social work, while its main body of content may be regarded as one of the arts of the application of sociological principles, derives principles from other arts and sciences. It is usually regarded by social workers themselves as a body of techniques rather than as an academic discipline.[1]

Public Relations Management deals chiefly with problems of the relationships of organizations with their publics. Originally utilized exclusively by business leaders as a systematic body of knowledge and technique, it has more recently been adapted to the needs of educational, social work, and ameliorative social pressure organizations. It constitutes an application of what is known concerning public opinion and sentiment, social psychology, and social organization to the aspirations of organized enterprises. It shares its area with publicity, public administration, business management, community organization, and a number of other types of activity.

---

1 See N. D. Humphrey, "The Concept of Culture in Social Case Work," *Sociology and Social Research* (1941), 26:53–60.

SELECTED READINGS

Barnes, Harry E., and O. M. Ruedi. *The American Way of Life*. 2nd ed. New York: Prentice-Hall, 1950.

Brown, Lawrence G. *Social Pathology*. New York: F. S. Crofts & Co., 1942. Chap. 1.

Crowther, J. G. *The Social Relations of Science*. New York: Macmillan Co., 1941.

Cuber, J. F., and R. A. Harper. *Problems of American Society*. New York: Henry Holt & Co., 1948. Chap. 1.

Elliott, Mabel A., and Francis E. Merrill. *Social Disorganization*. 3rd ed. New York: Harper & Bros., 1950. Chaps. 1, 2, 15, 22.

Faris, Robert E. L. *Social Disorganization*. New York: Ronald Press, 1948.

Friedrich, Carl J. *The New Image of the Common Man*. Boston: Beacon Press, 1950.

Fuller, Richard C., and R. R. Myers. "Some Aspects of a Theory of Social Problems," *American Sociological Review* (1941), 6:24–32.

Herman, Abbott. *An Approach to Social Problems*. Boston: Ginn & Co., 1949.

Holley, William C., Ellen Winston, and T. J. Woofter, Jr. *The Plantation South, 1934–37*. Washington: W.P.A. Division of Social Research; Government Printing Office, 1937.

Klein, Philip, and M. C. Burnette. "Social Work," *Encyclopaedia of the Social Sciences* (1934), 14:165–187.

Landis, P. H., and J. T. Landis. *Social Living*. Boston: Ginn & Co., 1949.

Lee, Alfred M. "Public Relations as Institutional Psychiatry," *Psychiatry* (1943), 6:271–276.

Lee, Alfred M., and Elizabeth Briant Lee. *Social Problems in America*. New York: Henry Holt & Co., 1949. Chaps. 1–3.

Mannheim, Karl. *Man and Society in an Age of Reconstruction*. New York: Harcourt, Brace & Co., 1940.

Merrill, Francis E., and others. *Social Problems*. New York: A. A. Knopf, 1950. Chaps. 1–4.

Mowrer, Ernest R. *Disorganization: Personal and Social*. Philadelphia: J. B. Lippincott Co., 1942. Chaps. 2, 5.

Nordskog, J. E., and others, eds. *Analyzing Social Problems*. New York: Dryden Press, 1950.

Odum, Howard W. *American Social Problems*. Rev. ed. New York: Henry Holt & Co., 1945.

Ogburn, W. F. *Social Change*. Rev. ed. New York: Viking Press, 1950.

Phelps, Harold A. *Contemporary Social Problems*. 3rd ed. New York: Prentice-Hall, 1947.

Queen, S. A., and J. R. Gruener. *Social Pathology*. New York: T. Y. Crowell Co., 1940. Chaps. 1–3.

Stroup, Herbert H. *Social Work*. New York: American Book Co., 1948.

Young, Kimball. *Personality and Problems of Adjustment*. New York: F. S. Crofts & Co., 1940. Chaps. 7, 30.

CHAPTER TWO

COMMUNITY CONDITIONING
OF SOCIAL PROBLEMS

Personal and Mass Aspects of Social Problems. Social problems may be viewed as mass phenomena subject to statistical
analysis and depiction, or they may be visualized in their directly
human proportions, in terms of selected human types. The vic-
tim of a social problem possesses attributes in common with
others in his group or class. Social problems which manifest
themselves in highly individualized forms find their settings in
community conditions making for problems. Unemployment,
racial tension, or theft is a social problem, but there is also the
highly personalized problem of the unemployed individual, the
persecuted Negro, or the thief. Some of the more important
community factors that condition social problems are examined
in this chapter.

Ecology of Social Problems. Social problems have loci of
greater or less intensity in social space and time which are functional consequences of social competition. Thus so-called
"natural" or unplanned areas develop in communities. In such
natural areas certain phenomena are found in greater numbers or
intensity than in others. Some homogeneity of types of activity,
in other words, exists in such areas.[1] If one maps the incidence
and determines the rates of such problem phenomena as prostitution, lower-class criminality, juvenile delinquency, illegitimacy,
insanity, and suicide, one finds characteristic urban distributions
of these problems. Identical distributions do not obtain for each
problem studied, and some forms, as for example manic-depressive
psychoses, will exhibit spatial configurations at variance with
many other phenomena of mental derangement.

---

[1] See A. B. Hollingshead's chaps. 9–14, part 2 of this outline below for a treatment of human
ecology.

The question arises as to whether the relationship of the division of labor and the land and its institutions produces a greater intensity of certain problems in one place than in another, or whether persons with comparable problems tend to congregate in certain areas. Ecological organization and distribution are the results of both environmental and cultural forces. Distribution studies, statistical indexes, and correlations between elements all simply provide a framework and propose problems for further sociological analysis.

NATURAL RESOURCES AND WASTE

The Situation in the United States. Insofar as the wealth of a nation equals the energy sources it commands multiplied by the technology it utilizes, the United States is the wealthiest country in the world. Its plane or actual mode of living, however inadequate, viewed from ideal standards, evidences that fact. But despite gains in technology and in fuel efficiency the United States is rapidly depleting its resources through ruthless and wasteful exploitation.

Present levels of exploitation, according to H. E. Barnes, have resulted in the waste of seven-elevenths of our timber, two-fifths of our fertile soil, one-third of our coal, and five-sixths of our oil. The depletion of American forests, the impoverishment and erosion of arable land, the inefficient exploitation of mineral resources, the waste of natural gas, the lack of control over water, its pollution and our failure adequately to utilize its energy resources, all point to increasing future problems of maintaining our plane of living.

Consciousness of the Problem. Since inefficient exploitation and waste of natural resources have usually been profitable to the dominant moral group in the community, problem consciousness in this area has been largely limited to the specialist. Such dramatic events, however, as the midwestern dust bowl of 1937, with its attendant westward migration of onetime farmers and townsmen, aided in bringing these problems to public discussion and activity. Yet, despite such efforts as the Tennessee Valley Authority, flood control, and Congressional acts concerning migratory water fowl, little has been done to control waste except where natural resources have been threatened with direct depletion. Just what will be the consequences of the tremendous drains of World War II have not been determined as yet. Perhaps the coincident discovery of ways of releasing atomic power will more than offset such drains.

POPULATION DISLOCATIONS

Rate of Population Increase. Discussions of population problems have both academic and social problematic aspects. The general decline in the rate of population increase in western Europe and the United States has resulted in forecasts of population stagnation after 1980. A stationary condition also points to problems accruing from an older and more conservative population, and from an economy which will be less dynamic and more subject to restrictions. There is growing popular awareness of class and geographic differentials in the birth-rate. The poorer classes and sections of the country contribute disproportionately to the next generation. This has led to questions of population quality, with the frequent major assumption that if persons are submerged economically they possess inferior hereditary endowments. This is an unproven assumption, but it is obvious that those persons who can least afford to provide opportunities for offspring are members of the class which produces the greatest number for the next generation.

Medical and Public Health Problems concerning population center in accentuating the remarkable decrease in infant mortality and especially in maternal mortality through a spread of prenatal and postnatal care. Since those sections of the United States and of the world which are the least developed industrially contribute disproportionately to the world's population and consequently create pressures on the food supply and other resources of those areas, population pressure and a desire for migration toward areas of greater economic opportunity result.

Migrations. Opportunity and economic gains in a new area frequently are only temporary in character, and the economic adjustment of the migrant is fraught with difficulties. Migration, unidirectional movement from one locus of adjustment to another, tends to relate to vertical mobility, movement upward or downward in status position either within the ranks of a particular class or between classes. Both migration (horizontal mobility) and vertical mobility require adjustments to problems in terms of personality, housing, minority group status, language, and vocational skills.

Housing. About 60 per cent of urban homes in the United States in 1939 were "substandard" according to an extensive survey conducted by the Works Progress Administration. Those cities, such as Detroit, which experienced a tremendous influx of war workers during the period 1940–45 found the overcrowding which resulted a dynamic factor in the industrial and social unrest of that period. Overcrowding is a factor in virtually all of the so-called pathologies of urban living. Since private builders generally find low-cost housing unprofitable, and since, on the other hand, slum conditions may result in disproportionately profitable rentals, little is done on a private level to alleviate this condition. Public low-cost housing is an arena of conflict. Many of those with vested interests in the present situation regard public housing as socialism and therefore as undesirable.

Public Health and Housing. Specialists in public health are aware of correlations between poor housing, sanitation, and high rates of communicable disease. Slum clearance, the development of workers' suburbs, and city planning as a whole are partially predicated on the relationship between adequate housing, adequate health, and consequent economic gain.

MENTAL DISORDERS AND MENTAL HYGIENE

Amentia and Dementia Defined. Lack of mental capacity, amentia or feeble-mindedness, is to be distinguished from derangement of mental capacities. Dementia, or what in extreme cases is sometimes legally adjudged insanity, unlike feeble-mindedness is not due to lack of innate intelligence but to an innate or post-natal disturbance in the emotional life. Mental derangement differs in degree from so-called normality through psychoneuroses to the various psychoses. In psychoneurosis the individual has exaggerated responses to normal stimuli. The psychoses range from those with organic involvements, like cerebro-arterio-sclerosis and senile dementia to the functional psychoses lacking known organic causes such as manic-depressive, dementia praecox, schizophrenia, and paranoia.

Feeble-Mindedness as a Problem. The feeble-minded in the American population may number as many as ten million. A conservative estimate puts the definitely feeble-minded persons at a minimum of 1,250,000. Fewer than 100,000 of these defectives receive institutional care currently.

Mental Illness as a Problem. The mentally ill in the United States number around three million at any given time, of whom about one-half million are patients for mental disease "on the books" of reporting public and private hospitals and about 80 per cent of these are hospitalized. State hospitals for the deranged alone cost some $100,000,000 a year, not to mention the even more important nonmonetary costs.

Environmental Factors in Mental Disorders. Recent emphasis in diagnosis has been placed less exclusively on the organic basis of mental disorder and more on the warped conditioning and emotional malfunctioning of the person and the situational demands made upon him. There has been a recognition of such facts as those indicating that urban rates of mental disease are higher than rural rates, and that large cities have higher mental disease rates than do small cities.

Treatment of Mental Illnesses. Psychoanalysis is useful as a therapeutic technique only in dealing with psychoneurotics. Other forms of psychiatric practice, such as various types of "shock treatment," are employed in dealing with psychotics. As a result of the spread of the mental hygiene movement, much of the stigma formerly attached to mental derangement has been reduced. The movement has aided in developing clinics for diagnosis and early treatment of personality disorders.

PROBLEMS OF REFORM AND PLANNING

Political Aspects. Corrupt politics have long been regarded in themselves as a pressing social problem. The political machine with its boss, graft, business-political, and criminal-political interrelationships has received uniform public moral condemnation and almost equally as uniform private moretic acceptance in powerful social groups. Because of this fact, as Lincoln Steffens noted in his *Autobiography* (1931), reform administrations which are evidences of "problem consciousness" often succumb to the same influences which they had fought against and which had led voters to place them in power. Even if a reform administration should remain virtuous, powerful groups are likely to tire of literal interpretations of societal morality and turn themselves and their dependents to the task of turning out the "lily whites," of electing a "practical" government. Because of its generality, people have greater patience it seems with virtue in the symbol of our national government, embodied in the President, than in lesser officials, national, state, and local.

This political situation, only too hastily sketched here, has to be borne in mind by those who wish to work through governmental organizations in planning and reform activities.

Problems of Planning do not center so much in our ability to provide means to ends as in the difficulty of motivating people, especially those in positions of power, to regard certain ends as desirable of achievement. It is at this point that reformers find it wise to utilize the most modern techniques of public relations planning and management. Planning in the past took a limited form and was motivated primarily by the goal of private profit. State planning, such as is evidenced by the Tennessee Valley Authority, which aims at developing and preserving resources from the viewpoint of total community welfare, is usually opposed by vested interests whose profits will be interfered with, and by the lethargy and ignorance of the public.

Planning and Cultural Complexity. Planning tends to come to the fore as a solution to problems of crisis, and recedes into the hands of a few specialists in periods of peace and prosperity. But with the growing complexity of modern culture, and with the growing consciousness of total community welfare as a desirable end, the subject of planning not only on a national but also on an international level can be expected to receive greater discussion and activity in the future. As David E. Lilienthal, chairman of the Tennessee Valley Authority, has put it in *TVA—Democracy on the March* (1944), a great planning effort "is democracy's answer both to our own home-grown would-be dictators and foreign anti-democracy alike. . . . Not one goal, but a direction. Not one plan, once and for all, but *the conscious selection by the people of successive plans.*"

SELECTED READINGS

Anderson, Camilla M. *Emotional Hygiene: The Art of Understanding.* 4th ed., rev. Philadelphia: J. B. Lippincott Co., 1948.

Anderson, John F. *The Psychology of Development and Personal Adjustment.* New York: Henry Holt & Co., 1949.

Barnes, H. E. *Society in Transition.* New York: Prentice-Hall, 1946.

Bernard, Jessie. *American Community Behavior.* New York: Dryden Press, 1949.

Brown, Lawrence G. *Social Pathology.* New York: F. S. Crofts & Co., 1942. Chaps. 29, 30.

Burgess, J. S. "Study of Modern Social Movements as a Means for Clarifying the Process of Social Action," *Social Forces* (1944), 22:269–275.

Carr-Saunders, A. M. *World Population: Past Growth and Present Trends.* Oxford: Clarendon Press, 1936.

Clarke, Helen I. *Social Legislation.* New York: D. Appleton-Century Co., 1940.

Colcord, Joanna C. *Your Community.* Rev. ed. New York: Russell Sage Foundation, 1947.

Cuber, J. F., and R. A. Harper. *Problems of American Society.* New York: Henry Holt & Co., 1948.

Dickinson, R. E. "Social Basis of Physical Planning," *Sociological Research* (1942), 34:51–67, 165–182.

Elliott, Mabel A., and F. E. Merrill. *Social Disorganization.* 3rd ed. New York: Harper & Bros., 1950. Chap. 22.

Hollingshead, A. B. "Community Research," *American Sociological Review* (1948), 13:136–156.

Horney, Karen. *Neurosis and Human Growth.* New York: W. W. Norton & Co., 1950.

Laski, H. J. *Where Do We Go from Here?* New York: Viking Press, 1940.

Lee, Alfred M., and Elizabeth Briant Lee. *Social Problems in America.* New York: Henry Holt & Co., 1949. Chap. 6.

McKean, D. D. *The Boss: The Hague Machine in Action.* New York: Houghton Mifflin Co., 1940.

MacRae, R. H. "Organized Labor in Social Planning," *National Conference on Social Work* (1944), 219–227.

Merrill, Francis E. *Social Problems on the Home Front.* New York: Harper & Bros., 1948.

Morgenthau, H. J. "Limitations of Science and the Problem of Social Planning," *Ethics* (1944), 54:174–185.

Mowrer, Ernest R. *Disorganization: Personal and Social.* Philadelphia: J. B. Lippincott Co., 1942. Chap. 5.

Rosenquist, Carl. *Social Problems.* New York: Prentice-Hall, 1940.

Salter, J. T. *Boss Rule: Portraits in City Politics.* New York: Whittlesey House, 1935.

Salter, J. T., ed. *The American Politician.* Chapel Hill: Univ. of North Carolina Press, 1938.

Sigerist, H. E. *Medicine and Human Welfare.* New Haven: Yale Univ. Press, 1941.

Sorokin, P. A. *Social Philosophies of an Age of Crisis.* Boston: Beacon Press, 1950.

Stern, Bernhard J. *Society and Medical Progress.* Princeton: Princeton Univ. Press, 1941.

Thorpe, Louis P. *The Psychology of Mental Health.* New York: Ronald Press, 1950.

U. S. Dept. of Agriculture. *Achieving a Balanced Agriculture.* Washington: Government Printing Office, 1940.

Young, Kimball. *Personality and Problems of Adjustment.* New York: F. S. Crofts & Co., 1940.

CHAPTER THREE

CHILDREN AND YOUTH

The Problem of Children. Children have virtually no control over the physical and psychological environment into which they are born and in which they grow up. The child is a flexible instrument capable of being molded physically and psychologically into one of numerous patterns. And the child who finds himself in a situation in which emotional and economic insecurity exists has greater likelihood for insecurity in adulthood than one who grows up in a secure and healthy environment. Persons, of course, are not mechanical products of situations. What is important is the definition the child ascribes to a situation. But, nonetheless, viewed in terms of averages and actuarial likelihood, situations groove children into probable forms. There are probabilities then which determine what meanings persons will be likely to attach to situations, with attendant probable results. The child born out of wedlock in a poverty-stricken rural home has different probabilities for escaping from truancy at school and avoiding delinquency and child labor than the child of a middle-class urban family.

PROBLEM CHILDREN AND PROBLEM PARENTS

Problem Homes Produce Problem Children. Just as in a real sense there are no illegitimate children, only illegitimate parents, so there are no problem children. Problem children invariably are products of problem homes, that is, homes in which the socio-psychological relationships between parents, and between parents and children, are not conducive to morally defined normality. Problem children, by and large, are unhappy and insecure children. They are not only problems to children and adults around them, but to themselves. They manifest inner tensions by over-aggression in forms such as stealing, or by various regressive acts such as bed wetting.

21

What Is Problem Behavior in Children? Definitions of what constitutes problem behavior vary since they are morally defined. Those things, for example, which teachers may regard as problems, such as a child's boisterous conduct in the classroom, may simply be signs of healthy energy expenditures. The child who quietly daydreams, who is extremely conforming and never causes a disturbance in the classroom may actually be evidencing pre-psychotic symptoms. Workers in child-guidance clinics, school social workers, and pediatricians are aware of the gap between morally defined and scientifically diagnosed problem behavior. It is recognized in these areas, if not popularly, that work with children manifesting behavior problems invariably requires additional therapy with the parents of such children.

The "Illegitimate" Child—say, rather, the child of illegitimate parents—has fewer "chances in life" than other children from the moment of conception. More illegitimate pregnancies result in abortions and stillbirths, infant mortality rates are higher, and the chances for subsequent adjustment to life-conditions are generally less favorable. No word carries greater stigma than the word *bastard*. In his inborn capacities, of course, the illegitimate child is on the average not different from the legitimate. But his social adjustment, granted knowledge of his situation, usually is problem-laden. The illegitimate child is legally related only to his mother, and state laws are oriented toward the mother's assumption of responsibility for his support and upbringing. The mother may, of course, institutionalize him, or place him for adoption or for foster home care.

Foster Home Care is rapidly superseding institutional care both in the treatment of illegitimate children and in that of neglected and delinquent children. Frequently, however, a physically neglected child, who is loved, is better situated in his own home than the cared-for child in a foster home who is unloved. A child in a foster home has advantages for normality denied the child in the traditional "orphan asylum" or industrial school. Foster home placement usually involves thorough investigation of both the home and child preceding placement, and as far as possible a "matching" of child and foster home.

Adoption normally is an end product which takes place only after a trial foster home placement. Such placement is being increasingly employed by the more enlightened juvenile courts in the cases of really neglected children and even in that of juvenile offenders where the source of delinquency is the home environment.

CHILD LABOR AND EDUCATIONAL DISADVANTAGES

Educational Opportunities. Over the past fifty years, the provision of educational opportunities for all children has come to be recognized morally as a right of the child and a duty of the community. Actually, however, schools and educational advantages vary greatly with respect to the character and position of the community and of the child's family in the community. By and large those sections of the country with the least income have the smallest gross appropriations for education, so that in the areas with high reproductive rates where education is needed most it is provided least. The very fact that early in the selective service draft some 250,000 persons had been rejected on the grounds of illiteracy, and that the armed services themselves were forced to set up teaching programs for illiterates is proof of the present general inadequacy of American education. The differential provisions on the basis of race and region have led to attempts to provide federal funds for education to reduce regional and racial differentials, but these have received much opposition from elements in the country with vested interests in racism and child labor or control.

Today, in contrast with the situation fifty years ago, there is much more civic consciousness of the results of failure to provide adequately for the educational development of the child, in terms of his discernible capacities. Growing knowledge of individual differences in capacities and interests has led progressive school systems to differentiate types and levels of education. Thus, in large cities, special programs and schools are provided to best meet individual needs of the child.

Child Labor. Lack of educational opportunity is correlated with the extent of child labor. State and federal laws which contain sections prohibiting or controlling the labor of children in mines and manufacturing have, by and large, been tangential to the central problem. In an attempt to overcome adverse U. S. Supreme Court rulings on acts containing controls over child labor, a Child Labor Amendment to the federal Constitution was written and presented to the states for adoption. Today it is necessary for eight more states to act favorably on the proposal before it becomes part of the federal organic law. The Children's Bureau of the U. S. Department of Labor, and such laws as the Fair Labor Standards Act (Wages and Hours Act) have had an effect on industrial employment of children, but the vast bulk of harmful child labor continues in the street trades, including the work of newsboys, in agriculture, and in domestic service.

Child labor is regarded as harmful to the child in that it tends to hinder continuing education, to increase opportunities for delinquency, to result in a larger amount of industrial accidents and ill-health, to depress adult wages, and thus actually to lower family income.

PROBLEMS OF ADOLESCENTS

Defined. The problems of adolescents nucleate in the process of the termination of protected childhood and the assumption of adult responsibility. The adolescent is beset with physical and physiological changes which, because of their fundamental character and the cultural definitions placed on them, require a more intensely conscious adjustment than any which have occurred previously in the life of the individual. The storm and stress of adolescence, however, is much more cultural than physiological in character. The redefinitions of self and role that take place are simply hung onto the hook of physical transformation.

A Period of Crisis and Revolt. Adolescence is a period of crisis. Frequently, therefore, it is also a time of revolt, of a quest for experience and certainty, and a period of religious and political conversion. With the growing consciousness of self the roots of a philosophy of life develop and these orient the adolescent toward patterns to be followed in adulthood. The values of age-mates frequently conflict with those of parents, teachers, and other ancients. The cultural patterns and sanctions of one generation rarely, in an era of accelerated change, obtain for another. Hence, there is a conflict of generations. This conflict is particularly accentuated in the children of immigrants, but it is present in all families in some degree.

Occupational Preparation. One recurrent question posed by adults to the adolescent youth which the youth also raises as frequently to himself is that of what work he is going to do as an adult. It is a rare adolescent who knows the answer to the question in any satisfyingly final sense, and it is a rare adult who could have known it at a similar stage in his own development. Occupations in a stationary society are more or less foreordained by parental pursuits, but this is much less probable in a dynamic one. The modern American parent of lower- or middle-class status usually wants his child to aim at something "higher" than his own calling. The answer of youth is often one of confusion. An added element in this process is the failure on the part of parents to realize that living out their own frustrated wishes through their children usually leads to their own and their children's unhappiness.

Occupational Guidance. In some cities the problem of occupational preparation is approached by school testing and placement programs in which capacities and interests are considered. But more often than not a youth's occupational preparation is a matter of personal accident. Under such circumstances much adult occupational misplacement and consequent dissatisfaction occur. Adolescents may aim at goals beyond their capacities with consequent frustrations and probable aggressions in other areas of living.

Heterosexual Adjustment. Contrary to popular conceptions, sexual inclinations and activities do not suddenly erupt in the person at adolescence. Puberty, to be sure, provides the organism with the capacity for reproduction, and it heightens sexual desire and consciousness. Coincident with this development an increasing amount of autoeroticism or of repression and sublimation of sexual urges may take place. These phenomena, in turn, granted European and American codes of sexual morality, carry anxieties and guilt feelings or further sexual deviancy as their correlates.

Adolescent Sex Problems. But overt sexuality is only one problem of youth's heterosexual adjustment. What is much more consciously a personal problem is that centering in the adolescent's wish to be regarded as attractive and desirable by the opposite sex and by his fellows. The adolescent boy or girl is as much beset with problems of attractive clothing, sufficient money, freedom during hours of recreation, and the like, as he is with guilt feelings concerning masturbation or with "heedlessness." Most of these problems are "solved" either by outgrowing them or by sharing anxieties with age-mates. The problems are much more real for girls, whose parents and whose own phantasies run from the extremes of fallen womanhood to old maidhood, than for boys. Young men, given the double standard of American morality, are sometimes expected to "sow their wild oats." The tensions generated in areas of heterosexual adjustment may be partially released by participation in school, church, and other activities which result in status and which themselves tend to mediate the sources of tension. Personal counselling by trained and truly empathetic teachers, social workers, and ministers can go far toward alleviating these problems.

RECREATION

What Youth Wants. The personalized problems of recreation for youth again emphasize the gap between morals and mores. Youth desires outlets for libidinal and other energies which frequently run counter to those of parents and adults. Youth is a period of adventure and exploration, a time of quest for new experiences.

What Society Offers. In this age of rapid transportation and communication, recreation has become increasingly commercialized and secularized, and consequently youth tends to find its recreation in such areas. At the same time mechanical developments have changed recreation from providing active participation to one of passive and vicarious stimulation. Movies have tended to exaggerate the value of rapid movement and gay adventure. Automobiles have changed the conditions for courtship. Hence, while there is no intrinsic problem in the recreational activities of youth, the dominant moral group in the community is likely to regard drinking, dancing, "necking," and car driving as subject to disapproval, condemnation, and, when possible, control.

The Perennial "Revolt of Youth." The older generation, vaguely cognizant of its own previous foibles and sins of commission, tends to oppose comparable activity on the part of youth. The conflict between youth and age, the perennial "revolt of modern youth," finds no more central battleground than in the recreational activities of youth. This problem has in part been ameliorated in some places through supervised play in so-called teen-age canteens and in churches and schools which are opened for secularized social activities.

DELINQUENCY

Juvenile Crime Examined. Juvenile delinquency is largely a matter of community definition. The amount of delinquency as measured by juvenile court statistics is usually greater in the city than in the country, and in the blighted areas of the city it exceeds the record of the middle-class suburbs. Statistics, however, are related to what the community regards as delinquent conduct, and to what the policy of the police and juvenile court authorities refers as an offense. There is no single "cause" of delinquency. Even such a predisposing factor as a broken home has been shown by C. R. Shaw and H. D. McKay[1] not necessarily to be causally related to delinquent acts. Boys have much higher rates of delinquency than girls, although the factor of moral definition is seen when one notes that girls commit proportionately more sex offenses. The age when one ceases to be a delinquent and becomes a wayward minor or an adult criminal varies from state to state.

Types of Delinquents. Assuming delinquency to be a characterizable phenomenon, delinquents fall largely into two categories. One contains the youth who grows up in a neighborhood where in order to be regarded favorably by his age-mates involves his performance of delinquent acts. Here being a delinquent is being a statistically normal member of the juvenile community. The second type of delinquent is the emotionally unstable youngster who grows up in an area where delinquency is morally and statistically abnormal but who commits unwarrantable acts because his own conflicting inner drives require unsanctioned satisfactions. The solution to the first type of delinquent conduct is based upon the provision of sanctioned outlets into which energy going into delinquent acts can be channeled. The solution to the second type of delinquency is case work, guidance, or psychiatry which results in conscious and socially acceptable management of inner tensions.

In Wartime, Prosperity, and Depression. America became alarmed at the seeming rise of delinquency on a national scale during World War II. While sex delinquency by younger girls appeared actually to increase, the general rise in delinquency in war-boom areas, such as Detroit, was difficult to ascertain because the increase in population and its changed composition could not be determined accurately. Delinquency rates show some tendency to rise in periods of economic prosperity and fall in periods of depression.

---

[1] "Social Factors in Juvenile Delinquency," National Commission on Law Observance and Enforcement, *Report on the Causes of Crime* (Washington: Government Printing Office, 1931), no. 13, vol. 2, p. 266.

Ethnic and Racial Factors in Delinquency. Rates tend to be disproportionately high among slum dwellers, and since Negroes and children of foreign parentage tend to occupy such areas in cities, rates for these groups have in the past been high. Shaw and McKay have shown, however, that the same neighborhood areas, over a period of time and successively occupied by different nationality groups, tended to continue with much the same delinquency rates. It is unlikely, therefore, that ethnic background is a fundamental predisposing factor for delinquency, whereas socio-cultural community conditions do contain such factors.

SELECTED READINGS

Bettelheim, Bruno. *Love Is Not Enough: The Treatment of Emotionally Disturbed Children.* Glencoe, Ill.: Free Press, 1950.

Bossard, James H. S. *The Sociology of Child Development.* New York: Harper & Bros., 1948.

Brameld, Theodore. *Ends and Means in Education; a Midcentury Appraisal.* New York: Harper & Bros., 1950.

Bro, M. H. *When Children Ask.* Chicago: Willett, Clark, 1940.

Butler, G. D. *Introduction to Community Recreation.* 2nd ed. New York: McGraw-Hill Book Co., 1949.

Cantor, Nathaniel F. *Crime and Society.* New York: Henry Holt & Co., 1939.

Cole, Louella. *Psychology of Adolescence.* 3rd ed. New York: Rinehart & Co., 1948.

Coyle, Grace Longwell. *Group Work with American Youth.* New York: Harper & Bros., 1948.

Davis, Kingsley. "The Sociology of Parent-Youth Conflict," *American Sociological Review* (1940), 5:523–535.

Elliott, Mabel A., and F. E. Merrill. *Social Disorganization.* 3rd ed. New York: Harper & Bros., 1950.

Folsom, Joseph K. *Youth, Family, and Education.* Washington, D. C.: American Council on Education, 1941.

Friedlander, Kate. *The Psycho-analytical Approach to Juvenile Delinquency.* New York: International Universities Press, 1947.

Gillette, J. M., and J. M. Reinhardt. *Problems of a Changing Social Order.* New York: American Book Co., 1942. Chaps. 23, 24.

Havighurst, R. J., and H. Taba. *Adolescent Character and Personality.* New York: John Wiley & Sons, 1949.

Healy, William, and Augusta F. Bronner. *Delinquents and Criminals, Their Making and Unmaking.* New York: Macmillan Co., 1926.

Hindus, Maurice. *Sons and Fathers.* New York: Doubleday, Doran & Co., 1940.

Kinsey, A. C., W. B. Pomeroy, and C. E. Martin. *Sexual Behavior in the Human Male.* Philadelphia: W. B. Saunders, 1948.

Landis, P. H. *Adolescence and Youth.* New York: McGraw-Hill Book Co., 1945.

Lundberg, Emma O. *Children of Illegitimate Birth and Measures for Their Protection.* U. S. Children's Bureau Publication No. 166. Washington: Government Printing Office, 1926.

McKown, H. B. *A Boy Grows Up.* Rev. ed. New York: McGraw-Hill Book Co., 1949.

Moodie, William. *The Doctor and the Difficult Child.* New York: Commonwealth Fund, 1940.

Morgan, John J. B. *Psychology of the Unadjusted School Child.* New York: Macmillan Co., 1946.

Mowrer, Ernest R. *Disorganization: Personal and Social.* Philadelphia: J. B. Lippincott Co., 1942. Chaps. 6, 13.

Myers, A. F., and C. O. Williams. *Education in a Democracy.* 3rd ed. New York: Prentice-Hall, 1948.

Rasey, Marie I. *Toward Maturity.* New York: Barnes & Noble, Inc., 1947.

Reckless, Walter C. *Criminal Behavior.* New York: McGraw-Hill Book Co., 1940.

Shaw, Clifford R. *The Natural History of a Delinquent Career.* Chicago: Univ. of Chicago Press, 1931.

Shaw, Clifford R., H. M. Zorbaugh, H. D. McKay, and L. S. Cottrell. *Delinquency Areas.* Chicago: Univ. of Chicago Press, 1929.

Smith, Harvey. *The Gang's All Here.* Princeton: Princeton Univ. Press, 1941.

Sutherland, Edwin H. *The Professional Thief.* Chicago: Univ. of Chicago Press, 1937.

Tappan, P. W. *Juvenile Delinquency.* New York: McGraw-Hill Book Co., 1949.

Teeters, Negley K., and John O. Reinemann. *The Challenge of Delinquency.* New York: Prentice-Hall, 1950.

Thomas, W. I. *The Unadjusted Girl.* Boston: Little, Brown & Co., 1927.

Thomas, W. I., and Dorothy Swaine Thomas. *The Child in America.* New York: A. A. Knopf, 1928.

Thorpe, Louis P. *The Psychology of Mental Health.* New York: Ronald Press, 1950.

Thrasher, Frederick M. *The Gang.* Chicago: Univ. of Chicago Press, 1927.

Thurston, Henry W. *The Dependent Child.* New York: Columbia Univ. Press, 1930.

U. S. Dept. of Labor, Children's Bureau. *White House Conference on Children in a Democracy, 1940.* Washington: Government Printing Office, 1940.

White House Conference on Child Health and Protection. *Dependent and Neglected Children.* New York: D. Appleton-Century Co., 1933.

Young, Kimball. *Personality and Problems of Adjustment.* New York: F. S. Crofts & Co., 1940. Pp. 622–685.

Zimand, Gertrude F. *Child Labor Facts.* New York: National Child Labor Committee Publication No. 379, 1940.

CHAPTER FOUR

ADULTS AND THE AGED

The Problems of Adults. The basic problems of adults center in making an adequate living within the bounds of legality, avoiding physical and psychological ill-health, and making sexual and other interpersonal adjustments possessing sufficient satisfactions to allow for an uncomplicated old age. Such at least are the problems as they are defined by the dominant moral view of American society. But persons deviate from these patterns, and because they do they are judged and regard themselves as possessed of personalized social problems.

OCCUPATIONAL ADJUSTMENT

Problem Areas. Two problem centered areas exist with reference to employment. One is that of getting a job which will provide secure income, and the other is that of satisfaction in work. A limited survey of men in industry showed that only 70 per cent of those studied found satisfaction in the jobs they held. Such dissatisfaction is evidenced in labor turnover, in absenteeism, and in union organization, strikes, and lockouts.

Causes. It is not surprising that dissatisfaction exists when the average job carries no tenure or security, when for every year and a half of business prosperity in the history of the United States there has been a year of depression. Full employment has never been a reality. From 2 to 25 per cent of the working force in the United States has always been unemployed. Unemployment is rarely a matter simply of personal insecurity. The average wage earner supports others besides himself. Especially since the American frontier was closed about 1890 and despite higher real wages, economic insecurity has threatened the farmer and wage earner.

Skills and Mass Production. Inadequate training for jobs available is a minor element in the problem of job adjustment.

Industry over the past fifty years has moved toward the elimination of highly skilled tradesmen. Mass production requires few craftsmen with long apprenticeships. It requires more trained engineers, who identify themselves with management. Mass production of standardized commodities has meant utilization of easily replaceable mass men. Hence, despite the rise in real wages the average American adult worker is constantly threatened with economic insecurity.

HEALTH

Nature of Health Problems. Ill-health impedes a satisfactory adjustment to work and to one's associates. The average person in the United States finds it difficult to afford medical care, finds himself unable to work a portion of the year, and dies before his time. Ill-health, then, is not simply a medical matter. It has large sociological components.

Physical illness and mental ill-health are correlative, for it is a rare person physically ill whose attitudes and values are not affected by the condition. Ill-health, of course, also provides the basis for an inability to meet normal responsibilities, but it may be feigned so as to escape responsibilities. The former situation may be obvious enough; the latter may assume such a disguised form as that of an invalid wife, who takes to bed shortly after her marriage and becomes chronically irresponsible thereafter.

From a broad point of view the problem is not so much that of further developments in the techniques of medicine as it is of the application of medical and public health knowledge to the areas and masses of people needing it. Organizational efforts in this direction are on the increase, and popular opinion for an extension of the Social Security Act to cover medical care is being developed.]

Extent of Sickness and Accidents. About 6 per cent of the American population daily is unable to proceed with its normal activities because of illness, and on any one day some one-half million persons are incapacitated because of accidents. Twice as many persons died from accidents in civilian pursuits as were killed in the American Army during World War I, and the situation was comparable during World War II. And accidents and illness strike hardest at those who can least afford them.

Cost of Medical Care. An average family requires an income of at least $60 a week in order to provide out of it sufficient to pay

for adequate private medical services. The average cost per
family of medical care, $108 in the prosperous year 1929, could
not be borne by the mass of the people, who either went without
care, engaged quacks, or employed self-medication.

Distribution of Medical Care. The lack of medical care is
not so much a result of the paucity of physicians as of the geographic distribution of physicians and of the "sliding-scale" fee
system in medicine. While the American Medical Association has
steadfastly opposed the development of group medicine, which
would ensure a better income for the average physician and a
wider spread of medical services, various organizations have
inaugurated plans of this sort, and their future growth seems
probable.

Alcoholism. For some moral groups in the community the
consumption of alcohol in any form is regarded as a problem.
For others, social drinking is permissible but excessive drinking
is decried. No disagreement exists either among laymen or professionals as to the undesirableness of true alcoholism. Chronic
alcoholism is a form of mental illness, and even the alcoholic
usually regards himself as a problem. Disagreement does exist,
however, as to the effects of alcohol consumption and its relation
to chronic alcoholism. The sequence frequently assumed to lead
to chronic alcoholism is that of occasional drinking for purposes
of heightening social intercourse, followed by increasing alcohol
consumption, and finally the arrival of a condition in which the
need for alcohol either periodically or constantly surpasses all
other values in the person's existence. Actually the number of
chronic alcoholics is small, and the mortalities from alcoholism
are less than 1 per cent of the total deaths.

Excessive drinking has a great number of personal sources.
Basically the most common motivation for chronic alcoholism
seems to lie in the person's strong feelings of inferiority, in a sense
of personal inadequacy while sober, and in an infantile conception
of revenge. The effects of overdrinking on an alcoholic's work,
family, and associates are so well known as not to require elaboration here.

Treatment of excessive drinking in the form of moral suasion
functions largely to increase the alcoholic's feelings of guilt and
his desire to escape these feelings through more drinking. For
those who are convinced they must stop, psychiatry and the

group therapy of Alcoholics Anonymous have done much to alleviate the problem. Those who approach the problem with the attitude of prohibiting the drinking of alcoholic beverages "or nothing" have contributed largely the latter. Fortunately, both the "dries" and the "wets" have come to see that compromises, including a certain amount of local-option prohibition, offer the wisest course.

Drug Addicts. Drug addiction is a problem the importance of which has been grossly exaggerated. There are from 100,000 to 500,000 addicts in the United States. Some experts contend that the real social problem is not the addict himself but rather the milieu into which he is forced. With federal regulation of the sale of drugs, addicts are forced into illegal channels for their supply.

Drugs are taken as a means of escape from odious realities and to achieve a state of euphoria. Drug addiction functions for the user in much the same way as alcohol for the imbiber. Drug addiction may result from a person's conversion to the use of drugs by others who already have the habit. Continued therapeutic employment of drugs on patients in hospitals may furnish a first step toward addiction. The patient must be aware that he is being given drugs, for addiction to take place. Addicts, by and large, however, are persons with deep-seated emotional conflicts which are curbed while the drug is in use. As long as an addict has the drug he can behave outwardly in a more or less normal fashion.

Deprivation of opiates (but not of cocaine derivatives) results in "withdrawal symptoms" characterized by muscle spasms, nausea, and the so-called aches. It has been contended that the addict prefers to keep his habit rather than to suffer the withdrawal symptoms, although addicts have been known voluntarily to hospitalize themselves so as to reduce their body tolerance to the drug and thus decrease the cost of the habit. Opium and cocaine addicts are not *per se* criminals in other respects. Only a fourth of the addicts in prisons have committed other offenses than sale or possession of the drugs. Marijuana (or hashish) smoking, which until recently was increasing in use, is associated to a much larger extent with crime commitment, however, and is much more difficult to control since the "loco-weed" may be grown domestically and made into cigarettes at home. The most effective cures for drug addicts lie not in prohibition or deprivation but in psychological depth therapy which eliminates the emotional conflicts allayed by the use of the drugs.

INTERPERSONAL ADJUSTMENT

Problems of Interpersonal Adjustment. All social problems have roots in inharmonious relations between persons, which in substance amount to discordant junctures of the sense of self of one person with the sense of self of one or more others. While social problems exist disproportionately in connection with poverty it is a commonplace that the *economically* secure can be unhappy single or married, become mentally ill, or resort to suicide. To be sure, politico-economic situations do provide the framework in which problems can arise, are accentuated, and are alleviated. Situations, then, and the definitions obtaining for them, promote or retard problems of interpersonal adjustment.

Unmarried Adults. The problems of unmarried adults lie primarily in the realms of sexual and social adjustment. Historically stigma has been attached to the unmarried state. With a loosening of the rigidity in taboos on extramarital sexual relations, a sex life outside of marriage is possible for a few adults. But such a sex life is much more possible for men than for women. The socially sanctioned career woman or "bachelor girl" has only recently made her appearance.

Unmarried adults normally provide support for persons other than themselves. The rates of mental disease, suicide, transiency, and homelessness are greater, as one might expect, for the unmarried adult than for the married.

The Problems of Marriage center in getting married, being happy in marriage, and staying married. Little training for marriage is now provided in either secondary schools or colleges. Despite the tendency during this century for the sexual morals to be relaxed, some men but especially women appear to possess little knowledge of the role of sex previous to entering the marriage contract. Such ignorance may be responsible for lack of marital adjustment. Marriage has been romanticized in the movies and literature to the point where it is often anticipated as a condition of heavenly bliss. Under these circumstances young people are frequently disappointed with the realities of married life and unhappiness, separation, and divorce may follow.

The Changing Family. In the past fifty years the structure of the American family has been changing. The status-role of the husband and father has declined, and that of the wife and mother has risen. From an ideal-typical patriarchate, the American family is moving toward an equalitarian form. But cultural definitions as to what the status-roles should be, have not been crystallized, and this is one of the several sources of family tensions which lead to disintegration of the marriage bond.

Types of Tensions. Classifications of marriage tensions vary from that of Harriet R. Mowrer [1] in which tensions are categorized as those of sex conflict, response conflict, and cultural conflict to those of E. T. Krueger,[2] who noted thirteen distinctive sources of domestic discord. Incompatibility in sexual intercourse and differentials in response to one's mate may themselves reflect differences in cultural backgrounds, temperamental inclinations, or value-systems of the marriage partners, and may accentuate hostilities and aggression in other areas of family life. Any particular factor such as the health of one or both of the partners, his earning capacities and spending habits, his age and status in the community, have significance for family harmony or discord, not as mechanical factors but in terms of the meanings the marriage partners attach to them. Insofar as factors are capable of being determined, however, and adequate actuarial tables constructed, probabilities for success or failure can be predicted, as Terman [3] and Burgess and Cottrell [4] have indicated.

Desertion has been called the poor man's divorce, for it occurs much more frequently among the working class than among others. The deserter is usually a man in the prime of life who leaves a wife and one or two children to fend for themselves during his absence. Desertions are often crisis-invoked departures which are of a temporary character, as in the case of the male deserter who is unable or unwilling to assume the temporary intensification of responsibility attendant on his wife's pregnancy.

Problems of the Deserted. Family welfare agencies or relatives usually afford aid to the deserted family. But the effects of desertion on children in such forms as curtailment of schooling, their premature employment, and the malorientation of their family roles cannot be measured by the relief costs which ensue.

---

1 *Personality Adjustment and Domestic Discord* (New York: American Book Co., 1935), chaps. 9, 10.
2 "A Study of Marriage Incompatibility," *The Family* (1928), 9:53–60.
3 Lewis M. Terman, *Psychological Factors in Marital Happiness* (New York: McGraw-Hill Book Co., 1938), p. 373.
4 E. W. Burgess and L. S. Cottreli, Jr., *Predicting Success or Failure in Marriage* (New York. Prentice-Hall, 1939), p. 225.

The Aid to Dependent Children feature of the federal Social Security Act has tended to mediate economic family difficulties attendant on desertion.

Divorce—Its Extent. Divorce has come to be a common feature of American life. One marriage in five now ends in divorce, the frequency having increased more than threefold since 1890. The rise in the rural rate, of course, has not kept pace with the mounting urban rate of divorce.

Divorce—Real vs. Nominal Causes. The real causes of divorce are obscured by the fact that bills of divorce are framed within what a particular state regards as legal grounds. But changed moral attitudes are reflected even here. Adultery, for example, has declined relatively as a grounds for divorce, and cruelty has increased. Courts and legislatures generally have become more liberal in divorce matters. South Carolina, for many years the only state that granted no divorces, passed a law in 1949 permitting divorce on four grounds. Some trend is also discernible toward a longer waiting period before an absolute divorce can be obtained.

Remedies for Divorce. Many persons who obtain divorce do so within seven years, are childless, and themselves remarry. The readjustment to a single state involves reordering of one's life, of relationships with friends, and of established habits. Children frequently constitute an area of conflict; parents fight over their custody, support, and affectional relations. Remedies for divorce center in more realistic programs of sex education, waiting periods between applications for licenses and marriage rites, and a uniform divorce law.

CRIMINALITY

Definition. The term criminal normally does not apply to all lawbreakers, for all persons violate laws, but only to those persons who commit heinous acts or who engage habitually and professionally in crime. What constitutes crime, of course, varies from place to place and from age to age. The collection and the utilization of crime statistics are thus subject to difficulties similar to those mentioned for juvenile delinquency. Crimes known to the police cover a broader area than those for which convictions occur. And criminals who can be studied are further restricted since it is largely prisoners who can be subjected to

verifiable research. The costs of crime are equally difficult to ascertain, because criminal activities interlock with legitimate
activities. Edwin H. Sutherland has called attention to the fact
that "white-collar criminality," carried on under the mores of
acceptable business practice, constitutes a segment of criminal
conduct which has been largely neglected in sociological studies
of crime and criminals.

Types of Criminals. Criminals may be typified as occasional
and habitual. The occasional criminal may commit crime when
an opportune situation arises but normally he maintains control
over latent, lawbreaking values. Under this category one would
place the emotionally unstable person who is driven to criminal
acts by inner compulsions over which he has little conscious control, as, for example, the individual embezzler. The habitual
criminal, often the confirmed delinquent grown up, has assimilated what is regarded as a criminal culture, and he receives
sanctions for his conduct from like-minded fellows. The chronic
repeater, or recidivist, falls in this category. Most offenders are
under thirty, motivated by desires for status through economic
gain, and are not significantly different in measurable features
from the noncriminal members of the social classes from which
they derive.

Theories of Treatment of criminals are in process of change.
Rationalizations of crime causation range from free will to determinism. The viewpoint that the criminal exercises free will in
committing acts, that the punishment should fit the crime, and
thus function as a deterrent, is gradually being superseded.
Modern ideas center in notions of the segregation of the criminal
from society until rehabilitation has been effected. The conceptions of the indeterminate sentence and of probation and parole
accord with this latter viewpoint. Sentences which are mandatory
in character emphasize the crime, but the newer approaches
emphasize not the crime but the criminal as a reformable human
being. Modern penology aims at separating offenders, to lessen
the probable disservices of prisons and reformatories as schools of
crime, and at training to achieve vocational and personal rehabilitation.

Sex Offenders. The most tabooed area of human behavior
is that centering in sex expression. Under these circumstances,
it is understandable that deviants in sex conduct are subject to

emotionalized public disapproval. Sex offenders such as rapists, sodomists, and homosexuals apparently have had life experiences to which strikingly deviant meanings came to be attached. Morally deviant meanings develop in the life experience of the person and become persistent and seemingly desirable ends for him. Since the roots of these values lie largely in the unconscious of the offender, they are subject to treatment through the various forms of psychotherapy.

Prostitutes. An understanding of prostitution and the prostitute is possible on a more readily understandable surface level. Prostitution exists because men desire overt heterosexual satisfaction for which they are willing to pay a price, and because some women are willing to make a commodity of sexual satisfaction. Houses of prostitution are frequently operated on a national scale by illegal business syndicates. The incidence of venereal disease among prostitutes in such houses is smaller than is generally assumed. Venereal disease rates are much higher among "charity girls," those who perform as a favor, and among the lowest grade of prostitutes, the streetwalkers.

Attitudes of Prostitutes. Prostitutes regard their work in much the same way that a physician regards his, as a profession. The typical prostitute is a girl who has never been very conscience-stricken in the area of sexual deviation and who entered her profession as a means of improving her economic status. Such conditioning factors as charitable promiscuity or illegitimacy may have paved the way for entrance into the profession, but few girls are lured into the work. In any literal sense they are not "white slaves." Once "in the racket," however, income and role-accommodation function to keep them in line. The threshold between prostitution and other employment is not a high and difficult one to cross. Prostitutes often leave the profession married to men of acceptable social standing. Prostitutes usually maintain male "pimps" whose function it is to protect them from legal and other unwanted entanglements and to provide them with clients.

Decline of Prostitution. The increased freedom, mobility, and "liberation" of American women has resulted in a decline in organized prostitution as well as in an increase in the percentage of the population married and in the divorce rate. The number of "protected" vice areas in cities has correspondingly declined. Undoubtedly there has been an increase in "semi-prostitutes" and in "call houses." Call houses are apartments to which a girl, often a clerk or stenographer during the day, is called so that she may ply her clandestine trade at night. The patrons of prostitutes are not only single men but also dissatisfied and adventure-seeking husbands.

OLD AGE

Increasing Number. The proportion of aged persons in the American population is gradually increasing. The declining birth-rate and stoppage of immigration together with progress in medical science have raised the ratio of older adults to young people. But with the heightened tempo of life, the growth of cities, and the increase in the factory system and mass production, the aged have been made more economically insecure than they were in an agricultural America.

Problems of Dependency and Care. Industrial superannuation in automobile plants before World War II, for example, was at forty-five years of age, but old-age assistance or insurance benefits under the Social Security Act did not begin until age sixty-five. Private pension schemes previous to the enactment of this legislation covered no more than 10 per cent of the population over sixty-five, and fewer than 50 per cent of the aged possessed savings for their old age. Moreover, ill-health, broken homes, and mental disorders are most prevalent in this age group. The mores of children's responsibility for support of aged parents have also undergone change. The provisions of the Social Security Act regarding the aged provide a basis for greater security than existed theretofore, but the areas left untouched by this legislation are still large.

SUICIDE

Extent. Suicide, as insurance actuaries know, results in more deaths annually than do automobile accidents. More than half of the suicides are men over forty-five years of age. Men kill themselves three times more readily than women do, urban rates are higher than rural rates, and Catholics have lower rates than Protestants.

Causes. The causal complex for suicide ties in with the maintenance of self in the eyes of others. When it seems to some persons that pride and honor and physical well-being cannot be maintained in life, self-destruction appears as a solution to their problems. Pride and position may suffer greatly as a consequence of economic debacle and consequent decline in status role. Hence, some correlation exists between the inception of business depression and rates of self-destruction. Correlations of suicide with climate appear to reflect temperature less than they do the relation between the individual and the group.

Types. Emile Durkheim classified suicides into the following types: (1) *altruistic*, in which the integration of the individual and the group was too pressing; (2) *egoistic*, where the relationship was too loose; and (3) *anomique*, resulting from catastrophic changes in the equilibrium of living.

Prevention. Persons who commit suicide, while not maniacs, undoubtedly have deep-seated emotional conflicts. Prevention of suicide, therefore, lies in widespread mental hygiene which encourages persons to have harmonious relations with others in an integrated community.

SELECTED READINGS

Adamic, Louis. *A Nation of Nations.* New York: Harper & Bros., 1945.

Beard, Mary. *Woman: Co-Maker of History.* New York: Longmans, Green & Co., 1940.

Beers, Clifford W. *A Mind That Found Itself.* New York: Doubleday, Doran & Co., 1928.

Bernard, Jessie. *American Family Behavior.* New York: Harper & Bros., 1942.

Bowman, H. A. *Marriage for Moderns.* New York: McGraw-Hill Book Co., 1942.

Burgess, E. W., and L. S. Cottrell, Jr. *Predicting Success or Failure in Marriage.* New York: Prentice-Hall, 1939.

Carpenter, Niles. *Hospital Service for Patients of Moderate Means.* Chicago: Univ. of Chicago Press, 1932.

Cavan, Ruth S. *The Family.* New York: T. Y. Crowell Co., 1942.

Chevigny, Hector, and Sydell Braverman. *The Adjustment of the Blind.* New Haven: Yale Univ. Press, 1950.

Clarke, Helen I. *Social Legislation.* New York: D. Appleton-Century Co., 1940.

Davies, Stanley P. *Social Control of the Mentally Deficient.* New York: T. Y. Crowell Co., 1930.

Elliott, Mabel A., and F. E. Merrill. *Social Disorganization.* 3rd ed. New York: Harper & Bros., 1950.

Gillette, J. M., and J. M. Reinhardt. *Problems of a Changing Social Order.* New York: American Book Co., 1942. Chaps. 9–10, 12, 15–17, 22, 27–29.

Gillin, John L. *Criminology and Penology.* New York: D. Appleton-Century Co., 1945.

Glueck, Sheldon, and Eleanor T. Glueck. *Juvenile Delinquents Grown Up.* New York: Commonwealth Fund, 1940.

Groves, Ernest R., and G. H. Groves. *The Contemporary American Family.* Philadelphia: J. B. Lippincott Co., 1947.

Groves, Ernest R., and others. *The Family and Its Relationships.* Rev. ed. Philadelphia: J. B. Lippincott Co., 1949.

Haggard, H. W., and E. M. Jellinek. *Alcohol Explored.* Garden City: Doubleday, Doran & Co., 1942.

Hart, Hornell, and Ella B. Hart. *Personality and the Family.* New York: D. C. Heath and Co., 1935.

Hill, Reuben, and others. *Families under Stress.* New York: Harper & Bros., 1949.

Knox, S. T. *The Family and the Law.* Chapel Hill: Univ. of North Carolina Press, 1941.

Landman, J. H. *Human Sterilization.* New York: Macmillan Co., 1932.

Lee, Alfred M. "Techniques of Social Reform: An Analysis of the New Prohibition Drive," *American Sociological Review* (1944), 9:65–77.

Mayo, Elton. *The Social Problems of an Industrial Civilization.* Boston: Harvard Univ. Graduate School of Business Administration, 1945.

McWilliams, Carey. *Brothers under the Skin.* Boston: Little, Brown & Co., 1943.

McWilliams, Carey. *Prejudice: Japanese Americans.* Boston: Little, Brown & Co., 1944.

Menninger, Karl A. *Man against Himself.* New York: Harcourt, Brace & Co., 1938.

Moore, Harry H. *American Medicine and the People's Health.* New York: D. Appleton-Century Co., 1927.

Mowrer, Ernest R. *Disorganization: Personal and Social.* Chicago: Univ. of Chicago Press, 1942. Chaps. 7, 8, 12–16.

Quarterly Journal of Studies on Alcohol. New Haven, 1940-date.

Reckless, W. C. *Criminal Behavior.* New York: McGraw-Hill Book Co., 1940.

Reed, Louis. *The Healing Cults.* Chicago: Univ. of Chicago Press, 1932.

Reed, Louis. *Midwives, Chiropodists, and Optometrists.* Chicago: Univ. of Chicago Press, 1932.

Sellin, Thorsten. *Culture Conflict and Crime.* New York: Social Science Research Council, 1938.

Taft, Donald R. *Criminology.* Rev. ed. New York: Macmillan Co., 1950.

Tibbitts, Clark, and W. Donahue, eds. *Planning the Older Years.* Ann Arbor: Univ. of Michigan Press, 1950.

Truxal, A. G., and F. E. Merrill. *The Family in American Culture.* New York: Prentice-Hall, Inc., 1947.

Wharton, John F. *The Theory and Practice of Earning a Living.* New York: Simon & Schuster, 1945.

Wood, A. E., and J. B. Waite. *Crime and Its Treatment.* New York: American Book Co., 1941.

Young, Kimball. *Personality and Problems of Adjustment.* New York: F. S. Crofts & Co., 1940. Chaps. 24, 25.

Zilboorg, G. *Mind, Medicine, and Man.* New York: Harcourt, Brace & Co., 1943.

CHAPTER FIVE

CASTE AND MINORITY PROBLEMS

Caste and Class. There are two main types of status structuring in the United States, those of caste and of class, each subdivided and both overlapping each other. A class is a social grouping in which members possess roughly equivalent culturally-valued attributes. A class is "open" in the sense that one can escape from a class or fall into it or climb into it by acquiring attributes comparable to those already in it. A caste, on the other hand, is a closed matter with limitations to status clearly demarcated. One is born into a caste, marries in it, and has benefits and handicaps to status determined by the fact of birth.

Caste in the United States. There is a white caste and a Negro caste in the United States. The terms race and ethnic group are used to label and suggest the character of the Negro caste, but neither is adequate. Caste status is not directly caused by race, but rather it is generated by socio-economic conditions and comes to be attached to visible physical features. Race prejudice is not inborn; it is acquired. It is not race, then, but cultural definition which is basic to discrimination, segregation, and conflicts between groups.[1]

Ethnic Minorities. Any ethnic or religious group, such as the Chinese, Irish, Japanese, Jews, Mexicans, or Poles, capable of being discerned on physical or cultural grounds, may be denied opportunities for employment, housing, or education on such grounds, and thus may be characterized as a problem minority group. The extent of segregated ethnic minorities is a measure of the absence of democracy. To possess a minority status does not necessarily mean numerical inferiority. Mexicans, for example, or persons of Mexican descent, in some parts of the Southwest outnumber Anglo-Americans, and they, the Mexicans, have a subordinate status.

---

[1] N. D. Humphrey, "American Race and Caste." *Psychiatry* (1941), 4:159–160.

The Morals-Mores Clash. Officially the ethical ideals or morals of the United States oppose minority discrimination. Segments of the population adhere to the view expressed in the U. S. Constitution. But the mores of powerful groups define the extent of such so-called problems as that of the Negro, the Japanese-American, and the like.

Problems of Social Structure center in value judgments as to wealth, power, and status and in the opportunities available to acquire and share these attributes. Social problems traverse status lines, but most of the phenomena in which conflicts of morals and mores converge have to do directly or indirectly with status and its achievement.

The social structure of the United States consists of at least two pyramids of status. One is larger than the other, and its base is higher. This is the white status pyramid. The other is the colored pyramid. The colored pyramid merges into the white in the area occupied by the Mexicans and the Chinese. Their relationship to the Negro-white caste system, however, is still indefinite.

PEOPLE OF COLOR

The Role of Visibility. Visibility or physical distinctiveness allows ready identification, once prejudicial attitudes and discriminatory practices have developed. Normally discrimination functions as a device to restrict competition in the labor market, to maintain a cheap source of labor, and incidentally—although this is popularly magnified—to limit social contact and intercourse. Visibility allows and aids segregation, the mark of a caste situation. Distinctions, then, only seem to be made on the basis of color. A person who possesses known Negro ancestry yet who has the appearance of a Caucasoid, is usually defined and discriminated against as a Negro.

Costs of a Caste System. Discrimination and segregation are costly phenomena. They are costly economically since they promote overlapping services, and the disease and criminality they foster must be borne by the whole community. They are destructive to full personality growth upon the part of both groups, and they allow only the most superficial community of interest. But since these devices afford status to the superordinate group, and since they have come to be surrounded with rationalizations and heartfelt meanings by that group, they are extremely difficult to change through the instrument of moral suasion.

Change through Changed Life-Conditions. In the long run discriminatory practices may be most basically changed through the same forces which have changed the position of women in the last one hundred years, namely, the dynamic elements of an industrial culture. On a world scale the changed balance of power which will be effected through the industrialization of such colored nations as China and India will do much toward altering American attitudes.

Organizations Working for Improvement. The race riots of 1943 in several American cities brought sharper community focus on the problem than had existed for some time. One result was that interracial committees sprang up all over the country, and a co-ordinating body, the American Council on Race Relations, was instituted as a clearinghouse and service-dispensing center. Long-time efforts by such interracial bodies as the National Association for the Advancement of Colored People, the National Urban League, and the Southern Regional Conference have shown progress over the years.

Government Action. The President's Committee on Fair Employment Practices, instituted by President F. D. Roosevelt during World War II, legally recognized the most inequitable gap between morals and mores, that of inequality of opportunity for making a livelihood. While federal legislation in this regard appears unlikely in the near future, New York has led the way on a state level with an act prohibiting discrimination in employment on the grounds of race, creed, or national origin.

NEGROES

One out of every ten Americans is a Negro. This ratio is proportionately smaller than the ratio of Negroes to whites in the early history of the nation. The abolition of slavery, except for legal definition, did little to affect the status position of the bulk of Negroes in the Southern United States. Since 1910 Negroes have increasingly moved northward and cityward. In the urban North they have suffered only slightly less discrimination and segregation than they do in the Jim Crow South. Historically restricted largely to agricultural pursuits or to domestic service, the Negro has made employment gains, especially since World War II began, but he is still on the lower levels of employment generally.

Strong class lines exist within the Negro community, but Negro professionals and businessmen are virtually limited to a Negro clientele. Negroes are subject to discrimination in almost every phase of public life, although schools, transportation, and voting facilities are open to them in the North on a relatively equal basis with whites.

The crime of lynching, which is not limited to the South or to Negroes, has shown a downward trend in the past thirty years. This downward trend contrasts with the upward trend Negroes exhibit in such status-giving attributes as ownership of wealth and in the years of education undergone by the Negro population. Negroes are becoming more conscious of their situation and more militant in their efforts to eliminate the Negro-white caste system.

MEXICANS, JAPANESE, AND INDIANS

Mexican-Americans. The problems of persons having Mongoloid ancestry vary from region to region. Anti-Mexican sentiment, especially for the mestizo population, is strongest in Texas and California, the areas where the largest number of the two million persons of Mexican origin or descent are congregated.

Japanese-Americans. The concentration of Japanese on the West Coast, the white prejudice against them, and their ability to compete successfully in agriculture, were basic factors besides military expediency to their unconstitutional relocation after Pearl Harbor. The Japanese and their American offspring constitute little more than one-tenth of 1 per cent of the population of the United States. But, despite the loyalty and bravery of Japanese-Americans in the American Army in World War II, they have received much more than their share of venomous hatred and discrimination.

The Amerinds. Anti-American Indian sentiment is largely concentrated in Oklahoma and the Southwest. Incongruously, men in public life point proudly to Indian strains in their ancestry. The American patterns of segregation toward discernibly different persons of Mongoloid descent who are concentrated in a particular area differ only in degree from those accorded Negroes.

ASSIMILATION OF IMMIGRANT GROUPS

Each successive immigrant group from the Irish and Germans of the 1840's to the Slavs and Mexicans of the 1920's has been subjected to similar broad problems of adjustment. Each group has occupied the lowest levels in the economy, with some segment of the immigrant group and in turn their children assimilating American culture and distributing themselves in various niches in the economy. Immigrant groups which were once regarded as threats to wage levels, and whose further immigration was opposed by organized labor, often in the second generation furnished the recruits and leadership for organized labor.

Before 1880 a large portion of the "old immigrant" groups (Germans, Irish, Scandinavians) turned to the land for their economic opportunities. The newer immigrants (Slavs, Latins, Jews) tended to congregate in cities where, after the closing of the frontier, a market for their labor existed. In the cities, what had been German, Irish, and Scandinavian slums, were in turn occupied by Latins and Slavs and then, in the North, by Negroes, Mexicans, and rural Southern whites.

Not so much the immigrants themselves, but the dual-cultured children of immigrants, contributed disproportionately to lower-class crime and other problems. And the farther removed an immigrant group was from possessing attributes idealized in the Anglo-Saxon myth as those possessed by Old Americans, the greater the likelihood that discrimination would be practiced against it. But within the white caste (save for Jews) the melting pot has continued to boil as amalgamation and integration of persons and cultures occurred.

The dominant white gentile group continues, however, to speak of the French-Canadians, the Italians, and the Poles as "problems." The "problem consciousness" of this elite group seems to be accentuated the higher the ratio of other groups to it, and the greater the threat to its economic security and dominance. Each immigrant group in turn has attempted to gain status by identifying with the prejudices of the older residents and by opposing and stereotyping the later migrants. A trend is discernible today whereby, with the decline in immigration, national groups persisting within the United States are being urged to salvage and perpetuate their cultures.

JEWS

Anti-Semitism, or more correctly anti-Jewism, is a world-wide phenomenon. It has been contended that anti-Semitism in the United States is greater than it was in pre-Nazi Germany. In many respects American Jews constitute a caste-like segment within the white caste. In part this situation has functioned to allow Jews to contribute disproportionately to scientific knowledge and to human welfare. But through the role of Jews as a socio-political scapegoat it has also provided fertile ground in recent years for the nucleation and growth of absolutistic governmental movements.

Like Negroes, Jews represent every shade of political opinion and income levels and run the gamut of personality and racial types. But such facts have little meaning to the frustrated individual who lumps them together, and who utilizes them as scapegoats to whatever antisocial end he desires. The Jewish problem, like that of colored minorities, is one of being understood and finding acceptance in an alien world.

SELECTED READINGS

Allport, Gordon W. *ABC's of Scapegoating.* Rev. ed. New York: Freedom Pamphlet, Anti-Defamation League of B'nai B'rith, 1948.

Benedict, Ruth F. *Race: Science and Politics.* Rev. ed. New York: Viking Press, 1943.

Brown, F. J., J. S. Roucek, and others. *One America: Our Racial and National Minorities.* New York: Prentice-Hall, 1945.

Cook, Lloyd Allen, ed. *College Study in Intergroup Relations.* Washington, D. C.: American Council on Education, 1950.

Corrigan, J. M., and G. Barry O'Toole, eds. *Race: Nation: Person: Social Aspects of the Race Problem.* New York: Barnes & Noble, 1944.

Davie, Maurice R. *Negroes in American Society.* New York: McGraw-Hill Book Co., 1949.

Dollard, John. *Caste and Class in a Southern Town.* New Haven: Yale Univ. Press, 1937.

Dollard, John. *Personality and Psychotherapy.* New York: McGraw-Hill Book Co., 1950.

Dubois, W. E. B. *Color and Democracy.* New York: Harcourt, Brace & Co., 1945.

Feldman, Herman. *Racial Factors in American Industry.* New York: Harper & Bros., 1931.

Fineberg, S. A. *Overcoming Anti-Semitism*. New York: Harper & Bros., 1943.

Frazier, E. Franklin. *The Negro in the United States*. New York: Macmillan Co., 1949.

Gamio, Manuel. *The Mexican Immigrant*. Chicago: Univ. of Chicago Press, 1930.

Graeber, Isacque, and S. H. Britt, eds. *Jews in a Gentile World*. New York: Macmillan Co., 1942.

Hay, Malcolm. *The Foot of Pride: The Pressure of Christendom on the People of Israel for 1900 Years*. Boston: Beacon Press, 1950.

Johnson, Charles S. *Patterns of Negro Segregation*. New York: Harper & Bros., 1943.

LaFarge, John. *Race Question and the Negro*. New York: Longmans, Green & Co., 1943.

Lasker, Bruno. *Race Attitudes in Children*. New York: Henry Holt & Co., 1929.

Lee, Alfred M. *Race Riots Aren't Necessary*. 3rd ed. Public Affairs Pamphlet No. 107. New York: Public Affairs Committee, Inc., 1947.

Lee, Alfred M., and Elizabeth B. Lee. *The Fine Art of Propaganda*. New York: Harcourt, Brace & Co. and Institute for Propaganda Analysis, 1939.

Leighton, Alexander H. *The Governing of Men: The Lessons of Japanese Relocation*. Princeton: Princeton Univ. Press, 1945.

Locke, Alain, and Bernhard J. Stern. *When Peoples Meet: A Study in Race and Culture Contacts*. Rev. ed. New York: Barnes & Noble, Inc., 1946.

Lowenthal, Leo, and Norbert Guterman. *Prophets of Deceit*. New York: Harper & Bros., 1949.

MacIver, Robert M., ed. *Group Relations and Group Antagonisms*. New York: Harper & Bros., 1944.

Montagu, M. F. A. *Man's Most Dangerous Myth*. New York: Columbia Univ. Press, 1942.

Montagu, M. F. A. *On Being Human*. New York: Henry Schuman, Inc., 1950.

Myrdal, Gunnar, and others. *An American Dilemma*. New York: Harper & Bros., 1944. 2 vols.

O'Brien, R. W. "Selective Dispersion as a Factor in the Solution of the Nisei Problem," *Social Forces* (1944), 23:140–147.

Odum, Howard W. *Race and Rumors of Race*. Chapel Hill: Univ. of North Carolina Press, 1944.

Panunzio, Constantine. *Immigration Cross Roads*. New York: Macmillan Co., 1927.

Reuter, E. B. *The American Race Problem*. New York: T. Y. Crowell Co., 1938.

Rose, Arnold. *The Negro in America*. New York: Harper & Bros., 1948.

Rose, Arnold and Caroline. *America Divided*. New York: A. A. Knopf, 1949.

Shalloo, J. P., and Donald Young, eds. "Minority Peoples in a World at War," *Annals of the American Academy of Political and Social Science* (September 1942), 223.

Stonequist, Everett Y. *The Marginal Man*. New York: Chas. Scribner's Sons, 1937.

Young, Donald. *American Minority Peoples*. New York: Harper & Bros., 1932.

CHAPTER SIX

SOCIAL CLASS PROBLEMS

When the United States had little industry and much free land, class lines were not very sharply drawn or clearly demarcated. With the industrialization of the country and the occupational relocation of its sources of economic power, class lines have become more accentuated, and social movements revolving about status- or class-consciousness have increased. From the viewpoint of the dominant moral group these problems center in the factory system, the distribution of income, the trade-union movement, and the canalization of class conflict.

FACTORY SYSTEM

Problems of Mass Production. The factory system has been aimed at efficient production of commodities so as to make profits for ownership. Because of the specialization of jobs and of other demands of mass production, technical growth has occurred to the point where most men in factories are virtually bound to the machines or conveyors they operate. They find little or no creative activity in their labor. Since the worker performs a limited number of strength-taking operations during his working day, with little change in pace or performance, he suffers among other things from fatigue. One consequence of fatigue is industrial accidents.

Industrial Accidents, taken as a whole, result in many more deaths than all of America's wars. They are abetted by carelessness and also in part by managemental efforts to speed up conveyors or belts. State workmen's compensation laws which provide benefits in the case of some forms of job-developed injuries or illnesses, ameliorate the problem to some extent. In many factories, however, conditions of work are such as to result in the assimilation of dusts and bodily poisons, many of which are not recognized under workmen's compensation laws. Because of accidents and the greater incidence of disease among laborers the average factory worker at twenty has a seven-year-less expectancy of life than the average office worker.

Factory Problems and Trade-Unionism. The worker's growing consciousness of inadequate wages and working conditions, and of the fact that once a worker he is likely to remain one, has led to an acceleration in the growth of trade-unionism, especially since the middle of the great depression of the 1930's. This growth was founded in part on the legal recognition of the right of a worker to join a union of his own choosing. The right was established nationally through the enactment of the National Labor Relations Act in 1935. The Fair Labor Standards Act of 1938 established rights to maximum hours and minimum wages for workers in industries engaged in interstate commerce.

Collective Bargaining. Organized labor aims at restricting the labor market in such fashion as to obtain a greater share of the fruits of production, to shorten hours of labor, and to better working conditions for its members. In the United States, the American Federation of Labor (AF of L), an organization primarily composed of semi-independent craft unions, dominated the trade-union movement from its inception in 1885 until the rapid growth of the Congress of Industrial Organizations or CIO. The latter association split off from the AF of L in 1934 and began organizing unions in the previously unorganized mass production industries (steel, automobiles). Rather than on a craft basis, which restricted membership to workers of a particular skill, the vertical or industrial CIO unions took in all eligible workers involved in producing a particular product. Negotiations for merging the two labor organizations were completed in 1955.

The Strike. The major instrument, and in a sense the only instrument the trade-union has to achieve its ends, is the strike. Strikes, however, may be begun either by legitimate union leaders or by *agents provocateurs* who aim at destroying union organization drives. In opposition to union tactics, the individual employer has the backing of his employers' association and such tools as the *lockout* and the *boycott* or *blacklist*. Usually commercial newspapers and radio stations and the police work sedulously on the side of management and ownership on the occasion of an industrial dispute.

Mediation Situation. Industrial unrest may be mediated in various known ways, chiefly through joint arbitration boards with impartial chairmen. But it is unlikely that the march toward unionism or the fight against it will be soon abated or stripped of "rough stuff." As a unity measure for the war period both the AF of L and CIO national officers supported a temporary "no strike" pledge. With the decline in the demand for labor, however, greater and greater pressure generated to abrogate this pledge. Mass industrial unrest became extensive following the termination of World War II.

Women in Industry. In one-sixth of urban families the only breadwinner is a woman. This situation contrasts sharply with that of one hundred years ago when virtually the only occupations for woman were those of housewife and schoolteacher. And during World War II, the five hundred occupations women in cities had previously held, expanded severalfold, an expansion at least comparable to that during World War I. While the position of women in industry at present is in flux and it has declined temporarily since World War II ended, there is no question that the status of women will remain at new high levels and that their areas of employment will continue to expand. Under these circumstances the percentage of married women employed outside the home should surpass the prewar figure of 45 per cent. The percentage of married Negro women employed in menial, low-paying, and domestic jobs is even greater.

Differential Treatment of Women. Low wages for women have been justified by employers on the grounds that the work they did was temporary, held only until marriage, and that they worked not to support themselves but in order to buy finery and to pay incidental expenses. Industrial unions, however, have raised the slogan of equal pay for equal work, and consequently through union contracts have aided greatly in raising women's wages in industry. Historically women have received discrimination under policies of some craft unions. They have been protected, however, by state legislation controlling standards in women's wages, industrial homework, hazardous industries, nightwork, and hours of labor. By and large, however, federal legislation concerned with goods and services involved in interstate commerce (and hence concerned with the conditions of work for women) has been more progressive than comparable state legislation.

PLANES OF EMPLOYMENT AND LIVING

The Productive Capacity of the United States is at present greater than that of any other nation, and the people's recognized desire for goods is equally great. But a considerable gap exists between America's capacity to produce and its current ability to distribute income in such a fashion as to allow consumers' needs tangibly to be expressed.

The Depressed Two-Thirds. In the prosperity year of 1929, 70 per cent of American families had incomes of less than $1,500. In 1935–36, the average income of the American family was about $1,070. It is estimated that, if in prosperous 1929, twenty million families had had their incomes raised to $2,500 each, they would have spent 40 per cent more for food, 65 per cent more for clothing, and would have made comparable purchases in other areas. Actually, the depressed two-thirds of American families look up to an ideal standard of living estimated by experts as necessary to "health and decency," which is beyond their present means. It is possible of achievement only if they have more adequate salaries and wages.

Unemployment. Wages result from employment, and unemployment, symptom as it is of a malfunctioning economy, has always been the fate of at least 2 per cent of the wage-earning class. At times during the depression of 1929–38 as much as 25 per cent of America's wage earners were unemployed, and in some areas as much as 75 per cent of the families were receiving relief.

Unemployment is usually categorized as seasonal (during certain periods), technological (resulting from labor-displacing inventions), and cyclical (resulting from recurring depressions). Apart from the physical deprivation unemployment affords, its morale-destroying effects in the forms of hopelessness, sickness, family discord, and the like are significant in showing the gap between actualities and our society's somewhat loftier moral pretensions.

Amelioration of Unemployment. The problem of unemployment has been approached largely from the viewpoint of ameliorating its effects rather than from that of eliminating its causes. Such programs as relief through temporary public works, unemployment compensation, and the like help to make unemployment less disastrous, but they actually do little to *prevent* unemployment. Prevention lies in programs of full employment at adequate wages which would allow workingmen to make adequate purchases of the products of their labor.

SELECTED READINGS

Adamic, Louis. "Sitdown," *Nation* (1936), 143:652–654, 702, 704.

Altmeyer, A. J. "Outlook for Social Security," *National Conference for Social Work* (1937), 634–644.

Anderson, Nels. *Men on the Move.* Chicago: Univ. of Chicago Press, 1940.

Arnold, Thurman W. *The Bottlenecks of Business.* New York: Reynal & Hitchcock, 1940.

Arnold, Thurman W., and others. *The Future of Democratic Capitalism.* Philadelphia: Univ. of Pennsylvania Press, 1950.

Beard, Mary. *Woman: Co-Maker of History.* New York: Longmans, Green & Co., 1940.

Bendix, Reinhard. "Bureaucracy: The Problem and Its Setting," *American Sociological Review* (1947), 12:493–507.

Best, Ethel, and Rebecca Smaltz. *Women Workers in Their Family Environment.* Washington: U. S. Dept. of Labor, Women's Bureau, 1941.

Blaisdell, Donald C., and Jane Greverus. *Economic Power and Political Pressures.* Temporary National Economic Committee Monograph No. 26. Washington: Government Printing Office, 1941.

Blatz, W. E., *Hostages to Peace: Parents and Children of Democracy.* New York: William Morrow & Co., 1940.

Brady, Robert A. *Business as a System of Power.* New York: Columbia Univ. Press, 1943.

Burnham, James. *Managerial Revolution.* New York: John Day, 1941.

Centers, Richard. *The Psychology of Social Classes.* Princeton: Princeton Univ. Press, 1949.

Chase, Stuart. *Idle Money, Idle Men.* New York: Harcourt, Brace & Co., 1940.

Coker, F. W. *Democracy, Liberty, and Property.* New York: Macmillan Co., 1942.

Daugherty, C. R. *Labor Problems in American Industry.* 3rd ed. Boston: Houghton Mifflin Co., 1948.

Davis, Jerome. *Capitalism and Its Culture.* New York: Farrar & Rinehart, 1935.

Douglas, Paul H., and Aaron Director. *The Problem of Unemployment.* New York: Macmillan Co., 1931.

Douglas, W. O. *Democracy and Finance.* New Haven: Yale Univ. Press, 1941.

Eliot, Thomas D. *American Standards and Planes of Living.* Boston: Ginn & Co., 1931.

Elliott, Mabel A., and Francis E. Merrill. *Social Disorganization.* 3rd ed. New York: Harper & Bros., 1950.

Epstein, Abraham. *Insecurity: A Challenge to America.* New York: Random House, 1938.

Feldman, Herman. *The Regularization of Employment.* New York: Macmillan Co., 1931.

Gillin, John L., and others. *Social Problems.* 3rd ed. New York: D. Appleton-Century Co., 1943. Chaps. 3, 10, 11, 20.

Green, William. *Labor and Democracy.* Princeton: Princeton Univ. Press, 1939.

Hansen, A. H. *Fiscal Policy and Business Cycles.* New York: W. W. Norton Co., 1940.

Harrison, Shelby M., and others. *Public Employment Office.* New York: Russell Sage Foundation, 1924.

Hiller, E. T. *The Strike.* Chicago: Univ. of Chicago Press, 1928.

Hollingshead, A. B. *Elmtown's Youth: The Impact of Social Classes on Adolescents.* New York: John Wiley & Sons, 1949.

Hoxie, R. F. *Trade Unionism in the United States.* New York: D. Appleton-Century Co., 1943.

Jones, A. W. *Life, Liberty and Property.* Philadelphia: J. B. Lippincott Co., 1940.

Kuznets, Simon. *National Income and Its Composition, 1919–1938.* New York: National Bureau of Economic Research, 1942. 2 vols.

Lee, Alfred M. *The Daily Newspaper in America.* New York: Macmillan Co., 1937. Chaps. 6, 17.

Lewis, John L. "The Future of Labor," *New Republic* (1936), 84:234–236.

Mayo, Elton. *The Social Problems of an Industrial Civilization.* Boston: Harvard Univ. Graduate School of Business Administration, 1945.

Meadows, Paul. *The Culture of Industrial Man.* Lincoln, Neb.: Univ. of Nebraska Press, 1950.

Merton, Robert K. *Social Theory and Social Structure.* Glencoe, Ill.: Free Press, 1949.

Millis, Harry A., and Royal E. Montgomery. *The Economics of Labor.* New York: McGraw-Hill Book Co., 1938. Vols. 1 and 4.

Minton, Bruce, and John Stuart. *Men Who Lead Labor.* New York: Modern Age Books, 1937.

Myers, M. G. *Monetary Proposals for Social Reform.* New York: Columbia Univ. Press, 1940.

Reynolds, L. G., and others. *Labor and National Defense.* New York: Twentieth Century Fund, 1941.

Rose, Arnold. *The Negro's Morale.* Minneapolis: Univ. of Minnesota Press, 1949.

Rosenfarb, Joseph. *The National Labor Policy.* New York: Harper & Bros., 1940.

Schumpeter, J. A. *Capitalism, Socialism, and Democracy.* 3rd ed. New York: Harper & Bros., 1947.

Selekman, B. M., and others. *Problems in Labor Relations.* New York: McGraw-Hill Book Co., 1950.

Simon, Herbert A. *Administrative Behavior.* New York: Macmillan Co., 1950.

Snyder, Carl. *Capitalism the Creator.* New York: Macmillan Co., 1940.

Stolberg, Benjamin. *The Story of the CIO.* New York: Viking Press, 1938.

Taylor, A. G. *Labor Problems and Labor Law.* 2nd ed. New York: Prentice-Hall, 1950.

Warner, W. Lloyd, and others. *Social Class in America: A Manual of Procedure for the Measurement of Social Status.* Chicago: Science Research Associates, Inc., 1949.

Whyte, W. F. *Industry in Society.* New York: McGraw-Hill Book Co., 1946.

Wilson, T. *Modern Capitalism and Economic Progress.* New York: Macmillan Co., 1950.

CHAPTER SEVEN

WAR AND REVOLUTION

Since the fruition of the free-enterprise system there has been a gradual rapprochement between industry and the political state. The trend of cultural evolution has been toward larger, more centralized organizations, not only in industry but also in religious, political, and other areas of culture. Business interests and political interests have become increasingly intertwined.

When privately controlled activities have failed to function to the satisfaction of powerful groups, the state has moved in, either to bolster business or to substitute governmental functions for those of private industry. Business itself has given lip service to the policy of having as little control or interference by the state in its activities as was profitably possible. On an international level, one business-state has found itself in conflict with other business-states in its search for and maintenance of markets.

National states have frequently resorted to war against each other and in coalition with each other in order to aggrandize themselves through conquest and to protect and increase markets. Wars are fought, of course, for many more reasons than bare economic ones. War has occurred so frequently as to be a statistically "normal" albeit a morally abnormal feature of human life. And to date no fool-proof machinery has been built to prevent war or adequately to settle international disputes.

The rise of Fascism, as a world-wide phenomenon, tended to accentuate the probabilities of war. Fascism, or intense and irresponsible nationalism, with all its social-psychological accoutrements, glorified the state and through its aggressive policies helped to instigate wars betweeen nations. The fact that Germany, Italy, and Japan have been defeated and their Fascist ideologies of government discredited in World War II, may eliminate the term Fascism, but it does not eliminate many of its causes and its threat to world peace.

Unlike the situation a hundred years ago, warfare today is total war. It is the total war of the "buzz bomb" and vast armor and the atomic bomb which affects all segments of the population whether military or civilian. War is terrifically destructive. World War I cost enough to supply every inhabitant of the major countries involved with adequate homes and the physical conditions for education. Harry E. Barnes notes that 2,500,000 persons lost their lives in wars in 1932–39, between the signing of the Kellogg Peace Pact by virtually all nations of the world and the outbreak of World War II.

PROBLEMS OF THE VETERAN

The civilian-turned-soldier is required to make adjustments to army life which are at variance with his role in civil life. He assimilates a military culture which momentarily alters his economic and social valuations and his sexual adjustments, and he thus comes to make virtues of emotional attitudes which are decried in peace times. He undertakes risks and undergoes hardships which the civilian under conditions of peace would regard as unendurable. His return to civilian life involves difficult readjustments to institutions and persons, especially to work and to his family and friends.

Victorious nations usually provide benefits and advantages for their veterans. But the effects of war on returning soldiers often continue to manifest themselves far beyond the time of return to civilian life, in the health, latent attitudes, and values of the veteran.

CLASS CONFLICT AND REVOLUTION

Class conflict, characterized in its extremes by strikes and riots, is regarded by the dominant moral group in a community as a serious problem in times of social change and industrial unrest. For example, the history of Great Britain in 1919–39 can best be understood in terms of the constant concern with revolution experienced by upper-class Britons. It finally began, by ballots, in 1945. Unity and internal peace are felt to be desirable ends, and mediation and negotiation are thought to be the proper means for settling disputes as they arise. The dominant moral group seems to feel that there can be no valid reasons for open conflict over the distribution of the results of production.

As long as there is no conscious mass judgment of unequal distribution of the economic values of production, or even granted awareness, an acceptance by the masses of the forms of unequal distribution, no class conflict occurs. If, however, exploitation is recognized as such by the subordinately statused groups, and union organization develops to force a reconsideration of the hours of work, the amount done, and the proceeds accruing, then class conflict is inevitable. It is inevitable so long as its energies are not diverted into racial, religious, political, or other channels.

A class revolution is simply an acceleration and intensification of class conflict in which the old order is overthrown and a new one is instituted. While revolutions are a long time in the making and are normally accompanied by violence and civil war, some revolutions are not as violent as others. A real revolution, in contrast to a "palace revolution," relocates the sources of political power. The French and American democratic revolutions succeeded in establishing the power of the rising business class, and the Russian transferred power to the Communist segment of the working class. The Nazi and Fascist upsurges, while they lasted in Germany and Italy, gave power to a new aristocratically-oriented political elite. All revolutionary movements, since they threaten the *status quo*, are defined as constituting social problems.

CAN WAR BE ABOLISHED?

Students of war and peace-planning are agreed that moves to abolish war must be based upon a concise knowledge of the causes of war. The only difficulty in this agreement is that propagandists for special interests have more influence than social scientists in convincing people what those causes might be. Also, it might be pointed out that while the allied governments of United States and Great Britain spent some $2,000,000,000, it is said, to develop the atomic bomb and the related release of atomic power for industrial purposes, only casual attention was given by the governments at least to the political and economic consequences of such developments, and no comparable allocation for social science research was made. On the contrary, the U. S. Congress had destroyed its only social planning instrument in 1944, the National Resources Planning Commission!

As Maurice R. Davie says in his *Evolution of War* (1925), "It is so much easier and more alluring to speculate as to the how and why of war than to grub for the facts." To suggest the complexity of the situation, S. A. Queen and others, in their *Social Organization and Disorganization* (1934), list the following factors as contributing to modern disharmony between nations: *ecological factors*, chiefly the pressure of population and inadequate natural resources, evidenced by the cases of Italy, Japan, Germany, Poland, and Great Britain's home islands; *cultural factors*, includ‚ ing nationalism, patriotism, imperialism (dynastic and economic), militarism, and the extreme form of all these, fascism; and *personal factors*, such as appeal by propagandists to human emotions of fear, revenge, self-respect, lure of prestige gain.

In commenting on the question of whether or not war can be abolished, Richard C. Fuller, in an earlier edition of this outline, observed, "War is associated with a cultural state of mind which has deep roots in the social heritage of almost every nation. From the cradle, children are indoctrinated in the expectations of war. Because war is a collective habit and hence institutionalized, it will be extremely difficult to eradicate. On the other hand, since war is cultural and not biological it is over-simplifying the matter to predicate the collective war of one nation against another on human instincts of pugnacity. Thus, if war is not determined by hereditary patterns, it can be controlled and per‚ haps eventually annihilated just as have other cultural institutions been modified or done away with."

SELECTED READINGS

Bernard, L. L. *War and Its Causes*. New York: Henry Holt & Co., 1944.

Brown, F. J. "Organizing for Total War," *Annals of the American Academy of Political and Social Science* (March 1942), 220.

Case, Clarence M. "Conscientious Objectors," *Encyclopaedia of the Social Sciences* (1931), 4:210–212.

Case, Clarence M. *Non-Violent Coercion: A Study in Methods of Social Pressure*. New York: Century Co., 1923.

Clarkson, J. D., and T. C. Cochran. *War as a Social Institution*. New York: Columbia Univ. Press, 1941.

Davie, Maurice R. *Evolution of War*. New Haven: Yale Univ. Press, 1925.

Dennis, Lawrence. *The Dynamics of War and Revolution*. New York: Weekly Foreign Letter, 1940.

Dodson, Leonidas, ed. "The Shadow of War," *Annals of the American Academy of Political and Social Science* (September 1934), 175.

Dollard, John. *Fear in Battle*. Washington: Infantry Journal, 1944.

Donahue, Wilma T., and Clark Tibbitts, eds. "The Disabled Veteran," *Annals of the American Academy of Political and Social Science* (May 1945), 239.

Eagleton, Clyde. *Analysis of the Problem of War*. New York: Ronald Press, 1937.

Einzig, Paul. *Economic Warfare*. New York: Macmillan Co., 1941.

French, Paul. *We Won't Murder: The History of Non-Violence*. New York: Hastings House, 1940.

Handman, Max. "War, Economic Motives, and Economic Symbols," *American Journal of Sociology* (1939), 44:629–649.

Hunter, Robert. *Revolution: Why, How, and When?* New York: Harper & Bros., 1940.

Kardiner, Abram. *The Traumatic Neuroses of War*. Washington: National Research Council, 1941.

Kennedy, E. D. *Dividends to Pay*. New York: Reynal & Hitchcock, 1940.

Laski, H. J. *Authority in the Modern State*. New Haven: Yale Univ. Press, 1919.

Lorwin, L. L. *The Economic Consequences of the Second World War*. New York: Random House, 1942.

Mann, Thomas. *This War*. New York: A. A. Knopf, 1940.

May, Mark A. *A Social Psychology of War and Peace*. New Haven: Yale Univ. Press, 1943.

Meadows, Paul. "Sequence in Revolution," *American Sociological Review* (1941), 6:702–709.

Melvin, Bruce. *Youth—Millions Too Many*. New York: Association Press, 1940.

Miller, Emanuel. *The Neuroses in War*. New York: Macmillan Co., 1941.

Moon, Parker T. *Imperialism and World Politics*. New York: Macmillan Co., 1926.

Nef, J. U. *War and Human Progress*. Cambridge, Mass.: Harvard University Press, 1950.

Patterson, E. M., ed. "Agenda for Peace," *Annals of the American Academy of Political and Social Science* (July 1944), 234.

Patterson, E. M., ed. "Our Muddled World," *Annals of the American Academy of Political and Social Science* (July 1945), 240.

Sharp, W. R., and Grayson Kirk. *Contemporary International Politics*. New York: Farrar & Rinehart, 1940.

Soule, George. *The Strength of Nations*. New York: Macmillan Co., 1942.

Spiegel, H. W. *The Economics of Total War*. New York: D. Appleton-Century Co., 1942.

Stouffer, S. A., and others. *The American Soldier*. (Studies in Social Psychology in World War II, vols. 1 and 2) Princeton: Princeton Univ. Press, 1949.

Taylor, Edmond. *The Strategy of Terror*. Boston: Houghton Mifflin Co., 1940.

Toynbee, A. J. *War and Civilization*. Oxford: Oxford University Press, 1950.

Waller, Willard. *The Veteran Comes Back*. New York: Dryden Press, 1944.

Waller, Willard, ed. *War in the Twentieth Century*. New York: Dryden Press, 1940.

Warren, R. L. "Fascism and the Church," *American Sociological Review* (1941), 6:45–51.

Watson, Goodwin, ed. *Civilian Morale*. Boston: Houghton Mifflin Co., 1942.

Webbink, Paul. "Postwar Jobs for Veterans," *Annals of the American Academy of Political and Social Science* (March 1945), 238.

Wright, Quincy. *The Causes of War and the Conditions of Peace*. New York: Longmans, Green & Co., 1935.

CHAPTER EIGHT

SOCIAL PLANNING

Definition of the Concept. Social planning implies conscious direction of group or societal life along predetermined lines. It may be done co-operatively or by special interests. Economic planning is one type of social planning, but a great deal of social planning is not necessarily economic. Planning is done by business organizations for production, scientific product development, labor relations, political relations, financing, and distribution. It is done by governmental units and related civic bodies to plan the use of physical resources, to organize for total war, to control crime, to care for defective and deranged persons, to promote public health, to control city and regional growth through zoning, and to do many other things.

A Planned Economy. Social planning may or may not be carried to the point implied by the term "a planned economy." The latter ideally suggests assurances of full employment, a degree of governmental control over industry, finance, and labor, and both political and economic democracy.

Chief Problems in Planning. The late Edward A. Filene believed that men of good will, regardless of conflicting interests and viewpoints, could get together and agree on "the next step forward" in social policy. Beyond "the next step," he believed such co-operative planning would bog down, but he believed that sound democratic procedure consisted in a continuing program of planning such "next steps." Upon this basis, he instituted and endowed his Twentieth Century Fund of New York, an organization sponsoring and subsidizing economic investigations. Such broadly conceived planning, however, necessitates careful assessments of facts and of long-held opinions as well as compromises on policies, and many representatives of special interests are unwilling to concede anything to their opposition, to retreat at all from their highly polarized positions.

The chief problems of planning become largely, not fact-gathering techniques and suitable methods for summarizing the facts, but the answers to the questions: For whom? By whom? When research and planning are done for and by the "wrong people," the dominant moral group has plentiful rationalizations to demonstrate why this should not be done. The National Association of Manufacturers and its affiliated trade associations spend a great deal of money on planning along both economic and political lines, but these same bodies oppose planning by the federal and state governments when that planning is not controlled by representatives (actual or intellectual) of business interests.

FOR WHOM?

Regardless of the instrumentalities and efforts by special-interest groups to oppose the process, all social decisions of importance are made by the masses of the people. As W. G. Sumner stated in his *Folkways* (1907), the masses in the long run define societal morals and place coercions upon the mores of every class and group in society. Sound social planning must, therefore, be in terms of the broad interests and demands of an increasingly more literate societal rank and file. This holds whether the planning is done by an instrument of democratic government, by a body co-operatively instituted by opposing pressure groups, or by special interest groups themselves.

BY WHOM?

Social planning for the public interest can only be assured so long as the interests of all sizable publics are made influential in the decisions of the planners. Because of the infallible manner in which men justify their own personal and group interests as being morally right, as being best for society, such pressures must be exerted directly and consciously rather than indirectly. For these reasons, those concerned with the mitigation of social problems through social planning have usually attempted to gain some sort of democratic governmental structure through which to institute and carry out the planning program.

Governmental Limitations. In the United States, at least three limitations are imposed upon those who seek to carry out planning through a governmental agency. These are those (1) inherent in the mores and morals of our people; (2) inherent in the divided nature of our governmental system, from federal to local, both functionally and hierarchically; and (3) inherent in the operations of special-interest pressure groups. Totalitarian countries avoid the second and third limitations but become self-limiting in a far more disastrous fashion because of their lack of knowledge of and responsiveness to the sentiments and interests of the people.

WHAT CAN PLANNING DO FOR US?

Enthusiastic advocates of social planning and especially of a planned economy have promised relief from practically all human woes by the simple process of turning our decisions over to a central planning body. Such extremists make easy targets for the opposition.

Social planning by responsible democratic agencies can help us to apply to the vastly complex problems of government, business, war, peace, and living in the twentieth century, the contributions of sound social scientists to our descriptive knowledge of man and his world. It can help a literate electorate to exert its pressures in more informed directions. It need not deal with over-all interpretations and programs. Those are the business of pressure groups—for labor, industrial management, distributive interests, professional men, and the many others.

Social and economic planning, however expert, as Richard C. Fuller once noted, "can be successful only to the degree that it is suited to the general temperament and consistent with the fundamental cultural attitudes of the group which it seeks to control."

SELECTED READINGS

Alexander, Franz. *Our Age of Unreason*. Philadelphia: J. B. Lippincott Co., 1942. Part 3.

Barnes, Harry E. *Intellectual and Cultural History of the Western World*. New York: Reynal & Hitchcock, 1941.

Burgess, E. W., and Herbert Blumer, eds. *Human Side of Social Planning*. Chicago: American Sociological Society, 1935.

Burgess, J. S. "Study of Modern Social Movements as a Means for Clarifying the Process of Social Action," *Social Forces* (1944), 22:269–275.

Burnham, James. *The Machiavellians: Defenders of Freedom*. New York: John Day Co., 1943.

Cantril, Hadley. *The Psychology of Social Movements*. New York: John Wiley & Sons, 1941.

Chafee, Zechariah, Jr. *Free Speech in the United States*. Cambridge: Harvard Univ. Press, 1941.

Cook, Lloyd Allen. *Community Backgrounds of Education.* New York: McGraw-Hill Book Co., 1938.

Coons, Arthur G. "The Nature of Economic Planning in Democracy," *Plan Age* (1939), 5:2.

Doob, Leonard W. *Plans of Men.* New Haven: Yale Univ. Press, 1940.

Field, Marshall. *Freedom Is More than a Word.* Chicago: Univ. of Chicago Press, 1945.

Fodor, M. W. *The Revolution Is On.* Boston: Houghton Mifflin Co., 1940.

Frank, Lawrence K. "Science and Culture," *Scientific Monthly* (1940), 50:491–497.

Galloway, George B. *Congress at the Crossroads.* New York: T. Y. Crowell Co., 1946.

Gordon, Manya. *How to Tell Progress from Reaction: Roads to Industrial Democracy.* New York: E. P. Dutton & Co., 1944.

Gouldner, A. W., ed. *Studies in Leadership.* New York: Harper & Bros., 1950.

Greer, Thomas H. *American Social Reform Movements since 1865.* New York: Prentice-Hall, Inc., 1949.

Laski, H. J. *Liberty in the Modern State.* Rev. ed. New York: Viking Press, 1949.

Lemert, E. M. *Social Pathology.* New York: McGraw-Hill Book Co., 1951.

Lilienthal, David. *TVA — Democracy on the March.* New York: D. Appleton-Century Co., 1944.

Lilienthal, David. *This I Do Believe.* New York: Harper & Bros., 1949.

Lundberg, George A. *Can Science Save Us?* New York: Longmans, Green & Co., 1947.

Lynd, Robert S. *Knowledge for What? The Place of Social Science in American Culture.* Princeton: Princeton Univ. Press, 1939.

McClenahan, B. A. "Sociology of Planning," *Sociology and Social Research* (1944), 28:182–193.

Mannheim, Karl. *Freedom, Power, and Democratic Planning.* New York: Oxford Univ. Press, 1950.

Mannheim, Karl. *Man and Society in an Age of Reconstruction.* New York: Harcourt, Brace & Co., 1940.

Odum, Howard W., and Harry E. Moore. *American Regionalism.* New York: Henry Holt & Co., 1938.

Odum, Howard W., and others. "Regional Planning Technique," *Plan Age* (1936), 2:3.

Riemer, Svend. "Social Planning and Social Organization," *American Journal of Sociology* (1946–47), 52:508–516.

Ross, E. A. *New-Age Sociology.* New York: D. Appleton-Century Co., 1940. Chap. 49.

Schesinger, Arthur M. *The American as Reformer.* Cambridge, Mass.: Harvard Univ. Press, 1950.

Simpson, G. "The Assault on Social Science," *American Sociological Review* (1949), 14:303–310.

Taft, P. *Movements for Economic Reform.* New York: Rinehart & Co., 1950.

Vance, R. B. "Place of Planning in Social Dynamics," *Social Forces* (1945), 23:331–334.

Ward, C. Henshaw. *Builders of Delusion.* Indianapolis: Bobbs-Merrill Co., 1931.

Part Two

—

Human Ecology

By

A. B. HOLLINGSHEAD
Yale University

PART TWO

HUMAN ECOLOGY
By A. B. Hollingshead

TOPICS

Chapter IX. The Ecological Order.

Ecology as a Scientific Discipline.
The Ecological Order.
Plant and Animal Ecology Differentiated from Human Ecology.
The Ecological View of the Human Community.

Chapter X. Aggregation.

The Problem of Numbers.
Demography.
The Population Pyramid.
Occupational Pyramid.
Spatial Distribution of Population within Human Habitats.

Chapter XI. Ecological Organization.

The Evolution of Ecological Organization.
Contemporary Ecological Organization.
Territorial Units in Metropolitan Organization.
The City: Organization and Structure.
Individual Specialization within Territorial Units.

Chapter XII. Dominance.

Dominance and Ecological Organization.
Dominance and Ecological Position.
Characteristics of an Important Center of Dominance.
Dominance and Stability.

Chapter XIII. Migration and Mobility.

The Problem of Dispersal.
The Migration Process.
Migration a Concomitant of Mobility.

Chapter XIV. Succession.

Types of Succession.
Succession as a Process.

CHAPTER NINE

THE ECOLOGICAL ORDER

ECOLOGY AS A SCIENTIFIC DISCIPLINE

Origin of the Term *Ecology*. The term *ecology* was coined in 1869 by the biologist Haeckel from the Greek word οἶκος, which means house, abode, dwelling. In the Greek sense the term means not only the dwelling-place, but also the inhabitants and the everyday maintenance activities they carry on in it. In this sense, then, ecology is the study of living things, not as individuals, but as members of a complex network of interconnected organisms (that range from the filterable virus to man) as these organisms function in multiform environments. The environments include the realm of physical nature, other plant and animal species, and other organisms of the same species.

Divisions of Ecology. Little attention was paid to the new discipline, ecology, during the ten or fifteen years succeeding Haeckel's pioneer work; however, as the years have passed, more and more interest has been focused on the study of the relationships existing between organisms and their environments, so that today there are three well-defined branches of ecology: *plant*, *animal*, and *human*. Plant ecology is the oldest and best developed, and animal ecology is somewhat less highly developed; little work was done on human ecology until about twenty-five years ago.

THE ECOLOGICAL ORDER

Research has revealed that there is an order among all living things, including man; an order that is the result of the competitive struggle for existence. The effect of this struggle is to bring about a distribution of the species and the individual, so that each lives finally in the place where he can live best and where he can best meet the competition with other organisms and

67

species. The plants and animals living together in a relatively stable order constitute a *community*, in the ecological sense of this term.

The Web of Life. All living organisms are bound together in a vast system of multiform, intricate, and ever-changing interdependencies. Interrelationships of organisms are territorial, functional, and temporal. This has been called "the web of life." Darwin's famous instance of the cats and the clover is the classic illustration of this interdependence.[1] He showed that bumblebees, fertilization of heartsease and other kinds of clover, field mice, cats, villagers, and old maids are all related in the network of life. Later studies have extended this fundamental principle to all types of organisms.

Competition. Within human society, as well as in plant and animal life, the competitive struggle for existence acts as a regulator of the number of individuals. It controls their distribution, and develops more or less of a balanced relation between their numbers and available resources.

Equilibrium. Competitive factors produce relative equilibria between numbers of the population and the resources of their sustenance base. Changes resulting in imbalance may be brought about by a famine, an epidemic, or an invasion of the habitat by some alien species. Such changes may be caused by introduction of a different nationality or class, by a change in technology or in the standard of living. Invasion may lead to a rapid increase of the invading population and a sudden decline in numbers of the original population, if not the total destruction of the latter. Under ordinary circumstances, any minor fluctuations that occur in the biotic balance are mediated and absorbed without profoundly disturbing the existing equilibrium and routine of life. When a sudden and catastrophic change occurs, it upsets the biotic balance and releases energies that have previously been held in check.

The Biotic Community is the functional and structural organization of life that results from the interrelation and interdependence of species within a common habitat. The essential characteristics of a community, so conceived, are those of a population (1) territorially organized, (2) more or less completely

---

1 Charles Darwin, *On the Origin of Species* (New York: Oxford University Press, 1902), pp. 58–63, 68–72.

rooted in the soil it occupies, (3) with its individual units living in a relationship of mutual interdependence that is symbiotic rather than social.

PLANT AND ANIMAL ECOLOGY DIFFERENTIATED FROM HUMAN ECOLOGY

Plants live in communities which have been studied extensively by plant ecologists, but there is apparently no form of social relationship between plants that can be described as familial. The relationships between the different species are purely symbiotic, and competition tends to be unrestrained. In contrast, such relations as exist among lower *animals*, particularly among the *social insects*, seem to be of the familial type.[1] In the case of the social insects, relations are not based on tradition and maintained by consensus, but are fixed in the structure of the organism and transmitted by hereditary instincts. One further point, among others, is the fact that animals communicate with each other and are able, under certain circumstances, to act in concert and collectively.

In the case of human beings certain social relations, at least those between the sexes, are predetermined in a very general way by structure and supported by glandular potentialities. Certain other relations, especially those that have to do with acquiring sustenance, are symbiotic in character, i.e., they are determined by the association of competitive individuals.[2] But in the case of man, as distinguished from plants and animals, economic relationships are invariably conditioned by understandings, customs, and law, rather than structure or instinct. Besides this, man—at least civilized man—keeps records and is, as Korzybski put it, "a time building animal," so that he lives in the past and future as well as in the present. The customary and social order in man, which is transmitted not as a biological but as a cultural heritage, performs somewhat the same function in human society as that performed in animal society by instinct. In human society, therefore, the social order is embodied in customs and formal laws, rather than in the physiological structure of the members.

---

1 W. M. Wheeler, *Social Life among the Insects* (New York: Harcourt, Brace & Co., 1920).
2 H. G. Wells and others, *The Science of Life* (New York: Doubleday, Doran & Co., 1931), book VI, chapter V, "The Science of Ecology," par. 1.

THE ECOLOGICAL VIEW OF THE HUMAN COMMUNITY

Reduced to its elements then, the human community may be considered to be ecologically the product of five interacting factors: a population (1) living in an area, (2) possessing artifacts (technological culture), and (3) customs and beliefs (nonmaterial culture), which determines (4) the use of the natural resources, and (5) the functions performed in the social division of labor.

In the human community these factors operate to produce its (1) spatial distribution, (2) functional organization, (3) position in a constellation of communities, and (4) changes, within the community, both ecological and social.

Human ecology deals with society in its biological and symbiotic aspects, that is, those aspects brought about by competition and by the struggle of individuals, in any social order, to survive and to perpetuate themselves. The social order includes that in which individual freedom is limited by the rules of a political society, or by the customs and conventions of a purely personal and moral order such as exists in the family. Human ecology is, therefore, concerned with (1) *population* in all its vital aspects; (2) *aggregation;* (3) *ecological organization;* (4) the position and function of *dominance;* (5) *migration;* and (6) *succession.* These points are taken up in succeeding chapters.

SUMMARY

Ecology may be defined as the study of the vital and spatial relations existing between organisms of the same, similar, and divergent species and their environment. In the broad Greek sense ecology analyzes not only how these organisms make their living and the influences this process has on their mode of life, but also the effects the organism has on the environment and the environment on the organism.

Ecological studies may be classified within the three realms of plants, of animals, and of the unique mammal, man. Human ecology began to develop when men looked about them and discovered that human activities trace definite spatial patterns, and form well-defined sustenance linkages that are in part a response to biological processes, in part a reaction to culture. These discoveries led to the view that plant, animal, and human ecology are interrelated within the framework of life, but that human activities, because of the influence of culture, must be viewed separately from those of plants and animals. This is not to say that human ecology is completely different from the other branches, but rather that all three are correlatives in a biotic whole called life.

SELECTED READINGS

Alihan, Milla A. *Social Ecology.* New York: Columbia Univ. Press, 1938.

Bernard, L. L. "A Classification of Environments," *American Journal of Sociology* (1925–1926), 31:318–322.

Firey, Walter. *Land Use in Central Boston.* Cambridge, Mass.: Harvard Univ. Press, 1947.

Hawley, A. H. *Human Ecology.* New York: Ronald Press, 1950.

Landis, Paul H. *Population Problems.* New York: American Book Co., 1943.

McKenzie, R. D. "The Ecological Approach to the Study of the Human Community," in R. E. Park and others. *The City.* Chicago: Univ. of Chicago Press, 1925. Pp. 63–79.

McKenzie, R. D. "Ecology, Human," in *Encyclopaedia of the Social Sciences* (1931), 5:314–315.

McKenzie, R. D. "The Scope of Human Ecology," *Publications of the American Sociological Society* (1926), 20:141–154.

Mezerik, A. G. *The Pursuit of Plenty.* New York: Harper & Bros., 1950.

Mukerjee, R. *Social Ecology.* New York: Longmans, Green & Co., 1945.

Park, R. E. "Human Ecology," *American Journal of Sociology* (1936–1937), 42:1–15.

Quinn, James A. *Human Ecology.* New York: Prentice-Hall, Inc., 1950.

Thompson, Warren S. *Plenty of People.* Lancaster, Pa.: Jacques Catteil Press, 1944.

Wirth, Louis. "Human Ecology," *American Journal of Sociology* (1944–1945), 50:483–488.

Zipf, George K. *Human Behavior and the Principle of Least Effort.* Cambridge, Mass.: Addison-Wesley Press, 1949.

Chapter Ten

AGGREGATION

THE PROBLEM OF NUMBERS

The Population Paradox. Population changes in size and composition take place, as Herbert Spencer pointed out long ago, as a result of two fundamental and apparently conflicting physiological urges: one urge leads each organism to struggle continuously toward preserving its individual existence to the utmost limits of its life span; the other urge leads the organism to continue, by procreation, the existence of the species, and, in the case of man, the race or nationality to which it belongs. The two urges were earlier conceptualized by Malthus when he referred to them as the "food quest" and "sex passion." In response to these two deep-seated tendencies each species has developed the capacity to reproduce in a geometric ratio, whereas the area of the earth and the sustenance resources on, in, and around it are definitely limited.

Capacity of Every Species to Reproduce beyond the Food Supply. If a species does not overincrease by producing a large number of surplus individuals in each generation, it will be in danger of extinction through the encroachments of its natural enemies; if it does, it creates the counterproblem of overeating its food supply, thereby destroying large numbers through starvation, disease, and enforced migration. The dilemma of overproduction, which continually faces all organisms, is normally solved by each species being prevented from overincreasing because of positive checks, disease, famine, drought, carnivorous and parasitoid enemies, and war.

The Balance between Numbers and Sustenance. The operation of the principle of over-reproduction and the counterprinciple of positive checks tends to create and maintain in communities a balance between (1) numbers and (2) available

72

sustenance in terms of (3) the group's culture, as it defines its standards of living. In every community, numbers tend to oscillate from year to year around a mean figure we call the "optimum." Furthermore, this optimum figure tends to remain relatively constant so long as the available sustenance is not appreciably increased or decreased. However, if the sustenance is increased, an increase in numbers or in the standards of living occurs; if it is decreased, numbers dwindle and the standards of living fall until a new balance is struck between numbers and food supply.

Unbalance between Numbers and Resources. A radical increase or decrease in the utilizable sustenance resources of a plant or animal species presumably results in an increase or decrease in numbers. This constantly recurring unbalance is, at any rate, the essential factor in the creation of population problems. The remarkable growth of population in Europe and the Americas in the last two centuries was conditioned by the release of energy through new manufacturing, agricultural, transportation, and communication techniques. New resources were made available to man, and the sustenance base was widened by steam-powered water and rail transportation. Contemporary population problems were created by the unequal distribution of sustenance resources among the nations. England, the Netherlands, France, Belgium, Russia, and the United States were more successful in the nineteenth-century scramble for territories than the nations who entered the industrial field in the last third of the nineteenth century—Germany, Italy, Poland, and Japan.

DEMOGRAPHY

Definition. The study of the vital processes of population aggregates has come to be known as demography. There are two aspects to the study: first, *the static*, which describes the number and composition of the aggregate at a given time for a stated unit of area; second, *the dynamic*, which analyzes the movement, growth, or decline, and changes in the composition of the aggregate over a period of time for a stated unit of enumeration. From another point of view, demography might be defined as biosocial bookkeeping. Its function would, thus, be to record and analyze the vital-social changes, over a temporal span, in the number and composition of the human units in communities.

Bases of Demography. Reliable demographic knowledge depends entirely upon accurate, detailed inventories of population (census enumeration), and careful, complete, and continuous registration of vital processes (births, marriages, divorces, and deaths). Rarely, if ever, do demographic data collected within arbitrary units of territory or time coincide with an ecological unit of population distribution. Ecologists are, therefore, definitely limited in their use of the data compiled by the census and by bureaus of vital statistics.

THE POPULATION PYRAMID

Definition. The population pyramid is a technique used to represent in a concise, graphic manner the complex variations of age, sex, physical, racial, social, and economic conditions in a given population aggregate, that is, the social segments of which a population is composed. Population pyramids are constructed to show the distribution of the several composites in the total population within arbitrarily determined class limits. Ordinarily, two or three variables are depicted in a single pyramid diagram, for instance, age, sex, and nativity, or age, sex, and color.

Distribution of Population in the Pyramid and Ecology. Every well-defined ecological area (for a definition of an ecological area see pp. 84–87) is characterized by a typical distribution of the population composing it, along age, sex, nativity, and occupational lines; in short, ecological areas may be in part defined in terms of the spatial, biological, and social distribution of the population inhabiting them. The ecologist assumes that the characteristics of the population in any given area are the result of competitive factors operating in the area, and the given distribution can be taken as an index of the ecological factors operative in the area. Thus, a given distribution of biosocial characteristics can be taken as suggestive of cultural organization. From this point of view, analysis of age, sex, race, nativity, and occupation is indispensable to a knowledge of the vital ecological, social, economic, cultural, and political processes which operate to form the structure and function of human communities.

In the city the age-sex distribution correlates with the different functional areas. The "down-town district" tends to have a high ratio of males to females; the residential suburbs have a high ratio of females to males. The range of age varies from almost all adults in the center of the city, to fewer adults (and many children) on the periphery of the city.

OCCUPATIONAL PYRAMID

Occupation and Stratification. Modern social organization has an occupational basis. Occupation may be defined "as that specific activity with a market value which an individual continually pursues for the purpose of obtaining a steady flow of income." [1] Occupation serves as a link that holds individuals to the social order. It joins each individual to many others in three ways: *technologically*—through the specific manual and mental operations implied in the execution of work; *economically*—by the income yield of an occupation which provides a livelihood; and *socially*—through the prestige attached to the occupation in accordance with the mores of the community. The income yield and the prestige attached to an occupation create functional and structural stratifications in the social order. Social and economic evaluation of occupations determines differences in: (*a*) an individual's function in the ecological order; (*b*) his proportion of the group's sustenance (wealth); and (*c*) his social status, plane of living, and ecological position in the community.

Strata in Social Pyramid. Technological, economic, and social relations which obtain among members of occupational groups bind them into an interdependent ecological unity known as the social pyramid. Numerically, a smaller and smaller number occupy each class as one ascends the pyramid. Psychologically, the classes are characterized by a developing *esprit de corps*, from the inarticulate, fluid, unskilled stratum up to the closely organized corporate existence found in the higher strata.

SPATIAL DISTRIBUTION OF POPULATION WITHIN HUMAN HABITATS

Human aggregation is a product of the active interrelationships between (1) cultural groups seeking sustenance and (2) their geographic base. Population must, therefore, be territorially, as well as functionally, distributed into patterns that correspond to the competitive factors operative in the area organized by the market. Ecologists, economists, geographers, and sociologists,

---

1 Arthur Salz, "Occupation," *Encyclopaedia of the Social Sciences* (1933), 11:424. Used by permission of the publishers, Macmillan Co., New York.

by pooling their knowledge, have found that the size, shape, and density of a given distribution area are products, in the main, of ecological organization; and, in turn, they have found that the ecological organization of a given people is a function of their culture. This intimate relationship between ecology, population, and culture is just beginning to be realized and adequately studied.

Four patterns can be objectively identified in the spatial distribution of the human species: (1) the world, (2) nations and states, (3) the region, and (4) the functional community.

The World Pattern. A map of world population shows seven areas of high density—the Japanese Archipelago, Java, eastern China, northeastern India, Italy, northwestern Europe, and the east coast of the United States from Richmond to Boston. Six of these seven areas are on islands and the mainland of Eurasia. Stretching inland from western Europe toward the eastern part of European Russia, there is a gradual drop in density. Central, northern, and southwestern Asia, Australia, most of Africa, South America, and North America, except eastern United States, are areas of low density. Areas of high and medium density follow coastal regions, and areas of low density are inland portions of the continents.

The National Pattern. If the nation is taken as a unit of aggregation we find many variations in the density of its population. In the United States population is variously distributed, in the different divisions. In 1930, 69.6 per cent of the total population lived east of the Mississippi River, and 30.4 per cent west of the Mississippi; 59.5 per cent of the population was in the North, 30.8 per cent in the South, and 9.7 per cent in the West. The density per square mile ranged from 262.6 in the Middle Atlantic states to 4.3 in the Mountain states. The national pattern of distribution is taking the form of definite metropolitan areas of agglomeration on the margin of navigable waters or adjacent to rich mineral and oil deposits.

The Region. Population distribution within a region tends to follow relatively homogeneous geographic conditions of soil, climate, topography, and natural resources. Exclusive of metropolitan agglomerations the density of population closely corresponds to food producing areas. In the United States areas of high density of the agricultural population are found east of a line drawn from Brownsville (Texas) through Wichita (Kansas) and Lincoln (Nebraska), to Winnipeg (Canada). West of this line, except in irrigated river valleys, large-scale grazing is the rule until the Pacific Slope is reached. This vast region is very sparsely populated. In the valleys of the Pacific Coast states an intensive agriculture is accompanied by a high density of population.

The Functional Community. Scattered throughout the nation are functional communities with their population distributed in spatial patterns around nucleated centers where lines of communication and transportation converge. Spreading out from great metropolises are smaller centers strung along lines of transportation in an apparently haphazard way. Thus, population clusters into spatial patterns ranging in size from the many-millioned metropolis, with a density of thousands per square mile, down to the isolated ranches in the western mountains and plains.

SUMMARY

Aggregation, in the *first* place, is not a mere statistical grouping, but the vital and functional distribution of the inhabitants of a discrete area into a characteristic demographic structure commonly referred to as its "composition." *Second*, that the number and type of inhabitants is determined by the struggle for sustenance within the competitive network of a market area. *Third*, that the social and vital characteristics of the population in a natural area reflect the operation of competitive factors which repel, attract, segregate, and limit numbers in terms of the available resources. *Finally*, that the population structure of a natural area may be conveniently analyzed by the use of the population pyramid, as well as other graphic and statistical techniques.

SELECTED READINGS

Aurousseau, M. "The Distribution of Population," *Geographical Review* (1921), 11:579–585.

Frazier, E. Franklin. *The Negro in the United States.* New York: Macmillan Co., 1949.

Hawley, A. H. *Human Ecology.* New York: Ronald Press, 1950.

Keller, A. G. *Societal Evolution.* Rev. ed. New York: Macmillan Co., 1931. Chaps. 1, 7.

Loomis, C. P., and J. A. Beegle. *Rural Social Systems.* New York: Prentice-Hall, 1950. Part 2.

McKenzie, R. D. "The Field and Problems of Demography, Human Geography, and Human Ecology," in L. L. Bernard, ed. *Fields and Methods of Sociology.* New York: Farrar & Rinehart, 1934. Pp. 52–57.

Newsholme, Sir Arthur. *Elements of Vital Statistics in Their Bearing on Social and Public Health Problems.* New York: D. Appleton & Co., 1924. Pp. 216–221.

Odum, Howard W., and Harry E. Moore. *American Regionalism.* New York: Henry Holt & Co., 1938.

Quinn, James A. *Human Ecology.* New York: Prentice-Hall, Inc., 1950.

Reuter, E. B., and C. W. Hart. *Introduction to Sociology.* New York: McGraw-Hill Book Co., 1933. Pp. 277–296.

Salz, Arthur. "Occupation," *Encyclopaedia of the Social Sciences* (1933), 11:424–435.

Smith, T. Lynn. *Population Analysis.* New York: McGraw-Hill Book Co., 1948.

Steward, Julian H. *Area Research: Theory and Practice.* New York: Social Science Research Council (Bulletin 63), 1950.

Thompson, Warren S. *Plenty of People.* Lancaster, Pa.: Jacques Cattell Press, 1944.

Vidal de La Blanche, P. M. J. "Distribution of Population," in his *Principles of Human Geography.* New York: Henry Holt & Co., 1926. Pp. 28–48.

Willcox, Walter F. "Census," *Encyclopaedia of the Social Sciences* (1930), 3:294–300.

Wolfe, A. B. "Demography," *Encyclopaedia of the Social Sciences* (1931), 5:85–86.

CHAPTER ELEVEN

ECOLOGICAL ORGANIZATION

INTRODUCTION

Ecological Organization refers to the distribution and ordering of organisms within a region or otherwise delimited territory for the fulfillment of their physiological needs.

Culture and Territorial Distribution. Man's widespread distribution on the earth is due, in the main, to his ability to adapt his culture to meet his needs under a wide range of physical environments. Man's ability to adjust himself to his environment and at the same time to utilize his environment for his own ends is reflected in the expansion of his economy from primitive collectional to modern metropolitan (industrial) organization.

Culture and Ecological Organization. In human society the amount of technical knowledge available among a given people determines their capacity to organize and utilize their environment for the satisfaction of physical and cultural needs. Consequently, the organization of territory is shifting constantly as the nature and form of the competitive factors change. Changes in culture generate changes in the forms of competition between men, and these factors, in turn, result in modifications in the spatial relations of human beings.

Man's Linkage to Nature. The "relation between man and nature is fundamental and at no time can he break the bond."[1] Furthermore, there is ample evidence that the distribution of the existing races of the human species has come about in essentially the same way as the distribution of other living organisms, namely, by the effort of each racial stock to find a locus, a niche, and a position in which it fits and, because it fits, survives.

It is evident as man rises in the scale of civilization that his dependence upon the soil and the natural resources of his habitat

1 Clark Wissler, *The Relation of Nature to Man in Aboriginal America* (1926), p. xi. Used by permission of the publishers, Oxford University Press, New York.

is mediated by his increasing dependence upon other men. Evidence of this dependence is the existence of a steadily expanding world market and the increasingly effective and increasingly extensive division of labor among the many nations, races, and peoples of the earth.

Aspects of Ecological Organization. The student of ecological organization may approach his task historically and anthropologically as Bews, Gras, and Forde do, or from the standpoint of contemporary organization as most American students have done, such as Park, Burgess, Galpin, McKenzie, and others. The latter sociologists have, in turn, confined their researches to (1) the investigation of the organization within and between territorial units, and (2) the distribution of population within the social pyramid and their residence in the different territorial areas or habitats. The remainder of this chapter is concerned with outlining the main concepts involved in each approach.

THE EVOLUTION OF ECOLOGICAL ORGANIZATION

Economic historians have traced five phases in the evolution of man's organization of the environment: collectional, nomadic, village, town, and metropolitan economy. Each economic type is characterized by a unique functional relation between the geographic environment, the economic organization of the sustenance resources, the density of the population aggregate, the size of the area organized for exploitation, the type of exploitation, and, finally, the spatial distribution of communities, and the distribution of the population within communities. The general trend in the sequence of factors enumerated is toward the development of more effective techniques to organize and exploit the geographic environment. Concomitants of this trend are an increase in cultural specialization, an increase in population density, an increase in the size of the area organized for exploitation, and differentiation of function within and between communities.

Collectional Economy. Nomadic collectors who wandered over a wide territory gathering their supplies from a plentiful or niggardly environment represent the simplest form of economic life known to us. These early men supplied their needs by appropriating what nature had to offer. The population must have been sparse, because they certainly lacked the knowledge necessary for efficient exploitation of their environment. In the latter part of the collectional phase, emergent specialization occurred along sexual and occupational lines. Men fished and made weapons, and the women dug roots, collected insects, seeds, and fruits, made clothing, cared for the young, and bore the burdens of the hearth. Occupational specialization existed both within and between tribes. One man made arrows, another spears, a third medicine and charms, still another hunted rather consistently, and each exchanged his product with another for the item he needed. Tribal specialization took form with one tribe gathering seeds, berries, and insects, another making salt, still others chipping flint and fishing. Intertribal exchange took place through barter in a neutral spot, usually on the boundary between tribal lands, on a definite day, with day and place protected by custom, and reinforced by religious sanctions.

Nomadic Economy is divided into two aspects—the cultural and the pastoral.

CULTURAL NOMADIC ECONOMY emerged from the collectional when men began to domesticate animals and cultivate plants. In this phase collection continued, but men planted and tended their garden plots systematically, and herded live stock, relying on them for a larger part of the things they needed than upon collecting the bounty of nature. Men cared for the animals, hunted, fished, made weapons, and compounded medicine; women were horticulturists, food gatherers, and bearers of the household burdens noted in the preceding section. Tribal specialization was more fully advanced with more trading at a regular market.

PASTORAL NOMADIC ECONOMY evolved out of cultural nomadic economy with the development of a well-marked differentiation between herders and tillers. Some peoples settled down on the land whereas others followed their flocks and herds and thus became nomadic husbandmen drawing their sustenance from domesticated animals and trade. Peoples in this latter class wandered over wide areas, coming into contact with many tribes; when necessary these nomads traded animal products for the food and manufactures produced by tillers. During this era the market was periodic, usually held on the boundaries of territory claimed by both the pastoralists and the horticulturists. (The Negritos of the Malay Peninsula, the pygmies of Central

Africa, and the Eskimos of North America have remained in one
or the other of these phases of primitive economy.)

Settled Village Economy was the counterpart of pastoral
nomadic economy. Historically it traces back to the time,
possibly 20,000 years ago, when kinship groups located in a
favorable environment combined the two pursuits of horticul-
ture and husbandry. The center of communal and economic
life became the compact, nucleated village built for protection
and association. Outside the village extended the open fields
used for tillage, pasture, and gathering, with paths radiating
from the village across the fields to other villages. Here we find
territory organized for the first time into nucleus and hinterland.

The economic function of the village community was plant
and animal cultivation for the satisfaction of sustenance needs.
Each village aimed to be self-sufficient, but probably none were.
Within the village, cloth, leather, shoes, pottery, metal, and
tools might be manufactured by artisans who had become more
advanced specialists than were the workers under nomadic
economy. Foods were also processed and stored. Most villages
remained agricultural, although some showed definite signs of
becoming centers of trade, commerce, and manufacture.

Town Economy developed historically in Europe from village economy when a trader class came into existence in a
market village. The trader did business in his combined home
and shop, both buying and selling there when possible. Often,
however, he was forced to attend the market to purchase his
wares, and to wander from village to village peddling them while
his wife remained at home managing the shop. The trader
located in the town, organized consumers and producers into
a functional unit which worked out its interdependence within
itself, and in relation to the outside world through the mechanism
of commerce.

The organized market area of the average town extended
over a radius of fifteen or twenty miles from the integrating
center; within this hinterland many villages were located which
served as the source of supply and the distribution area.

Two types of towns gradually emerged: *first*, the local town
described above; *second*, the prominent town with an extended
trade. A favorable ecological position, with respect to trade
routes, waterways, hinterland, and natural resources, determined
whether a town grew large or remained small. The large town

became a commercial center dominated by specialized traders and manufacturers, who formed guilds or associations to protect their interests, and to facilitate the organization of their market for exploitive purposes. Elaborate trade associations developed in the large commercial towns for the purpose of efficiently organizing the market.

Metropolitan Economy. Gradually, large commercial towns grew into metropolises. The metropolis is the dominant center which organizes over a wide region, commerce, manufactures, finance, and business enterprise. Its function is to integrate and control as many market activities as possible, over as wide a territory as communication and transportation permit within a competitive system. Economic dominance over its tributory hinterland characterizes the metropolis.

Metropolitan economy is the organization of producers and consumers mutually dependent for goods and services, wherein their wants are supplied by a system of exchange concentrated in a large city which is the focus of local trade and the center through which normal economic relations with the outside are established and maintained.[1]

Subordinate to the metropolis are cities, towns, villages, and the open country. These dependent units perform different functions in the elaborately organized network of ecological interdependence between metropolitan center and hinterland. Today under metropolitan economy all forms of aggregation from the metropolis to the isolated farmstead are spatially organized into a vast complex sustenance unit by the competitive interactions between the factors operative within the area organized by the market. Minute specialization in trade functions is found from wholesalers through buyers, sellers, exchanges, common carriers, corporate organization, to finance.

Recapitulation. By way of recapitulation we may point out that, historically, ecological organization has been characterized by two types of economy: The first was organized on a familial and tribal basis, and the second was integrated on a political and territorial basis. Furthermore, there was apparently no definite period in Occidental history when society which had been organized originally on a familial and tribal basis, made the fundamental change by which it assumed the character of

---

1 N. S. B. Gras, *An Introduction to Economic History* (1922), p. 186. Used by permission of the publishers, Harper & Bros., New York.

a territorial and eventually a political organization. The transition appears to have taken place at different times and under different circumstances among different people. The transaction is still in process.

CONTEMPORARY ECOLOGICAL ORGANIZATION

The Market Integrates Competition. In a competitively organized society, the distribution of population and of economic and cultural functions is integrated around the market. Because not every location, culture element, or individual has equal competitive ability, we find human beings and human activities segregated into different territorial distributions and population aggregations. Moreover, competitive interaction operative between individuals, cultural groups, and their habitat gives rise to specialization of function in human society. In general, two forms of specialization may be differentiated in ecological organization: (1) territorial and (2) individual. In the succeeding sections these will be discussed.

TERRITORIAL UNITS IN METROPOLITAN ORGANIZATION

Every territorial unit represents a functional area organized about a market. Furthermore, each is related to many others through specialization of cultural functions. Occupational specialization coupled with lines of transportation and communication are the bonds which tie territorial units into an interdependent network. Because of this web of functional specialization, communication, and transportation, every individual occupied in a specialized pursuit is connected with other individuals for the satisfaction of his wants. Spatially distributed as consumers and producers, these individuals constitute the trade area.

Criteria for Determining the Units. Three fundamental standards must be recognized in the analysis of what constitutes an ecological unit: (1) man's utilization of the land; (2) the structural-functional organization of institutional agencies with respect to the market; and (3) the spatial distribution of institutional activities and population over the landscape.

Ecological Areas.

THE METROPOLITAN REGION is a functionally organized unit made up of many interdependent communities integrated by a metropolis. Structurally the region tends to be radial in form.

It is composed of the central metropolis surrounded by its suburbs, satellite cities, then farther out the smaller semidependent cities, towns, villages, and open countryside. Its size and shape are determined by several factors, the most important being physiographic configurations, position of other metropolises, and lines and modes of transportation and communication. Modern modes of communication and transportation have organized the integral units in the functional complex so that each community is territorially differentiated, often specialized, yet all are inextricably connected by commercial, industrial, agricultural, cultural, and social bonds into a structural-functional pattern.

THE METROPOLITAN AREA includes the central city, its suburbs, and independent satellites within a radius of approximately thirty miles from the downtown area of the metropolis. These localities comprise the built-up areas of daily commutation between work and place of residence.

METROPOLIS is the term applied to a city which economically and culturally dominates a region. The *first* requisite of a metropolis is its ability to draw into itself the products of the region for storage, trade, and transport. The *second* requisite is that its financial institutions must dominate activities in the hinterland. Manufactures are usually situated in or near the city, but this is not a necessity, for often large manufacturing centers are independent cities located at a distance from the metropolis, as for example in the case of Detroit or Pittsburgh.

SATELLITE CITIES are grouped around the metropolis within the metropolitan area. The mother city with her suburbs and satellites composes a city group. Satellite cities grow up adjacent to the metropolis as land values in the city rise, congestion occurs, and tax rates become prohibitive for industry. Ordinarily a satellite city is created by the establishment of an industry or a group of industries on unimproved cheap land outside the corporate city limits. The *centrifugal* factors of cheap land, low taxes, and space for operation and for expansion push industry into these locations. Rapid transportation, easy communication, and electrical power facilitate this result. On the other hand, a series of *centripetal* factors, which include a large labor supply, nearness to a market, belt-lines, and financial and administrative aid, draw industries close to the city. Thus, clustered around every metropolis are its satellite cities, politically independent, but subordinate units in the interdependent economic and cul-

tural life of the metropolis. Strictly speaking, rather than the
metropolis alone, the metropolitan area, with central city and
satellites, is the center which integrates the life of a region.

THE REGIONAL CITY integrates and dominates the economic
life of a metropolitan region. On the basis of function they may
be grouped into three types: (*a*) extractive-industrial, Birming-
ham and Pittsburgh; (*b*) commercial, Atlanta and Dallas; (*c*) com-
mercial-food processing, Omaha and Kansas City.

Two sets of factors entered into the development of regional
cities: *first*, the development of the railways brought remote
areas into contact and competition. Economic specialization
ensued and cities arose at focal points where rail lines converged,
bulk was broken, tariffs changed, giving this location favorable
position in the competitive network or where deposits of natural
resources made manufacture on a large scale profitable. Rail
lines extend out from the city into the hinterland, connecting
small cities, towns, and villages into an interdependent unity.
Motor transport has accommodated itself to this pattern, inten-
sifying the relationship between the city and its hinterland.

The *second* factor in the regional city's rise to power is the
growth of chain organizations administered through regional
headquarters located in a large key city. In these cities are located facilities for handling the activities of the regional office.
Today there is a strong tendency for different national concerns
to select the same city as their regional headquarters. This
binds the territory more closely to the regional metropolis.

THE SMALL PROVINCIAL CITY is strictly local in its influence
and organization. Its position with respect to larger centers
enables it to develop and dominate a district which includes
its own immediate area, plus a number of towns and their trade
areas. Small cities function in the integration of economic and
cultural life between the regional city and the more remote
urban and rural territory. They are minor links in the metropolitan network. Motor transport, by filling in the gaps created
during the railway era, has increased the number, size, and power
of cities in this class.

RURBAN AREA. The rurban town of from approximately
3,000 to 5,000 inhabitants with its outlying trade area forms
an ecological structure which stands midway between the city
and country, combining characteristics and functions of each.
Functionally, it unites the farm producer with the city and
the country consumer with the city producer.

For a town to be in this class it must support a minimum of one service agency along each of the following lines: merchandising, marketing and finance, communication and transportation, processing of local products, education (including a high school), professional, religious, and social organizations. The smaller centers are little specialized, bordering on the rural village which performs many functions in a single establishment. The larger towns are partially specialized. Most of their trade, however, continues to come from farmers. Ordinarily the rurban center is a county seat town, or at least the second town in the county.

RURAL TERRITORY. In the United States this is composed of three kinds of ecological units: (1) the village, (2) the neighborhood hamlet, and (3) the farmstead.

The *village* or small town is more rural or agricultural in its structure and function than the rurban center. Yet it functions as a link connecting farmers with the larger urban centers. In size it ranges from about 250 to 1,000 inhabitants. Farmers living close to villages patronize them for immediate needs such as groceries, overalls, work shoes, gasoline, and light repairs which cannot be done on the farm. Their children attend school there and many social activities center in them.

The *neighborhood hamlet* is a simple service center usually located at the juncture of two highways, or at a railroad station. In size it ranges from 25 to around 250 persons. A general store or two, grammar school, church, garage, service station, small lumberyard, repair shop, and a warehouse ordinarily complete the list of service agencies.

The *farmstead* is the final consumption unit and the elemental production unit in American agriculture. From it go raw materials and foodstuffs to be fabricated and processed in world commerce, manufacture, and consumption. To it come finished commodities from the cities which it helps support; the cities in turn make possible the farm life of today.

These ecological units are not isolated or self-sufficient. Each is but an interdependent unit in the complex metropolitan organization for life. Their size and structure are products of their functions in the competitive order of an organized series of markets.

THE CITY: ORGANIZATION AND STRUCTURE

The structure of the city is a product of competitive interaction between people, market facilities, transportation and communication agencies, type of functions performed, and the site, as the city develops from a rurban nucleus into a metropolis; furthermore, the processes operative in the growth of cities are the same from the small provincial city to the large metropolis. Its organization varies with its size, economic functions, cultural peculiarities, and its position in the ecological network. Its physical structure tends to follow the same distributive pattern, with minor modifications due to topography and other unique factors. Processes operative in the organization of the city create this common type structure.

Processes Operative in Its Organization.[1]

CONCENTRATION is the massing of human beings and human utilities in areas where nature or man has made conditions favorable to the satisfaction of sustenance needs. The principal factors responsible for concentration are the development of machinery and industrial techniques, and their application, in the market area, to production, transportation, and communication.

CENTRALIZATION is the integration of human beings and facilities around pivotal points at which social, economic, and cultural interaction occurs most frequently. These focal centers are located where lines of transportation and communication converge. The center of community activities is associated with these points, inasmuch as the basic types of community agencies locate here. Centralization has been called the community forming process.

SEGREGATION is the sifting of like social and population types, as well as industrial and commercial facilities, into specific districts. Competitive selection operative in the city forms hundreds of these small apparently isolated clusters, which in reality make up the substructure of the city's zones. Here we find automobile rows, financial agencies, second-hand stores, wholesale districts, hobo stems, slums, ethnic and racial minorities, and gold coasts all placed like the gaudy sections of a jigsaw puzzle.

INVASION is the penetration of a segregated area by an institutional function or population group different from the one already there. It is a universal process in city growth. Its operation is a result of changes in competitive relationship among

---

1 R. D. McKenzie, "The Scope of Human Ecology," in E. W. Burgess, *The Urban Community* (Chicago: Univ. of Chicago Press, 1926), pp. 172–177.

institutional agencies and population types within the city's framework.

SUCCESSION is the end product of an invasion cycle. (See Chapter XIV.)

DECENTRALIZATION is the term used to characterize the tendency for human beings and institutional agencies to move away from the center of the city and locate on the outskirts where land values are low and spaces are available. Rapid motor transportation and electric power are accelerating the process.

ROUTINIZATION is the repetitious daily movement back and forth from place of work to place of residence, or the shift into and out of the retail business, amusement, and wholesale districts by the city's population and those who use its services. The term also refers to the shunting about of goods within the city, from storage warehouses to manufacturing plants or to retail outlets. This process is a product rather than a creator of city structure.

City Structure is contingent upon the operation of the ecological processes, for they create its pattern of distribution in space and time. The spatial pattern is integrated around the point of centralization where the largest number of individuals interact for the satisfaction of needs. Under modern cultural conditions the city's spatial structure tends to follow definite patterns modified by local geographic and cultural conditions.

City growth occurs both from the center outward, *central growth*, and along local lines of communication and transportation, *radial growth*. Within the city the basic distribution pattern is a series of concentric zones extending from the center outward. In the expansion process each zone encroaches on the contiguous outer one creating the invasion-succession cycle.

City Zones.[1]

THE HEADQUARTERS AREA OR CENTRAL BUSINESS DISTRICT is located in the center. Here exist the centers for transportation, finance, wholesaling, mercantile offices, administrative offices for industry, hotels, theaters, municipal buildings, newspapers, specialty shops, and department stores, but few grocery stores. It is the integrative area for the city's life and function. The city's highest land values are found here along with the lowest population density.

1 E. W. Burgess, "The Growth of the City; An Introduction to a Research Project," in Park and Burgess, *The City* (Chicago: Univ. of Chicago Press, 1925), pp. 47–62.

The "Interstitial Area" lies immediately outside the center zone. It is characterized by high land values, but the buildings are old deteriorated relics of the days before the center's functions began to invade the area. Light manufactures, delinquency, vice, poverty, and personal disorganization exist here. Disciplinary and reorganizing agencies such as police stations, missions, settlement houses, and relief agencies are scattered in it. Here are the headquarters of vice, crime, and the homeless men and women who frequent cities.

The Area of Workingmen's Homes is an area of flats where shop and factory workers live. Ordinarily it is the second place of residence for immigrants who have been successful. The paternal family is the characteristic social unit. Grocery stores, bakeries, drugstores, shoe-repair shops, notion stores, and taverns are the principal businesses.

High-Class Apartment and Residential Zone. This zone lies between the workingmen's and the commuter's homes; it is fifteen to twenty minutes from the heart of the city. Along the central traffic arteries the apartment houses are strung out like high fences on either side of a road. Behind them, on the quieter streets, are the private homes of the upper middle class. Chain groceries, drugstores, specialty shops, and local theaters are the principal business forms.

Suburban Zone. This is composed of many specialized districts. Frequently on one side of the central city are found manufacturing satellite cities; on another, railroad yards; on a third, specialized residential suburbs; and completing the circle, there may be intensified truck farms. This zone is from thirty to sixty minutes from the center of the city. There is a strong tendency for wealthy families to live in the exclusive residential suburbs; and the heads of these families commute to the central city each day.

Cultural Districts (Natural Areas).[1] Within each broad zone are found many specialized segregated districts (areas) characterized by: (1) *a few specific functions*, as in the financial and hotel district; (2) *physical differentiation*, e.g., by skyscrapers, or by dilapidated frame and brick buildings in the slums; (3) *social distinctiveness*, with great wealth in the exclusive suburbs, and extreme poverty and squalor in the slum sector; (4) *natural*

---

[1] Harvey W. Zorbaugh, "The Natural Areas of the City," in E. W. Burgess, *The Urban Community* (Chicago: Univ. of Chicago Press, 1926), pp. 219–229.

selection of population elements, with single young adults in the rooming houses, or many children in the workingmen's district; and (5) *institutional adjustments*, as in the vice district where delinquent conduct is "normal." These are only a few of the many contrasts in the city's cultural districts. Each district is a "natural area," for it is a product of competitive factors which draw into it appropriate functions and population elements, and repel from it those who do not fit into its scheme of specialization or culture.

INDIVIDUAL SPECIALIZATION WITHIN TERRITORIAL UNITS

Division of Labor and Social Selection. As culture becomes more complex, an individual's function within it becomes more specialized, and definite differentiations into occupations and classes occur. This form of specialization creates the internal organization of the community into residential patterns occupied by easily recognized individual types, and social classes. In this way competition more or less determines both the social niche (class) and the spatial niche (area of residence) an individual will occupy. In any event, the occupation by which an individual makes his living defines more or less adequately his place in the ecological and social order.

In our civilization the separation of place of work from place of residence has brought about most of the segregation in the community. A man functions within the economic sphere where he is needed, because of the nature of his occupation; but within the noneconomic or familial sphere he lives where his tastes and interests dictate.[1]

Studies of ecological organization have revealed that every type of human activity investigated to date has a distinct pattern of distribution within and between the many natural areas. Investigations have revealed, for example, such a distribution of various types of mental diseases.[2] The explanation of this orderly distribution of mentality types is not wholly

---

1 In this connection see: R. D. McKenzie, *The Neighborhood* (1923); Louis Wirth, *The Ghetto* (1929); Frederic M. Thrasher, *The Gang* (1927); Harvey Zorbaugh, *Gold Coast and Slum* (1929); W. F. Whyte, *Street Corner Society* (1943); all preceding are Univ. of Chicago Press publications; John Dollard, *Class and Caste ir a Southern Town* (New Haven: Yale Univ. Press, 1937); Robert S. and Helen Lynd, *Middletown* (New York: Harcourt, Brace & Co., 1929), Part I; Robert S. and Helen Lynd, *Middletown in Transition* (New York: Harcourt, Brace & Co., 1937), Ch. I–III.

2 H. Warren Dunham, "The Ecology of Functional Psychoses in Chicago," *American Sociological Review* (1937). 2:467–479.

clear but may, perhaps, be regarded as an illustration of the general ecological principle that different types of human beings tend, with more or less inevitability, to drift into the particular niches in the territorial and cultural order in which they can most easily survive, then build up a variant culture within the framework of their interests.

SELECTED READINGS

Bews, J. W. *Human Ecology*. London: Oxford Univ. Press, 1935.

Breese, Gerald W. *The Daytime Population of the Central Business District*. Chicago: Univ. of Chicago Press, 1949.

Burgess, E. W. "The Growth of the City," in R. E. Park and others. *The City*. Chicago: Univ. of Chicago Press, 1925. Pp. 47–62.

Gallion, A. B., and S. Eisner. *The Urban Pattern: City Planning and Design*. New York: D. Van Nostrand Co., 1950.

Galpin, Charles J. "The Trade Function of the American Village," in R. D. McKenzie. *Readings in Human Ecology*. Ann Arbor: George Wahr, 1934. Pp. 294–297.

Gras, N. S. B. *An Introduction to Economic History*. New York: Harper & Bros., 1922.

Hatt, Paul. "The Concept of Natural Areas," *American Sociological Review* (1946), 11:423–427.

Hawley, A. H. *Human Ecology*. New York: Ronald Press, 1950.

Kolb, J. H., and E. de S. Brunner. *A Study of Rural Society*. New York: Houghton Mifflin Co., 1936.

Landis, Paul H. *Population Problems*. New York: American Book Co., 1943.

Loomis, C. P., and J. A. Beegle. *Rural Social Systems*. New York: Prentice-Hall, 1950.

McKenzie, R. D. *The Metropolitan Community*. New York: McGraw-Hill Book Co., 1933.

McKenzie, R. D. "The Scope of Human Ecology," in E. W. Burgess. *The Urban Community*. Chicago: Univ. of Chicago Press, 1926. Pp. 172–177.

Milbank Memorial Fund. *Demographic Studies of Selected Areas of Rapid Growth*. Proceedings of the Round Table on Population Problems (pamphlet). New York: The Fund, 1944.

Mitchell, Robert B., ed. "Building the Future City," *Annals of the American Academy of Political and Social Science* (November 1945), 242.

Mowrer, Ernest R. *Disorganization: Personal and Social*. Philadelphia: J. B. Lippincott Co., 1942. Pp. 99–191.

Quinn, James A. *Human Ecology*. New York: Prentice-Hall, Inc., 1950.

Shaw, Clifford R., and Henry D. McKay. *Juvenile Delinquency and Urban Areas*. Chicago: Univ. of Chicago Press, 1942.

Teggart, Frederick J. *The Processes of History*. New Haven: Yale Univ. Press, 1918. Pp. 79–85.

Thompson, Warren S. *Population Problems*. 3rd ed. McGraw-Hill Book Co., 1942.

Zorbaugh, Harvey W. "The Natural Areas of the City," in E. W. Burgess. *The Urban Community*. Chicago: Univ. of Chicago Press, 1926. Pp. 219–229.

CHAPTER TWELVE

DOMINANCE

INTRODUCTION

Relation between Numerical and Territorial Dominance.
In its most primordial and elementary manifestations man's
competition with other men takes the form of a natural increase
of births over deaths, in the course of which a race or a people,
by the mere force of increasing numbers, will occupy successively an ever larger territory within the common habitat or
within a territory over which another people has established
some claim. Thus, a concomitant of natural increase may be
territorial control or dominance as well as numerical predomi-
nance.

In this way, there has been a rapid expansion of European
peoples overseas, since the period of the great discoveries and
explorations, beginning in the latter part of the fifteenth century.
During this epoch the peoples of European origin have increased
about twice as rapidly as the peoples in other parts of the world.
For instance, in the period from 1800 to 1930, the population of
Europe increased from about 180 to 480 millions, to which should
be added 160 millions contributed by European peoples to the
populations outside of Europe. Other examples of this natural
process are the increasing preponderance of the French-Canadian
population in Quebec and eastern Ontario, an increase which is
due entirely to the natural growth of the French population
by the excess of births over deaths. Still another illustration is the
growth of the Boer population in South Africa, due as in the case
of the French-Canadian, almost wholly to the natural increase of
the original immigrants who came to South Africa in the early
part of the eighteenth century.

The form which dominance assumes in this and similar
instances has its origin in the ability of a people to increase and
flourish under conditions imposed by the soil, climate, and the
existing social order, rather than in its ability to enforce its claims

to the soil by military prowess. This struggle of competing peoples to expand within the limits of the human habitat ordinarily terminates in the most elementary form of dominance which the struggle of living organisms everywhere produces, the dominance of mere numbers. But the economic and political dominance of one people over others can be achieved and long maintained by military power and cleverness in spite of numerical inferiority.

Dominance, so far as human ecology is concerned, stated briefly, *is the integration of diverse activities into a co-ordinated unity* through competition as, for example, *the control of market functions,* through competition of buyer and seller.

DOMINANCE AND ECOLOGICAL ORGANIZATION

Center of Dominance. In our culture and in civilized societies generally the center of dominance is the city. As far as concerns dominance in commerce and industry, the center is the urban business section with its network of transportation and communication. A center of dominance has been defined as "the focal point of transportation and communication where are assembled the specialized agencies which are most active in integrating it with outlying centers and their constituencies on the basis of subordination and division of labor." [1]

Dominance normally extends as far as social, cultural, economic, and political agencies centered in the city radiate in their control of activities located in the subordinate or peripheral area. Dominance in human society, finally, depends upon the ability of persons and groups to act on the basis of funded experience and the news of changing events, to control the activities and functions of persons, groups, and institutions both within the center of dominance and the subordinate area. Illustrations of dominance in this sense are: (1) British control of the money market through the medium of loans throughout the world; (2) Mecca as the dominant religious center in the Mohammedan world. Economic dominance arises from the control of transportation, communication, and market functions; whereas ideological dominance results from focusing attention on a particular item or idea in a certain place at a given time. Our general recognition that Paris and Hollywood are the sources of feminine fashions illustrates this latter idea.

---

1 C. A. Dawson and W. E. Gettys, *An Introduction to Sociology* (1935; 2nd ed.), p. 172. Used by permission of the publishers, Ronald Press Co., New York.

Gradients of Intensity of Dominance. It is characteristic of dominance, as it manifests itself in the processes of the market place, that control resides at the center or at least at the point of greatest activity and change (the city's business section), but control declines gradually towards the periphery. This principle is evident in both the growth of the city and in the expansion of the area it dominates. Field investigations have shown that the intensity of dominance decreases proportionately as one moves outward from the center toward the margin of the area of dominance. This principle is in general known as the *dominance gradient*, and it holds good for many items, but more particularly, because they have been most thoroughly investigated, newspaper circulation, trade, and traffic. Incidentally, the area of dominance for all three is almost coterminous. Since the same forces which produce the interdependence between center and margin for the three indices have operated to create and maintain the existing territorial distribution of social and economic functions, they may be taken as indices of the degree of dominance which the center exerts over subordinate parts of the area it organizes.

Dominance and the News. The organization and distribution of news and newspapers may be taken as a good illustration of the dominance gradient in metropolitan organization. One of the functions of the modern newspaper has been the extension of the area of urban dominance over an increasingly wider territory through the control of the news and advertising carried on its pages. This is a development made possible by the perfection of instantaneous communication and high speed transportation.

In short, wherever there is a center of trade there is also a center of dominance, but it is the dominance of the central marketing and banking areas which exerts the most positive and pervasive influences upon the growth of metropolitan cities, and the areas subordinate to them.

DOMINANCE AND ECOLOGICAL POSITION

The competitive position of a given location in an area of interaction is determined either by natural resources, that is, geographic conditions, or by the technological culture of a people. Usually both factors actively enter into the situation in such a way that it is impossible to separate the geographic from the cultural; likewise it is rather naïve to attribute determinism to one or the other. In its pristine state a site may possess every conceivable advantage, but it will not attract human activities and institutions necessary for its development unless it comes into the competitive arena dominated by some distant center. For instance, New York City did not develop until its site became a frontier outpost in the metropolitan economy centered in London. Moreover, Chicago developed the potentialities of its site only after the railroad from New York connected the central continental hinterland through it with the world market.

Centralization of Control; Decentralization of Operation. The development of modern instantaneous long-distance communication, such as the radio, telephone, and teletype, has created a wide time differential between transportation and communication that is bringing about a reorganization of industrial and commercial activities. It has made for, as McKenzie states, a "centralization of control and decentralization of operation." Control is concentrated in a dominant center where foci of communication converge; here the management of distant enterprises plans and directs operations in accordance with market demands. Industrial plants and commercial enterprises are so situated that they can most effectively meet competition throughout the area organized by the market.

Two trends are being produced by the centralization of control, and the decentralization of operations: *First*, centers of dominance are becoming more powerful, and serve as integrating activities over wider and wider areas. The stock and produce exchange, the executive office, the financial agencies, the transportation headquarters and the central communicative offices integrating the far-flung ganglia of modern intelligence, are the effective, dynamic integrators which dominate activities throughout the market area. *Second*, spatial separation of intelligence center from work center is developing direct trade between place of production and area of marketing and distribution.

CHARACTERISTICS OF AN IMPORTANT CENTER OF DOMINANCE

Specialization of Function. In the dynamic center every kind of function becomes highly specialized. While the physical parts of a spatially distributed ecological area integrated by the dominant metropolis are apparently far from the center, actually they are connected with it in three ways. *First*, through the transportive and communicative techniques built and controlled by financial interests located in the city. *Second*, through the organization of the market located in the specialized dominant center. *Third*, through specialization in economic, political, or cultural functions, which produces interdependence. Specialization reaches its highest form in the center but its influence extends to the margin of activity. The primary function of the integrative center is to create an articulate relationship between the specialized dependent parts.

Another product of intensive interrelationship, existent between the functional parts of our integrated ecological order, has been the rise of specialized centers of dominance. This is illustrated in the manufacturing phases of the automotive industry. For instance, Duluth ships ore; Toledo makes tools and gears; Niagara, aluminum; Akron, tires; Southern mill towns, upholstery; and so on for many automotive parts, in many other cities. In the Detroit area the multiplicity of parts are assembled into the machine and made ready for market. The advertising and financial ends of the industry are in New York. Machines assembled in the Detroit area are, finally, purchased by consumers in all parts of the United States and in many parts of the world market.

In summary, thousands of productive, distributive, and servicing processes are located in hundreds of specialized centers spatially separated, but functionally integrated through a few key centers which control all phases of the industry. One of the most significant trends in present metropolitan economy is the development of these specialized cities and the subordinate areas they dominate. The industrial city is, in turn, subordinate to the world metropolis which integrates the multiform activities performed in its subordinate cities and their tributary areas.

Ecological Position. The place (in an area of competitive interaction) which can be most easily, quickly, and cheaply reached from the many radial points in it by ideas, goods, services, and human beings becomes the heart of the center of dominance. Thus, in New York City, the core of the metropolis is Manhattan Island, south of Fifty-ninth Street. In Chicago it is the Loop. Briefly stated, each city has its dynamic center, usually typified as "the business district."

Cultural Climax. The concept "dominance" implies that within a territorially distributed culture complex, cultural achievements are concentrated in a few centers. Here the conditions which make achievement possible are found. In these centers the highest levels of culture are consolidated; from them they are diffused to lesser centers and to the open country. Centers where high cultural achievements are made, generally represent the centers of dominance.

Thus, the highest cultural achievements have almost always been identified with the city. The city supplies a much larger percentage of distinguished men than its population ratio warrants, for most of a nation's leadership is developed in the city. The city influences politics more than its population justifies; moreover, it leads the fashions in morals, manners, attire, and language. In it are located the cultural institutions which supply creative leadership in all branches of art, science, business, politics, and religion. Sanitation, health, and welfare institutions have been developed in the city. Today the great universities, research foundations, art centers, libraries, museums, hospitals, are almost all located in ecologically dominant centers. The great wealth thus centralized represents a surplus which can be and is used for the further creation of capital, as well as the advancement of culture.

DOMINANCE AND STABILITY

Theoretically considered, if a center of dominance produced by the operation of a complex set of factors in an area of competition integrates the activities pursued in it, and the competitive factors remain constant, a condition of stability would result. The center would then remain dominant so long as the factors which produced it continue to operate. In actuality, this condition is never realized, for the conditioning factors which produce a center are variably changing. Consequently, the world's centers of dominance and the areas dominated constantly shift and are always in process of change. Old centers decline, as new ones arise in response to emergent factors that disturb the competitive processes.

The development of a dominant center is closely associated with a successional series (discussed in Chapter XIV). Each center, in its rise to dominance, passes through a series of growth and change cycles which tend both to integrate its activities and at the same time to disintegrate them. In this developmental series there occurs a period of rapid changes, succeeded by one in which the number of changes declines; then there emerges a phase of relative fixity characterized by few changes. This latter period may last for a considerable time, but it tends inevitably to give way to another change cycle as sketched above. As the city develops toward a climax its role as dominant integrator increases with each phase of the succession. But as a new competing center arises to challenge the old center successfully and the old center gradually declines, the attributes of dominance associated with the old tend to be transferred to the new center. Competition plays a variant role in this general process. During the interim phases of change in the life of a city, an area, or a region, competition increases in importance, but as adjustments are made to the new situation the role of custom and tradition again actively enters the scene to dominate the situation. Competition tends to decline as society becomes rigid and fixed; the roles of custom and tradition become more important in its organization. When such a stable condition develops, the activities of persons operating in the process are routinized in response to custom and consensus. Thus, there emerges a fixed social order that will eventually be broken down by the intrusion of new factors of a competitive nature.

Briefly and abstractly we have presented an interpretation of the apparent antithesis between competition as an ecological process and customary consensus as a social process. Actually the two are antithetical correlatives—both are ordering processes. Competition, in ecological relations, gives rise to a balance between competing factors in a situation; whereas custom, as a social process, tries to regulate and fix the equilibrium attained by competition, and gives rise to a stable condition. Competition as a process is constantly trying to order ecological relationships within a moving equilibrium, whereas custom assumes a relatively stable condition, once it has been attained, is final, and can be controlled more or less permanently by rationalizing activity in a fixed manner.

Historically considered, centers of dominance in a given culture have maintained their position as long as the culture they integrated has remained the climax culture in the portions of the world connected by transportation and communication systems which the centers control. Gilfillan[1] has shown how

---

[1] S. C. Gilfillan, "The Coldward Course of Progress," *Political Science Quarterly* (1920), 30:393–409.

the world's centers of dominance have shifted northward and westward as one culture declined and a new one arose to integrate activities. In this process, the dominant cities have moved from the centers to the rims of the continents, while water-borne commerce has supplanted overland trade between one world market center and another. The areas the dominant cities integrate have gradually increased until today we have a few world metropolises. But such giants as New York and London are being successfully challenged by the rise of Continental and Oriental centers. The former cities are trying to rationalize their positions by appealing to treaties, past policies, et cetera, when actually there is occurring a new regrouping in world affairs in response to new conditions.

SUMMARY

It was pointed out in Chapter XI that the competitive process operates to place individuals and cultural artifacts where they are best able to survive; moreover, it forces them to specialize their activities in order to compete more effectively with their fellows and with other cultural elements. In this sense, then, competition is the ordering process which characterizes the symbiotic community.

Ecological dominance as outlined in this chapter is only one kind of dominance existent in our culture. Other, and of course more familiar, forms are moral, economic, and political in nature. These forms are generally spoken of as "social controls" because they arise from social relations which are based upon consensus; that is, we like to think of them as rational. It is evident that these more sublimated and sophisticated forms of control—if one may use the term "sophisticated" in this context—are ultimately related to the more elementary form of dominance described in the preceding pages.

SELECTED READINGS

Fairchild, H. P. *People: The Quantity and Quality of Population.* New York: Henry Holt & Co., 1939.

Ferenczi, Imre. "Modern Migrations," *Encyclopaedia of the Social Sciences* (1933), 10:429–440.

Hawley, A. H. *Human Ecology.* New York: Ronald Press, 1950.

Hobbs, Albert H. *Differentials in Internal Migration.* Philadelphia: Univ. of Pennsylvania, The Author, 1942.

McKenzie, R. D. *The Metropolitan Community*. New York: McGraw-Hill Book Co., 1933.

Quinn, James A. *Human Ecology*. New York: Prentice-Hall, Inc., 1950.

Smith, T. Lynn. *Population Analysis*. New York: McGraw-Hill Book Co., 1948.

Thompson, Warren S. *Plenty of People*. Lancaster, Pa.: Jacques Cattell Press, 1944.

Weigert, Hans W., and V. Stefansson, eds. *Compass of the World*. New York: Macmillan Co., 1944. Esp. arts. by Quincy Wright, F. W. Notestein and Frank Lorimer, pp. 408–460.

CHAPTER THIRTEEN

MIGRATION AND MOBILITY

INTRODUCTION

Commentators upon human affairs, who are disposed to take a broad and philosophic view of the human scene, have for more than two centuries been impressed by the profound historical significance and pervasive influence upon culture and society of man's wanderings from habitat to habitat. This point of view is being fortified by his steadily increasing mobility under contemporary socio-cultural conditions. The fact that migrations involve new contacts and conflicts of peoples and cultures led Ratzel, Bücher, and more recently, Teggart and Reuter, among others, to emphasize the importance of migrations, and the wars that are so frequently associated with them, as fundamental factors in the advancement of civilization. From the efforts of these students and others, it is now generally thought that relative permanence and fixity, where they exist in society and culture, are largely a consequence of the isolation or absence of contacts between people with divergent cultures, a condition which a stable population seems to produce. As Reuter has remarked, an isolated immobile people tends to develop a homogeneous culture "in which the institutional structure is highly integrated, the social rules definite and uniform and the individual's life activities standardized and his place in the social order predetermined."[1] Turgot long ago pointed out that man is emancipated by migration and conflict from this slowly evolving fixity in social institutions and this unconscious tyranny of tradition and custom which characterize an isolated people.

From the point of view of human ecology, relative stability results from an adjustment of numbers to the physical environment, to each other, and to the culture they live in; consequently, as the population in an isolated area becomes relatively stabilized,

[1] E. B. Reuter, *Race and Culture Contacts* (New York: McGraw-Hill Book Co., 1934), p. 2.

life becomes ordered by customs and tradition. An adjustment between numbers and resources is then the natural sequence. This adjustment between numbers and resources is maintained by approximately equal birth- and death-rates over a long time span. The natural balance between numbers and resources, resulting in a relatively stable spatial and sustenance relation, found in almost all isolated peoples, no matter what phase of culture they live in, has been called *biotic equilibrium.*

Migration Defined. Migration may be defined as movements of people, individuals, or groups from one locality to another. This process usually entails the transmission of cultural artifacts, traits, ideas, and techniques from individual to individual, group to group, and culture to culture. When a people becomes mobile, it carries its old culture with it and creates both a migration and a culture drift. A culture drift may also occur through culture contacts resulting from individual emissaries going out from one people to another people for the purposes of adventure, trade, and religious proselytism. In this way a Western culture drift has been diffused to Asiatic countries without extensive migration occurring.

Effects of Migration. The customary and traditional ways of life give way to new forms as the individual is freed from the repressive regime of custom. His energies are released for creative as well as destructive thinking and acting. He is free to roam in search of adventure. Thus, migration is a conditioning factor in the inception and development of new social and cultural forms.

Intrusions disturb well-established adjustments of numbers to each other, and to the sustenance base. New adjustments must take place. Meanwhile, competition operates in one of three ways to determine the number and distribution of population units in any given area: (1) it tends to readjust the same approximate number of habitants in the area along the lines of old or new functions, unless new knowledge and techniques have been developed for the exploitation of the sustenance base; (2) new units may be attracted under a new form of adjustment to the habitat; and (3) if the conditions created by the intrusion are adverse, excess numbers will be expelled.

THE PROBLEM OF DISPERSAL

There is every reason to believe that man, like other animal species, came into existence in a single area from which, in the course of human history, he has spread to every other part of the world. What racial differences now exist are to be attributed, however, less to the direct effects of physical environment than to the effects of isolation and of the inbreeding which this isolation imposed. Now that this isolation has so completely broken down under the influence of modern means of transportation, one of the historical conditions under which the races of mankind came into existence has effectively disappeared. The result is that there is not now, if there ever was among human beings, any such thing as a pure race. The purest races are those that have been longest and most completely isolated. Thus, the Nordics who most nearly approach the ideal Nordic type are in Iceland. On the other hand, the Jews, who are supposed to possess definite and distinguishable racial traits, are as mixed as any racial stock of which we have a history. This is attributed to the wide dispersal of the Jews.[1]

Relation between Migration and Settlement. Dispersion involves not merely migration but settlement. Man, like every other animal, must come to terms with his environment. He must become acclimated; he must find the particular niche in the biotic community in which he can live. Man's reactions to his environment are so vast and disturbing that they have covered the earth effectively with a web of his reconstructions and modifications of nature. He has not only altered the face of the earth but he has also recreated plants and animals and modified the natural conditions and order in which the different species came into existence. In addition to the process of naturalization in the biotic community, man has to find a place in the human environment and in the economic and social order which his association with other human beings imposes upon him.

Migration and Assimilation. The process by which the individual is incorporated in this customary and institutional social order is perhaps best described as a process of socialization. The assimilation cycle involves successively, under ordinary conditions, competition, conflict, accommodation, assimilation, and eventually biological amalgamation.

Much the same cycle of changes takes place with the incorporation of every new generation into a society to which its members are indigenous.

---

1 Maurice Fishberg, *The Jews: A Study of Race and Environment* (New York: Chas. Scribner's Sons, 1911).

THE MIGRATION PROCESS

Writers of the eighteenth and early nineteenth centuries attributed importance to migration and cultural conflicts as agencies by which a rational order has progressively superseded a customary and nonrational order. There has, however, been very little effort by either geographers or sociologists to analyze and distinguish the manner in which the different forms of migration actually take place or, for that matter, to define precisely what is included under the term mobility. Ordinarily, migrations fall into three general classes: (*a*) *nomadic shifting* of people over wide areas for sustenance purposes; (*b*) *occupation of an area* for military, political, and economic purposes but, because most of the invading occupants are males, without normal reproduction occurring within the conquering migrant group; and (*c*) *true migration*, which involves both change of habitat and settlement, possibly, and frequently, when another people are invaded, assimilation. The second and third types involve breaking home ties and the contacts of peoples with variant cultures.

Primitive Migrations were essentially mass shiftings of whole tribes from one area to another. More often than not, they were motivated by a search for food or plunder. Usually they were warlike migrations, resulting in the clash of divergent peoples. Out of these struggles came new adjustments. In short, these early migrations were mass movements like the westward expansion in the United States and the great trek of the Boers in South Africa, a kind of swarming of the peoples, seeking in the wide open spaces a new freedom where family, tribe, and sect might have opportunity to live, each according to its own conception of the good life. This was the form of migration that is characteristic of what E. T. Mason has called "the age of dispersion."[1]

The Great Classical Migrations were one wave of population following upon another—by which Asia, Europe, Africa, and the Americas were peopled in the beginning of our era. They were movements out into a strange land, movements which, using a term that has been associated with Hebrew migrations of the ancient world, one may describe as the great Diaspora, the almost universal dispersion. It is in this Diaspora that the races and

---

[1] E. T. Mason, "Migration and the Food Quest, A Study in the Peopling of America," *Annual Report of the Smithsonian Institution*, July 1894. pp. 523–539.

peoples whose racial characteristics and tribal cultures, which were probably formed in isolation, have finally come together. It is out of this conjunction that civilization, as distinguished from the local and tribal cultures which have contributed to it, has arisen.

Mediaeval Migration. The migrations of the Middle Ages were of a different kind. They were not movements of masses but, as Bücher puts it, of classes. These people were merchants and middlemen, journeymen, landworkers, wandering knights, jugglers and minstrels, gypsies, and itinerants of all kinds— every kind of man, in fact, who was footloose and free, including scoundrels in search of protection within town walls. This type of migration represented for the most part the movements of men in search of adventure and profit, not of pioneers destined to extend the area of permanent settlement.

In the course of time as the country became settled and migration was chiefly of the type just mentioned, extensive migration was succeeded by travel. The merchants settled about the market place, and these centers became towns. Commerce, which began with the exchange of luxuries, was followed by a wider exchange of necessities. Thus, the expansion of trade extended the area of specialization and furthered the division of labor. So far as the trade was free it increased the area of economic interdependence and undermined the economic independence of the different regions.

Modern Migrations, in the main, have assumed the form of *individual* and *family* movements from one home to another. The effect of this form of migration has been to disperse peoples and to undermine traditional ancestral cultures. The modern migrant is normally a proletarian, an industrial or agricultural worker, who from necessity has to seek his fortune among strangers.

In scope modern migrations are: (1) *intercontinental,* involving the movement of peoples not only across national boundaries and cultural areas, but also oceans; (2) *intracontinental,* these may be international migrations, such as the penetration of Italians into Switzerland, Germans into Poland, Mexicans into the United States; or they may be (3) *intranational,* as the shifting of population from rural to urban districts, from east to west, north to south, and vice versa, as in the United States and other large continental countries, also Brazil, Russia, and the Union of

South Africa. Ecologically and culturally all three kinds of migration are important.

Modern migrations have been characterized by *two movements:* (1) the expansion of peoples from fixed centers to the unexploited margins of the area organized by the market; and (2) concentration in cities.

Conditions of Migration. The general compulsives discernible in migrations, both primitive and modern, continue to operate universally, although they vary in intensity and form depending upon the specific conditions under which they operate at a given time. Usually conditions underlying migrations are grouped into two broad categories: (1) *changes in the physical environment,* such as cataclysms in nature; and (2) *changes in the socio-cultural environment.* Changes in either environment may act as expulsive or attractive factors in the migrations of peoples. Under primitive conditions most migrations were probably caused by a combination of both. Most modern migrations, however, have been conditioned by *changes in the socio-cultural environment.* The motivation of an individual's decision to migrate may be traced to general cultural, economic, political, and social conditions both in the country of emigration and in the country of immigration, as well as to personal desires for gain or for adventure.

The general conditioners of migrations since the Columbian era of discoveries have been mainly economic (sustenance) in origin and development. The expansion of peoples in the past four centuries has been world-wide in scope and significance. The form of expansion has generally been the establishment of a frontier settlement by an European or Asiatic country on the rim of an undeveloped continent. These settlements were usually political or economic outposts, oftentimes both.

Capital from the homeland was sent out to exploit the open resources in the new lands. Along with capital went overseers, engineers, and workers; later came settlers in areas where Europeans could settle successfully. Where they could not, Negroes or Asiatics were imported. Migration has tended to follow the path of capital in the exploitation of the new continents. Once the settlement structure developed, any modification in the techniques of organizing the economic life in these areas resulted in migration of workers and settlers to places where new exploitation was occurring. Old areas of exploitation lost or gained population when a new cycle of development began. Thus, capital development, economic specialization, division of labor between interdependent areas, and general economic and political conditions have motivated modern population movements, both intercontinental and intracontinental, internationally and intranationally.

MIGRATION A CONCOMITANT OF MOBILITY

Mobility Defined. Mobility, as the term has come to be used in ecological studies, means, in the simplest interpretation, measurable movement in a time, a space, or a social framework. In general, population movements, both spatial and social, may be classified, as we have done in this chapter, into two broad categories: (1) migration and (2) mobility. In a strict sense migration is mobility, that is, a specific kind of movement, but mobility does not necessarily have to be migration. In fact, in the modern world, movements of people, goods, and ideas within a cultural system have in many respects become substitutes for migration.

In general, one may say that with the development of communication and standardization, there is relatively less migration of person and more mobility of ideas and commodities. We must distinguish, however, between those movements, whether migrations or not, which are habitual and those which involve some break in the routine of the individual habits and the customs of a society. For instance, one cannot call the daily cycle of movement of workers from their homes, perhaps in the suburbs, to their shops and offices in or near the center of the city, a migration; on the contrary, it is a simple routine, habitual process. Such routine movements tend to crystallize and fix the structure of society. On the other hand, movements which interrupt routine and create the necessity for some intelligent and creative action, tend thus to undermine tradition and keep institutions active and alive.

By contrast, the civilized man who, through the medium of trade and barter, has made the world tributary to him, is searching not for a place, in the wilderness, which no hunter has disturbed, nor for some remote stretch of steppe, or pasture where a shepherd can tend his sheep without fear of disturbance. On the contrary, the civilized man goes to the city to seek his fortune, to sell an idea, or to get a job. The place he looks for is somewhere in the ranks of an established social and economic order — preferably a city — and not in the wilderness. This is why most modern movement represents mobility as we have defined it, in contrast to migration as it exists among primitives.

Mobility and " Social Mobility." Sorokin makes a distinction between mobility or movement in physical space, and social mobility or "social circulation." He defines social mobility as "the movement of individuals or groups from one social position to another and the circulation of cultural objects, values and traits among individuals and groups."[1] Sorokin further delimits social mobility into horizontal and vertical aspects. *Horizontal* mobility is the transition of an individual or group from place to place within the same culture complex and on the same social plane, or the diffusion of a culture trait within a given social class in the same culture. *Vertical* mobility, on the other hand, is the transition of an individual, group, or culture element from one social stratum to another. The mobility may be ascending or descending. It proceeds along several social ladders within the institutional framework of a people.

SUMMARY

The migration of peoples brings cultures into collision. Changes result from the shock. Previously established equilibria are destroyed or greatly modified, and integration in the social structure gives way to disintegration. Individuals and groups are freed from customary restraints. A condition of status characteristic of a relatively stable culture is replaced by a condition of competitive freedom. The old relations no longer tie the individual into the cultural order. He becomes mobile and is forced to make new adjustments to the changed conditions. For the individual to survive he must reorient his activities to the disorganization about him. Out of the flux emerges a new synthesis, a new order, which molds numbers and culture elements into a functioning complex of interrelated, correlated, and integrated parts. The phases of change which occur when a disruption takes place are known as *succession*.

SELECTED READINGS

Bernard, William S., and others. *American Immigration Policy: A Reappraisal.* New York: Harper & Bros., 1950.

Brown, L. G. *Immigration.* New York: Longmans, Green and Co., 1933.

---

[1] P. A. Sorokin, "Social Mobility," *Encyclopaedia of the Social Sciences* (1933), 10:554. Used by permission of the publishers, Macmillan Co., New York.

Bücher, Karl. *Industrial Evolution.* (Trans. from 3rd German ed.) New York: Henry Holt & Co., 1901.

Davie, Maurice R. *World Immigration.* New York: Macmillan Co., 1936.

Drake, St. Clair, and H. R. Cayton. *Black Metropolis.* New York: Harcourt, Brace & Co., 1945.

Ferenczi, Imre. "Proletarian Mass Migration, 19th and 20th Centuries," in *International Migrations.* New York: National Bureau of Economic Research, 1929. 1:81–88.

Forde, C. Daryll. *Habitat, Economy and Society: A Geographic Introduction to Ethnology.* New York: Harcourt, Brace & Co., 1934.

Hammond, J. L. "Commerce since the Industrial Revolution," *Encyclopaedia of the Social Sciences* (1931), 4:10–13.

Hawley, A. H. *Human Ecology.* New York: Ronald Press, 1950.

McKenzie, R. D. "Movement and the Ability to Live," *Proceedings of the Institute of International Relations* (1926), pp. 175–180.

McKenzie, R. D. *Readings in Human Ecology.* Ann Arbor: George Wahr, 1934.

Park, R. E. "Human Migration and the Marginal Man," *American Journal of Sociology* (1928), 33:881–893.

Park, R. E., and E. W. Burgess. *Introduction to the Science of Sociology.* 2nd ed. Chicago: Univ. of Chicago Press, 1924. Pp. 505–784.

Quinn, James A. *Human Ecology.* New York: Prentice-Hall, Inc., 1950.

Reuter, E. B. *Race and Culture Contacts.* New York: McGraw-Hill Book Co., 1934. Pp. 1–18.

Schmid, Calvin F. *Social Trends in Seattle.* Seattle, Wash.: Univ of Washington Press, 1944.

Smith, T. Lynn. *Population Analysis.* New York: McGraw-Hill Book Co., 1948.

Sorokin, P. A. *Society, Culture, and Personality.* New York: Harper & Bros., 1947.

Taft, D. R. *Human Migration.* New York: Ronald Press, 1936. Pp. 3–48, 555–578.

Teggart, F. J. *Theory of History.* New Haven: Yale Univ. Press, 1925. Pp. 187–197.

Zipf, George Kingsley. "The $\frac{P_1 P_2}{D}$ Hypothesis: On the Intercity Movement of Persons," *American Sociological Review* (1946), 11:677–686.

CHAPTER FOURTEEN

SUCCESSION *

TYPES OF SUCCESSION

The term *succession* applies to movements of population and to such social and cultural changes as these movements entail. All forms of succession occur in specific places, take place in time, and involve changes in relationships of a vital, spatial, and functional nature. As such, from one point of view, succession may be regarded as a universal historical phenomenon characteristic of every human group that ever existed on the earth's surface during a given era. On the other hand, many ecologists are interested only in the changes that are primarily physical and vital. These include migrations of people, diffusion of artifacts, ideas, and techniques, changes in spatial location and in occupations of individuals and groups; in short, any type of change which affects an existing division of labor or which influences the relation of population to their sustenance base. Succession, from this point of view, is classified into five types: (1) cultural, (2) territorial, (3) demographic, (4) occupational, and (5) land utilization. These types overlap.

1. Cultural Succession. In this class fall those phenomena known to the anthropologist as the "stages of culture" and to the historian as the "succession of empire" which embrace the rise of one civilization and the decline of another. For instance, the vicissitudes that comprise the Christian Era are usually spoken of as the Decline of the Roman Empire, the Mediaeval, the Early Modern, and the Modern Periods. This type also refers to the long series of successions the anthropologists include in the sequential development of culture from the eolithic to the present.

---

* With his permission, some of the material in this chapter was taken from the late R. E. Park's "Succession, an Ecological Concept," *American Sociological Review* (1936), 1:171–179.

2. Territorial Succession. Territory is subject to invasion and change of occupants in the same way as any aspect of culture. The long procession of peoples who have invaded and settled South Africa is illustrative of this fact. First, the Bushmen. They were hunters who left, in caves in the mountains, interesting rock pictures as records of their presence. Then came the Hottentots. They were hunters, to be sure, but herdsmen also, and they had a great deal of trouble with the Bushmen, who killed their cattle with poisoned arrows. So the Hottentots drove the Bushmen into the Kalahari desert. The Bantu were next. They were hunters and herdsmen but they also cultivated the soil and raised Kaffir corn.

Later still came the Boers, particularly the Trek Boers, who settled the Transvaal and the Orange Free State, conquered and enslaved the natives, settled on the land, raised large families, and lived on their extensive lands in patriarchal style. Although they were descendants, for the most part, of the Dutch, with a sprinkling of Huguenots and other Europeans, they became, as a result of their isolation and their long association with the country, a separate folk, with their own language, their own customs and culture.

Then, finally, came the English. They were sophisticated city folk, who came in force only after the discovery of diamonds (Orange Free State in 1872) and gold (Transvaal in 1884). They built Johannesburg, a cosmopolitan city; a world city, in fact, like Calcutta, Shanghai, or London. In this way they drew South Africa out of its isolation into the current of international trade and into the new world civilization.

What makes this instance of succession ecologically interesting is the fact that it illustrates the principle that the more primitive the culture of a people the larger the territory needed, in proportion to its numbers, to support its population. A corollary of this fact is the principle that the land eventually goes to the people who can get the most out of it.

What, finally, makes the settlement of South Africa relevant and significant, as an example of succession, is the fact that it represents all the forms of succession we are now considering.

3. Demographic Succession. This aspect of succession is intricately interwoven with the territorial aspect. Actually the former cannot be separated from the latter, for with a change of territorial occupancy comes a change in population type and composition. Both the territorial and the demographic uses of succession are apparent in descriptions of the intramural movements and shiftings of population incident to the growth of the city and of its various "natural areas." Immigrant peoples ordinarily settle at first in or near the centers of cities, in the so-called areas of transition, and from there are then likely to move by stages, perhaps one might better say by leaps and bounds, from an area of first to areas of second and third settlement. This movement is generally in the direction of the periphery of the city and eventually into the suburban area, in any case from a less to a more stable section of the metropolitan region.

In the same sense, the term has been applied to the successive waves by which the American frontier advanced from the Atlantic Seaboard westward across the plains to the Pacific Coast, each advance marked by a different type of culture and by a different occupational and personality type.

4. Occupational Succession. In metropolitan economy the occupational pyramid is formed on the basis of economic and social functions. Within an industry or a region the pyramid's composition as it is represented in social classes remains relatively stable over long periods; but the individual units in each class are highly variable and mobile. As is well known, the base of the pyramid is composed of unskilled laborers, who are usually representatives of a compact unassimilated ethnic or racial group; whereas, the apex of the pyramid is composed of representatives of the assimilated ruling class, who are the owners or managers of industry.

As one ethnic or racial group succeeds another in the exploitive process the new one generally enters the occupational pyramid at the base. In such a system, succession is characterized by the rise of individual members of a given group, who move up the strata of the pyramid through the selective processes represented by vertical and horizontal mobility. As the individual members of one group become accommodated to the culture they have entered, and consequently rise in the social scale, another group must be introduced at the base of the pyramid to carry on the activities of unskilled labor. At this point, a new invasion takes place, followed by the inevitable succession from the bottom of the pyramid toward the top. As soon as the upward process begins, new forms of competition produce ethnic and racial concentrations in occupations, and spatial redistributions.

5. Land Utilization Succession. Land is utilized differently under different conditions of settlement and market organization. In fact, land utilization may be taken as an index of the phase of development of metropolitan economy in a region. Within the confines of the city, the use and value of its land indicate the position of the city with respect to the point of dominance. Land values are likely to be highest in the centers of trade, and values, other things being equal, tend to decline with increasing distance from the central market. Furthermore, land values reveal a definite succession as land utilization shifts from one use to another. McKenzie pointed out that in the Puget Sound Region the use of agricultural land has passed through four successions; namely, hop growing, dairying, poultry raising, and finally, intensive market gardening. Each succession was marked by changes in population type, and in spatial, sustenance, and social relations.[1]

Succession Defined. A succession represents the sequential phases of an historical process, created by factors operating in the inanimate, animate, and the socio-cultural environments, as well as in the interactions and reactions of one on the other. Park includes in succession, "every possible form of orderly change so far as it affects the interrelations of individuals in a community or the structure of the society of which these individual units are a part." [2]

Three significant ideas are included in the term *succession*, as we have used it in this outline: (1) The human community is composed of symbiotic and cultural relationships. (2) Changes in the relationships of the components take place as competitive conditions change. (3) The changes that occur compose a series leading to either the development or the disintegration of the community. Such changes ordinarily do not follow a rhythmic or cyclical pattern. There is a tendency, however, for a phase of relative stability to be followed by a period of rapid change, which, in turn, is succeeded by another period of relative stability.

SUCCESSION AS A PROCESS

The descriptions and illustrations cited indicate in a general way the things ecologists and sociologists are disposed to call

---

1 R. D. McKenzie, "Ecological Succession in the Puget Sound Region," *Publications of the American Sociological Society* (1929), 23:60–80.
2 R. E. Park, "Succession, an Ecological Concept," *American Sociological Review* (1936), 1:171–179.

succession. What remains obscure is the nature of the process, and the conditions under which it works. From this point of view, an understanding of the process must take into consideration two aspects of the changes associated with succession: (1) conditions precipitating the changes, and (2) the morphological aspect, or the forms which the changes exhibit when passing from one relative equilibrium to another.

Etiology of Change. Etiological elements in succession always include: (1) An invasion upsets the existent equilibrium in a given symbiotic-cultural complex. (2) A set of historical conditions are created by the interactions between cultures, classes, and institutions, in terms of their cultural heritages. (3) The demographic complex has been molded into a pattern of spatial and sustenance relationships through the adjustment of numbers to the sustenance base. (4) Finally, the conditions obtaining in the biotic and physical environments must be taken into consideration. Intrusive factors may enter any of these elemental aspects of an existent condition and disturb the biotic balance and cultural equilibrium. An invasion in one aspect may, and often does, initiate change in all other aspects.

The fact seems to be that change of some sort is everywhere continuous, although the rate and pace of change may and does vary, sometimes greatly. Under ordinary circumstances, such minor changes as occur may be mediated without profoundly disturbing the existing equilibrium and routine of communal life. When, on the other hand, a sudden and catastrophic change occurs—it may be a war, a famine, or pestilence, some change at any rate that upsets the biotic balance and breaks "the cake of custom"—it releases energies which up to that time had been held in check. A series of rapid and even violent changes may ensue which may profoundly alter the existing organization of communal life and give a new direction to the future course of events.

Etiology of Change, from Cultural Standpoint. Human ecology, in approaching the study of society, assumes that the origin of social change, if one could trace it to its source, would be found in the struggle for existence, and the migration, mobility, and the territorial and occupational distribution of peoples, which this struggle has brought about. Ecology conceives society as fundamentally a territorial as well as a cultural organization. So far as this conception is valid, it assumes that most, if not all, cultural changes in society will be correlated with changes in its territorial organization, and every change in the territorial and occupational distribution of the population will effect changes in the existing cultures. The evolution of society is, therefore, in one of its aspects, the evolution of a territorial organization.

Social change seems invariably to have its origin in some sort of crisis, some break or interruption in the established routine. In fact, succession may be regarded as resulting from a series of recurrent crises. These crises have a general character and a natural history that make a comparative study of them possible, and, for the purpose of social theory, interesting and profitable.

Morphology of Succession. What we ordinarily call a crisis, whether it is a war, a revolution, or a business boom, almost invariably has a place in a definite configuration of events. The crisis is the point from which events take a turn in a new direction.

There are, as a matter of fact, two types of what we have termed crisis—crises, in the interrelation of human beings— which have been studied systematically and statistically. These are (1) on the biotic level, the outbreak and recurrence of epidemics of infectious diseases and (2) on the social level, the occurrence and recurrence of business booms and depressions.

In some aspects, a business boom is not unlike an epidemic, just as an infectious disease, when it becomes epidemic, is not unlike an invasion of the boll weevil or some other insect pest. The difference is that the microbe which is responsible for a business boom is psychic, and in the early days of stock jobbery as in the case of the tulip mania in Holland, the South Sea Bubble in England, and the John Law speculation in France, before the investing public had developed sales resistance, the consequences were often amazing as well as disastrous.

It was the dramatic aspects of business booms, as it was the catastrophic consequence of the great plagues, that first attracted the attention of students. They were regarded at this time as chance events, due to wars, revolutions, and other "acts of God." Later it was discovered that business crises, like an epidemic or any other occurrences that apparently upset the balance of nature, invariably occur not by chance but as an incident or phase of a clearly defined configuration of events. Every business cycle includes "a phase of revival, expansion, recession, and contraction." It was found, also, that the cycles were recurrent, though not periodic, and that "their average duration varied in different communities at different stages of economic development."[1]

The difficulties in finding a mathematical formula which would describe the course of a business cycle, as of an epidemic, arose, it seems, from the necessity of analyzing, from the movement as a whole, the four different components of the cycle: (1) random perturbations, (2) seasonal variations, (3) cycles, and (4) secular trends.

SUMMARY

By way of summary, we may point out that succession as it has been used by human ecologists may be viewed as a sequence of changes associated with the development of community or region. Furthermore, changes evolved in a successive developmental series are related to each other, and must be studied in terms of their interdependence. When this procedure is followed, well-defined characteristic patterns become apparent to the researcher. The form and rapidity of successive changes are, in the main, consequent upon the component biotic and cultural factors active in the development succession. In most successions, at least three types of changes occur which transform the affected area: *First*, alterations take place in the spatial distribution of population units and institutional services; these alterations are accompanied by changed sustenance functions and relations. *Second*, many times a new socio-cultural order is formed, with fundamental changes occurring in many aspects of the pre-existent order. *Third*, there is formation of a new population type which, with a characteristic composition, normally accompanies each succession. Succession generally develops along one or all of the following lines: classes, occupations, age, sex, race, or ethnic groups.

SELECTED READINGS

Burgess, E. W. "The Natural Area as the Unit for Social Work in the Large City," *Proceedings of the National Conference of Social Work* (1926), 53:504–510.

Carpenter, J. R. *An Ecological Glossary.* Norman: Univ. of Oklahoma Press, 1938.

Davie, Maurice R. "The Pattern of Urban Growth," in G. P. Murdock, ed. *Studies in the Science of Society.* New Haven: Yale Univ. Press, 1937. Pp. 133–161.

---

[1] Wesley C. Mitchell, "Business Cycles," *Encyclopaedia of the Social Sciences* (1930), 3:92–107. Used by permission of the publishers, Macmillan Co., New York.

Hawley, A. H. *Human Ecology*. New York: Ronald Press, 1950.

Johnson, Charles S. *Patterns of Negro Segregation*. New York: Harper & Bros., 1943.

Kenngott, George F. *The Record of a City*. New York: Macmillan Co., 1912.

Lind, Andrew W. *Island Community: Ecological Succession in Hawaii*. Chicago: Univ. of Chicago Press, 1938.

McKenzie, R. D. "Ecological Succession in the Puget Sound Region," *Publications of the American Sociological Society* (1929), 23:60–80.

Mitchell, Wesley C. "Occupational Succession," in Committee on Recent Economic Changes, *Recent Economic Changes*. New York: McGraw-Hill Book Co., 1929. 2:876–879.

Mukerjee, R. "The Concepts of Distribution and Succession in Human Ecology," *Social Forces* (1932), 11:1–7.

Mukerjee, R. *Man and His Habitation*. New York: Longmans, Green & Co., 1942.

Quinn, James A. *Human Ecology*. New York: Prentice-Hall, 1950.

Smith, T. Lynn. *Population Analysis*. New York: McGraw-Hill Book Co., 1948.

Thompson, Edgar T. "Mines and Plantations and the Movement of Peoples," *American Journal of Sociology* (1931), 37:314–326, 603–611.

Vance, Rupert B. "Frontiers: Geographical and Social Aspects," in *Encyclopaedia of the Social Sciences* (1931), 5:503–505.

Vance, Rupert B. *Research Memorandum on Population Redistribution within the United States*. New York: Social Science Research Committee, 1938.

Wirth, Louis. "Localism, Regionalism, and Centralization," *American Journal of Sociology* (1937), 42:493–509.

Part Three

Race and Culture

By

EDWARD B. REUTER
Late of Fisk University

PART THREE

RACE AND CULTURE
By Edward B. Reuter

TOPICS

Chapter XV. The Relations between Race and Culture.
Organic and Cultural Variability.
Independence of Concepts.
Interdependence of Concrete Reality.

Chapter XVI. Races and Culture Groups.
The Concept of Race. Race Differences.
The Sociological Significance of Race.
The Mixture of Racial Groups.
Racial Determinism. Racial Doctrines.

Chapter XVII. Culture.
The Concept of Culture. The Origin of Culture.
The Content of Culture. The Conditioning Effects of Culture.
The Diffusion of Culture. Culture Change.

Chapter XVIII. Race and Culture Contacts.
Historical Contacts. Contacts and Race Relations.
The Intermixture of the Races. The Fusion of Cultures.
Marginal Groups. Race Problems.

CHAPTER FIFTEEN

THE RELATIONS
BETWEEN RACE AND CULTURE

Race and culture are in separate orders of reality: one is biological, the other is social. Genuine understanding of race and culture, therefore, depends upon clear comprehension of the distinction between biological and social processes, and of the interrelations among these processes in concrete reality.

ORGANIC AND CULTURAL VARIABILITY

Uniformity and Stability. In the racial character and cultural organization of human beings there is a high degree of uniformity and stability. All individuals are alike in original nature in that each embodies the same complex of physical, mental, and temperamental traits; the individuals of each generation are like those of each preceding one. In its fundamental aspects, the culture of every group is like that of every other group. Human nature, a product of primary group relations, is a common characteristic of mankind.

Along with uniformity and stability in racial character and cultural organization, there are also wide and important differences, as well as variation and change, in original characters and social traits. On the side of original nature, the three major independent variations are sex, race, and individual differences; in the social realm, variations may be classed as personal and cultural.

Organic Variability. In the organic realm, individual variability is continuous within the limitations of the species. Individuals of the same species vary from one another in height, weight, stature, and all other physical characters, but the fluctuations are always within a narrow range and cluster about a median point. Such differences are variations of the kind that may be produced by combinations of traits that vary quantitatively. In mental ability the range of variation is somewhat wide between the dullards and the men of talent, but intelligence is of the same quality in all; the differences are matters of degree. The range in temperament is probably as wide as in physique and mentality.

Cultural Variability. The range of variability is greater in the cultural than in the organic realm. The only limits in the former are those set by the physical structure of the organism, which makes impossible various types of life and behavior, and the nature of the material with which man must work. There are wide differences among peoples in their arts, techniques, and material culture; the differences are still greater in language, systems of thought, law, government, social organization, sentiments and attitudes, standards, and other elements of an immaterial nature.

INDEPENDENCE OF CONCEPTS

The Racial and Cultural Processes. It is essential to clarity of thought that the racial and cultural phenomena and processes be conceived as lying on different planes of reality. They are of independent origin, involve unlike mechanisms of transmission, and function to separate ends.

Race a Physical Concept. Races are products of the biological processes. The term *race* refers to a variety of mankind composed of individuals of common descent, a group with heritable traits sufficiently pronounced to set it apart from other human subdivisions. Races are indefinitely interfertile and intergrade with others of the same species.

A race arises as a single abrupt step or a series of sudden steps. Its origin is in a mutation, a biological accident, that produces an individual with transmissible physical structures new to the species. These characters are transmitted through the germ plasm and reappear unchanged in successive generations. The race thus begun may undergo change only by selective substitution in the process of biological adaptation. The whole genetic process culminates in the production of a biological individual: the origin is in mutation; the method of change is selection; the medium of transmission is the germ plasm; the mechanism is the chromosomes; the content is integrated structures; and the end result is a biological organism.

Culture a Social Concept. Culture is an outcome of social experience. It refers to the sum and organization of human invention and discovery, to the accumulated results of human effort. It includes the great variety of tools and other artifacts evolved during man's continued efforts to satisfy his needs; the subsidiary complex of sentiments and attitudes; the institutional structures and other control techniques operating to perpetuate the social order and make general the approved types of behavior; and the bodies of philosophical explanations of the world which help to make life intelligible and existence, in a measure, tolerable.

The culture process is thus separate from and contrasted at every point with the racial process. From small beginnings, culture grows through additions; it develops and changes through the incorporation of new items and the modification of the old practices, during use and transmission. Culture is transmitted through social contact and communication. Its origin is in human discovery and invention, its manner of growth is accumulation, its medium is communication, its mechanism is imitation and inculcation, its content is patterns of behavior, and its end results are types of personality and bodies of interrelated belief and practice.

INTERDEPENDENCE OF CONCRETE REALITY

Relationship between Racial and Social Processes. The racial and social processes are distinct and relatively independent and it is necessary to analyze each process apart from the concrete reality by means of which it gets expression. But at certain points they come together and interact, or operate simultaneously, to the same or different ends. It is necessary, therefore, to consider the relationships of the processes conceptually abstracted.

On a common-sense level, racial and cultural phenomena are coexistent, intimately interrelated, and mutually conditioned. Race facts are culturally defined and racial changes are brought about by social factors; on the other hand, culture facts are always observed as the possession of concrete racial groups.

There is, however, more than this superficial order of interdependency. The processes are not separated in concrete reality. The human being has a dual inheritance: a complement of appetites and capacities characteristic of the organism transmitted biologically, and a body of habits resulting from present and past associated life.

Race as Conditioned by Culture. The individual is a biological unit whose nature is determined by the organic hereditary processes. But he comes at birth into a social environment, lives an associative life, and acquires a heritage and a personality as a result of interaction with other human beings. The subsequent working of the biological process is conditioned and controlled by the culture into which he is born and by the fact of associative life. The manner in which biological facts emerge from and are controlled by cultural facts may be shown by a simple example.

Domestication is a biological process. It is an alteration, by selective survival, of the native endowment of a race. The process presupposes heritable differences among individuals and a selective birth- or mortality-rate. The change resulting from individual differences and varying rates of birth or mortality is strictly biological. But the selection of survivors may be consciously controlled, be deliberate and purposeful, as in the case of political measures designed to reduce the number of feeble-minded persons in a population. Here, a purely social fact controls the biological process, and domestication becomes as much a historical as a biological matter.

Similar control and direction of biological phenomena by social and cultural facts exist generally. The social and cultural facts fix the conditions of survival and so determine the direction and result of organic processes. Births and deaths are organic facts but their incidence is determined by cultural conditions. War is a social phenomenon that leads to racial transformation and decline. Slavery is a form of social organization determined by economic conditions but it leads directly to racial consequences. Marriage customs have direct and obvious racial consequences. Commerce and international trade are cultural phenomena, but they have racial consequences in the biological amalgamation of diverse stocks.

A low order of mentality is a biological fact. The social exclusion and the consequent association of the mentally deficient, and the appearance among them of characteristic folkways and divergent behavior patterns are purely cultural phenomena. But these cultural phenomena determine their marriage contacts which in turn determine racial phenomena.

Culture as Conditioned by Race. Certain biological facts bear a constant relation to cultural phenomena. The capacity of individuals determines the level of the human nature and culture that may be acquired and transmitted from one generation to the next; by controlling the level of individual achievement, the original equipment of human beings at birth controls the culture and social organization.

Sex, for example, is a biological fact probably without direct cultural connotation. But sex is an obvious basis for social organization and for the restriction and exclusion of individuals. In this way, sex gives rise to a wide range of subsidiary cultural phenomena.

Blindness is a physical or biological fact. But this fact limits the number and determines the kind of social contacts and, consequently, sets limits to personal development and group organization. Deafness, physical defect, mental deficiency, disease, and other biological facts and conditions limit contacts, and the consequent isolation may result in distorted personalities and retarded culture.

Race phenomena and processes are biological; cultural phenomena and processes are social. They are distinct types of reality and must be understood separately if they are to be understood at all. But in concrete reality the biological and social processes exist together and each influences the other. Hence the interrelations and mutual conditioning of the processes must also be understood in order to understand behavior phenomena.

SELECTED READINGS

Count, Earl W., ed. *This Is Race: An Anthology.* New York: Henry Schuman, 1950.

Faris, E. *The Nature of Human Nature.* New York: McGraw-Hill Book Co., 1937.

Hankins, F. H. *Introduction to the Study of Society.* New York: Macmillan Co., 1935. Pp. 218–397.

Krogman, Wilton M. "The Concept of Race," in Ralph Linton, ed., *The Science of Man in the World Crisis.* New York: Columbia Univ. Press, 1945.

Locke, Alain, and Bernhard J. Stern. *When Peoples Meet: A Study in Race and Culture Contacts.* Rev. ed. New York: Barnes & Noble, Inc., 1946.

Park, R. E. *Race and Culture.* Glencoe, Ill.: Free Press, 1950.

Park, R. E., and E. W. Burgess. *Introduction to the Science of Society.* Chicago: Univ. of Chicago Press, 1924. Pp. 64–149.

Reuter, E. B. "Racial Theory," *American Journal of Sociology* (1945), 50:452–461.

Reuter, E. B. "The Relation of Biology and Sociology," *American Journal of Sociology* (1926–1927), 32:705–718.

Reuter, E. B., and C. W. Hart. *An Introduction to Sociology.* New York: McGraw-Hill Book Co., 1933. Pp. 26–46.

Shapiro, H. L. "Society and Biological Man," in Ralph Linton, ed., *The Science of Man in the World Crisis.* New York: Columbia Univ. Press, 1945.

Sutherland, E. H. "The Biological and Sociological Processes," in E. W. Burgess, ed., *The Urban Community.* Chicago: Univ. of Chicago Press, 1926.

CHAPTER SIXTEEN

RACES AND CULTURE GROUPS

In the human realm, race has not been a particularly fruitful category. In common usage the concept is undefined and is used loosely to designate culture groups, language groups, or even political or class divisions as well as large groups which possess distinctive appearance because of common descent.

THE CONCEPT OF RACE

The Biological Concept. The biological conception of race is that of a permanent variety of mankind composed of individuals descended from a common ancestor who diverged, by mutation, from the previously existing racial type. A race is a division inferior to a species, yet possessed of constant transmissible traits sufficiently pronounced to characterize it as a distinct type. The distinguishing marks are of less constant character and of less biological significance than the traits which divide animals into species.

Few human groups meet these biological specifications necessary to form a distinct race. Human contacts throughout the human era have been such that racial groups when formed have not been long continued. In the modern world there are no clear-cut divisions, no human groups that meet the requirements of reasonably rigid biological definition. Local groups of remote districts are readily distinguishable but they are everywhere surrounded by scarcely distinguishable variants, and the remote local groups are united by various intermediate forms.

Hypothetical Races. Because of the biological impurity of the various existing racial stocks, the problem of classification is sometimes conceived as one of determining the original races from which the existing groups were produced by intermixture. This is a problem of determining the ancestors from the heritable traits present in the mixed stock of the present day. The term *race* then refers not to existing concrete groups but to hypothetical constructs sharply divorced from tangible reality. The problems thus presented are important but they are purely speculative and aside from the present discussion.

Concrete Racial Groups. It is immediately obvious that no valid classification in biological terms of modern racial groups is possible. There are no sharp and stable lines of demarcation. Within any major group there are wide variations in stature, head form, pigmentation, facial angle, body proportions, and other physical characters. Individuals may be classified with any one of these as a criterion but, since there is no constant relation among the various physical traits, classification made with one as a criterion will not correspond to classification made on the basis of any other.

Biological traits are marks of individual organisms; biological facts are individual phenomena. A concrete race is a grouping of individuals having the same combination of heritable traits. But each individual in the modern world represents a mixture of traits, hence is not classifiable in any rigidly defined set of racial categories.

Race as a Statistical Concept. Because each individual differs from every other, there is no limit to the number of subtypes that may be set up in any large group. They may be classified according to any physical trait or any combination of physical traits. Since there is an indefinite overlapping of traits, there are as many races as one may desire to set up. Classifications are based on varying characters and there is no generally accepted system.

In this sense race is merely a statistical concept, and not a reality; there is no individual that conforms to type. Race is a statistical abstraction, an idealized set of characters, derived from the concrete, complex reality.

Races as Culturally Defined Groups. In sociological usage a race is a physical subtype of cultural formation. The biological origins and affiliations are relatively unimportant. It is a group with more or less permanent distinguishing characters to which the persons concerned, the members themselves or the members of outside groups, attach certain interpretations. The physical marks are meaningful only as a basis of identification that permits a type of cohesion.

RACE DIFFERENCES

Shared and Heritable Traits. However defined, the term *race* directs attention to the physical and biological aspects of man that are heritable in character and common to the members of a group.

Physical Characters. The individual variations among human beings in stature, body weight, skin color, and other biologically determined traits are within a very narrow range. Such differences, in all cases, are quantitative; they are differences in degree, not in kind.

Between concrete racial groups, however defined, the physical differences are less than the individual differences within a single racial group. The racial characters are averages of individuals comprising the group. The differences among such averages from one group to another are relatively slight. There is much overlapping. In pigmentation, for example, certain individuals of a dark race are of lighter complexion than many individuals of the lighter race.

The differences in physical characters seem in all cases to be biologically unimportant. It is not possible to show, for example, that the kinky hair, everted lips, long forearm, highly pigmented skin, and other physical traits of the Negro peoples, or the contrasted traits of the North European groups, are either good or bad.

The common idea that certain races or peoples are superior to others in some important traits is undemonstrated and appears to be without foundation. Such differences as exist are individual differences. Persons of keen senses and persons with defective senses are common in all groups. It may very well be that at a given time the percentages vary from one racial group to another. But the differences between groups as such, if and when shown to exist, are matters of statistical distribution; they are not racial traits.

Mental Characters. The members of each racial group have the same equipment of psychological characters. Perception, memory, the ability to form abstract conceptions, the capacity to inhibit impulses, and the other main mental characters of human beings appear to be the same in all racial groups. No qualitative differences, in the sense that some have mental capacities that others lack, have ever been shown to exist.

Such differences as may be observed are individual differences. Differences between and among groups are merely statistical averages; there are individuals of various degrees of mental ability in every group. If one racial group is mentally superior to another it is only in the sense of chance distribution. At a particular time one group may contain more superior individuals or fewer mentally incompetent individuals than another. That one group is able to produce a surplus of superior men each generation is conceivable, but neither historical nor biological evidence supports this theory.

The tendency to speak of superior and inferior races appears to do violence to the fact that these are concepts about individuals; applied to races or groups, such terms are either meaningless or carry a different, a merely statistical, connotation. It seems to be only in a statistical sense that one racial group may be said to be superior to another in mental capacity; there is apparently no racial group with any mental deficiency that would prevent cultural advance comparable with that of any other group.

Psychological Tests and Racial Differences. The crude findings of the early psychological tests showed marked differences among racial groups. Superficial interpretation, premature publication, and journalistic exploitation of such findings popularized the idea, in line with common prejudices and class biases, that gross racial differences exist in mentality.

But the results of the psychological tests, when adequately interpreted and competently understood, do not reflect group differences attributable to a racial factor. The tests in vogue are standardized on the basis of Anglo-Saxon and urban experience and education, hence they show differences in groups to the extent of differences in social experience and tradition. Differences in showings made on the tests are to be attributed to variations in the social heritage. That race is merely a chance element is shown by the fact that in the Army Tests the Negroes of certain Northern states ranked above the whites of certain Southern states.

The measures of individual intelligence ratings, if granted to be valid, do not give the rating of a race. It is not possible to arrive at the qualities of a race by the addition of individual qualities or by taking an average of individual qualities. Differences between race groups exist as the tests show, but the tests do not show the differences to be attributable to race, if by race is meant the biological make-up apart from social experience.

THE SOCIOLOGICAL SIGNIFICANCE OF RACE

The Independence of Cultural Capacity The physical differences among racial groups are slight and biologically unimportant. It has not been shown that the traits used by anthropologists in their classifications bear any constant relation to cultural capacity; mental differences among the racial groups have not been demonstrated.

The Isolating Effects of Race. The physical and visible marks of race are of great social and cultural significance. They differentiate between groups of people, and they condition contact and interaction by operating as barriers to communication across the group lines.

Visible marks of race are convenient criteria for classifications; they automatically assign individuals to categories. To the extent that these categories are social and cultural as well as physical, such classification defines personal experience, and conditions and limits participation in social life.

The cultural phenomena, caused by the fact that racial marks are treated as social values, are in no sense biological. They are not the result of race differences directly; they are the result of social attitudes directed toward the physical facts. The taboos and sanctions, not the biological facts, prevent full participation and achievement.

Race Marks as Social Values. Social attitudes may arise toward physical and biological traits. Each isolated racial group, and provincial men of all racial groups, look upon their own type as the only fully human form and tend to fear or despise men of other races. There is a vague, undefined fear of the strange, a spontaneous negative reaction from the unusual. This antipathy, an organic reaction largely below the conscious level, is a basis for negative attitudes towards individuals and groups of individuals who possess an outward appearance, food habits, moral customs, social beliefs, or behavior that differs from those familiar to the group.

In practically all places in the modern world the conspicuous marks of race, particularly skin color, are made the object of favorable or unfavorable estimation. They are the basis for differential treatment and for social and cultural exclusion.

Isolation and Retardation. The immediate effect of isolation, regardless of the conditions that induce it, is to prevent personal development and to retard the cultural advance of the excluded people. It narrows the range of contact and communication and makes difficult the meeting and association of men on the plane of equality and self-respect.

The relative slowness of change in primitive groups is due to the paucity of stimulating contacts, the lack of access to ideas current elsewhere, brought about by the fact of physical separation. The relative retardation of excluded individuals and groups—the Negroes, the working-class groups, and others within larger culture areas—is due to a similar narrowing of contacts brought about by social restrictions.

Group Solidarity. Individuals and groups excluded because of race and divergent appearance, whether it be by means of unformulated common understanding or by a legislative fiat of the ruling class, fraternize and develop a distinctive type of mind. The special environment inculcates a similarity of habits, manners, interests, beliefs, and traditions that facilitates contact and communication within the group and retards communication with other groups. The excluded individuals develop a distinctive folklore, and distinctive social and cultural traits.

This distinctive culture complex helps to augment the isolation of the group and to increase its internal cohesion. The traits peculiar to the group become the objects of ridicule and other types of persecution. Unable to discard them and gain membership in the dominant group, individuals strive for self-respect by exalting the qualities in which they differ. These marks thus become things of importance, emotionally charged symbols of of group unity, that are defended with sectarian zeal. The new peculiarities lead to further exclusion and so to greater unity.

THE MIXTURE OF RACIAL GROUPS

The Process of Intermixture. The mixture of ethnic stocks is one of the uniform consequences of contacts among peoples. In all places where divergent peoples have come into contact for a period of time they have produced a hybrid offspring. The intermixture may be by way of formal intermarriage, sometimes by way of more casual, informal, and unsanctioned unions. If the association of the groups be long continued, the lines of demarcation disappear; one or the other or both of the originally divergent peoples are lost in the resulting mixed population.

The mixture of races has been in process throughout most of the human era. Its early incidence is indicated by the fact that many of the fossil remains of prehistoric man show that the individuals were descended from ancestors of different racial stocks, and the mixing of blood has continued in every area of contact to the present time.

Attitudes toward Racial Intermixture. The attitudes toward racial mixture vary from approval, through indifference or even apparent unawareness that race mixture is in process, to violent opposition that expresses itself in prohibitory legislation and mob violence. In the former situation the intermixture normally goes on by means of marriage forms that are conventional in the particular area. In the latter case intermarriage is rare, and contact and intermixture are for the most part outside of the marriage institution. The attitudes of approval and disapproval change the social aspects of the phenomenon; they apparently have no appreciable effect on miscegenation itself.

Every area of race contact is a particular historic situation characterized by unique economic and political conditions, and the racial attitudes in any area must be understood in terms of the historic development of the economic and political order.

Approval and Encouragement of Intermixture. When the social stocks are somewhat closely related and not strongly contrasted in physical type or culture, as are the various immigrant peoples of the American population, intermarriage commonly attracts little attention and arouses little opposition. It is often looked upon with positive approval, as an indication that the newcomers are being fully incorporated into the national group.

In certain areas and at certain times, marriage of European colonists or settlers into the native populations has been encouraged as a means of incorporating the natives into the existing culture, and of maintaining friendly relations with the native people.

The French in Canada manifested little antagonism toward the American Indians. They mingled freely with the Algonquin tribes, both on the coast and in the interior. Intermarriage was encouraged by the officials and by the Catholic missionaries. Mixed marriages were numerous and a relatively large French-Indian population established a bond between the races.

In the Spanish colonies, for the most part, friendly relations were never established between the races; the conquerors were interested primarily in exploiting the area and the people. But there was a paucity of white women, and racial intermixture continued throughout the era without official or moral opposition. Intermixture was so extensive that it became the outstanding phenomenon of race contacts in Spanish America.

Popular Opposition. In other areas of contact, the mixture of races arouses more or less violent opposition. This is frequently the case where the physical and cultural differences between the races in contact are wide and obvious. But the explanation lies in the social relations rather than in the physical contrasts.

In colonial and settlement areas, opposition to miscegenation typically arises only after the introduction of white women.

The desire of the white women to keep a monopoly on the sex activities of the white men is frequently reinforced by the activities of the missionaries. The conditions of miscegenation violate the formal standards of the missionaries—which standards they are concerned to propagate—and arouse their violent and active condemnation.

Intermixture tends to break down the caste relations between groups. It thus generates opposition from two sources: the disturbance of the caste pattern of accommodation (the division into independent castes) arouses emotional resentment, and the control of the economically and politically dominant group is put in jeopardy by the weakening of the pattern.

For these or other reasons, opposition to racial intermixture may arise in areas in which the early attitudes were tolerant or positively favorable. Efforts to prevent miscegenation vary, according to the political exigencies of the situation, from the formally unacknowledged inculcation of caste prejudice, as in present-day Hawaii, to formal and legal as well as mob procedures, as in the Southern states of America.

Cultural Effects of Race Mixture. In popular and propagandist literature, great cultural importance is frequently attributed to race mixture.

The intermixture of races has often been associated with cultural phenomena of great human moment. The amalgamation of divergent racial strains seems everywhere to have preceded, accompanied, or followed profound changes in culture and social organization. The historic facts have been variously interpreted: in one view, it has been cited as a cause of cultural progress; in another, it has been cited in explanation of cultural decadence.

Either position involves a misconception of the relation between biological and cultural phenomena; the two do not stand in a causal relation to each other. The actual relation between race mixture and cultural phenomena is discussed in a later paragraph.

Biological Effects of Race Mixture. So far as the biological evidence goes, neither in-marriage nor out-marriage has any beneficial or injurious effects. The traits of individuals are determined by the genetic factors received from the immediate ancestry. The transmissible traits reappear in the offspring without regard to whether the parents are of the same or different racial strains. The marriage of closely related persons makes more likely the appearance in offspring of recessive traits; cross-mating decreases the likelihood that such traits will reappear. This, however, is a matter that has to do with the heritable traits of the parents; it is not a question of whether they belong to the same or different racial strains. Neither endogamous nor exogamous mating is able to produce any traits in the offspring that are not expressed or latent in the individual ancestry. Racial intermarriage, on the basis of the biological evidence from animal breeding as well as on the evidence from human marriage, is a matter of biological indifference.

Social Effects of Race Mixture. The immediate social effects of race mixture are to bring the races closer together in sympathy and understanding and to facilitate the process of assimilation.

The effect of biracial ancestry on individual status and personality depends upon the attitude people take toward racial intermixture. The fact of biracial origin makes the individual conspicuous and, where intermarriage is forbidden, self-conscious. The role and status of mixed bloods are stated in a later chapter.

RACIAL DETERMINISM

The Doctrine of Racial Determinism. The doctrine of racial determinism holds that the culture differences among population groups are expressions of innate factors. The racial, that is, biological, differences determine the possibilities of cultural advance; because of the biological differences, an advanced culture is possible for some groups but is not possible for others.

Culture as a Function of Race. The doctrine of racial determinism errs in making culture a function of race. The culture differences that have existed for many centuries between the Negroids, Mongoloids, and Caucasoids are advanced as proof of the existence in racial groups of a determining factor other than diversity of historic experience.

In some cases the physical differences are posited as the foundation of the culture differences; the culturally backward peoples are believed to be more closely akin to the anthropoid apes than are the European stocks. But a greater similarity of the culturally backward peoples to the apes cannot be demonstrated and, if it could, it would justify no inference in regard to social qualities and mental abilities. The fact of physical resemblance demonstrates only the fact of physical resemblance. There is no known correlation between specific physical and mental qualities in the individual and so none in the race, which, in this respect, is simply a totality of individuals.

In some cases there is a direct assumption of mental inferiority. But the various attempts to discover racial differences in innate mental constitution have been uniformly unsuccessful.

It is the social background and the culture heritage that determine a race's status. Races have not lived in the same world and have not had the same experiences and opportunities. Hence their accomplishments cannot be attributed solely to innate characters, and cannot be attributed to race at all until the differences in opportunities and experiences have been equated. Culture is only casually associated with race, and such association as exists must be understood in historical terms.

Race Change and Culture Continuity. A culture has a high degree of continuity, a tendency to resist change and to change but slowly unless it be profoundly disorganized. This stability remains in the presence of heterogeneous biological changes of type. Heterogeneous types may be carriers of homogeneous cultures: all of western, central, and eastern Europe represents a general homogeneity of culture but a heterogeneity of racial type. In a smaller area, such as France or the United States, the same fact is yet more obvious.

The same is true of the various elements of culture that migrate separately. The English language, for example, persists in spite of the fact that it is used and transmitted by a large percentage of the people of the world and by the most diverse racial types.

Culture Change and Racial Stability. The converse is likewise true: homogeneity of biological type may go with heterogeneity of culture. This fact may be illustrated from almost any area of the modern world. The aborigines of the new world are fairly homogeneous as to racial type. But the culture differences as one goes from the Aztec to the Eskimo are as great as those between the African and the Eskimo or the African and the ancient Greek.

The specific racial type appears to be only a chance carrier of specific cultures. The language, technology, and other culture facts carried by a group are matters of historic accident. The change in culture of the American and the African branches of the Negro racial group is historical. Biologically the groups are the same; culturally they are different. The innate characters of the North European peoples are not essentially different today from those of 2,000 years ago, but the cultures are radically different.

RACIAL DOCTRINES

The Nature of Racial Doctrines. Racial doctrines are very numerous and very diverse, and they are held with the greatest of emotional certitude. These doctrines are to be understood as in part rationalizations of folk beliefs and in part as constructions of utilitarian origin.

Primitive Ethnocentrism. Most uncivilized peoples apply to themselves terms meaning men; for others they have less exalted terms. These are usually not rationalized; they are merely direct observation and report of differences between themselves and others unlike them. Sometimes the differences are accounted for by myths indicating the special favor of some deity.

In much of the current literature the same ethnocentric feeling appears and the same order of rationalization, with the exception that the rationalization is likely to run in terms of science rather than of deities. The superiority of the white man is accepted; the discussion revolves about the relative superiority of the branches of the white race, about the degree of inferiority of the other groups, or about the cause and explanation of the white man's superiority.

Political Constructs. In many cases the racial doctrines have been invented and propagated in the interests of some group or party. Count Arthur Gobineau, for example, produced his work to support the class and theological biases. In the preface to his work on racial inequality he points out that his theory was fabricated in support of certain clerical and social views, deliberately constructed as a tool to combat the "theorists of subversion" and the "eccentric liberalism" of his day and thereby uphold biblical revelation and the status and rights of the aristocratic caste. In spite of this frank and more or less naïve admission, the doctrine had a wide vogue; it was in line with the prejudices of the audience to which he spoke.

A great part of the more modern racial doctrines has been built up, consciously or naïvely, in the modern struggle against democracy. The whole eugenic doctrine, for example, unknown to most of its expounders and converts, is an aspect of race biology and a powerful antidemocratic tool. The mental tests, and this result was not anticipated by most of the practitioners, are valuable political tools for race control. The correlation of race with intelligence quotient was an inference elicited from the assumption of race superiority and inferiority, not the reverse.

SELECTED READINGS

Adorno, T. W., and others. *The Authoritarian Personality.* New York: Harper & Bros., 1950.

Benedict, Ruth, and Gene Weltfish. *The Races of Mankind.* New York: Public Affairs Pamphlet No. 85, 1943.

Boas, Franz. "Race," *Encyclopaedia of the Social Sciences* (1934), 13:25–36.

Boas, Franz. *Race, Language and Culture.* New York: Macmillan Co., 1940.

Dahlberg, Gunnar. *Race, Reason and Rubbish.* New York: Columbia Univ. Press, 1942.

Garth, T. R. *Race Psychology.* New York: McGraw-Hill Book Co., 1931.

Hankins, F. H. *The Racial Basis of Civilization.* New York: A. A. Knopf, 1931.

Haring, Douglas G. *Racial Differences and Human Resemblances.* Syracuse, N. Y.: Syracuse Univ. Bookstore, 1947.

Herskovits, Melville J. *Man and His Works: The Science of Cultural Antropology.* New York: A. A. Knopf, 1948.

Herskovits, Melville J. "Race Mixture," *Encyclopaedia of the Social Sciences* (1934), 13:41–43.

Hertz, F. *Race and Civilization.* New York: Macmillan Co., 1928.

Klineberg, Otto. *Race Differences.* New York: Harper & Bros., 1935.

Lee, Alfred M. *Race Riots Aren't Necessary.* Public Affairs Pamphlet No. 107· New York: Public Affairs Committee, Inc., 1945.

Locke, Alain, and Bernhard J. Stern. *When Peoples Meet: A Study in Race and Culture Contacts.* Rev. ed. New York: Barnes & Noble, Inc., 1946.

Montagu, M. F. A. *Man's Most Dangerous Myth.* New York: Columbia Univ. Press, 1942.

Montagu, M. F. A. *On Being Human.* New York: Henry Schumann, Inc., 1950.

Park, Robert E. "Mentality of Racial Hybrids," *American Journal of Sociology* (1931), 36:534–551.

Park, Robert E. "Personality and Culture Conflict," *Publications of the American Sociological Society* (1931), 25:95–110.

Reuter, E. B. *Race Mixture.* New York: McGraw-Hill Book Co., 1931.

Woofter, T. J. *Races and Ethnic Groups in American Life.* New York: McGraw-Hill Book Co., 1933.

Young, Donald. *American Minority Peoples.* New York: Harper & Bros., 1932. Chaps. 11, 12.

Chapter Seventeen

CULTURE

No human group lives in a state of nature. Each group has a more or less elaborate and integrated social heritage, received from the ancestors and transmitted to the descendants. This heritage maintains the spatial and temporal solidarity of the group. Each new generation lives in and by the cultural remains of the earlier generations. The social heritage accounts for human nature and for its relatively unchanging character. Culture, which is coextensive with human life, is both a cause and an effect of the qualities that make life human.

THE CONCEPT OF CULTURE

Meaning of the Term. The term *culture* is used to signify the sum total of human creations, the organized result of group experience up to the present time. Culture includes all that man has made in the form of tools, weapons, shelter, and other material goods and processes, all that he has elaborated in the way of attitudes and beliefs, ideas and judgments, codes and institutions, arts and sciences, philosophy and social organization. Culture also includes the interrelations among these and other aspects of human as distinct from animal life. Everything, material and immaterial, created by man, in the process of living, comes within the concept of culture.

The Social Nature of Culture. No part of culture is inborn. It is a deposit from the activities of men as they endeavor to control reality for the satisfaction of their wishes. The members of each generation receive the cultural heritage from preceding generations and adapt themselves to it just as they do to climate and the other aspects of the physical environment. They use their inherited culture, add to it, and pass it on to their descendants. In an ultimate sense it exists only in men—in the habits, interests, and ideas of the members of the group. But it has a history of its own apart from any particular individual or group that receives, possesses, and transmits it. Culture may be treated as a reality independent of its present possessors. Language, for example, has objective reality as do religious dogmas, scientific theories, and law. Any given generation is a recipient and carrier. But the possession of the culture is a prerequisite to its transmission. It is not passed on in a merely physical sense; it becomes part of the life organization of each person who becomes a member of the group.

The Diversity of Culture Forms. Culture is characterized by its diversity; it takes a myriad of forms. The material devices and the idea systems vary from group to group; each people has its body of thought and custom, its characteristic way of life. Each culture goes its own way, persists in its own peculiar mode of life. The recorded differences between racial groups are often little more, sometimes nothing more, than culture differences. Each group is absorbed in its own culture; its thought and behavior are determined by the traditional materials. By the culture of a group, as distinct from culture in general, is meant the mode of life of the people. These culture differences among groups are in no way due to psychological and biological differences among peoples; they are caused entirely by external forces. They are the cause rather than the effect of racial differences.

Culture Diversity and Understanding. Culture is both an integrating and a segregating factor in human life and association. It makes for easy understanding and mutual appreciation among those who share the same heritage; it makes understanding difficult and appreciation rare among peoples of diverse heritages. A common language is necessary to communication. But even with a common language, the degree of understanding is limited except when there is a common background of belief, interest, and sentiment, a background that comes from participation in a common life.

The savage does not understand the white man; in the nature of the case he cannot do so. To understand the white man he must understand the white man's culture, or some considerable part of it. The converse is equally true: the white man does not understand the savage; he does not, in general, understand anything outside his own culture complex.

The same thing is true, in somewhat lesser degree, of men with closely related cultures as, for example, the people of two European states. A considerable lack of fundamental understanding exists between individuals and classes, such as an aristocracy and a peasantry, who possess different parts of a common culture. No individual possesses the whole of a complex culture. The particular part he possesses depends upon his social status and contacts. Thus, two individuals of the same culture may have in common only a few general elements, such as the supernatural beliefs, moral sentiments, and ethical ideas.

THE ORIGIN OF CULTURE

Culture as a Factor of Associative Life. The beginning of new culture facts at any given time or place is the result either of invention or of contact with and learning from other peoples; the culture facts are either created within the group or learned from outsiders. No part of the culture is inborn; no part is acquired or transmitted by way of the germinal inheritance. Culture originates from associative life and is elaborated in response to human need.

Invention. All culture facts begin as inventions. This is true regardless of the kind of achievement; ideas, types of behavior, and forms of social organization are as truly inventions as are the material devices. The new facts, produced in reaction to the previously existing situation, serve some definite immediate need, are added to the already existing body of culture, increasing its complexity, and are handed down to the following generations. The automobile, for example, in part replaces the horse; in part, it exists alongside. The living culture is therefore constantly changing and increasing in volume and complexity through the addition of new items.

The similarity of needs and the similarity of minds lead to the similarity of inventions in diverse areas. The bow and arrow, the invention of fire, the domestication of animals, and the fabrication of flood stories are illustrations of inventions independently created in different times and places.

In many cases inventions are in the nature of accidents—chance combinations of factors producing something new. In other cases failure or imperfection in transmission may produce a deviation that is in reality a new fact; the development of dialects through errors in speaking and the transmission of the errors are cases in point. Again, invention may come as an undesigned result of other activity; the domestication of animals, for example, which is one of the great inventions of the world, was probably an unforeseen outgrowth of the keeping of animal pets.

Where invention is something more than chance or accident, it is a personal achievement, usually of a superior mind; it involves the imaginative picturing of a group of relations before the relations have objective existence. An invention is a product of reflection leading to a new synthesis of elements. In the modern world invention is closely interwoven with science, and most of the modern contrivances are evolved; the steam engine, for example, is a combination of various minor, independently invented elements.

Borrowing. Once invented, culture facts spread: it is easier to copy and use things than to invent them. Within a particular group, so far as that group is concerned, culture comes chiefly from outside sources; wherever there is communication inventions spread. The spread may be in one direction; for example, the primitive group may have little to give but much to learn from the civilized group.

But there is always selection: only those things are accepted from the outside culture for which there is obvious need and which can be adjusted to the culture and the social patterns. The simple people readily accept the metal implements of the civilized group because of their obvious superiority to stone and bone tools, but in the realm of social organization and idea systems innovations are resisted and change is slow.

The Individual and the Group. In the last analysis all invention comes from individuals. Whether it be a word, an idea, an institutional detail, or a mechanical device, it originates as an individual expression. The group, as a group, never invents anything. Even in the case of such things as folk songs, which are frequently assumed to be of group origin, the inventor is a person; the illusion that they are group creations is due to the short interval of time between the invention and the group use.

The group performs two important functions in the culture invention. It provides the conditions conducive to the functioning of creative minds. In the case of a folk song, for example, the group gives the situation and the mental condition necessary to such creation. The act of invention is always related to the culture base: the innovating individual utilizes the existing culture facts and reshapes certain details into new combinations. It is in no case possible to go much beyond the culture base. The group furnishes the existing culture and gives the talented individual an opportunity to make a new contribution.

In addition to providing the cultural conditions in which the inventor works, the group performs a second essential function in the process of culture growth: it utilizes the inventions made, and preserves and transmits them to succeeding generations.

The Persistence of Culture Forms. A prime characteristic of culture is that it persists; most of the culture elements are passed on from generation to generation. Material objects outlive their creators and users. The habits determined by these objects or formed in response to the situation likewise persist and tend to reproduce the physical molds.

THE CONTENT OF CULTURE

Human Attitudes and Values. From the point of view of content, culture may be variously broken down into more or less complex subdivisions. Ultimate analysis of culture brings us to the examination of human attitudes and values, since it is these, in their various combinations and permutations, that constitute culture.

A common superficial distinction is often made between the material and the nonmaterial aspects of culture. The classification is not particularly helpful since it represents a somewhat arbitrary separation; external forms and material objects are in large measure meaningless when separated from the appropriate body of ideas and subjective reality.

A Classification of Culture Facts. According to one analysis, all the culture facts of any people are comprehended in nine fundamental divisions.

- *a.* Speech
  Languages, writing systems, etc.
- *b.* Material Traits
  - (1) Food habits
  - (2) Shelter
  - (3) Transportation and travel
  - (4) Dress
  - (5) Utensils, tools, etc.

      (6) Weapons
      (7) Occupations and industries
  c. Art
     Carving, painting, drawing, music, etc.
  d. Mythology and Scientific Knowledge
  e. Religious Practices
      (1) Ritualistic forms
      (2) Treatment of the sick
      (3) Treatment of the dead
  f. Family and Social Systems
      (1) The forms of marriage
      (2) Methods of reckoning relationship
      (3) Inheritance
      (4) Social control
      (5) Sports and games
  g. Property
      (1) Real and personal
      (2) Standards of value and exchange
      (3) Trade
  h. Government
      (1) Political forms
      (2) Judicial and legal procedures
  i. War [1]

An Alternative Classification. Another classification divides culture into three categories: the *inductive*, the *aesthetic*, and the *control*.

INDUCTIVE. In the first category are included all bodies of knowledge that are inductively derived and all devices that are tested by practice or experience. Specifically, it includes such material objects as tools, machines, and various utilitarian objects; and such nonmaterial things as crafts, skills, techniques, logic, and scientific knowledge and method.

AESTHETIC. The second category consists of such material objects as works of art and the symbols and vestments of ritual; and such nonmaterial things as forms of recreation, the conventions of social intercourse, and aesthetic aspects of the fine arts.

CONTROL. The third category contains all those things that exercise a control influence on the group members. This category includes such material things as patriotic emblems, the insignia of authority, and other coercive objects or symbols; and such

---

1 Clark Wissler, *Man and Culture* (New York: T. Y. Crowell Co., 1923), p. 74.

nonmaterial things as usages, moral standards, religious sanctions, and laws.[1]

The Types of Culture Content. The most obvious aspects
of culture are the material parts, such as the tools, buildings, and
utensils, used in the control of the external environment. Such
aspects are form and space relations unlike those of nature; they
are human rearrangements of matter. It is largely through the
preservation of these external products of human activity that
something of the nature of past cultures may be known.

A second distinguishable aspect of culture is the body of
behavior patterns—habits, activities, and skills—of the people
who produce and use the material objects. This habit system is
to be understood as a product of the total culture complex and
at the same time as a powerful factor in its perpetuation and
elaboration.

Mental patterns are as real and as definitely a part of culture
as are the material artifacts and the behavior patterns. The body
of sentiments and attitudes, the type of mind, is determined by
the culture and in turn reflects it. The human values—cleanliness, music, children, poetry, diamonds, nudity, and so on, and
the attitudes toward them, derive from the culture rather than
from original nature.

The social organization and institutional structures constitute a fourth aspect of culture. The relations to authority,
laws of property, and family relationships are typical of this part
of culture.

The symbolic elements of culture include all the nonmaterial
tools that give control over the world of reality. Here are included language, graphic representation, mathematics, and other
means of representing the outside world.

The organization of thought constitutes a final aspect of
culture. This includes the whole body of science and philosophy
as well as the beliefs of religion and magic.

THE CONDITIONING EFFECTS OF CULTURE

Stability and Persistence. The culture of a group, its mode
of life, is perhaps more stable and persistent than its physical
and racial character. The biological traits, as a result of selective birth- and death-rates or migration and intermixture, may

---

1 James W. Woodard, "A New Classification of Culture," *American Sociological Review* (1936),
1:89–102, and "The Role of Fictions in Cultural Organization," *Transactions of the New
York Academy of Sciences* (1944), Series II, 6:311–344.

undergo profound change in a relatively few generations. But the body of culture fact, in the absence of catastrophic phenomena, persists through successive generations with little alteration in fundamental character.

The Inflexibility of Culture Forms. The enduring nature of culture comes in part from the material persistence of the objective elements. Buildings, roads, books, machines, and like facts of relatively permanent character resist change and operate as facts of the geographic environment by setting a mold to which conformity is obligatory. The codes and institutions have a similar, if less obvious, inflexibility and enduring character.

The Formation and Persistence of Habit Patterns. To each individual culture comes from without. The existing pattern is a mold in which the plastic child is formed; inevitably the child acquires the mode of life of the group into which he is born. In all essential human traits the person is a product of the group and its mode of life. So early and complete is the conditioning of the child that many of the reactions to the restraints of culture are frequently ascribed to organic nature.

The habit patterns learned in the life of the group make difficult the formation of new habits. Early conditioning has a modifying effect on the organic structure, gives a set that is permanent. The acquisition of one mode of speech, for example, results in a development of the physiological speech mechanism that makes impossible the formation of certain other sounds. The same is true in regard to further acquisition of ideas; the learning of one thing may make impossible the subsequent learning of others.

The Culture Set and Personal Assimilation. The persistence of habits formed and the inhibiting effect they have on the formation of other habit complexes is readily seen in the case of individuals transplanted to a new culture situation. In a new environment the old habits, sentiments, and beliefs of the immigrant persist, and complete assimilation to the new culture is generally impossible. But the child of the immigrant acquires the new culture with the same ease as the native child; in general, it is extremely difficult to prevent his acquiring it.

THE DIFFUSION OF CULTURE

The Process of Diffusion. Culture facts are not only transmitted from generation to generation but they also spread from the place of origin and become incorporated in varying degrees in the culture of near and distant peoples.

The Culture Area. As a result, the culture forms current among a people generally bear considerable resemblance to those of neighboring peoples and a less close resemblance to those of more distant peoples. Within continental or other large areas there are broad resemblances; among the major geographic divisions there are sharp contrasts. In general, the cultural similarity is greatest where communication is easiest; the differences are pronounced where communication is limited.

The Culture Center. The first appearance of a culture fact is, of course, at some definite place, within some specific human group. From the place of origin, it spreads outward in the same way as the concentric circles on a pool spread from the point of disturbance. Ideally, the invention will reach its most highly developed form at the place of origin, this being at once the place where specific need led to its emergence and where it has the longest period of development. The invention will appear in increasingly diluted and modified form as distance increases from the point of origin.

But the area of diffusion is determined by contacts which, in turn, are determined in large measure by routes of travel. In consequence, the culture area tends to coincide with the geographic area. Certain traits of Eskimo culture, for example, with the center of dispersion about Hudson Bay, extend over a relatively narrow area east to Greenland and west through Alaska to Siberia, illustrating extreme distortion of the ideal pattern.

The Rate of Diffusion. Certain culture traits either do not spread spontaneously beyond the particular tribal group, or else they spread slowly and with difficulty. The language spoken by a group tends to remain its exclusive possession. Each group has its own language; one language may spread only by displacing another. Since the speech of each group is adequate to its needs, there is little tendency for one to displace another. The same thing is true of the forms of political and social organization and various other culture elements and complexes.

Some facts of culture diffuse widely and rapidly. This is particularly the case of elements that have an obvious superiority over items in current use, and of elements that supplement rather than displace items at present in use. The use of tobacco is a familiar illustration of quick and general diffusion. In the modern world, scientific discoveries spread so rapidly that the place of origin is a matter of indifference.

CULTURE CHANGE

The Pace of Culture Change. So long as a culture remains a living thing, it is in a state of growth and change. The pace of change is sometimes slow, as in a small and isolated primitive group, and sometimes rapid, as in the modern machine civilization. It is only the dead culture, as that of ancient Egypt or classical Greece, that remains as it was.

The Source of Change. Changes are due to the incorporation of new facts and relations. The new may come from without, by borrowing, as the phrase goes, from other peoples with whom the group is in contact. It may come as a consequence of indigenous invention or discovery. A good deal of change is in the nature of accident rather than of invention proper; as previously mentioned, many undesigned changes come about, as in language modification, partly in consequence of imperfections in the machinery for the inculcation of traditional forms.

The Order of Change. Change is usually most marked and rapid in the material and objective aspects of culture. It proceeds less rapidly and with increasing resistance through language, social customs, institutional forms, and thought systems, to modifications of the social organization and the moral order.

The unequal pace of social change is readily understood in simple terms. The deliberate adoption of a new element depends upon its simplicity, the degree to which its superiority to elements in current use is obvious, and the sentimental or other resistance its adoption encounters.

A new and simple material fact, as a new tool, weapon, word, or other utilitarian object adapted to the needs of the folk, is readily accepted and incorporated into the existing complex. It can be accepted as a single item supplementing or displacing other similar objects in current use. It involves, therefore, a minimum of habit resistance. The comparative efficiency of the new fact is obvious or readily demonstrable. Ordinarily, there is no sentiment surrounding utilitarian objects, hence no emotional resistance to change.

Apart from material elements, the superiority of the new to the old is seldom immediately obvious. In this case the new makes its way slowly even though its superiority may be easily demonstrated. Modern medicine, based on the germ theory of disease, displaces folk practices, based on alternative theories, very slowly as compared with the prompt folk acceptance and use of the automobile. This comparison shows how new inventions having an obvious use are accepted at a speedier rate than vitally important contributions not so easily recognized as superior. Where a degree of logical thought is necessary to understand or demonstrate the superiority of one value over another, as in economic and social discovery, there is generally no displacement of the old by the new.

In many cases the new invention or discovery meets emotional resistance because its adoption would disturb the old relations or institutions about which there exists more or less of sentiment. The opposition to rational changes in family arrangements, supernatural practices, economic organization, and governmental procedures arises in part from the fact that these institutions are grounded in sentiment and tradition. It arises, also, in part, from the fact that the existing order and its parts function to the welfare of the functionaries; the self-interest of the classes supports the conservatism of sentiment.

Finally, change is slow in all those aspects of culture that may not be atomized and adopted piecemeal.

The Direction of Social Change. The direction of change is determined, in the absence of catastrophe or major invention, by the inertia of the existing complex. There is ready acceptance of new items that supplement the present arrangements and further development along established lines; there is indifference to or active rejection of inventions that involve disturbance of habitual modes of thought and action or in any way run counter to the traditions and sentiments of the moral order.

The Undesigned Nature of Culture Change. A culture is an integrated system of objects and practices expressing the sentiments, attitudes, and philosophies of man. As a consequence, the invention or introduction of any new item effects, sooner or later, some modification and reorganization throughout the system. Such changes are generally neither designed nor anticipated.

On the level of mechanical invention the results are often direct and obvious. In a simple group the invention of the bow and arrow, or the adoption of firearms introduced from without, may result in an immediate economic prosperity and an increase in military power that change not only the mode of life of the group but also that of the surrounding peoples. The invention, or more properly the development, of the automobile brought changes not only in the transportation system but also in all aspects of the culture, including the mental and moral habits of the people.

Changes consequent upon material inventions are so easily seen as to give rise to a common idea that all culture change is initiated by mechanical discoveries. But discoveries in other realms of reality may be equally significant for culture and social change; not all the major inventions are in the mechanical realm. The germ theory of disease, with the resulting revolution in the whole dependent structure of medicine, and the theory of evolution have wrought changes in the whole mode of life of the people.

SELECTED READINGS

Barnett, H. G. "Culture Process," *American Anthropologist* (1940), 42:21–48.

Benedict, Ruth. *Patterns of Culture.* Boston: Houghton Mifflin Co., 1934.

Chapin, F. S. *Cultural Change.* New York: D. Appleton-Century Co., 1928.

Kluckhohn, C., and H. A. Murray, eds. *Personality in Nature, Society, and Culture.* New York: A. A. Knopf, 1948.

Kroeber, A. L. *Anthropology.* 2nd ed. New York: Harcourt, Brace & Co., 1948.

Lee, Alfred M. "Levels of Culture as Levels of Social Generalization," *American Sociological Review* (1945), 10:485–495.

Linton, Ralph. *The Science of Man in the World Crisis.* New York: Columbia Univ. Press, 1945.

Lowie, R. H. *Social Organization.* New York: Rinehart & Co., 1948.

MacIver, R. M. *The More Perfect Union.* New York: Macmillan Co., 1948.

Malinowski, Bronislaw. *The Dynamics of Culture Change.* New Haven: Yale Univ. Press, 1945.

Malinowski, Bronislaw. *A Scientific Theory of Culture.* Chapel Hill: Univ. of North Carolina Press, 1944.

Murdock, G. P. *Social Structure.* New York: Macmillan Co., 1949.

Ogburn, William Fielding. *Technology and International Relations.* Chicago: Univ. of Chicago Press, 1949.

Rader, M. *Ethics and Society.* New York: Henry Holt & Co., 1950.

Sapir, Edward. "Culture, Genuine and Spurious," *American Journal of Sociology* (1924), 29:401–429.

CHAPTER EIGHTEEN

RACE AND CULTURE CONTACTS

The contact and intermingling of divergent stocks result in two distinct but related types of phenomena: the biological inter-mixture of the previously separated strains, and the fusion of their culture heritages. The former breaks down whatever there may have been of racial integrity; the latter disturbs more or less profoundly the cultural equilibrium established in the pre-ceding period of isolation. Race problems arise in the transition from one period of racial and cultural equilibrium to another.

HISTORICAL CONTACTS

Primitive Peoples. Among the simpler peoples, wanderings and migratory movements seem always to have been the rule. The search for food or adventure, flights to escape attacks by enemies, spreading to escape the impoverishing results of their own multiplication, and other facts led to extensive wanderings. So general were these movements that the traditions of nearly every people are based on the story of a migration.

The wanderings resulted in contacts with neighboring peoples whose territory was invaded. In the resulting conflicts, old groups were broken up and new ones formed from the frag-ments. Powerful and aggressive groups overran the territory of smaller and weaker groups, imposed themselves as ruling classes, absorbed or were absorbed by the conquered peoples.

In the course of these conflicts resulting in the destruction of old stocks and the formation of new mixtures and blends, there was a more or less constant exchange of culture facts, the stimu-lation of invention, and the adaptation of old facts to new environments.

The Ancient World. So far as it is possible to follow the early history of peoples, they were constantly moving about. The peoples of eastern Asia migrated into Europe; those of central and western Asia moved into southern Asia; the North European peoples overran the Mediterranean area; the Central Africans overran southern Africa; the Alaskans migrated as far at least as Mexico, and the peoples of Mexico as far as Alaska. These and other similar movements and mixtures give a picture of prehistoric movements and contacts.

The civilization of the ancient world rose from the mixing of earlier groups and cultures. Babylon had its origin in the mixture of two different national and racial elements. Greece, Rome, and practically every other historic state were, in the beginning, mixtures of more or less heterogeneous ethnic elements, and their civilizations arose out of the culture fusion.

The ancient world continued and extended the mixing of blood and the fusion of heritages that characterized the earlier peoples.

The Period of the Discoveries. The period of the discoveries increased the race contacts that had been going on for countless ages. It was a period of contacts among groups previously separated, and of contacts on a larger scale than had anywhere existed previously.

The Modern Era. In the modern world the contact and intermingling of diverse ethnic and culture groups are incomparably greater than in any previous period; the mass contacts of diverse groups and divergent cultures are an essentially modern phenomenon.

Physical science and mechanical invention laid the basis for the modern world order. On the one hand, they brought power machinery and factory production which standardized and enormously increased the production of material goods; on the other, they perfected the means of rapid communication and developed cheap, easy, and rapid means of transportation. These made inevitable the present reduction of the world to a commercial and economic unit. The parallel development of popular education undermined the traditional controls. Science thus operated directly and indirectly for the economic and intellectual liberation and mobility of the individual man. The new freedom, physical and intellectual, in the presence of marked differentials in economic opportunity in different regions, got expression in an unprecedented migration, in the association of peoples previously widely separated, and in the exclusion or absorption of weaker peoples and the repopulation of whole continents by diverse and amalgamated stocks.

There were thus wholesale and indiscriminate contacts among ethnic strains wholly dissimilar, between peoples of varied degrees of development that had lived under widely different life-conditions. The highly civilized nations of Europe suddenly came into close relations with native races of contrasted culture and in contrasted climatic zones.

CONTACTS AND RACE RELATIONS

Universal Phenomena. However much the contacts of peoples may differ with time and place, there are certain phenomena of universal incidence. Below the multiplicity of detail in the concrete reality are the same stable factors. The disintegration of the native social order, the intermixture of racial strains, the fusion of cultures, and the disorganization of individual personality organization seem to recur in all areas of race and culture contact.

In the modern world, in the absence of insuperable political barriers to geographic mobility, population flows to those areas that offer or are thought to offer more tolerable conditions of life or superior opportunities for personal success. There is always an appreciable inertia; the differential between areas must be sufficient to overbalance the ties of sentiment binding the individual to his homeland, and to offset the provincial fear of the new and strange.

The racial and cultural consequences of immigration are fairly uniform and the final outcome easily predictable.

Immigration movements are commonly between countries of somewhat similar cultures and on friendly relations. The initial contacts between the immigrants and members of the established population of the area are often marked by fear and suspicion, but they are seldom overtly hostile; the early negative reactions commonly disappear as association leads to understanding and appreciation.

Almost from the beginning there are transfer and blending of the cultures. In making their accommodations to the new situation, the immigrants rapidly lose their peculiar folkways and superficially identifying cultural characteristics, and acquire the social heritage of the area through their participation in the common life.

Intermarriage generally begins early and increases with growth in cultural similarity. This process results in time in the biological absorption of the numerically subordinate group or in the formation of a mixed population. No immigrant group maintains its physical identity indefinitely and seldom does so for even a few generations.

The period of transition from the old to the new culture heritage is marked by more or less widespread personal disorganization. This accompaniment of transition declines as the conflicting heritages become harmonized in a single system of social rules.

The Contact between Divergent Groups. Different types of phenomena appear where the territory of a militaristically impotent or culturally retarded people is occupied by representatives of a colonizing nation. The initial relations are largely or wholly a function of economic and political expediency.

The objective of the intruders may be frankly and openly predatory, the intention being to occupy the territory and exploit its resources. In these circumstances there is a minimum of consideration for the claims or welfare of the native people. They are more or less ruthlessly excluded from the area, reduced to slavery if the resources to be exploited call for an acclimatized labor force, or, in the event of armed resistance, they may be destroyed. In any event, the working relations presently established assign to the weaker people a servile status and subordinate role in the area formerly theirs.

In other circumstances a crude display and use of major force, by arousing hostility and resistance, would hinder or defeat the purposes of the occupation. The immediate objective may be trade with the native population, as in the British-Indian fur trade of the American Northwest. Where the occupation is ostensibly to protect the interests of an exploited group, the tangible benefits are more likely to accrue if the relations are friendly. In such cases the attitudes of the invaders are conciliatory, at least until their position is consolidated or until the natives appreciate the underlying motives of the foreign protectors.

The ultimate outcome is clear; whether the relations are friendly or antagonistic, the native population is presently reduced to a subordinate status. This may come immediately by the exercise of superior force and the enslavement of the native people, or it may develop as the economic forces imperceptibly undermine the position of the native group.

The Class Order and Personal Accommodation. The particular type of class order that comes to prevail depends upon the temper of the exploiting group and the exigencies of the situation; the work relations imposed define the patterns of behavior possible in the situation.

Individuals of necessity accept the conditions they cannot control; they conform to the rules imposed and consciously adjust their lives on the new basis. In time, as they are conditioned through the habit mechanism to the restrictions the order imposes, the new life becomes less burdensome; there is an internal adjustment to the external conditions. Around the status, as an established fact, there gradually develops an appropriate body of interests, sentiments, and attitudes; presently it comes to be accepted by master and servant alike as in conformity with the natural order.

This process is rendered easier by the fact that the class order tends to perpetuate and exaggerate the differences on which it was originally founded. The type of life, work, and responsibility determines the external traits of dress and manner as well as the beliefs and attitudes appropriate to the station in life. Moreover, the order is rationalized, explained in such a way as to justify and perpetuate it; a mythological history is built up about it; and the established religion provides it with supernatural sanctions.

To the extent that accommodation is achieved there is a state of harmony between the classes and races; often there is a high degree of social and personal sympathy and understanding.

Once firmly established, the class order tends to perpetuate itself; both the subordinate and the superior status are taken for granted. The duties, obligations, and roles are recognized and respected. The slave not only accepts his status, but may actually take pride in it and resent any effort of his fellows to escape the status.

THE INTERMIXTURE OF THE RACES

The Effect of Continued Association. Wherever divergent groups are in contact and association for a period of time, they produce a more or less numerous hybrid progeny. There seems to be no historic exception. If the association be long continued, the lines of separation tend to disappear as one or the other of the originally divergent peoples is lost in the resulting mixed-blood population.

Similar Peoples. Where the stocks are somewhat closely related and not sharply contrasted in culture and physical type, intermarriage goes on rapidly and commonly attracts little attention or opposition. The American experience is fairly typical of what happens when a common residence brings friendly peoples of similar culture into close association. In the relatively short period of American life, the older immigrant groups have merged into a common group and the rate of intermarriage of individuals of more recent entrance is such that their complete biological absorption into the general population is a question of only a few generations.

Divergent Peoples. Where the races in contact are sharply differentiated in skin color or other physical characters, or in culture and social status, the amount of intermarriage is commonly small. But physical and social differences between races are not insuperable barriers to intermarriage. The white pioneers of America in many regions took Indian wives, and similar marriages are frequent in various areas characterized by a paucity of white women. In a slave regime, once a friendly accommodation has been reached, racial intermixture may go on easily and rapidly.

In areas of contact where the exploitation of native peoples or resources goes on without formal master-slave relations, intermarriage and intermixture are commonly retarded. The class differences tend to harden into caste divisions marked by chronic friction and traditionally antagonistic attitudes. But intermixture is never wholly absent; half-castes appear and increase in number in every colonial area as in every area of settlement.

THE FUSION OF CULTURES

The Results of Contacts. Contacts with strange peoples result, also, in the disorganization of the simpler culture, the gradual assimilation of the weaker people, the transfer and fusion of heritages, and the final achievement of a new cultural equilibrium.

Culture Change and Conflict. The simpler peoples adopt and use various material elements of the more advanced culture. This process enriches the simpler culture but at the same time disorganizes the native economy and mode of life and makes the simpler group dependent upon further contacts. To secure the desired articles there must be an exchange of native goods. To secure the native goods in quantity for exchange involves a shift of occupation, a disturbance of work habits, and a reduction of work interest.

The change in economic organization is followed in time by changes in the more basic elements of the culture. The religio-superstitious system is disorganized and corrupted, partly as a consequence of economic change, and partly (particularly if there are missionaries present to attack the native moral order) through the borrowing of practices and beliefs. Ultimately, through the decay or destruction of old institutions and traditional life-patterns, there is a more or less complete change in the fundamental social organization.

The transition is marked by competition between the alternative culture elements, particularly in those realms, such as religion and superstition, wherein there is no immediate objective measure of the relative efficiency of the competing units. In the course of culture fusion there is chronic conflict, overt or potential, between the sponsors of the competing systems. The defeated group strives to preserve or restore the lost or decaying standards, seeks to preserve its language and other signs of former unity, and builds an elaborate body of myth rationalizing the existing status.

Cultural Assimilation. The spread of culture resulting from the contact of unequally advanced peoples is largely a one-way movement; the subordinate or minority group in general has more to learn than the dominant group and the incentives to learning are greater and more obvious. The superiority of certain culture elements is patent and they are taken over immediately and without emotional resistance. Some familiarity with the technology and work techniques of the ruling group may be imposed as the work relations are established. An ability to use the language of the ruling group has obvious advantages.

Racial intermixture facilitates the process of personal assimilation and the culture fusion. The social heritages are in general most easily acquired in primary contacts and sympathetic association and are most readily and naturally transmitted to the young. The children of biracial ancestry are likely to be bilingual and to possess other elements of both cultures. In knowledge, habits, and sentiments they belong in some measure to each parent group.

Personal Disorganization. The foregoing in some part accounts for the fact that the period of cultural transition is one of wide personal disorganization. The change in work techniques and group practices disturbs the established habit systems and frees the individual, in a measure, from the traditional controls; it introduces new elements of insecurity into the life experience. The children of biracial ancestry in particular are exposed to two contrasting and conflicting sets of moral standards. With freedom and choice go personal disorganization and personal failure.

The breakdown of the control system favors the miscegenation of the races. The latter process is in itself, in most cases, a form of disorganization, being a violation of the customary practices and taboos. Irregularity in this respect, by weakening the control system, is conducive to the violation of other standards, and thus to further experimentation, failure, and possible personal demoralization.

A New Equilibrium. The assimilation of the native group is a protracted process always accompanied by disorder. It goes on at very unequal rates. Some individuals, because of fortunate chance circumstances, are brought into more or less close and personal relations with members of the ruling group and acquire an understanding and appreciation of its culture. This is particularly likely to be the case of children of biracial ancestry, and of all children in regions where native schools are established and missionaries active. Other individuals have little direct contact with the new culture, retain their traditional ways, and resist change long after the more mobile individuals have lost the old culture patterns.

The social disorder and cultural duality, incident to cultural fusion and assimilation, ultimately give way to a single set of enforced behavior patterns. The trend in every culture is toward equilibrium, toward order and status and uniformity. There may be a re-establishment of an old order through the assimilation of all individuals to it or there may be a new order resulting from fusion, but in any case one set of standards will in time replace the dual system. As this result ensues, personal disorganization and maladjustment decline and, when the equilibrium is complete, disappear.

MARGINAL GROUPS

Factors Leading to Marginal Groups. The effect of contact, operating through differential opportunity and through blood intermixture, is to produce cultural diversity; a larger or smaller number of individuals come to occupy, in status and heritage, a position between the contrasted cultures.

If the channels of cultural transition be unobstructed, the individuals who acquire the language and other cultural baggage of the dominant group pass into its ranks and participate in its life. This outcome is usual and typical of immigrant experience in America and elsewhere. Where caste or other barriers interfere with mobility, the cultural expatriates tend to form or to be formed into a special intermediate caste which may eventually assume the characteristics of a nationality.

When the physical marks of race are sufficiently pronounced so that the hybrid offspring are superficially distinguishable from the members of either parent group, the tendency to separation is stronger and more general. Unless the racial hybrids promptly disappear by intermarriage into one or the other parent group, they presently come to constitute a new racial strain in the population.

The Status of Mixed Bloods. These mixed-blood individuals are intermediate in physical type between the parents. As they increase in number the intermarriage and intermixture of the races are stimulated; the mixed bloods intermarry and intermix with both racial groups and a multiplicity of intermediate types bridges the gap between the parent races.

Socially and culturally, as well as biologically, the mixed-blood individuals commonly occupy positions intermediate between the two culture groups, thereby serving as cultural intermediaries between them. The mulattoes in the United States, the mestizos of Latin America, the Eurasians of Hawaii and elsewhere, and the part-native individuals in various colonial areas have an intermediate cultural position, and hybrid individuals everywhere achieve personal success higher than the more isolated and less mobile members of the subordinate group.

The two facts of (1) biracial ancestry and (2) distinctive status and achievement are often mistakenly assumed to stand in a cause and effect relationship. The intermediate social status, however, is not a direct result of the blood intermixture although the two facts are related.

The intermediate social status and the superior achievement are the results of social contacts. The hybrid individuals are more in contact with the dominant culture group, have greater mobility and freedom, and are more easily and quickly assimilated into the dominant culture than are the more isolated and less mobile members of the native population.

The Role of Mixed-Blood Groups. The social role of biracial marginal groups turns upon the administrative policy that obtains in the particular historical situation.

a) In the presence of two integrated and contrasted cultures, such as the Oriental and the European, there is no natural place and function for a marginal group. Unless the hybrids are absorbed into one or the other culture, they tend to become outcasts from both. If they are formed into a special caste it tends to be an inferior caste within one of the parent groups rather than a class intermediate between the two. The individuals who depart from the one civilization do not thereby approach the other; they simply lose status within the particular civilization. The hybrid individuals must content themselves with such status as is assigned them by the group with which they elect to be identified. In general they have no respected place and no special role in the biracial situation in the Oriental world.

b) In other areas, the presence of a mixed population is utilized to lessen the friction between the pure-blood groups. The independent organization of a hybrid middle-class may be encouraged and its growth fostered by catering to the aspirations of marginal persons without in full reality granting their wishes. The superior cultural worth of marginal persons may be recognized by preferential economic opportunities and by minor offices and inferior governmental positions, as in the British West Indies and in various Anglo-Indian areas. The result of this policy is to effect a fairly complete separation of the Europeanized and partly Europeanized individuals from the native population and to identify them with the ruling class by making them economically and morally dependent upon it. The native population is thus deprived of its natural leaders, and a middle-class cushion placed between the white aristocracy and the unassimilated native labor supply.

c) The ruling-class policy may be one of exclusion without special provision for the intermediate racial and cultural individuals. For the most part this is the method of dealing with the Negro population of the United States; it is essentially the policy of the self-governing colonies of South Africa; and it was the German native policy. No effort is made to establish relations that will secure harmony between the races; an impassable color line is drawn and no recognition given to the fact of cultural differences. The refusal to recognize superiority and to grant status and opportunity generates resentment and chronic discontent. The role of the marginal individuals tends to be that of leadership in the subordinate group.

RACE PROBLEMS

Nature of the Race Problem. Racial problems are expressions of disharmony between traditional status and current aspiration. They arise in areas wherein the attitudinal sets and the institutional patterns fail to comprehend the changing cultural and social phenomena. The nature of the race problem is an index of the stage that has been reached in the transition from the initial contacts and mixtures of groups to the final achievement of a new racial and cultural unity.

Race and Native Problems. Race problems, as distinct from the so-called native problem, seem to have their origin at the stage in the racial cycle at which biracial marginal groups become important and no adequate provision is made for satisfying their wishes. So long as the cultural lines between the races are distinct and clearly drawn, there may be a problem or a series of problems of an administrative order—problems of control, sanitation, labor, education, and the like—but there is no race problem. So long as the individuals are free to enter the dominant group and participate in its culture to the extent of their mastery of its elements, there is no race problem. Race problems proper arise at the point where the dominant culture group denies to individuals and groups who have mastered the culture an unobstructed opportunity to identify themselves with the dominant group and participate in its heritage.

Race Consciousness. When racial and cultural hybrids are excluded from full participation in the culture, resentment reinforces the sentimental bonds of unity. A sense of common interest arises; the conviction develops that their fortunes are involved in a common destiny. Like any natural group set apart in a population, they build up a characteristic body of sentiment, develop a provincial unity, and elaborate a mythology in the struggle for self-respect. Every minority that is excluded and persecuted tends to become militantly self-conscious.

Racial Separation. Where the lines of demarcation are entirely cultural they may be escaped by any individual who cares to conform to the majority standards. But where the differentiating characteristics are racial rather than cultural the individuals, regardless of personal traits and cultural achievements, cannot escape classification and the limitations of opportunity that go with it. The criteria of separation remain to the end of the racial cycle, that is, until such time as further intermixture erases the distinguishing marks of race.

Cultural Retardation. The discriminations by the dominant group lead to a disposition on the part of the excluded individuals to avoid cross-race contacts and the resulting humiliating experiences. There is established and maintained a more or less complete and voluntary segregation; isolating themselves, the hybrid and marginal individuals may undertake to work out a semi-independent social order.

Some degree of cultural retardation is an accompaniment and inevitable result of such separation. The pace of racial intermixture declines and the acceptance of cultural invention is impeded.

The excluded group elaborates a body of doctrine and fabricates a racial history to explain and justify its position in the inclusive social order. Its lack of power and prestige results in numerous compensatory phenomena that tend to intensify the isolation. The body of social opinion, for example, tends to be negative, to deny the values of the ruling group and to react adversely to all suggestions originating in it. In its extreme development, as in certain modern nationalistic minorities, the race-conscious minority becomes impervious to all facts conflicting with its emotional complex. Potential racial conflict is chronic and traditional.

SELECTED READINGS

Ackerman, Nathan W., and Maria Jahoda. *Anti-Semitism and Emotional Disorder.* New York: Harper & Bros., 1950.

Adorno, T. W., and others. *The Authoritarian Personality.* New York: Harper & Bros., 1950.

Burgess, E. W. "Accommodation," *Encyclopaedia of the Social Sciences* (1930), 1:403–404.

Davie, Maurice R. *Negroes in American Society.* New York: McGraw-Hill Book Co., 1949.

Dodson, Dan W. "Social Action and Education," *Journal of Educational Sociology* (1949–50), 23:345–351.

Dollard, John. *Caste and Class in a Southern Town.* New Haven: Yale Univ. Press, 1937.

Dollard, John, and Neal E. Miller. *Personality and Psychotherapy.* New York, McGraw-Hill Book Co., 1950. Chaps. 21–23.

Doyle, Bertram W. *The Etiquette of Race Relations in the South: A Study in Social Control.* Chicago: Univ. of Chicago Press, 1937.

Kohn, Hans. "Race Conflict," *Encyclopaedia of the Social Sciences* (1934), 13:36–41.

Lee, Alfred M. *Race Riots Aren't Necessary.* Public Affairs Pamphlet No. 107. New York: Public Affairs Committee, Inc., 1945.

Locke, Alain, and Bernhard J. Stern. *When Peoples Meet: A Study in Race and Culture Contacts.* Rev. ed. New York: Barnes & Noble, Inc., 1946.

Masuoka, J. "The Hybrid: A Reflection on Race Problem," *Phylon* (1945), 6:327–336.

Miller, H. A. *Races, Nations, and Classes.* Philadelphia: J. B. Lippincott Co., 1924.

Park, Robert E. "Education in Its Relation to Conflict and Fusion of Cultures," *Publications of the American Sociological Society* (1918), 13:38–63.

Park, Robert E., and E. W. Burgess. *Introduction to the Science of Sociology.* Chicago: Univ. of Chicago Press, 1924. Pp. 280–331, 663–725.

Powdermaker, Hortense. *After Freedom.* New York: Viking Press, 1939.

Reuter, E. B. *Race and Culture Contacts.* New York: McGraw-Hill Book Co. 1934.

Reuter, E. B. *Race Mixture.* New York: McGraw-Hill Book Co., 1931.

Shalloo, J. P., and Donald Young, eds. "Minority Peoples in a Nation at War," *Annals of the American Academy of Political and Social Science* (September 1942), 223.

Slavson, S. R. *Analytic Group Psychotherapy.* New York: Columbia Univ. Press, 1950.

Stonequist, Everett V. *The Marginal Man.* New York: Chas. Scribner's Sons, 1937.

Thompson, Edgar T., ed. *Race Relations and the Race Problem.* Durham: Duke Univ. Press, 1939.

Weatherford, W. D., and C. S. Johnson. *Race Relations.* New York: D. C. Heath & Co., 1934.

Young, Donald. *American Minority Peoples.* New York: Harper & Bros., 1932.

Part Four

———

Collective Behavior

By

HERBERT BLUMER
University of Chicago

PART FOUR

COLLECTIVE BEHAVIOR
By Herbert Blumer

TOPICS

CHAPTER NINETEEN

THE FIELD OF COLLECTIVE BEHAVIOR

The Term *Collective Behavior*. The nature of collective behavior is suggested by consideration of such topics as crowds, mobs, panics, manias, dancing crazes, stampedes, mass behavior, public opinion, propaganda, fashion, fads, social movements, revolutions, and reforms. The sociologist has always been interested in such topics, but it is only in recent years that efforts have been made to group them in a single division of sociological concern and to regard them as different expressions of the same generic factors. The term *collective behavior* is used to label this area of sociological interest.

Group Activity as Collective Behavior. From one point of view practically all group activity can be thought of as collective behavior. Group activity means that individuals are acting *together* in some fashion; that there is some division of labor among them; and that there is some fitting together of the different lines of individual conduct. In this sense, group activity is a collective matter. In the classroom, for example, there is a division of labor between the teacher and the students. The students act in expected ways and the teacher, likewise, has a different kind of activity which is expected of him. The activities of the different students and of the teacher fit together to form orderly and concerted group conduct. This conduct is collective in character.

The Basis of Collective Behavior. In the example which has just been used, the collective behavior occurs because students and teachers have common understandings or traditions as to how they are to behave in the classroom. The students are expected to act in certain ways and they are aware of such expectations; the teacher, likewise, is expected to act in a certain way, and he understands that expectation. This guidance of behavior by common expectations always marks group activity that is under the influence of custom, tradition, conventions, rules, or institutional regulations. Thus, two things may be said: *First*, that the great bulk of collective behavior among human beings occurs because people have common understandings and expectations. *Second*, that the major portion of the field of sociology is devoted to the study of such collective behavior. When the sociologist studies customs, traditions, folkways, mores, institutions, and social organization, he is dealing with the social rules and social definitions through which collective behavior is organized.

Collective Behavior as a Division of Sociology. The latter statement raises a question. If practically all sociology is concerned with collective behavior, in what sense can one speak of the study of *collective behavior* as a separate division of sociology? The answer to this question will enable us to state a little more clearly what the study of collective behavior deals with.

Elementary Forms of Collective Behavior. While most of the collective behavior of human beings exists in the form of regulated group activity, there is a great deal which is not under the influence of rules or understandings. A highly excited mob, a business panic, a state of war hysteria, a condition of social unrest represent instances of collective behavior which are of this character. In these instances, the collective behavior arises spontaneously and is not due to pre-established understandings or traditions. It is the study of just such elementary and spontaneous forms that constitutes one of the major interests in the field of collective behavior.

Organized Forms of Collective Behavior. The other major interest in the study of collective behavior is tracing the way in which the elementary and spontaneous forms develop into organized forms. Customs, conventions, institutions, and the social organization have a career, represented by the passage from a fluid and unorganized condition to a set and organized status. To determine the lines and manner of such development becomes a matter of important concern in the study of collective behavior.

Definition of Collective Behavior. Stated in the most general form, these remarks suggest that the student of collective be-

CHAPTER TWENTY

ELEMENTARY
COLLECTIVE BEHAVIOR

CIRCULAR REACTION AND SOCIAL UNREST

Nature of Circular Reaction. One gets a clue to the nature of elementary collective behavior by recognizing the form of social interaction that has been called *circular reaction*. This refers to a type of interstimulation wherein the response of one individual reproduces the stimulation that has come from another individual and in being reflected back to this individual reinforces the stimulation. Thus the interstimulation assumes a circular form in which individuals reflect one another's states of feeling and in so doing intensify this feeling. It is well evidenced in the transmission of feelings and moods among people who are in a state of excitement. One sees the process clearly amidst cattle in a state of alarm. The expression of fear through bellowing, breathing, and movements of the body, induces the same feeling in the case of other cattle who, as they in turn express their alarm, intensify this emotional state in one another. It is through such a process of circular reaction that there arises among cattle a general condition of intense fear and excitement, as in the case of a stampede.

The nature of circular reaction can be further helpfully understood by contrasting it with interpretative interaction, which is the form chiefly to be found among human beings who are in association. Ordinarily, human beings respond to one another, as in carrying on a conversation, by interpreting one another's actions or remarks and then reacting on the basis of the interpretation. Responses, consequently, are not made directly to the stimulation, but follow, rather, upon interpretation; further, they are likely to be different in nature from the stimulating acts, being essentially adjustments to these acts. Thus

havior seeks to understand the way in which a new so
arises, for the appearance of such a new social order is ec
to the emergence of new forms of collective behavior. 1
of stating the matter permits one to distinguish the
collective behavior from the rest of sociology. One may s:
sociology in general is interested in studying the social ord
its constituents (customs, rules, institutions, etc.) as the)
collective behavior is concerned in studying the ways by v
the social order comes into existence, in the sense of the emerg
and solidification of new forms of collective behavior.

SELECTED READINGS

Cooley, Charles H. *Social Process.* New York: Chas. Scribner's Sons, 191

Ginsberg, Morris. "Association," *Encyclopaedia of the Social Sciences* (1930
2:284–286.

LaPiere, R. T. *Collective Behavior.* New York: McGraw-Hill Book Co., 1938.

LaPiere, R. T., and P. R. Farnsworth. *Social Psychology.* 3rd ed. New York:
McGraw-Hill Book Co., 1949.

Mannheim, Karl. *Ideology and Utopia.* Trans. by Louis Wirth and E. A. Shils.
New York: Harcourt, Brace & Co., 1936.

Park, Robert E., "Collective Behavior," *Encyclopaedia of the Social Sciences*
(1930), 3:631–633.

Park, Robert E., and E. W. Burgess. *Introduction to the Science of Sociology.*
2nd ed. Chicago: Univ. of Chicago Press, 1924. Chap. 13. Selected
bibliography, pp. 934–950.

Reuter, E. B., and C. W. Hart. *Introduction to Sociology.* New York: McGraw-
Hill Book Co., 1933. Chaps. 17–19.

Sargent, S. S. *Social Psychology.* New York: Ronald Press, 1950.

Young, Kimball. *Social Psychology.* 2nd ed. New York: Appleton-Century-
Crofts, Inc., 1944. Part 3.

Young, Kimball. *Source Book for Social Psychology.* New York: F. S. Crofts
& Co., 1927. Part 6.

interpretative interaction might be likened to a game of tennis and has the character of a shuttle-like process instead of a circular process. It tends, in degree, to make people different; circular reaction tends to make people alike.

Circular Reaction in Collective Behavior. Circular reaction is very common among human beings. It is the chief form of inter-stimulation present in spontaneous and elementary collective behavior. Its role in this respect will be seen in the discussion of social unrest, collective excitement, social contagion, and in the instance of crowd activity. Here it may be pointed out that it gives rise to collective, or shared behavior, which is not based on the adherence to common understandings or rules. It is for this reason that circular reaction is the natural mechanism of elementary collective behavior.

The Genesis of Elementary Collective Behavior. Under what conditions does spontaneous and elementary collective behavior arise? Seemingly, under conditions of unrest or disturbance in the usual forms of living or routines of life. Where group life is carried on satisfactorily in accordance with rules or cultural definitions, there is clearly no occasion for the emergence of any new forms of collective behavior. The wishes, needs, and dispositions of people are satisfied through the ordinary cultural activities of their groups. In the event, however, of some disturbance of these established ways of acting, or in the event of the appearance of new dispositions which cannot be satisfied by the existing cultural definitions, elementary collective behavior is likely to arise.

The Factor of Restlessness. When people have impulses, desires, or dispositions which cannot be satisfied by the existing forms of living they are in a state of unrest. Their experience is one of feeling an urge to act but of being balked in doing so; consequently the experience is one of discomfort, frustration, insecurity, and usually of alienation or loneliness. This inner tension, in the absence of regulated means for its release, will express itself usually through random and unco-ordinated activity. This is a mark of restlessness. Externally, the activity is likely to be erratic, lacking in consistency, and rather similar to a sort of indefinite prowling; internally, it is likely to take the form of disordered imagination and disturbed feelings. In its more acute forms it is characteristic of neurotic behavior.

The Development of Social Unrest. The presence of restlessness among many individuals need not mean, however, the existence of a state of social unrest. It is only when restlessness is involved in circular reaction, or becomes contagious, that social unrest exists. One may view social unrest as the socialization of restlessness. Unless the restlessness of individuals has a reciprocally stimulating and reinforcing effect, it is neither shared nor collective. Such a condition seems to be true of modern neurotic restlessness. The neurotic individual can be regarded as isolated and socially apart—one who finds it difficult to be free, easy, and spontaneous in his association with other people. His disturbed feelings arise as a reaction against other individuals, rather than as a sympathetic sharing of their feelings. The display of neurotic restlessness is likely to irritate others and to alienate them. By contrast, in the instance of social unrest, restlessness has a reciprocal character, i.e., its display awakens a similar condition of restlessness on the part of others, and there occurs mutual reinforcement of this state as the individuals interact with each other. It follows that social unrest is most likely to exist where people are sensitized to one another, or prepared to enter readily into rapport, and also where they undergo together the derangement of their routines of living. These conditions are met in such instances of social unrest as revolutionary unrest, agrarian unrest, the unrest of women, religious and moral unrest, labor unrest—to mention but a few of the many forms. These instances bespeak fundamental disturbances in the feelings, thoughts, and behavior of people due to significant changes in their ways of living.

The Extent and Intensity of Social Unrest. Social unrest may range both in extent and in intensity. It may be confined to a small community as in a case of a small mining community at the time of a strike, or it may extend to a larger dispersed population as in the instance of contemporary Moslem unrest. It may be mild and general, as in the case of much of present-day moral unrest, or be specific and acute as in the revolutionary unrest immediately preceding the Russian Revolution of 1917. Whether narrowly confined or extensive, subdued or acute, social unrest has certain common characteristics which should be designated.

Characteristics of Social Unrest. One of the most interesting of these traits of social unrest is the random character of behavior.

People are likely to move around in an erratic and aimless way, as if seeking to find or avoid something, but without knowing what it is that they are trying to find or avoid. Indeed, it is just this lack of understood objectives that explains restless behavior. People are in a state of tension and uneasiness, and feel a strong urge to act. This urge to act, in the absence of goals, necessarily leads to aimless and random behavior.

Another significant mark of social unrest is excited feeling, usually in the form of vague apprehensions, alarm, fears, insecurity, eagerness, or aroused pugnacity. Such excited feeling is conducive to rumors and to exaggerated views and perceptions. Such features of behavior are usually to be found in all conditions of social unrest.

A third important characteristic of social unrest is the irritability and increased suggestibility of people. In a state of social unrest, people are psychologically unstable, suffering from disturbed impulses and feelings. Their attention is likely to be variable and shifting, and lacking in usual continuity. Their condition makes them much more sensitive to others, but also less constant and stable in their make-up and in their conduct. To recognize this increased instability and restlessness is to understand why people in a state of social unrest are suggestible, responsive to new stimulations and ideas, and also more malleable.

The Role of Social Unrest. These remarks indicate the important role of social unrest. On one hand, it is a symptom of disruption or breaking down of the order of living. On the other hand, it signifies incipient preparation for new forms of collective behavior. This latter point is particularly of importance. In a metaphorical sense, social unrest can be thought of as a condition which is unorganized, unregulated, fluid, and active. Usual routines of activity have broken down, and individuals have been rendered malleable. Social unrest may be regarded as the crucible out of which emerge new forms of organized activity—such as social movements, reforms, revolutions, religious cults, spiritual awakenings, and new moral orders. In itself, it may be thought of as having the potentiality of many diverse expressions; that is to say that the alternative forms of newly organized activity into which social unrest may resolve itself are many. We shall be interested in seeing how social unrest develops and expresses itself in new ways of behavior.

MECHANISMS OF ELEMENTARY
COLLECTIVE BEHAVIOR

Characteristics of Elementary Mechanisms. The behavior of people who are in a state of social unrest shows a number of typical forms of interaction which we can designate as the elementary mechanisms of collective behavior. They are elementary because they appear spontaneously and naturally, they are the simplest and earliest ways in which people interact in order to act together, and they usually lead to more advanced and complicated forms.

Milling. The basic type of such elementary forms is that of *milling*. Milling can be thought of as a pure instance of circular reaction. In milling, individuals move around amongst one another in an aimless and random fashion, such as in the interweaving of cattle and sheep who are in a state of excitement. The primary effect of milling is to make the individuals more sensitive and responsive to one another, so that they become increasingly preoccupied with one another and decreasingly responsive to ordinary objects of stimulation. It is such a condition to which the term *rapport* refers. We observe this state in a magnified form in the instance of hypnosis. The hypnotic subject becomes increasingly preoccupied with the hypnotist, in such a way that his attention becomes riveted upon the hypnotist and correspondingly he develops an immunity to most other types of stimulation to which he would ordinarily respond. Milling tends to induce this condition among people. Their attention becomes increasingly focused on one another and less on objects and events which would ordinarily concern them. Being preoccupied with each other they are inclined to respond to one another quickly, directly, and unwittingly. Because milling induces this preoccupation and this readiness to quick response, it clearly makes for collective behavior. People in this state are much more disposed to act together, under the influence of a common impulse or mood, than they are to act separately, under the influence of feelings that are not common to them. Viewed in this way, milling can be regarded as an elementary and natural means by which people are prepared to act together in a spontaneous way.

Collective Excitement. We may single out collective excitement as a more intense form of milling and treat it as a separate elementary mechanism conducive to collective behavior. While it may be regarded as a speeding up of the milling process and hence as having the general features of circular reaction, it has certain specific marks that deserve attention. First, one should appreciate the power of excited behavior in catching and riveting the attention of observers. In all societies, animal as well as human, individuals are particularly sensitive to the display of excitement upon the part of one another. It is difficult to ignore such excited behavior; to do so one must remove himself from the scene of action or force his attention to some other object by the aid of some verbal formulae. His natural tendency is to pay attention to the excited behavior and to take an interest in it. This power of excited behavior in compelling attention is of particular interest, for the extent to which one becomes preoccupied with an object, to that extent one comes under its control. A human being controls himself in the face of an object of attention to the extent that he is able to call up images which he can oppose to such an object. Yet excited behavior, as an object of attention, interferes with this process of directed imagery. Where people are collectively excited, as a result of some form of milling, this loss of normal control becomes pronounced, setting the stage for contagious behavior.

Another interesting feature of collective excitement is that under its influence people become more emotionally aroused and more likely to be carried away by impulses and feelings; hence rendered more unstable and irresponsible. In collective excitement, the personal make-up of individuals is more readily broken; and, in this way, the condition is prepared for the formation of new forms of behavior and for the reorganization of the individual. In collective excitement, individuals may embark on lines of conduct which previously they would not likely have thought of, much less dared to undertake. Likewise, under its stress, and with opportunities for the release of tension, individuals may incur significant reorganization in their sentiments, habits, and traits of personality.

These remarks suggest how influential collective excitement may be in bringing people together into new forms of collective association and in laying the basis for new forms of collective behavior.

Social Contagion. Where collective excitement is intense and widespread, there is every likelihood for some kind of social contagion to take place. Social contagion refers to the relatively rapid, unwitting, and nonrational dissemination of a mood, impulse, or form of conduct; it is well exemplified by the spread of crazes, manias, and fads. In its more extreme forms it has the character of a social epidemic, as in the instance of the tulip mania in Holland in the eighteenth century or of the dancing mania of the Middle Ages. In modern times, we see it clearly pronounced in the development of war hysteria or in the operation of financial panics.

Social contagion may be regarded as an intense form of milling and collective excitement; in it the development of rapport and unreflective responsiveness of individuals to one another becomes pronounced. What is most interesting and spectacular about social contagion is that it attracts and infects individuals, many of whom originally are merely detached and indifferent spectators and bystanders. At first, people may be merely curious about the given behavior, or mildly interested in it. As they catch the spirit of excitement and become more attentive to the behavior, they become more inclined to engage in it. This may be viewed as a lowering of social resistance brought about by the fact that they suffer some loss of self-consciousness and, accordingly, of ability to interpret the activity of others. Self-consciousness is a means of barricading oneself against the influence of others, for with it the individual checks his immediate, natural responses and impulses, and makes judgments before acting. Consequently, when people are under the stress of collective excitement, becoming more and more preoccupied with a given type of behavior, they are more likely to be subject to the impulses awakened in them. Where people already have a common disposition to act in a certain way, such as to seek gain, to flee from danger, or to express hatred, the display of such behavior under conditions of collective excitement easily releases the corresponding impulses on their part. Under such conditions the given kind of behavior will "spread like wild-fire," as one sees it in the case of a speculative orgy, a financial panic, or a wave of patriotic hysteria.

Stages of Spontaneous Behavior. Milling, collective excitement, and social contagion are present, in varying degree, in all instances of spontaneous group behavior. It is especially in the early stages of the development of such behavior, that they are to be found; but they may operate at any point in the career of such developing behavior. Thus in the instance of a social movement, we find that they are most pronounced in the early period, but they always continue to operate, though in a more minimal way, for a long time. This process can be understood in view of their social function, as it has been outlined above. They operate, as we have seen, to unite people on the most primitive level and so to lay the basis for more enduring and substantial forms of unification.

Our discussion so far has sought to show briefly the nature of collective behavior in its most elementary and spontaneous form and to explain the nature of the mechanisms by which it operates. Our immediate task is to discuss the different types of elementary collective groups; subsequently, we shall consider the manner in which collective behavior becomes organized and solidified in new forms of group and institutional conduct. Four types of elementary collective groups can be isolated: the acting crowd, the expressive crowd, the mass, and the public. These social groupings can be regarded as elementary since they arise spontaneously and their action is not set or determined by existing cultural patterns. Each has a distinctive character and each arises under a special set of conditions.

SELECTED READINGS

Britt, S. H. *Selected Readings in Social Psychology.* New York: Rinehart & Co., 1950.

Cleveland, C. C. *The Great Revival in the West, 1797–1805.* Chicago: Univ. of Chicago Press, 1916.

Davenport, F. M. *Primitive Traits in Religious Revivals.* New York: Truth Seeker Co., 1905.

Durkheim, Emile. *The Elementary Forms of Religious Life.* Trans. by J. W. Swain. New York: Macmillan Co., 1915.

Festinger, Leon, and others. *Social Pressures in Informal Groups.* New York: Harper & Bros., 1950.

Hecker, J. F. C. *Dancing Mania in the Middle Ages.* New York: Twentieth Century Publ. Co.

Lowenthal, L., and N. Guterman. *Prophets of Deceit: A Study of the Techniques of the American Agitator.* New York: Harper & Bros., 1949.

Mackay, Charles. *Extraordinary Popular Delusions and the Madness of Crowds.* Boston: L. C. Page & Co., 1932.

Newcomb, T. M. *Social Psychology.* New York: Dryden Press, 1950.

Park, Robert E., and E. W. Burgess. *Introduction to the Science of Sociology.* 2nd ed. Chicago: Univ. of Chicago Press, 1924. Pp. 866, 878, 924, 935.

Young, Kimball. *Social Psychology.* 2nd ed. New York: Appleton-Century-Crofts, Inc., 1944. Chap. 16.

CHAPTER TWENTY-ONE

ELEMENTARY
COLLECTIVE GROUPINGS

THE ACTING CROWD

Much of the initial interest of sociologists in the field of collective behavior has centered on the study of the crowd. This interest was lively particularly towards the end of the last century, especially among French scholars. It gained its most vivid expression in the classical work, *The Crowd*, by Gustave Le Bon. This work and others have provided us with much insight into the nature and behavior of the crowd, although much still remains unknown.

Types of Crowds. It is convenient to identify four types of crowds. The first can be called a *casual* crowd, as in the instance of a street crowd watching a performer in a store window. The casual crowd usually has a momentary existence; more important, it has a very loose organization and scarcely any unity. Its members come and go, giving but temporary attention to the object which has awakened the interest of the crowd, and entering into only feeble association with one another. While the chief mechanisms of crowd formation are present in the casual crowd, they are so reduced in scope and weak in operation, that we need not concern ourselves further with this type of crowd. A second type may be designated as the *conventionalized* crowd, such as the spectators at an exciting baseball game. Their behavior is essentially like that of casual crowds, except that it is expressed in established and regularized ways. It is this regularized activity that marks off the conventional crowd as a distinct type. The third type of crowd is the *acting*, aggressive crowd, best represented by a revolutionary crowd or a lynching mob. The outstanding mark of this type of crowd is the presence of an aim or objective toward which the activity of the crowd is directed. It is this type of crowd which is the object of concern in practically all studies of the crowd. The remaining type is the *expressive* or "dancing" crowd, such as is so common in the origin of religious sects. Its distinguishing trait is that excitement is expressed in physical movement merely as a form of release instead of being directed toward some objective. In this chapter, we shall consider the acting crowd, and in the following chapter, the dancing crowd.

Formation of Crowds. The essential steps in the formation of a crowd seem to be quite clear. First is the occurrence of some exciting event which catches the attention and arouses the interest of people. In becoming preoccupied with this event and stirred by its excitatory character, an individual is already likely to lose some of his ordinary self-control and to be dominated by the exciting object. Further, this kind of experience, by arousing impulses and feelings, establishes a condition of tension which, in turn, presses the individual on to action. Thus, a number of people stimulated by the same exciting event are disposed by that very fact to behave like a crowd.

This becomes clear in the second step—the beginning of the milling process. The tension of individuals who are aroused by some stimulating event, leads them to move around and to talk to one another; in this milling the incipient excitement becomes greater. The excitement of each is conveyed to others, and, as we have indicated above, in being reflected back to each, intensifies his own excited condition. The most obvious effect of this milling is to disseminate a common mood, feeling, or emotional impulse, and also to increase its intensity. This really leads to a state of marked rapport wherein individuals become very sensitive and responsive to one another and where, consequently, all are more disposed to act together as a collective unit.

Another important result may come from the milling process, and may be regarded as the third important step in the formation of the acting crowd. This step is the emergence of a common object of attention on which the impulses, feelings, and imagery of the people become focused. Usually the common object is the exciting event which has aroused the people; much more frequently, however, it is an image which has been built up and fixed through the talking and acting of people as they mill. This image, or object, like the excitement, is common and shared. Its importance is that it gives a common orientation to the people, and so provides a common objective to their activity. With such a common objective, the crowd is in a position to act with unity, purpose, and consistency.

The last step may be thought of as the stimulation and fostering of the impulses that correspond to the crowd objective, up to the point where the members are ready to act on them. This nurturing and crystallizing of impulses is a result of the interstimulation that takes place in milling and in response to leadership. It occurs primarily as a result of images that are aroused through the process of suggestion and imitation, and reinforced through mutual acceptance. When the members of a crowd have a common impulse oriented toward a fixed image and supported by an intense collective feeling, they are ready to act in the aggressive fashion typical of the acting crowd.

Characteristics of the Acting Crowd. Now we may characterize the nature of the acting crowd, or as some writers also term it, the psychological crowd. It should be noted, first, that such a group is spontaneous and lives in the momentary present. As such it is not a society or a cultural group. It has no heritage or accumulation of tradition to guide its activity; it has no conventions, established expectations, or rules. It lacks other important marks of a society such as an established social organization, an established division of labor, a structure of established roles, a recognized leadership, a set of norms, a set of moral regulations, an awareness of its own identity, or a recognized "we-consciousness." Instead of acting, then, on the basis of established rule, it acts on the basis of aroused impulse. Just as it is, in this sense, a noncultural group, so likewise is it a nonmoral group. In the light of this fact it is not difficult to understand that crowd actions may be strange, forbidding, and at times atrocious. Not having a body of definitions or rules to guide its behavior and, instead, acting on the basis of impulse, the crowd is fickle, suggestible, and irresponsible.

This character of the crowd can be appreciated better by understanding the condition of the typical member. Such an individual loses ordinary critical understanding and self-control as he enters into rapport with other crowd members and becomes infused by the collective excitement which dominates them. He responds immediately and directly to the remarks and actions of others instead of interpreting these gestures, as he would do in ordinary conduct. His inability to survey the actions of others before responding to them carries over to his own tendencies to act. Consequently, the impulses aroused in him by his sympathetic sharing of the collective excitement are likely to gain immediate expression instead of being submitted to his own judgment. It is just this condition which is the mark of suggestibility; it explains why the role of suggestion is so pronounced in the crowd. It should be noted, however, that this suggestibility exists only along the line of the aroused impulses; suggestions made contrary to them are ignored. This limiting of the area of suggestibility, but with an intensification of the suggestibility inside of these limits, is a point which is frequently overlooked by students of crowd behavior.

The loss of customary critical interpretation and the arousing of impulses and excited feelings explain the queer, vehement, and surprising behavior so frequent among members of a genuine crowd. Impulses which ordinarily would be subject to a severe check by the individual's judgment and control of himself now have a free passage to expression. That many of these impulses should have an atavistic character is not strange, nor, consequently, is it surprising that much of the actual behavior should be violent, cruel, and destructive. Further, the release of impulses and feelings which encounter no restraint, which come to possess the individual, and which acquire a quasi-sanction through the support of other people, gives the individual a sense of power, of ego-expansion, and of rectitude. Thus, he is likely to experience a sense of invincibility and of conviction in his actions.

The behavior of the crowd can be understood better with a realization of these aspects of the individual member: his loss of self-concern and critical judgment, the surging forth of impulses and feelings, many of which are usually suppressed, his sense of expansion and greatness, and his suggestibility to his fellows. It should be borne in mind that this state of the members of the crowd is due to their extreme rapport and mutual excitement; and, in turn, that this rapport in the acting crowd has become organized around a common objective of activity. Common focusing of attention, rapport, and individual submergence—these exist as different phases of one another, and explain the unity of the crowd and the general character of its behavior.

To prevent the formation of a mob or to break up a mob, it is necessary to redirect the attention so that it is not focused collectively on one object. This is the theoretical principle underlying crowd control. Insofar as the attention of the members is directed toward different objects, they form an aggregation of individuals instead of a crowd united by intimate rapport. Thus, to throw people into a state of panic, or to get them interested in other objects, or to get them engaged in discussion or argumentation represents different ways in which a crowd can be broken up.

Our discussion of the crowd has presented the psychological bond of the crowd, or the spirit, that may be called "crowd-mindedness" to use a felicitous phrase of E. A. Ross.[1] If we think in terms of crowd-mindedness, it is clear that many groups may take on the character of a crowd without having to be as small in size as in the instance of a lynching mob. Under certain conditions, a nation may come to be like a crowd. If the people become preoccupied with the same stirring event or object, if they develop a high state of mutual excitement marked by no disagreement, and if they have strong impulses to act toward the object with which they are preoccupied, their action will be like that of the crowd. We are familiar with such behavior on a huge scale in the case of social contagion, like that of patriotic hysteria.

THE EXPRESSIVE CROWD

The Dominant Mark of the Expressive Crowd. The distinguishing feature of the acting crowd, as we have seen, is the direction of the attention toward some common objective or goal; the action of the crowd is the behavior gone through to reach that objective. As opposed to this characteristic, the dominant mark of the expressive crowd is that it is introverted. It has no goal or objective—its impulses and feelings are spent in mere expressive actions, usually in unrestrained physical movements, which give release to tension without having any other purpose. We see such behavior in a marked form in the saturnalia, the carnival, and the dancing crowds of primitive sects.

Comparisons with the Acting Crowd. In explaining the nature of the expressive crowd we should note that in formation and fundamental character it is very much like the acting crowd. It consists of people who are excited, who mill, and who in doing so, spread and intensify the excitement. There develops among them the same condition of rapport marked by quick and unwit-

---

[1] E. A. Ross. *Social Psychology* (New York: Macmillan Co., 1908).

ting mutual responsiveness. Individuals lose awareness of themselves. Impulses and feelings are aroused, and are no longer subject to the constraint and control which an individual usually exercises over them. In these respects the expressive crowd is essentially like the acting crowd.

The fundamental difference is that the expressive crowd does not develop any image of a goal or objective, and, consequently, suggestion does not operate to build up a plan of action. Without having an objective toward which it might act, the crowd can release its aroused tension and excitement only in physical movement. Stated tersely, the crowd has to act, but it has nothing toward which it can act, and so it merely engages in excited movements. The excitement of the crowd stimulates further excitement which does not, however, become organized around some purposive act which the crowd seeks to carry out. In such a situation the expression of excited feeling becomes an end in itself; the behavior, therefore, may take the form of laughing, weeping, shouting, leaping, and dancing. In its more extreme expression, it may be in the form of uttering gibberish or having violent physical spasms.

Rhythmic Expression. Perhaps the most interesting feature of this expressive behavior, as it is carried on collectively, is that it tends to become rhythmical; so that with sufficient repetition and with the existence of sufficient rapport, it takes on the form of people's acting with unison. It is easy to see that it may come to be like a collective dance; it is this aspect that leads one to designate the expressive crowd as a dancing crowd. It may be said that just as an acting crowd develops its unity through the formation of a common objective, the expressive crowd forms its unity through the rhythmical expression of its tension.

This feature is of outstanding significance, for it throws considerable light on the interesting association between "dancing" behavior and primitive religious sentiment. To illustrate this point, let us consider the experience of the individual in the dancing crowd.

The Individual in the Expressive Crowd. The stimulation that the individual receives from those with whom he is in rapport lessens his ordinary self-control and evokes and incites impulsive feelings which take possession of him. He feels carried away by a spirit whose source is unknown, but whose effect is acutely appreciated. There are two conditions which are likely to make this experience one of ecstasy and exaltation, and to seal it with a sacred or divine stamp. The first is that the experience is cathartic in nature. The individual who has been in a state of tension, discomfort, and perhaps anxiety, suddenly gains full release and experiences the joy and fullness that come with such relief. This organic satisfaction unquestionably yields a pleasure and exhilaration that makes the experience momentous. The fact that this mood has such complete and unobstructed control over the individual easily leads him to feel that he is possessed or pervaded by a kind of transcendental spirit. The other condition which gives the experience a religious character is the approval and sanction implied in the support coming from those with whom he is in rapport. The fact that others are sharing the same experience rids it of suspicion and enables its unqualified acceptance. When an experience gives complete and full satisfaction, when it is socially stimulated, approved, and sustained, and when it comes in the form of a mysterious possession from the outside, it easily acquires a religious character.

The Development of Collective Ecstasy. When an expressive crowd reaches the height of such collective ecstasy, the tendency is for this feeling to be projected upon objects which are sensed as having some intimate connection with it. Thereupon such objects become sacred to the members of the crowd. These objects may vary; they may include persons (such as a religious prophet), the dance, a song, or physical objects which are felt to be linked with the ecstatic experience. The appearance of such sacred objects lays the basis for the formation of a cult, sect, or primitive religion.

Not all expressive crowds attain this stage of development. Most of them do not pass beyond the early milling or excited stage. But implicitly, they have the potentiality of doing so, and they have most of the characteristic features, even though they be in a subdued form.

Like the acting crowd, the expressive crowd need not be confined to a small compact group whose members are in immediate physical proximity of one another. The behavior which is characteristic of it may be found on occasion in a large group, such as the nation-wide public.

Evaluation. A brief evaluation of the acting crowd and the expressive crowd can be made here. Both of them are spontaneous groupings. Both of them represent elementary collectivities. Their form and structure are not traceable to any body of culture or set of rules; instead, such structures as they have, arise indigenously out of the milling of excited individuals. The acting crowd focuses its tension on an objective and so becomes organized around a plan of action; the expressive crowd merely releases its tension in expressive movement which tends to become rhythmical and establishes unity in this fashion. In both crowds the individual is stripped of much of his conscious, ordinary behavior, and is rendered malleable by the crucible of collective excitement. With the breakdown of his previous personal organization, he is in a position to develop new forms of conduct and to crystallize a new personal organization along new and different lines. In this sense, crowd behavior is a means by which the breakup of the social organization and personal structure is brought about, and at the same time is a potential device for the emergence of new forms of conduct and personality. The acting crowd presents one of the alternative lines for such reorganization—the development of aggressive behavior in the direction of purposive social change. We shall view this line of reorganization as giving rise to a political order. The expressive crowd stands for the other alternative—the release of inner tension in conduct which tends to become sacred and marked by deep sentiment. This might be regarded as giving rise to a religious order of behavior.

THE MASS

We are selecting the term *mass* to denote another elementary and spontaneous collective grouping which, in many respects, is like the crowd but is fundamentally different from it in other ways. The mass is represented by people who participate in mass behavior, such as those who are excited by some national event, those who share in a land boom, those who are interested in a murder trial which is reported in the press, or those who participate in some large migration.

Distinguishable Features of the Mass. So conceived, the mass has a number of distinguishable features. *First*, its membership may come from all walks of life, and from all distinguishable social strata; it may include people of different class position, of different vocation, of different cultural attainment, and of different wealth. One can recognize this in the case of the mass of people who follow a murder trial. *Second*, the mass is an anonymous group, or more exactly, is composed of anonymous individuals. *Third*, there exists little interaction or exchange of experience between the members of the mass. They are usually physically separated from one another, and, being anonymous, do not have the opportunity to mill as do the members of the crowd. *Fourth*, the mass is very loosely organized and is not able to act with the concertedness or unity that marks the crowd.

The Role of Individuals in the Mass. The fact that the mass consists of individuals belonging to a wide variety of local groups and cultures is important. For it signifies that the object of interest which gains the attention of those who form the mass is something which lies on the outside of the local cultures and groups; and therefore, that this object of interest is not defined or explained in terms of the understandings or rules of these local groups. The object of mass interest can be thought of as attracting the attention of people away from their local cultures and spheres of life and turning it toward a wider universe, toward areas which are not defined or covered by rules, regulations, or expectations. In this sense the mass can be viewed as constituted by detached and alienated individuals who face objects or areas of life which are interesting, but which are also puzzling and not easy to understand and order. Consequently, before such objects, the members of the mass are likely to be confused and uncertain in their actions. Further, in not being able to communicate with one another, except in limited and imperfect ways, the members of the mass are forced to act separately, as individuals.

Society and the Mass. From this brief characterization it can be seen that the mass is devoid of the features of a society or a community. It has no social organization, no body of custom and tradition, no established set of rules or rituals, no organized group of sentiments, no structure of status roles, and no established leadership. It merely consists of an aggregation of individuals who are separate, detached, anonymous, and thus, homogeneous as far as mass behavior is concerned. It can be seen, further, that the behavior of the mass, just because it is not made by pre-established rule or expectation, is spontaneous, indigenous, and elementary. In these respects, the mass is a great deal like the crowd.

In other respects, there is an important difference. It has already been noted that the mass does not mill or interact as the crowd does. Instead, the individuals are separated from one another and unknown to one another. This fact means that the individual in the mass, instead of being stripped of his self-awareness is, on the other hand, apt to be rather acutely self-conscious. Instead of acting in response to the suggestions and excited stimulation of those with whom he is in rapport, he acts in response to the object that has gained his attention and on the basis of the impulses that are aroused by it.

Nature of Mass Behavior. This raises the question as to how the mass behaves. The answer is in terms of each individual's seeking to answer his own needs. The form of mass behavior, paradoxically, is laid down by individual lines of activity and not by concerted action. These individual activities are primarily in the form of selections—such as the selection of a new dentifrice, a book, a play, a party platform, a new fashion, a philosophy, or a gospel—selections which are made in response to the vague impulses and feelings which are awakened by the object of mass interest. Mass behavior, even though a congeries of individual lines of action, may become of momentous significance. If these lines converge, the influence of the mass may be enormous, as is shown by the far-reaching effects on institutions ensuing from shifts in the selective interest of the mass. A political party may be disorganized or a commercial institution wrecked by such shifts in interest or taste.

When mass behavior becomes organized, as into a movement, it ceases to be mass behavior, but becomes societal in nature. Its whole nature changes in acquiring a structure, a program, a defining culture, traditions, prescribed rules, an in-group attitude, and a we-consciousness. It is for this reason that we have appropriately limited it to the forms of behavior which have been described.

Increasing Importance of Mass Behavior. Under conditions of modern urban and industrial life, mass behavior has emerged in increasing magnitude and importance. This is due primarily to the operation of factors which have detached people from their local cultures and local group settings. Migration, changes of residence, newspapers, motion pictures, the radio, education—all have operated to detach individuals from customary moorings and thrust them into a new and wider world. In the face of this world, individuals have had to make adjustments on the basis of largely unaided selections. The convergence of their selections has made the mass a potent influence. At times, its behavior comes to approximate that of a crowd, especially under conditions of excitement. At such times it is likely to be influenced by excited appeals as these appear in the press or over the radio—appeals that play upon primitive impulses, antipathies, and traditional hatreds. This should not obscure the fact that the mass may behave without such crowdlike frenzy. It may be much more influenced by an artist or a writer who happens to sense the vague feelings of the mass and to give expression and articulation to them.

Instances of Mass Behavior. In order to make clearer the nature of the mass and of mass behavior, a brief consideration can be given to a few instances. Gold rushes and land rushes illustrate many of the features of mass behavior. The people who participate in them usually come from a wide variety of backgrounds; together they constitute a heterogeneous assemblage. Thus, those who engaged in the Klondike Rush or the Oklahoma Land Boom came from different localities and areas. In the rush, each individual (or at best, family) had his own goal or objective, so that between the participants there was a minimum of co-operation and very little feeling of allegiance or loyalty. Each was trying to get ahead of the other, and each had to take care of himself. Once the rush is under way, there is little discipline, and no organization to enforce order. Under such conditions it is easy to see how a rush turns into a stampede or a panic.

Mass Advertising. Some further appreciation of the nature of mass behavior is yielded by a brief treatment of mass advertising. In such advertising, the appeal has to be addressed to the anonymous individual. The relation between the advertisement and the prospective purchaser is a direct one—there is no organization or leadership which can deliver, so to speak, the body of purchasers to the seller. Instead, each individual acts upon the basis of his own selection. The purchasers are a heterogeneous group coming from many communities and walks of life; as members of the mass, however, because of their anonymity, they are homogeneous or essentially alike.

Proletarian Masses. What are sometimes spoken of as the proletarian masses illustrate other features of the mass. They represent a large population with little organization or effective communication. Such people usually have been wrested loose from a stable group life. They are usually disturbed, even though it be only in the form of vague hopes or new tastes and interests. Consequently, there is a lot of groping in their behavior —an uncertain process of selection among objects and ideas that come to their attention.

THE PUBLIC

Nature of the Public. We shall consider the public as the remaining elementary collective grouping. The term *public* is used to refer to a group of people (*a*) who are confronted by an issue, (*b*) who are divided in their ideas as to how to meet the issue, and (*c*) who engage in discussion over the issue. As such, it is to be distinguished from a public in the sense of a national people, as when one speaks of the public of the United States, and also from a *following*, as in the instance of the "public" of a motion-picture star. The presence of an issue, of discussion, and of a collective opinion is the mark of the public.

The Public as a Group. We refer to the public as an elementary and spontaneous collective grouping because it comes into existence not as a result of design, but as a natural response to a certain kind of situation. That the public does not exist as an established group and that its behavior is not prescribed by traditions or cultural patterns is indicated by the very fact that its existence centers on the presence of an issue. As issues vary, so do the corresponding publics. And the fact that an issue exists signifies the presence of a situation which cannot be met on the basis of a cultural rule but which must be met by a collective decision arrived at through a process of discussion. In this sense, the public is a grouping that is spontaneous and not pre-established.

Characteristic Features of the Public. This elementary and spontaneous character of the public can be better appreciated by noticing that the public, like the crowd and the mass, is lacking in the characteristic features of a society. The existence of an issue means that the group has to act; yet there are no understandings, definitions, or rules prescribing what that action should be. If there were, there would be, of course, no issue. It is in this sense that we can speak of the public as having no culture—no traditions to dictate what its action shall be. Further, since a public comes into existence only with an issue it does not have the form or organization of a society. In it, people do not have fixed status roles. Nor does the public have any we-feeling or consciousness of its identity. Instead, the public is a kind of amorphous group whose size and membership varies with the issue; instead of having its activity prescribed, it is engaged in an effort to arrive at an act, and therefore forced to *create* its action.

The peculiarity of the public is that it is marked by disagreement and hence by *discussion* as to what should be done. This fact has a number of implications. For one thing, it indicates that the interaction that occurs in the public is markedly different from that which takes place in the crowd. A crowd mills, develops rapport, and reaches a unanimity unmarred by disagreement. The public interacts on the basis of interpretation, enters into dispute, and consequently is characterized by conflict relations. Correspondingly, individuals in the public are likely to have their self-consciousness intensified and their critical powers heightened instead of losing self-awareness and critical ability as occurs in the crowd. In the public, arguments are advanced, are criticized, and are met by counterarguments. The interaction, therefore, makes for opposition instead of the mutual support and unanimity that mark the crowd.

Another point of interest is that this discussion, which is based on difference, places some premium on facts and makes for rational consideration. While, as we shall see, the interaction may fall short by far of realizing these characteristics, the tendency is in their direction. The crowd means that rumor and spectacular suggestion predominate; but the presence of opposition and disagreement in the public means that contentions are challenged and become subject to criticism. In the face of attack that threatens to undermine their character, such contentions have to be bolstered or revised in the face of criticisms that cannot be ignored. Since facts can maintain their validity, they come to be valued; and since the discussion is argumentative, rational considerations come to occupy a role of some importance.

Behavior Patterns of the Public. Now we can consider the question as to how a public acts. This question is interesting, particularly because the public does not act like a society, a crowd, or the mass. A society manages to act by following a prescribed rule or consensus; a crowd, by developing rapport; and the mass, by the convergence of individual selections. But the public faces, in a sense, the dilemma of how to become a unit when it is actually divided, of how to act concertedly when there is a disagreement as to what the action should be. The public acquires its particular type of unity and manages to act by arriving at a collective decision or by developing a collective opinion. It becomes necessary to consider now the nature of public opinion and the manner of its formation.

PUBLIC OPINION

Public opinion should be viewed as a collective product. As such, it is not a unanimous opinion with which everyone in the public agrees, nor is it necessarily the opinion of a majority. Being a collective opinion it may be (and usually is) different from the opinion of any of the groups in the public. It can be thought of, perhaps, as a composite opinion formed out of the several opinions that are held in the public; or better, as the central tendency set by the striving among these separate opinions and, consequently, as being shaped by the relative strength and play of opposition among them. In this process, the opinion of some minority group may exert a much greater influence in the shaping of the collective opinion than does the view of a majority group. Being a collective product, public opinion does represent the entire public as it is being mobilized to act on the issue, and as such, does enable concerted action which is not necessarily based on consensus, rapport, or chance alignment of individual choices. Public opinion is always moving toward a decision even though it never is unanimous.

The Universe of Discourse. The formation of public opinion occurs through the give and take of discussion. Argument and counterargument become the means by which it is shaped. For this process of discussion to go on, it is essential for the public to have what has been called a "universe of discourse"—the possession of a common language or the ability to agree on the meaning of fundamental terms. Unless they can understand one another, discussion and argumentation are not only fruitless, but impossible. Public discussion today, particularly on certain national issues, is likely to be hampered by the absence of a universe of discourse. Further, if the groups or parties in the public adopt dogmatic and sectarian positions, public discussion comes to a standstill; for such sectarian attitudes are tantamount to a refusal to adopt the point of view of one another and to alter one's own position in the face of attack or criticism. The formation of public opinion implies that people share one another's experience and are willing to make compromises and concessions. It is only in this way that the public, divided as it is, can come to act as a unit.

Interest Groups. The public, ordinarily, is made up of interest groups and a more detached and disinterested spectator-like body. The issue which creates the public is usually set by contesting interest groups. These interest groups have an immediate private concern in the way the issue is met and, therefore, they endeavor to win to their position the support and allegiance of the outside disinterested group. This puts the disinterested group, as Lippmann has pointed out, in the position of arbiter and judge. It is their alignment which determines, usually, which of the competing schemes is likely to enter most freely into the final action. This strategic and decisive place held by those not identified with the immediate interest groups means that public discussion is carried on primarily among them. The interest groups endeavor to shape and set the opinions of these relatively disinterested people.

Viewed in this way, one can understand the varying quality of public opinion, and also the use of means of influence such as propaganda, which subvert intelligent public discussion. A given public opinion is likely to be anywhere between a highly emotional and prejudiced point of view and a highly intelligent and thoughtful opinion. In other words, public discussion may be carried on different levels, with different degrees of thoroughness and limitation. The efforts made by interest groups to shape public opinion may be primarily attempts to arouse or set emotional attitudes and to provide misinformation. It is this feature which has led many students of public opinion to deny its rational character and to emphasize instead, its emotional and unreasoned nature. One must recognize, however, that the very process of controversial discussion forces a certain amount of rational consideration and that, consequently, the resulting collective opinion has a certain rational character. The fact that contentions have to be defended and justified and opposing contentions criticized and shown to be untenable, involves evaluation, weighing, and judgment. Perhaps it would be accurate to say that public opinion is rational, but need not be intelligent.

The Role of Public Discussion. It is clear that the quality of public opinion depends to a large extent on the effectiveness of public discussion. In turn, this effectiveness depends on the availability and flexibility of the agencies of public communication, such as the press, the radio, and public meetings. Basic to their effective use is the possibility of free discussion. If certain of the contending views are barred from gaining presentation to the disinterested public or suffer some discrimination as to the possibility of being argued before them, then, correspondingly, there is interference with effective public discussion.

As mentioned above, the concerns of interest groups readily lead them to efforts to manipulate public opinion. This is particularly true today, when public issues are many and the opportunities for thorough discussion are limited. This setting has been conducive to the employment, in increasing degree, of "propaganda"; today most students of public opinion find that their chief concern is the study of propaganda.

PROPAGANDA

Propaganda can be thought of as a deliberately evoked and guided campaign to induce people to accept a given view, sentiment, or value. Its peculiarity is that in seeking to attain this end it does not give fair consideration to opposing views. The end is dominant and the means are subservient to this end. Hence, we find that a primary characteristic of propaganda is the effort to gain the acceptance of a view not on the basis of the merits of that view but, instead, by appealing to other motives. It is this feature that has made propaganda suspect. In the area of public discussion and public consideration, propaganda operates to mold opinions and judgments not on the basis of the merits of an issue, but chiefly by playing upon emotional attitudes and feelings. Its aim is to implant an attitude or value which comes to be felt by people as natural, true, and proper, and, therefore, as one which expresses itself spontaneously and without coercion.

Collective Action through Propaganda. It is important to realize that propaganda seeks to bring about collective action rather than mere individual action. In this sense it should be distinguished from advertising, since advertising tries to influence individual action. In propaganda, by contrast, there is the effort to create a conviction and to get action in accordance with this conviction. Those who share a conviction are more easily disposed to act together and to give one another support. From this point of view, everyone who preaches a doctrine or who seeks to propagate a faith is a propagandist, for his ultimate purpose is not to discuss the merits of an issue, but instead to implant a given conviction. With this character, it is clear that propaganda operates to end discussion and reflection.

Practical Rules of Propaganda. There are a few simple rules which are generally recognized to apply to propaganda. *First*, of course, to implant a desired view or attitude, it is necessary to attract the attention of people. *Next*, the object in which it is desired that they become interested should be given a favorable and appealing setting, as in the instance of advertising. *Third*, the images which are used to influence them should be simple and clean-cut. *Fourth*, there should be continuous repetition of the slogans or catchwords or of the presented images. *Fifth*, it is best never to argue, but simply to persist in assertion and reassertion. Such simple techniques are held to be particularly effective in the case of the bulk of people whose attention is ordinarily easily diverted and whose interest is easily flagged.

The Chief Procedures of Propaganda. The chief lines along which propaganda may operate, however, are broader and deserve more thorough consideration. We can distinguish three primary ways by which propaganda is likely to achieve its ends. The first is by simply misrepresenting facts and by providing false information. Judgments and opinions of people are obviously shaped by such data as are available to them. By manipulating the facts, concealing some and misrepresenting others, the propagandist can do much to induce the formation of a given attitude.

Another favorite means of propaganda is to make use of in-group–out-group attitudes. It is well known by sociologists that when two groups develop a keen sense of opposition, strong and unreasonable feelings are released. Each group tends to foster attitudes of loyalty and altruism among the members and to inculcate bitter feelings of hatred and enmity toward the outsiders. The ability to use this in-group–out-group pattern is a primary desideratum to the propagandist. He endeavors to get people to identify his views with their in-group feelings, and opposing views with out-group attitudes. It is the presence of this in-group–out-group setting that explains the extreme effectiveness of propaganda during times of war.

Perhaps the outstanding method of the propagandist is to utilize the emotional attitudes and prejudices which people already have. His purpose here is to build up an association between them and his propagandistic message. Thus, if he can link his views to certain favorable attitudes which people already have, these views will gain acceptance. Also, if opposing views can be associated with unfavorable attitudes, they are likely to be rejected. We see a great deal of this device in current discussions. Efforts are made to identify contentions with such beneficently toned stereotypes as "democracy," "save the Constitution," and "individual liberty," and opposing contentions with such stereotypes as "communism" and "anti-American." It is by playing upon the feelings and prejudices which people already have, that propaganda primarily operates.

The Ingenuity of Propagandists. While it is possible to indicate the simple rules which propaganda follows and the psychological mechanisms which it employs, it is important to realize that it depends primarily upon ingenuity. Each situation has to be met in terms of its peculiarities; a device which may be very successful in one situation may be of no value in another. In this sense, propaganda is like persuasion in face-to-face situations; much depends on intuitive impression and artful ingenuity.

Conflicting Propagandas. Without doubt, there is an increasing use of propaganda at the present time in the public arena, and undoubtedly, this factor has influenced both the nature of public opinion and the manner of its information. This consequence has led to despair on the part of many as to the serviceability of democratic machinery. However, it is important to realize that the presence of propaganda and counter-propaganda sets, again, an issue and ushers in the discussional process which we have spoken of above. For when there are conflicting and opposing propagandas at work, the stage is set for a logical duel, where facts have a premium and rational considerations enter. From this point of view one may understand the remark that propaganda is harmful and dangerous only when there is *one* propaganda.

THE PUBLIC, THE CROWD, AND THE MASS

Before concluding the discussion of the public, it should be pointed out that under certain conditions the public may be changed into a crowd. Most propaganda tends to do this, anyway. When the people in the public are aroused by an appeal to a sentiment which is common to them, they begin to mill and to develop rapport. Then, their expression is in the form of public sentiment and not public opinion. In modern life, however, there seems to be less tendency for the public to become the crowd than for it to be displaced by the mass. The increasing detachment of people from local life, the multiplication of public issues, the expansion of agencies of mass communication, together with other factors, have led people to act increasingly by individual selection rather than by participating in public discussion. So true is this, that in many ways the public and the mass are likely to exist intermingled with one another. This fact adds confusion to the scene of contemporary collective behavior and renders analysis by the student difficult.

COLLECTIVE GROUPINGS AND SOCIAL CHANGE

In the discussion of elementary collective groupings we have considered the acting crowd, the expressive crowd, the mass, and the public. There are other primitive groupings which we can mention here only briefly, such as the panic, the stampede, the strike, the riot, the "popular justice" vigilante committee, the procession, the cult, the mutiny, and the revolt. Most of these groupings represent variations of the crowd; each of them operates through the primitive mechanisms of collective behavior which we have described. Like the four major types which we have considered, they are not societies, but operate outside of a governing framework of rules and culture. They are elementary, natural, and spontaneous, arising under certain fit circumstances.

The appearance of elementary collective groupings is indicative of a process of social change. They have the dual character of implying the disintegration of the old and the appearance of the new. They play an important part in the development of new collective behavior and of new forms of social life. More accurately, the typical mechanisms of primitive association which they show have a significant role in the formation of a new social order.

It is to this problem of the formation of a new social order, that we shall now devote ourselves. Our task will be to consider primarily the social movements by which new kinds of collective behavior are built up and crystallized into fixed social forms.

SELECTED READINGS

Albig, William. *Public Opinion.* New York: McGraw-Hill Book Co., 1939. Esp. chaps. 1–6, 10, 13, 23.

Allport, G. W. *The Nature of Personality: Selected Papers.* Cambridge, Mass.: Addison-Wesley Press, 1950. Esp. pp. 1–47.

Allport, G. W., and L. Postman. *The Psychology of Rumor.* New York: Henry Holt & Co., 1947.

Bauer, Wilhelm. "Public Opinion," *Encyclopaedia of the Social Sciences* (1934), 12:669–674.

Berelson, Bernard, and M. Janowitz, eds. *Reader in Public Opinion and Communication.* Glencoe, Ill.: Free Press, 1950.

Bernays, Edward L. *Propaganda.* New York: Liveright Publ. Corp., 1938.

Burgess, E. W., ed. *Personality and the Social Group.* Chicago: Univ. of Chicago Press, 1929.

Chase, Stuart. *Democracy under Pressure.* New York: Twentieth Century Fund, 1945.

Dennis, Wayne, ed. *Current Trends in Social Psychology.* Pittsburgh: Univ. of Pittsburgh Press, 1948.

Dewey, John. *The Public and Its Problems.* New York: Henry Holt & Co., 1927.

Doob, Leonard W. *Public Opinion and Propaganda.* New York: Henry Holt & Co., 1948.

Durkheim, Emile. *Elementary Forms of Religious Life.* Trans. by J. W. Swain. New York: Macmillan Co., 1915.

Gallup, George, and Saul F. Rae. *The Pulse of Democracy.* New York: Simon & Schuster, 1940.

Gruening, Ernest. "Publicity," *Encyclopaedia of the Social Sciences* (1934), 12:698–701.

Hardman, J. B. S. "Masses," *Encyclopaedia of the Social Sciences* (1933), 10:195–201.

Hecker, J. F. C. *Dancing Mania of the Middle Ages.* New York: Twentieth Century Publ. Co.

Hovland, Carl I., and others. *Experiments on Mass Communication.* (Studies in Social Psychology in World War II, v. 3) Princeton: Princeton Univ. Press, 1949.

Institute for Propaganda Analysis. *Propaganda Analysis* (1937–1942), 1–4.

Krech, David, and R. S. Crutchfield. *Theory and Problems of Social Psychology.* New York: McGraw-Hill Book Co., 1948. Part 2.

Lasswell, Harold D. *Propaganda Technique in the World War.* New York: A. A. Knopf, 1927.

Lasswell, Harold D. "The Study and Practice of Propaganda." Pp. 3–27 in: Lasswell, R. D. Casey, and B. L. Smith. *Propaganda and Promotional Activities: An Annotated Bibliography.* Minneapolis: Univ. of Minnesota Press, 1935. See also continuing bibliography in this book and in *Public Opinion Quarterly* beginning in 1935, compiled by B. L. Smith and others.

Lasswell, Harold D., Nathan Leites, and others. *Language of Politics: Studies in Quantitative Semantics.* New York: George W. Stewart, 1949.

Lazarsfeld, P. F., and others. *The People's Choice: How the Voter Makes Up His Mind in a Presidential Campaign.* 2nd ed. New York: Columbia Univ. Press, 1948.

Le Bon, Gustave. *The Crowd: A Study of the Popular Mind.* London: T. F. Unwin, 1897.

Lee, Alfred M. "The Analysis of Propaganda: A Clinical Summary," *American Journal of Sociology* (1945), 51:126–135.

Lee, Alfred M. "Public Opinion in Relation to Culture," *Psychiatry* (1945), 8:49–61.

Lippmann, Walter. *The Phantom Public.* New York: Macmillan Co., 1925.

Lippmann, Walter. *Public Opinion.* New York: Macmillan Co., 1922.

Lowenthal, L., and N. Guterman. *Prophets of Deceit: A Study of the Techniques of the American Agitator.* New York: Harper & Bros., 1949.

MacDougall, C. D. *Hoaxes.* New York: Macmillan Co., 1938.

Mackay, Charles. *Extraordinary Popular Delusions and the Madness of Crowds.* Boston: L. C. Page & Co., 1932.

Mannheim, Karl. *Ideology and Utopia.* New York: Harcourt, Brace & Co., 1936.

Meusel, Alfred. "Proletariat," *Encyclopaedia of the Social Sciences* (1934), 12:510–518.

Miller, Hugh. *The Community of Man.* New York: Macmillan Co., 1949.

Mosteller, Frederick, and others. *The Pre-election Polls of 1948.* New York: Social Science Research Council, 1949.

Odegard, Peter. *The American Public Mind.* New York: Columbia Univ. Press, 1930.

Ortega y Gasset, José. *Revolt of the Masses.* New York: W. W. Norton, 1932.

Park, Robert E. "The Natural History of the Newspaper," Chap. 4 in Park and E. W. Burgess. *The City.* Chicago: Univ. of Chicago Press, 1925.

Park, Robert E., and E. W. Burgess. *Introduction to the Science of Sociology.* 2nd ed. Chicago: Univ. of Chicago Press, 1924. Chaps. 12–13.

Parten, Mildred. *Surveys, Polls, and Samples.* New York: Harper & Bros., 1950.

Rodgers, Lindsay. *The Pollsters.* New York: A. A. Knopf, 1949.

Ross, E. A. *Social Psychology.* New York: Macmillan Co., 1908.

Sidis, B. *Psychology of Suggestion.* New York: D. Appleton & Co., 1898.

Siepmann, Charles A. *Radio, Television and Society.* New York: Oxford Univ. Press, 1950.

Sorel, Georges. *Reflections on Violence.* New York: B. W. Huebsch, 1912.

Stouffer, S. A., and others. *Measurement and Prediction.* (Studies in Social Psychology in World War II, v. 4) Princeton: Princeton Univ. Press, 1950.

Tarde, Gabriel. *Laws of Imitation.* Trans. by E. C. Parsons. New York: Henry Holt & Co., 1903.

Wallas, Graham. *The Great Society.* New York: Macmillan Co., 1904.

Wiener, Norbert. *Cybernetics, or Control and Communication in the Animal and the Machine.* New York: John Wiley & Sons, 1948.

CHAPTER TWENTY-TWO

SOCIAL MOVEMENTS

Social movements can be viewed as collective enterprises to establish a new order of life. They have their inception in a condition of unrest, and derive their motive power on one hand from dissatisfaction with the current form of life, and on the other hand, from wishes and hopes for a new scheme or system of living. The career of a social movement depicts the emergence of a new order of life. In its beginning, a social movement is amorphous, poorly organized, and without form; the collective behavior is on the primitive level that we have already discussed, and the mechanisms of interaction are the elementary, spontaneous mechanisms of which we have spoken. As a social movement develops, it takes on the character of a society. It acquires organization and form, a body of customs and traditions, established leadership, an enduring division of labor, social rules and social values—in short, a culture, a social organization, and a new scheme of life.

Our treatment of social movements will deal with three kinds—general social movements, specific social movements, and expressive social movements.[1]

GENERAL SOCIAL MOVEMENTS

New Cultural Trends. By general social movements we have in mind movements such as the labor movement, the youth movement, the women's movement, and the peace movement. Their background is constituted by gradual and pervasive

---

1 Attention is called, in passing, to spatial movements, such as nomadic movements, barbaric invasions, crusades, pilgrimages, colonization, and migrations. Such movements may be carried on as societies, as in the case of tribal migrations; as diverse peoples with a common goal, as in the case of the religious crusades of the Middle Ages; or as individuals with similar goals, as in most of the immigration into the United States. Mechanisms of their collective operation will be dealt with in the following discussion of social movements. In themselves, such movements are too complicated and diversified to be dealt with adequately here.

changes in the values of people—changes which can be called cultural drifts. Such cultural drifts stand for a general shifting in the ideas of people, particularly along the line of the conceptions which people have of themselves, and of their rights and privileges. Over a period of time many people may develop a new view of what they believe they are entitled to—a view largely made up of desires and hopes. It signifies the emergence of a new set of values, which influence people in the way in which they look upon their own lives. Examples of such cultural drifts in our own recent history are the increased value of health, the belief in free education, the extension of the franchise, the emancipation of women, the increasing regard for children, and the increasing prestige of science.

Indefinite Images and Behavior. The development of the new values which such cultural drifts bring forth involve some interesting psychological changes which provide the motivation for general social movements. They mean, in a general sense, that people have come to form new conceptions of themselves which do not conform to the actual positions which they occupy in their life. They acquire new dispositions and interests and, accordingly, become sensitized in new directions; and, conversely, they come to experience dissatisfaction where before they had none. These new images of themselves, which people begin to develop in response to cultural drifts, are vague and indefinite; and correspondingly, the behavior in response to such images is uncertain and without definite aim. It is this feature which provides a cue for the understanding of general social movements.

Characteristics of General Social Movements. General social movements take the form of groping and unco-ordinated efforts. They have only a general direction, toward which they move in a slow, halting, yet persistent fashion. As movements they are unorganized, with neither established leadership nor recognized membership, and little guidance and control. Such a movement as the women's movement, which has the general and vague aim of the emancipation of women, suggests these features of a general social movement. The women's movement, like all general social movements, operates over a wide range—in the home, in marriage, in education, in industry, in politics, in travel—in each area of which it represents a search for an arrangement which will answer to the new idea of status being formed by women. Such a movement is episodic in its career, with very scattered manifestations of activity. It may show considerable enthusiasm at one point and reluctance and inertia at another; it may experience success in one area, and abortive effort in another. In general, it may be said that its progress is very uneven with setbacks, reverses, and frequent retreading of the same ground. At one time the impetus to the movement may come from people in one place, at another time in another place. On the whole the movement is likely to be carried on by many unknown and obscure people who struggle in different areas without their striving and achievements becoming generally known.

A general social movement usually is characterized by a literature, but the literature is as varied and ill-defined as is the movement itself. It is likely to be an expression of protest, with a general depiction of a kind of utopian existence. As such, it vaguely outlines a philosophy based on new values and self-conceptions. Such a literature is of great importance in spreading a message or view, however imprecise it may be, and so in implanting suggestions, awakening hopes, and arousing dissatisfactions. Similarly, the "leaders" of a general social movement play an important part—not in the sense of exercising directive control over the movement, but in the sense of being pace-makers. Such leaders are likely to be "voices in the wilderness," pioneers without any solid following, and frequently not very clear about their own goals. However, their example helps to develop sensitivities, arouse hopes, and break down resistances. From these traits one can easily realize that the general social movement develops primarily in an informal, inconspicuous, and largely subterranean fashion. Its media of interaction are primarily reading, conversations, talks, discussions, and the perception of examples. Its achievements and operations are likely to be made primarily in the realm of individual experience rather than by noticeable concerted action of groups. It seems evident that the general social movement is dominated to a large extent by the mechanisms of mass behavior, such as we have described in our treatment of the mass. Especially in its earlier stages, general social movements are likely to be merely an aggregation of individual lines of action based on individual decisions and selections. As is characteristic of the mass and of mass behavior, general social movements are rather formless in organization and inarticulate in expression.

The Basis for Specific Social Movements. Just as cultural drifts provide the background out of which emerge general social movements, so the general social movement constitutes the setting out of which develop specific social movements. Indeed, a specific social movement can be regarded as the crystallization of much of the motivation of dissatisfaction, hope, and desire awakened by the general social movement and the focusing of this motivation on some specific objective. A convenient illustration is the antislavery movement, which was, to a considerable degree, an individual expression of the widespread humanitarian movement of the nineteenth century. With this recognition of the relation between general and specific social movements, we can turn to a consideration of the latter.

SPECIFIC SOCIAL MOVEMENTS

Characteristics. The outstanding instances of this type of movement are reform movements and revolutionary movements. A specific social movement is one which has a well-defined objective or goal which it seeks to reach. In this effort it develops an organization and structure, making it essentially a society. It develops a recognized and accepted leadership and a definite membership characterized by a "we-consciousness." It forms a body of traditions, a guiding set of values, a philosophy, sets of rules, and a general body of expectations. Its members form allegiances and loyalties. Within it there develops a division of labor, particularly in the form of a social structure in which individuals occupy status positions. Thus, individuals develop personalities and conceptions of themselves, representing the individual counterpart of a social structure.

A social movement, of the specific sort, does not come into existence with such a structure and organization already established. Instead, its organization and its culture are developed in the course of its career. It is necessary to view social movements from this temporal and developmental perspective. In the beginning a social movement is loosely organized and characterized by impulsive behavior. It has no clear objective; its behavior and thinking are largely under the dominance of restlessness and collective excitement. As a social movement develops, however, its behavior, which was originally dispersed, tends to become organized, solidified, and persistent. It is possible to delineate stages roughly in the career of a social movement which represent this increasing organization. One scheme of four stages has been suggested by Dawson and Gettys.[1] These are the stage of social unrest, the stage of popular excitement, the stage of formalization, and the stage of institutionalization.

Stages of Development. In the first of these four stages people are restless, uneasy, and act in the random fashion that we have considered. They are susceptible to appeals and suggestions that tap their discontent, and hence, in this stage, the agitator is likely to play an important role. The random and erratic behavior is significant in sensitizing people to one another and so makes possible the focusing of their restlessness on certain objects. The stage of popular excitement is marked even more by milling, but it is not quite so random and aimless. More definite notions emerge as to the cause of their condition and as to what should be done in the way of social change. So there is a sharpening of objectives. In this stage the leader is likely to be a prophet or a reformer. In the stage of formalization the movement becomes more clearly organized with rules, policies, tactics, and discipline. Here the leader is likely to be in the nature of a statesman. In the institutional stage, the movement has crystallized into a fixed organization with a definite personnel and structure to carry into execution the purposes of the movement. Here the leader is likely to be an administrator. In considering the development of the specific social movement our interest is less in considering the stages through which it passes than in discussing the mechanisms and means through which such a movement is able to grow and become organized. It is convenient to group these mechanisms under five heads: (1) agitation, (2) development of *esprit de corps*, (3) development of morale, (4) the formation of an ideology, and (5) the development of operating tactics.

The Role of Agitation. Agitation is of primary importance in a social movement. It plays its most significant role in the beginning and early stages of a movement, although it may persist in minor form in the later portions of the life-cycle of the movement. As the term suggests, agitation operates to arouse people and so make them possible recruits for the movement. It is essentially a means of exciting people and of

---

1 C. A. Dawson and W. E. Gettys, *Introduction to Sociology* (Rev. ed.; New York: Ronald Press Co., 1935, chap. 19).

awakening within them new impulses and ideas which make them restless and dissatisfied. Consequently, it acts to loosen the hold on them of their previous attachments, and to break down their previous ways of thinking and acting. For a movement to begin and gain impetus, it is necessary for people to be jarred loose from their customary ways of thinking and believing, and to have aroused within them new impulses and wishes. This is what agitation seeks to do. To be successful, it must first gain the attention of people; second, it must excite them, and arouse feelings and impulses; and third, it must give some direction to these impulses and feelings through ideas, suggestions, criticisms, and promises.

Agitation operates in two kinds of situations. One is a situation marked by abuse, unfair discrimination, and injustice, but a situation wherein people take this mode of life for granted and do not raise questions about it. Thus, while the situation is potentially fraught with suffering and protest, the people are marked by inertia. Their views of their situation incline them to accept it; hence the function of the agitation is to lead them to challenge and question their own modes of living. It is in such a situation that agitation may create social unrest where none existed previously. The other situation is one wherein people are already aroused, restless, and discontented, but where they either are too timid to act or else do not know what to do. In this situation the function of agitation is not so much to implant the seeds of unrest, as to intensify, release, and direct the tensions which people already have.

Agitators seem to fall into two types corresponding roughly to these two situations. One type of agitator is an excitable, restless, and aggressive individual. His dynamic and energetic behavior attracts the attention of people to him; and the excitement and restlessness of his behavior tends to infect them. He is likely to act with dramatic gesture and to talk in terms of spectacular imagery. His appearance and behavior foster the contagion of unrest and excitement. This type of agitator is likely to be most successful in the situation where people are already disturbed and unsettled; in such a situation his own excited and energetic activity can easily arouse other people who are sensitized to such behavior and already disposed to excitability.

The second type of agitator is more calm, quiet, and dignified. He stirs people not by what he does, but what he says. He is likely to be a man sparing in his words, but capable of saying very caustic, incisive, and biting things—things which get "under the skin" of people and force them to view things in a new light. This type of agitator is more suited to the first of the social situations discussed—the situation where people endure hardships or discrimination without developing attitudes of resentment. In this situation, his function is to make people aware of their own position and of the inequalities, deficiencies, and injustices that seem to mark their lot. He leads them to raise questions about what they have previously taken for granted and to form new wishes, inclinations, and hopes.

The function of agitation, as stated above, is in part to dislodge and stir up people and so liberate them for movement in new directions. More specifically, it operates to change the conceptions which people have of themselves, and the notions which they have of their rights and dues. Such new conceptions involving beliefs that one is justly entitled to privileges from which he is excluded, provide the dominant motive force for the social movement. Agitation, as the means of implanting these new conceptions among people, becomes, in this way, of basic importance to the success of a social movement.

A brief remark relative to the tactics of agitation may be made here. It is sufficient to say that the tactics of agitation vary with the situation, the people, and the culture. A procedure which may be highly successful in one situation may turn out to be ludicrous in another situation. This suggests the problem of identifying different types of situations and correlating with each the appropriate form of agitation. Practically no study has been conducted on this problem. Here, one can merely state the truism that the agitator, to be successful, must sense the thoughts, interests, and values of his listeners.

The Development of *Esprit de Corps*. Agitation is merely the means of arousing the interest of people and thus getting them to participate in a movement. While it serves to recruit members, to give initial impetus, and to give some direction, by itself it could never organize or sustain a movement. Collective activities based on mere agitation would be sporadic, disconnected, and short-lived. Other mechanisms have to enter to give solidity and persistency to a social movement. One of these is the development of *esprit de corps*.

Esprit de corps might be thought of as the organizing of feelings on behalf of the movement. In itself, it is the sense which people have of belonging together and of being identified with one another in a common undertaking. Its basis is constituted by a condition of rapport. In developing feelings of intimacy and closeness, people have the sense of sharing a common experience and of forming a select group. In one another's presence they feel at ease and as comrades. Personal reserve breaks down and feelings of strangeness, difference, and alienation disappear. Under such conditions, relations tend to be of co-operation instead of personal competition. The behavior of one tends to facilitate the release of behavior on the part of others, instead of tending to inhibit or check that behavior; in this sense each person tends to inspire others. Such conditions of mutual sympathy and responsiveness obviously make for concerted behavior.

Esprit de corps is of importance to a social movement in other ways. Very significant is the fact that it serves to reinforce the new conception of himself that the individual has formed as a result of the movement and of his participation in it. His feeling of belonging with others, and they with him, yields him a sense of collective support. In this way his views of himself and of the aims of the movement are maintained and invigorated. It follows that the development of *esprit de corps* helps to foster an attachment of people to a movement. Each individual has his sentiments focused on, and intertwined with, the objectives of the movement. The resulting feeling of expansion which he experiences is in the direction of greater allegiance to the movement. It should be clear that *esprit de corps* is an important means of developing solidarity and so of giving solidity to a movement.

How is *esprit de corps* developed in a social movement? It would seem chiefly in three ways: the development of an in-group–out-group relation, the formation of informal fellowship association, and the participation in formal ceremonial behavior.

THE IN-GROUP–OUT-GROUP RELATION. The nature of the in-group–out-group relation should be familiar to the student. It exists when two groups come to identify each other as enemies. In such a situation each group regards itself as the upholder of virtue and develops among its members feelings of altruism, loyalty, and fidelity. The out-group is regarded as unscrupulous and vicious, and is felt to be attacking the values which the in-group holds dear. Before the out-group the members of the in-group not only feel that they are right and correct, but believe they have a common responsibility to defend and preserve their values.

The value of these in-group–out-group attitudes in developing solidarity in a social movement is quite clear. The belief on the part of its members that the movement is being opposed unjustly and unfairly by vicious and unscrupulous groups serves to rally the members around their aims and values. To have an enemy, in this sense, is very important for imparting solidarity to the movement. In addition, the "enemy" plays the important role of a scapegoat. It is advantageous to a movement to develop an enemy; this development is usually in itself spontaneous. Once made, it functions to establish *esprit de corps*.

INFORMAL FELLOWSHIP. *Esprit de corps* is formed also in a very significant way by the development of informal association on the basis of fellowship. Where people can come together informally in this way they have the opportunity of coming to know one another as human beings instead of as institutional symbols. They are then in a much better position to take one another's roles and, unwittingly, to share one another's experience. It seems that in such a relationship, people unconsciously import and assimilate into themselves the gestures, attitudes, values, and philosophy of life of one another. The net result is to develop a common sympathy and sense of intimacy which contributes much to solidarity. Thus, we find in social movements the emergence and use of many kinds of informal and communal association. Singing, dancing, picnics, joking, having fun, and friendly informal conversation are important devices of this sort in a social movement. Through them, the individual gets a sense of status and a sense of social acceptance and support, in place of prior loneliness and personal alienation.

CEREMONIAL BEHAVIOR. The third important way in which social movements develop *esprit de corps* is through the use of formal ceremonial behavior and of ritual. The value of mass meetings, rallies, parades, huge demonstrations, and commemorative ceremonies has always been apparent to those entrusted with the development of a social movement; the value is one that comes from large assemblages, in the form of the sense of vast support that is experienced by the participant. The psychology that is involved here is the psychology of being on parade. The individual participant experiences the feeling of considerable personal expansion and therefore has the sense of being somebody distinctly important. Since this feeling of personal expansion comes to be identified with the movement as such, it makes for *esprit de corps*. Likewise, the paraphernalia of ritual possessed by every movement serves to foster feelings of common identity and sympathy. This paraphernalia consists of a set of sentimental symbols, such as slogans, songs, cheers, poems, hymns, expressive gestures, and uniforms. Every movement has some of these. Since they acquire a sentimental significance symbolizing the common feelings about the movement, their use serves as a constant reliving and re-enforcement of these mutual feelings.

Esprit de corps may be regarded, then, as an organization of group feeling and essentially as a form of group enthusiasm. It is what imparts life to a movement. Yet just as agitation is inadequate for the development of a movement, so is mere reliance on *esprit de corps* insufficient. A movement which depends entirely on *esprit de corps* is usually like a boom and is likely to collapse in the face of a serious crisis. Since the allegiance which it commands is based merely on heightened enthusiasm, it is likely to vanish with the collapse of such enthusiasm. Thus, to succeed, especially in the face of adversity, a movement must command a more persistent and fixed loyalty. This is yielded by the development of morale.

The Development of Morale. As we have seen, *esprit de corps* is a collective feeling which gives life, enthusiasm, and vigor to a movement. Morale can be thought of as giving persistency and determination to a movement; its test is whether solidarity can be maintained in the face of adversity. In this sense, morale can be thought of as a group will or an enduring collective purpose.

Morale seems to be based on, and yielded by, a set of convictions. In the case of a social movement these seem to be of three kinds. First is a conviction of the rectitude of the purpose of the movement. This is accompanied by the belief that the attainment of the objectives of the movement will usher in something approaching a millennial state. What is evil, unjust, improper, and wrong will be eradicated with the success of the movement. In this sense, the goal is always overvalued. Yet these beliefs yield to the members of a movement a marked confidence in themselves. A second conviction closely identified with these beliefs is a faith in the ultimate attainment, by the movement, of its goal. There is believed to be a certain inevitability about this. Since the movement is felt to be a necessary

agent for the regeneration of the world, it is regarded as being
in line with the higher moral values of the universe, and in this
sense as divinely favored. Hence, there arises the belief that
success is inevitable, even though it be only after a hard struggle.
Finally, as part of this complex of convictions, there is the belief
that the movement is charged with a sacred mission. Together,
these convictions serve to give an enduring and unchangeable
character to the goal of a movement and a tenacity to its effort.
Obstructions, checks, and reversals are occasions for renewed
effort instead of for disheartenment and despair, since they do
not seriously impair the faith in the rectitude of the movement
nor in the inevitability of its success.

It is clear from this explanation that the development of
morale in a movement is essentially a matter of developing a
sectarian attitude and a religious faith. This provides a cue
to the more prominent means by which morale is built up in a
movement. One of these is found in the emergence of a saint
cult which is to be discerned in every enduring and persisting
social movement. There is usually a major saint and a series
of minor saints, chosen from the popular leaders of the movement.
Hitler, Lenin, Marx, Mary Baker Eddy, and Sun Yat-sen will
serve as convenient examples of major saints. Such leaders
become essentially deified and endowed with miraculous power.
They are regarded as grossly superior, intelligent, and infallible.
People develop toward them attitudes of reverence and awe,
and resent efforts to depict them as ordinary human beings. The
pictures or other mementos of such individuals come to have the
character of religious idols. Allied with the saints of a movement
are its heroes and its martyrs. They also come to be regarded as
sacred figures. The development of this whole saint cult is an
important means of imparting essentially a religious faith to the
movement and of helping to build up the kind of convictions
spoken of above.

Similar in function is the emergence in the movement of a
creed and of a sacred literature. These, again, are to be found
in all persisting social movements. Thus, as has been said frequently, *Das Kapital* and *Mein Kampf* have been the bibles
respectively of the communist movement and of the National
Socialist movement. The role of a creed and literature of this sort
in imparting religious conviction to a movement should be clear.

Finally, great importance must be attached to myths in the
development of morale in a social movement. Such myths may

be varied. They may be myths of being a select group or a chosen people; myths of the inhumanity of one's opponents; myths about the destiny of the movement; myths depicting a glorious and millennial society to be realized by the movement. Such myths usually grow out of, and in response to, the desires and hopes of the people in the movement and acquire by virtue of their collective character a solidity, a permanency, and an unquestioned acceptance. It is primarily through them that the members of the movement achieve the dogmatic fixity of their convictions, and seek to justify their actions to the rest of the world.

The Development of Group Ideology. Without an ideology a social movement would grope along in an uncertain fashion and could scarcely maintain itself in the face of pointed opposition from outside groups. Hence, the ideology plays a significant role in the life of a movement; it is a mechanism essential to the persistency and development of a movement. The ideology of a movement consists of a body of doctrine, beliefs, and myths. More specifically, it seems to consist of the following: *first*, a statement of the objective, purpose, and premises of the movement; *second*, a body of criticism and condemnation of the existing structure which the movement is attacking and seeking to change; *third*, a body of defense doctrine which serves as a justification of the movement and of its objectives; *fourth*, a body of belief dealing with policies, tactics, and practical operation of the movement; and, *fifth*, the myths of the movement.

This ideology is almost certain to be of a twofold character. In the first place, much of it is erudite and scholarly. This is the form in which it is developed by the intellectuals of the movement. It is likely to consist of elaborate treatises of an abstract and highly logical character. It grows up usually in response to the criticism of outside intellectuals, and seeks to gain for its tenets a respectable and defensible position in this world of higher learning and higher intellectual values. The ideology has another character, however—a popular character. In this guise, it seeks to appeal to the uneducated and to the masses. In its popular character, the ideology takes the form of emotional symbols, shibboleths, stereotypes, smooth and graphic phrases, and folk arguments. It deals, also, with the tenets of the movement, but presents them in a form that makes for their ready comprehension and consumption.

The ideology of a movement may be thought of as providing a movement with its philosophy and its psychology. It gives a set of values, a set of convictions, a set of criticisms, a set of arguments, and a set of defenses. As such, it furnishes to a movement (*a*) direction, (*b*) justification, (*c*) weapons of attack, (*d*) weapons of defense, and (*e*) inspiration and hope. To be effective in these respects, the ideology must carry respectability and prestige—a character that is provided primarily by the intelligentsia of the movement. More important than this, however, is the need of the ideology to answer to the distress, wishes, and hopes of the people. Unless it has this popular appeal, it will be of no value to the movement.

The Role of Tactics. We have referred to tactics as the fifth major mechanism essential to the development of a social movement. Obviously the tactics are evolved along three lines: gaining adherents, holding adherents, and reaching objectives. Little more can be said than this, unless one deals with specific kinds of movements in specific kinds of situations. For, tactics are always dependent on the nature of the situation in which a move-ment is operating and always with reference to the cultural background of the movement. This functional dependency of tactics on the peculiarity of the situation helps to explain the ludicrous failures that frequently attend the application of certain tactics to one situation even though they may have been successful in other situations. To attempt revolutionary tactics these days in terms of the tactics of two centuries ago would be palpably foolish. Similarly, to seek to develop a movement in this country in terms of tactics employed in a similar movement in some different cultural setting would probably bring very discouraging results. In general, it may be said that tactics are almost by definition flexible and variable, taking their form from the nature of the situation, the exigencies of the circumstances, and the ingenuity of the people.

We can conclude this discussion of the five mechanisms considered merely by reiterating that the successful development of a movement is dependent on them. It is these mechanisms which establish a program, set policies, develop and maintain discipline, and evoke allegiance.

Reform and Revolution. Mention has been made of the fact that specific social movements are primarily of two sorts:

reform and revolutionary movements. Both seek to effect changes in the social order and in existing institutions. Their life-cycles are somewhat similar, and the development of both is dependent on the mechanisms which we have just discussed. However, noteworthy differences exist between the two; some of these differences will now be indicated.

The two movements differ in the *scope of their objectives*. A reform movement seeks to change some specific phase or limited area of the existing social order; it may seek, for example, to abolish child labor or to prohibit the consumption of alcohol. A revolutionary movement has a broader aim; it seeks to reconstruct the entire social order.

This difference in objective is linked with a *different vantage point of attack*. In endeavoring to change just a portion of the prevailing social order, the reform movement accepts the basic tenets of that social order. More precisely, the reform movement accepts the existing mores; indeed, it uses them to criticize the social defects which it is attacking. The reform movement starts with the prevailing code of ethics, and derives much of its support because it is so well grounded on the ethical side. This makes its position rather unassailable. It is difficult to attack a reform movement or reformers on the basis of their moral aims; the attack is usually more in the form of caricature and ridicule, and in characterizing reformers as visionary and impractical. By contrast, a revolutionary movement always challenges the existing mores and proposes a new scheme of moral values. Hence, it lays itself open to vigorous attack from the standpoint of existing mores.

A third difference between the two movements follows from the points which have been made. A reform movement has *respectability*. By virtue of accepting the existing social order and of orienting itself around the ideal code, it has a claim on existing institutions. Consequently, it makes use of these institutions such as the school, the church, the press, established clubs, and the government. Here again the revolutionary movement stands in marked contrast. In attacking the social order and in rejecting its mores, the revolutionary movement is blocked by existing institutions and its use of them is forbidden. Thus, the revolutionary movement is usually and finally driven underground; whatever use is made of existing institutions has to be carefully disguised. In general, whatever agitation, proselytizing, and maneuvers are carried on by revolutionary movements have to be done outside the fold of existing institutions. In the event that a reform movement is felt as challenging too seriously some powerful class or vested interests, it is likely to have closed to it the use of existing institutions. This tends to change a reform movement into a revolutionary movement; its objectives broaden to include the reorganization of the institutions which are now blocking its progress.

The differences in position between reform and revolutionary movements bring in an important distinction in their *general procedure and tactics*. A reform movement endeavors to proceed by developing a public opinion favorable to its aims; consequently, it seeks to establish a public issue and to make use of the discussion process which we have already considered. The reform party can be viewed as a conflict group, opposed by interest groups and surrounded by a large inert population. The reform movement addresses its message to this indifferent or disinterested public in the effort to gain its support. In contradistinction, the revolutionary movement does not seek primarily to influence public opinion, but instead tries to make converts. In this sense it operates more like a religion.

This means some difference as to the groups among which the two movements respectively conduct their agitation and seek their adherents. The reform movement, while usually existing on behalf of some distressed or exploited group, does little to establish its strength among them. Instead, it tries to enlist the allegiance of a middle-class public on the outside and to awaken within them a vicarious sympathy for the oppressed group. Hence, generally, it is infrequent that the leadership or membership of a reform movement comes from the group whose rights are being espoused. In this sense a revolutionary movement differs. Its agitation is carried on among those who are regarded as in a state of distress or exploitation. It endeavors to establish its strength by bringing these people inside of its ranks. Hence, the revolutionary movement is usually a lower-class movement operating among the underprivileged.

Finally, by virtue of these characteristic differences, the two movements diverge in their functions. The primary function of the reform movement is probably not so much the bringing about of social change, as it is to reaffirm the ideal values of a given society. In the case of a revolutionary movement, the tendency to dichotomize the world between those who have and those who have not, and to develop a strong, cohesive, and uncompromising group out of the latter, makes its function that of introducing a new set of essentially religious values.

A concluding remark may be made about specific social movements. They can be viewed as societies in miniature, and as such, represent the building up of organized and formalized collective behavior out of what was originally amorphous and undefined. In their growth a social organization is developed, new values are formed, and new personalities are organized. These, indeed, constitute their residue. They leave behind an institutional structure and a body of functionaries, new objects and views, and a new set of self-conceptions.

EXPRESSIVE MOVEMENTS

Distinctive Feature of Expressive Movements. The characteristic feature of expressive movements is that they do not seek to change the institutions of the social order or its objective character. The tension and unrest out of which they emerge are not focused upon some objective of social change which the movement seeks collectively to achieve. Instead, they are released in some type of expressive behavior which, however, in becoming crystallized, may have profound effects on the personalities of individuals and on the character of the social order. We shall consider two kinds of expressive movements: religious movements and fashion movements.

Religious Movements. Religious movements begin essentially as cults; they have their setting in a situation which, psychologically, is like that of the dancing crowd. They represent an inward direction of unrest and tension in the form of disturbed feelings which ultimately express themselves in movement designed to release the tension. The tension does not then go over into purposive action but into expression. This characteristic suggests the nature of the situation from which religious movements emerge. It is a situation wherein people are upset and disturbed, but wherein they cannot act; in other words, a situation of frustration. The inability to release their tension in the direction of some actual change in the social order leaves as the alternative mere expressive behavior.

It is well to recall here the most prominent features of the dancing crowd. One of these is a feeling of *intense intimacy* and *esprit de corps*. Another is a heightened feeling of *exaltation* and ecstasy which leads individuals to experience personal expansion and to have a sense of being possessed by some transcendental spirit. Individuals feel inspired and are likely to engage in prophetic utterances. A third mark is the *projection of the collective feelings on outside objects*—persons, behavior, songs, words, phrases, and material objects—which thereby take on a sacred character. With the recurrence and repetition of this crowd behavior, the *esprit de corps* becomes strengthened, the dancing behavior formalized and ritualized, and the sacred objects reinforced. It is at this stage that the sect or cult appears. Since the growth of a religious movement is patterned after that of the sect, let us consider some of the important features of the sect.

First it should be noted that the members of a sect may be recruited from a heterogeneous background, showing differences in wealth, rank, education, and social background. These differences and distinctions have no significance in the sect. In the milling and in the development of rapport everyone is reduced to a common level of brotherhood. This fact is shown not only by the feelings and attitudes which the members have for one another, but also by the manner in which they refer to one another and the way in which they address one another.

Around the feelings of exaltation and the sacred symbols in which these feelings become crystallized, there grow up a series of beliefs and rites which become the *creed and the ritual of the sect*. The whole life of the sect becomes centered around this creed and ritual which, in themselves, come to acquire a sacred character. Since they symbolize the intense feelings of the group, they become absolute and imperative. The prophet plays an important role here. He is a sacred personage and he tends to symbolize in himself the creed and ritual of the group. Also, he is the primary guardian of this creed and ritual.

The creed of the group becomes elaborated into an extensive body of doctrine as the sect becomes cognizant of criticisms made by outsiders and as it seeks to justify its views. It is in this way that a *theology* arises; a large part of it is in the form of an apologia. Accompanying this is some change in the ritual, primarily in the form of addition. Those features of its practices and modes of living which subject the sect to criticism and even persecution at the hands of outsiders are likely to be cherished by the sect as the marks of its own identity and thus acquire a special significance.

Another important feature of the sect that arises from its peculiar experience and sacred character is the belief that it is divinely favored, and that it consists of a *select group of sacred souls*. The transformation experienced by members of the sect and the new moral and communal vistas that it yields, readily lead them to this conviction. People on the outside of the sect are regarded as lost souls; they have not been blessed with this rectifying experience.

The feeling which the sect has of itself as a community of saved souls easily disposes it to aggressive proselyting of outsiders. Frequently, it feels it has a divine mission to save others and to "show them the light." Hence it seeks *converts*. In order to become a member, an outsider has to have a conversion experience—a moral transformation similar in character to that of the original members. The public confession is a testimonial of such an experience, and is a sign that the individual is a member of the select. These remarks point to a particularly significant characteristic of the sect—the intense conflict relation in which the sect stands with reference to the outside world. The sect may be said to be at war with the outside world, yet it is a peculiar kind of conflict relation, in that the sect is not concerned with seeking to change the institutions or the objective social order, but instead seeks the moral regeneration of the world. It aims, at least originally, not to change the outside existence, but to change the inner life. In this sense, the sect might be thought of as profoundly revolutionary, in that it endeavors to inculcate a new conception of the universe instead of merely seeking to remake institutions or the objective structure of a social order.

A religious movement tends to share these features of the sect. Its program represents a new way of living and it aims at a moral regeneration of the world. As it develops from the amorphous state that it is likely to have in the situation of the dancing crowd, it tends to acquire a structure like that of the sect, and so develops into a society. In this way it becomes analogous to specific social movements except that its aims are of a profoundly different nature.[1]

Fashion Movements. While fashion is thought of usually in relation to clothing, it is important to realize that it covers a

---

[1] There are political as well as religious sects. The difference is that the political sect seeks to bring about olitical revolution as well as change in the fundamental philosophy of life.

much wider domain. It is to be found in manners, the arts, literature, and philosophy, and may even reach into certain areas of science. In fact, it may operate in any field of group life, apart from the technological and utilitarian area and the area of the sacred. Its operation requires a class society, for in its essential character it does not occur either in a homogeneous society like a primitive group, or in a caste society.

Fashion behaves as a movement, and on this basis it is different from custom which, by comparison, is static. This is due to the fact that fashion is based fundamentally on differentiation and emulation. In a class society, the upper classes or so-called social elite are not able to differentiate themselves by *fixed* symbols or badges. Hence the more external features of their life and behavior are likely to be imitated by classes immediately subjacent to them, who, in turn, are imitated by groups immediately below them in the social structure. This process gives to fashion a vertical descent. However, the elite class finds that it is no longer distinguishable, by reason of the imitation made by others, and hence is led to adopt new differentiating criteria, only to displace these as they in turn are imitated. It is primarily this feature that makes fashion into a movement and which has led one writer to remark that a fashion, once launched, marches to its doom.

As a movement, fashion shows little resemblance to any of the other movements which we have considered. While it occurs spontaneously and moves along in a characteristic cycle, it involves little in the way of crowd behavior and it is not dependent upon the discussion process and the resulting public opinion. It does not depend upon the mechanisms of which we have spoken. The participants are not recruited through agitation or proselyting. No *esprit de corps* or morale is built up among them. Nor does the fashion movement have, or require, an ideology. Further, since it does not have a leadership imparting *conscious* direction to the movement, it does not build up a set of tactics. People participate in the fashion movement voluntarily and in response to the interesting and powerful kind of control which fashion imposes on them.

Not only is the fashion movement unique in terms of its character, but it differs from other movements in that it does not develop into a society. It does not build up a social organization; it has no personnel or functionaries; it does not develop a division of labor among its participants with each being assigned a given status; it does not construct a set of symbols, myths, values, philosophy, or set of practices, and in this sense does not form a culture; and finally, it does not develop a set of loyalties or form a we-consciousness.

Nevertheless, the movement of fashion is an important form of collective behavior with very significant results for the social order. First, it should be noted that the fashion movement is a genuine expressive movement. It does not have a conscious goal which people are trying to reach through collective action, as is true in the case of the specific social movements. Nor does it represent the release of excitement and tension generated in a dancing crowd situation. It is expressive, however, of certain fundamental impulses and tendencies, such as an inclination toward novel experience, a desire for distinction, and an urge to conform. Fashion is important especially in providing a means for the expression of developing tastes and dispositions; this feature establishes it as a form of expressive behavior.

The latter remark provides a cue for understanding the role of fashion and the way in which it contributes to the formation of a new social order. In a changing society, such as is necessarily presupposed for the operation of fashion, people are continually having their subjective lives upset; they experience new dispositions and tastes which, however, are vague and ill-defined. It seems quite clear that fashion, by providing an opportunity for the expression of dispositions and tastes, serves to make them definite and to channelize them and, consequently, to fix and solidify them. To understand this, one should appreciate the fact that the movement and success of fashion are dependent upon the acceptance of the given style or pattern. In turn, this acceptance is based not merely upon the prestige attached to the style but also upon whether the style meets and answers to the dispositions and developing tastes of people. (The notorious failures that attend efforts to make styles fashionable upon the basis of mere prestige provide some support for this point.) From this point of view, we can regard fashion as arising and flourishing in response to new subjective demands. In providing means for the expression of these dispositions and tastes, fashion acts, as suggested before, to shape and crystallize these tastes. In the long run fashion aids, in this manner, to construct a *Zeitgeist* or a common subjective life, and in doing so, helps to lay the foundation for a new social order.

REVIVAL MOVEMENTS AND NATIONALISTIC MOVEMENTS

The Merging of Specific Movements. In our discussion so far, we have been treating separately specific social movements, religious movements, and fashion movements. Yet it should be clear that they can be merged, even though in very different degrees. Thus a revolutionary movement may have many of the features of a religious movement, with its success dependent to some extent upon the movement's becoming fashionable.

Revival Movements. Revival movements and nationalistic movements are particularly likely to have this mixed character. We shall devote a few remarks to them. In revival movements people idealize the past, venerate the ideal picture that they have, and seek to mold contemporary life in terms of this ideal picture. Such movements are explainable, apparently, as a response to a situation of frustration. In this situation people are experiencing a loss of self-respect. Since the future holds no promise for them to form a new respectful conception of themselves, they turn to the past in an effort to do so. By recalling past glories and achievements they can regain a modicum of self-respect and satisfaction. That such movements should have a strong religious character is to be expected. Nationalistic movements are very similar in these respects.

Nationalistic Movements. Most nationalistic movements have a strong revivalistic character in which the past of the people is glorified. This aspect is intimately associated with the motivation that is so characteristic of this kind of movement—namely a feeling of inferiority. Those who initiate the movement usually have had distressing personal experiences in which they have been made to feel inferior and as not privileged enough to enjoy a respectable status. Their wounded self-feelings and their desire to re-establish self-respect lead them to efforts to improve the status of the group with which they are identified. In such a movement there is not only the creation of an objective, such as the gaining of national autonomy, but usually also an idealization of some past epoch in the lives of the people.

SELECTED READINGS

Adams, Brooks. *The Theory of Social Revolutions.* New York: Macmillan Co., 1913.

Burns, C. D. *The Principles of Revolution.* London: Allen & Unwin, 1920.

Cantril, Hadley. *The Psychology of Social Movements.* New York: John Wiley & Sons, 1941.

Cleveland, C. C. *The Great Revival in the West, 1797–1805.* Chicago: Univ. of Chicago Press, 1916.

Davenport, F. M. *Primitive Traits in Religious Revivals.* New York: Truth Seeker Co., 1905.

Down, T. C. "The Rush to the Klondike," *Cornhill Magazine* (1898), 4:33–43.

Edwards, L. P. *The Natural History of Revolutions.* Chicago: Univ. of Chicago Press, 1927.

Farquhar, J. N. *Modern Religious Movements of India.* New York: Macmillan Co., 1915.

Greer, Thomas H. *American Social Reform Movements since 1865.* New York: Prentice-Hall, 1949.

Haberle, Rudolf. "Observations on the Sociology of Social Movements," *American Sociological Review* (1949), 14:346–357.

Hertzler, J. O. "Religious Institutions," *Annals of the American Academy of Political and Social Science* (March 1948), 256:1–13.

Hocking, William E. *Morale and Its Enemies.* New Haven: Yale Univ. Press, 1918.

Holcombe, Arthur N., and others. "Parties, Political," *Encyclopaedia of the Social Sciences* (1933), 11:589–639.

Johnson, Alvin, and others. "Agrarian Movements," *Encyclopaedia of the Social Sciences* (1930), 1:489–515.

Kropotkin, P. *Memoirs of a Revolutionist.* Boston: Houghton Mifflin Co., 1899.

Le Bon, Gustave. *The Psychology of Revolution.* New York: G. P. Putnam's Sons, 1913.

Neumann, Franz. *Behemoth.* Oxford: Oxford Univ. Press, 1942.

Nystrom, Paul. *The Economics of Fashion.* New York: Ronald Press, 1928.

Rader, M. *Ethics and Society.* New York: Henry Holt & Co., 1950.

Rainwater, Clarence E. *The Play Movement in the United States.* Chicago: Univ. of Chicago Press, 1921.

Reed, John. *Ten Days That Shook the World.* New York: Modern Library, 1935.

Tracey, J. *The Great Awakening.* Boston, 1842.

Van Langenhove, F. *The Growth of a Legend.* New York: G. P. Putnam's Sons, 1916.

Wagner, D. O. *Social Reformers.* New York: Macmillan Co., 1934.

Wallas, G. *Human Nature in Politics.* 4th ed. New York: Macmillan Co., 1950.

Wittenmyer, A. *History of the Woman's Temperance Crusade.* J. H. Earle Co., 1878.

CHAPTER TWENTY-THREE

CONCLUSIONS CONCERNING COLLECTIVE BEHAVIOR

A social order can be regarded as consisting of the following elements, among others. *First*, a body of common expectations, upon the basis of which people are able to co-operate and regulate their activities to one another. This procedure yields them customs, traditions, rules, and norms. *Second*, a set of values which are attached to these expectations and which determine how important they are, and how readily people will adhere to them. *Third*, the conceptions which people have of themselves in relation to one another and to their groups. And, *fourth*, a common subjective orientation in the form of dispositions and moods.

This conception of a social order enables one to understand more readily the statement made at the beginning of the discussion that in studying collective behavior we were concerned with the process of building up a social order. In the early stages of this process, collective behavior is uncertain in character and relatively unorganized. The elementary and spontaneous types appear. In them, one sees most clearly the primary mechanisms of association. As the interaction between people continues, collective behavior secures form and organization. There appear new expectations, new values, new conceptions of rights and obligations, and new tastes and moods. We have sought to show in this process the role of collective behavior mechanisms and the function of social movements. In general, we can say that movements centering around the mechanisms of the public give rise to the political phase of the social order; those using primarily the mechanisms of the crowd and of rapport give rise to a moral order and a sacred order; and those, like fashion, which stress the mechanisms of the mass, yield subjective orientations in the form of common tastes and inclinations

SELECTED READINGS

LaPiere, R. T. *Collective Behavior*. New York: McGraw-Hill Book Co., 1938.

LaPiere, R. T., and P. R. Farnsworth. *Social Psychology*. 3rd ed. New York: McGraw-Hill Book Co., 1949.

Lee, Alfred M., and Elizabeth Briant Lee. *Social Problems in America*. New York: Henry Holt & Co., 1949. Chaps. 23, 24.

Park, Robert E. "Collective Behavior," *Encyclopaedia of the Social Sciences* (1930), 3:631-633.

Reuter, E. B. *Handbook of Sociology*. New York: Dryden Press, 1941. Pp. 205-210.

Ross, E. A. *Social Psychology*. New York: Macmillan Co., 1915.

Roucek, Joseph S., and others. *Social Control*. New York: D. Van Nostrand Co., 1947. Chaps. 23-27.

Sargent, S. S. *Social Psychology*. New York: Ronald Press, 1950.

Young, Kimball. *Social Psychology*. 2nd ed. New York: Appleton-Century-Crofts, Inc., 1944. Part 3.

Part Five

Institutions

By

EVERETT CHERRINGTON HUGHES
University of Chicago

PART FIVE

INSTITUTIONS
By Everett Cherrington Hughes

TOPICS

CHAPTER TWENTY-FOUR

INSTITUTIONS DEFINED

THE FACTOR OF PERSISTENCE

We are apt, says MacIver,[1] to call anything socially established an institution. Even persons are so thought of, as is the faithful janitor who, with affectionate gruffness, keeps many succeeding generations of students in order in the old college building. He stays on where others merely sojourn.

More commonly the term *institution* is applied to those features of social life which outlast biological generations or survive drastic changes that might have been expected to bring them to an end. A holy place, such as Jerusalem or the hills of Rome, may be visited by religious pilgrims long after the original gods have been succeeded by others. A ceremony may be celebrated by people who no longer know its origin and would repudiate its first meaning, if they but knew it. A once useful means of achieving some known end persists as an accepted and even sacred practice after better technical devices have been invented.

These examples show the tendency of human beings to get set in their ways. Other animals undoubtedly show a similar tendency, but man alone transmits to future generations a great number of his acquired ways of behaving, gives reasons for his ways, makes a virtue of them, and glorifies them for their very antiquity. This phenomenon appears truly paradoxical when one recalls man's capacity for inventing new ways of doing things. It is in this realm of things socially—rather than biologically—established and transmitted in a world of succeeding generations and events that institutions are to be found.

THE CONCEPT IN OTHER FIELDS OF STUDY

Other fields of study, as well as sociology, are concerned with institutions. Psychologists use the term to distinguish

---

‡ R. M. MacIver, *Society: A Textbook of Sociology* (New York: Farrar & Rinehart, 1937), p. 14.

the socially communicated and socially sanctioned aspects of human behavior from those which can be described without necessary reference to society. Philosophers speak of institutions when they wish to distinguish the historical from the timeless aspects of ideas, ethics, and politics. Likewise, institutional economics deals with the historical forms within which economic behavior takes place, rather than with propositions which are presumed to hold good universally.

THE VIEWS OF SOCIOLOGISTS

The sociologist, whose special object of study is precisely the processes by which modes of human behavior are established and change, must carry his distinctions further. Among the American sociologists, Sumner and Cooley have defined social institutions by distinguishing them from other social phenomena.

Sumner and Cooley. Sumner considered *folkways* the elementary social phenomena. These popular usages are at once the product of past collective behavior and the mold for present and future behavior. In following them, the individual is acting under a constraint of which he is not always aware. It was the co-ordinating, constraining aspect of society that Sumner took as his starting point.

Cooley approached the problem from the subjective side. Yet it was not in the individual as such, but in the *primary group* in which a distinctively human nature is developed, that he found his elementary social phenomenon. The primary group, as he conceived it, has no formulated rules, but the individual in it is sensitive to the gestures and opinions of his fellows. This sensitivity to the regard of the others of a primary group is the basis of that social constraint which becomes set in the folkways.

Sumner distinguishes *institutions* from the folkways.[1] In addition to the consistency of behavior implied in the folkways, institutions are more consciously utilitarian, and have a structure within which people co-operate in prescribed ways on certain occasions. In short, institutions differ from folkways in that they require a more conscious and formal co-operation. Cooley, in turn, speaks of primary groups as "springs of life not

---

1 W. G. Sumner, *Folkways* (Boston: Ginn and Co., 1907), pars. 40, 41, 56, 61, 53, 67, *et passim;* C. H. Cooley, *Social Organization* (New York: Chas. Scribner's Sons, 1909), chaps. 3, 28; E. Faris, "The Primary Group: Essence and Accident," *American Journal of Sociology* (1932), 38:41–50.

only for the individual, but for social institutions." The latter are "mature, specialized, and comparatively rigid parts of the social structure." Faris, commenting on Cooley's conception of the primary group, says that in the institution, unlike the primary group, a person "acts in an *office*."

Continuous Formal Group Behavior. Thus, both Sumner and Cooley distinguish institutions in terms of the conscious fulfilling of defined offices. MacIver[1] makes a similar, although not identical, distinction between institutions and associations. An association is a group of persons pursuing some interest in common. Institutions are the established forms of procedure by which group activity is carried on. But the institutions can arise only by means of continued group behavior. In short, in the study of institutions we focus our attention upon the formally established aspects of collective or group behavior.

DEVELOPMENT OF INSTITUTIONS

Marginal to social institutions are phenomena of collective behavior which occur contrary to, or outside of, accepted and expected social usage. These marginal forms are crucial for an understanding of institutional processes, for every established form of collective behavior was once not so. Our interest is in precisely those processes by which collective behavior which begins outside formal offices and without formal rules, engaged in by unconventional groups of people, in unexpected situations, or in ways contrary to use and wont, develop formal offices, organized groups, defined situations, and a new body of sanctioned use and wont. Institutions do not spring full-formed from the head of Zeus. Before they are institutions they are institutions in process. Some of the forms of collective behavior from which they spring are celebrations, festivals, great days, social movements such as strikes, religious and national revivals, and reform movements; other forms are essentially enterprises.

ELEMENTARY INSTITUTIONS

Before considering how institutions arise and change in our society, it is well to have in mind the elementary form of institutions as found in the simple, stable societies studied by anthropologists. "The real component units of culture which have a considerable degree of permanence, universality and indepen-

---

1 MacIver, *op. cit.*, pp. 15–16.

dence are the organized systems of human activities called institutions. Every institution centers around a fundamental need, permanently unites a group of people in a cooperative task and has its particular body of doctrine and its technique or craft. Institutions are not correlated simply and directly to their functions; one need does not receive one satisfaction in one institution. But institutions show a pronounced amalgamation of functions and have a synthetic character." [1] Elementary institutions, as described by Malinowski, do not show that singleness of function which is the ideal of so many people in an efficiency-minded society. Each of them satisfies a variety of needs.

Two features of such elementary institutions are (1) a set of mores or formal rules which can be fulfilled only by (2) people acting collectively in traditional complementary capacities or offices. The first of these represents *consistency;* the second, *concert* or *organization.* Together they give us a way of observing the dynamics of institutions.

Examples of elementary social institutions are the *fiesta* of Mayan villages in Yucatan, as described by Redfield, and the English rural parish of the past, as described by the Webbs. [2]

Both these institutions were in simple communities. Everyone in the community had some part in them. The moral consensus was so complete that no one, apparently, was opposed to their operations; they were *expected* to operate.

Such distinctions of social *status* as existed in the community determined the parts played by individuals in these institutions. The accepted leaders of the community expected, in turn, to assume the burdens and to enjoy the honors of office. It was their moral and civic right and duty to do so. The offices involved both the performance of ritual and the exercise of some authority and initiative.

The voluntary and conscious assumption of offices by persons of the appropriate status is a feature of a well-established institution. The criteria and the mechanisms by which officers are selected, trained, and charged may be much more complicated than in these simple cases. On the other hand there are situations in which the collective action is led by prophets,

---

1 B. Malinowski, "Culture," *Encyclopaedia of the Social Sciences* (1931), 4:621–46, p. 626 quoted.

2 Robert Redfield, *The Folk Culture of Yucatan* (Chicago: Univ. of Chicago Press, 1941), chap. 10, "From Holy Day to Holiday"; B. and S. Webb, *English Local Government* (New York: Longmans, Green & Co., 1927).

upstarts, or promoters whose authority is not sanctioned by tradition or laws; such situations show collective behavior which is not yet "instituted" and "sanctioned."

The procedures and rituals involved in carrying on these institutions were, in a general way, known to all members of the community. They knew what to expect. This does not mean that any member of the community could have carried them out or that there was no mystery about them, but simply that they knew when to expect them and how to react to each part of the procedure. This was true, not only of the people of a given village or parish, but of all the people of the region. For these institutions were common to an area, although each community had its own officers and participants as well as its own peculiarities of tradition and practice.

It would have been difficult to say what the purposes of these institutions were, for they were so well established in tradition as to be unquestioned. Purposes occur *within* human behavior and are but an aspect of it. Institutions which are established are not subject to a single purpose. They may perform many functions, but the functions are implicit, rather than explicit.

As civilization proceeds, social organization becomes much more complicated. Institutions multiply; some arise whose workings are mysterious to the general mass of people. Their mechanisms are elaborated. Social sanctions become confused. But wherever institutions are found, the features mentioned are present, although not always in the complete yet simple form here described.

SELECTED READINGS

Allport, F. H. *Institutional Behavior*. Chapel Hill: Univ. of North Carolina Press, 1933. Chaps. 1, 2.

Angell, R. C. *Integration of American Society: A Study of Groups and Institutions*. New York: McGraw-Hill Book Co., 1941. Chap. 2.

Ballard, L. V. *Social Institutions*. New York: D. Appleton-Century Co., 1936. Chap. 1.

Chapin, F. S. *Contemporary American Institutions*. New York: Harper & Bros., 1935. Chap. 16.

Hamilton, W. H. "Institution," *Encyclopaedia of the Social Sciences* (1932), 8:84–89.

Hertzler, J. O. *Social Institutions*. New York: McGraw-Hill Book Co., 1929. Chaps. 1–3.

Lundberg, George A. *Foundations of Sociology*. New York: Macmillan Co., 1939. Chap. 10.

MacIver, R. M. *Society: A Textbook of Sociology*. New York: Farrar & Rinehart, 1939. Chap. 1.

CHAPTER TWENTY-FIVE

INSTITUTIONS CLASSIFIED

THE FUNCTIONS OF INSTITUTIONS

Institutions are generally classified according to some central function of each. Herbert Spencer used the following categories: domestic, ceremonial, political, ecclesiastical, professional, and industrial.[1] Current authors use similar categories, but generally add educational and social welfare institutions.

Multiplicity of Function. It must not be assumed that an institution performs but one function. The central and peculiar function of the family evidently is the maintenance of special affectional relations between people who are kin according to the usage of the given culture. But the family is, in various ways and degrees, an economic institution. In some societies it furnishes the accepted structure for religious observance. It is so notoriously an educational institution that professional educators often blame the failures of formal education upon the short-comings of parents.[2]

Functions Shared among Institutions. Nor can it be assumed that a given social function is performed exclusively by any one institution. If we conceive education as all the activities by which children learn or are taught the techniques, customs, and sentiments of the society in which they live, it is obvious that the school has no monopoly upon education. Indeed, some societies produce leaders for their enterprises, experts in their arts, and masters of their folklore, ritual, and custom without any schools at all. In our own society, certain types of knowledge, such as sex lore, the technique of professional stealing, and even religion, persist in spite of their exclusion from school curricula. Schools,

---

1 H. Spencer, *The Principles of Sociology* (3rd ed.; New York: D. Appleton-Century Co., 1901),
2 See K. Young, *Sociology: A Study of Society and Culture* (New York: American Book Co. 1942), pp. 399–447, for a discussion of the functions of the family in our society.

says Sumner, teach the current orthodoxy rather than all of the knowledge and beliefs on which a society really rests. It is even more obvious that not all the playing is done in playgrounds nor all the charity given by social agencies.

Certain functions are performed by elaborate systems of interconnected institutions. The traditional doctor's office, which once served as clinic, medical school, surgery, and laboratory, is today but one among many institutions concerned with healing. In addition to those already named there are hospitals for various kinds of people and various ailments, the schools and professional associations of various auxiliary occupations, the associations and examining boards of special branches of medicine, as well as the governmental, philanthropic, and private institutions for distributing medical care and protecting the health of the public. To say that the function of any one of these institutions is healing, without specifying its particular function in the whole healing system, would be a truism without meaning.

The discovery of the specific functions of institutions is the aim of sociological study. Radcliffe-Brown gives us a definition of function useful for this purpose:

> By the function of an institution I mean the part it plays in the total system of social integration of which it is a part. By using that phrase, social integration, I am assuming that the function of culture as a whole is to unite individual human beings into more or less stable social structures; i.e., stable systems of groups determining and regulating the relation of those individuals to one another, and providing such adaptation to the physical environment, and such internal adaptation between the component individuals or groups, as to make possible an ordered social life.[1]

Social Interrelations. A society is an integrated system which can continue to exist only under certain conditions. There must be replacement of the member individuals by others. There must be provision and distribution of the means of life. The incoming members must learn and carry on the techniques and rules of the society. These conditions all depend upon another; viz., consensus with respect to a body of beliefs or sentiments. These are but bare bones. Actually, a social system consists of particular ways of doing all these things. The functions of an institution are its part in such a system.

It follows that no institution, however classified, may be understood in isolation. The church, we say, is a religious insti-

---

1 A. R. Radcliffe-Brown, "The Present Position of Anthropological Studies," *British Association for the Advancement of Science, Centenary Meeting* (London, 1931), section H., p. 13.

tution. But its existence depends upon other institutions and upon informal parts of our culture. Religious attitudes, fostered by churches, have as their objects not only deities but also features of the economic order, the political system, and the family. A celibate priesthood is unthinkable without pious families in which mothers encourage their sons to listen to the divine call. Furthermore, the members of the religious body have other interests and other points of contact with the social system. The church gets only a part of their time, attention, money, and loyalty. The functions of the church are to be understood only by analyzing its many relations with the total social system. The same is true of any institution.

CLASSIFICATION OF INSTITUTIONS

Claims of Participants. Institutions may also profitably be classified according to the nature and limits of the claims of the participating individuals upon each other. In the family, for instance, the claims are deep and implicit, a part of one's very being. At the opposite pole stand certain types of social groupings in which the individuals concerned are not emotionally involved, but are consciously and voluntarily banded together with relation to some clearly defined and limited common interest. Trade associations are a common institution in our society, but no one is expected to bleed and die for them. If, however, some group of people continues to act together, even with regard to a secular matter, claims are likely to develop. Even in a business enterprise moral and personal claims may arise. This may, indeed, be its undoing. A family, on the other hand, may conduct a business enterprise for the mutual profit of its members; but if the enterprise destroys the bonds of affection and the sense of common fate of its members, it is scarcely a family any longer. This suggests that the nature of mutual claims is subject to change, but that change beyond certain limits may disrupt the entire institution. There are also, probably, typical changes such as from contractually limited claims toward deep, implicit expectations.

Type of Organization. Another way of classifying institutions is by type of organization, that is, by the configurations of officers, leaders, and participants of various kinds. In the family, members have various functions to perform and various claims upon each other according to age, sex, and kinship. In the *col-*

legium, or guild, a group of equals who have been subjected to common specialized training co-operate on a democratic basis within, but are sharply differentiated from other types of persons of the society to which they belong. In other institutions, there is a hierarchy of individuals arranged in pyramidal form about a central, enhanced figure; such is the Roman Catholic Church. In the modern business enterprise, a person or small group of associated persons carry on certain activities to which other persons give intermittent support as customers; but there is little in the way of persistent mutual claims between the entrepreneur and the occasional customer, although each recognizes the position of the other. There is a great variety of such configurations.

It will be noted that in the last two ways of classifying institutions the emphasis is not upon a supposed end or aim, but upon the manner in which the institution operates. Such classifications are, like others, useful only in so far as they are of assistance in studying the manner in which institutions arise and operate within the total framework of a society.

MAJOR TYPES OF INSTITUTIONS

It is of interest, since the student is primarily concerned with our own society, to note some of the major types of institutions within it.

The Family. To understand the family in our society it is not sufficient to think of the family in its universal aspect, stripped of its historical peculiarities. So simplified, Sumner suggests that we would find a woman with an infant in her arms.[1] But in our society, the family is much more than that. It implies wedlock, and the unwed mother is often separated from her child either by her own will or by that of other agencies. The married couple is expected to establish a household and to live there in a co-operation whose terms are largely prescribed by custom and law. Their children are a part of the parental household for a time, but generally leave at an age that varies according to occupation and other circumstances of their parents. However, they remain bound to the family, by sentiment or by property interests. The activities carried on co-operatively by the family vary from social class to social class, from country to city, from region to region, and from time to time.[2]

---

1 "The Family and Social Change," *American Journal of Sociology* (1909), 14:577–91.
2 W. F. Ogburn, and M. F. Nimkoff, *Sociology* (Boston: Houghton Mifflin Co., 1940), chap. 23, "The Family."

Any particular state of the family may be so established as to become idealized; then changes are noted with horror and it is predicted that the family is about to disappear. To study the family in our society it is necessary to know the manner of marriage selection by race, religion, class, occupation, etc., the kind of household that is maintained, the kinds of mutual aid that are demanded of and given to relatives of various degree, and the effects of family life upon the personality and career of the individual. By implication, the relations of the family to other institutions must be understood, for schools, churches, and other institutions depend in various ways upon the nature of family life. It is of interest to know the circumstances which apparently favor continuance of the marriage of a couple; those which are associated with breakup of marriage; those which favor birth of children and the success of parents in inculcating into the children the standards of conduct of the parents themselves and of the surrounding society; and those things which favor the fiscal success of the household as a co-operative enterprise, for when a family cannot feed its members or pay its rent, other agencies take over a large measure of the control generally vested in it.

Political Institutions. The sociologist has not ordinarily made detailed study of the state, or of other political bodies. This has been the job of the political scientist. But there is an increasing tendency for political scientists to study those aspects of political institutions which would be of interest to the sociologist; namely, the state as collective behavior and action within the framework of a continually changing social structure. This is the new political science of collective behavior and public opinion, and of the functions of the state, which is supplementing the older study of formal constitutions.

Economic Institutions. The economist studies production and distribution of commodities. Certain economists, in the course of writing the history of modern economic institutions, have become sociologists and have made important contributions to the theory of institutions in their noneconomic as well as their economic aspects. In America, Sumner, an economist, found it advisable to investigate other aspects of human behavior and laid the basis for much of current sociological theory.

Likewise, sociologists have found it necessary to study certain features of economic life. The family, for instance, is a consumer's co-operative of a sort. In every economic institution, the main social processes go on. For instance, the stock market is a good arena for the study of selection of participants, and of the growth of codes with reference to the most secular of all human activities. The factory, the chain store, the bank, and many other institutions, although they are specialties of the economist, are also being studied in sociological terms.

The Church. The church, while perhaps not so dominant in political and economic affairs as it once was, is still important. Faced by a growing secularization of life and by indifference of a large part of the population, its functionaries resort to secular study of the church in the hope of discovering means of checking its decline. A good deal of this study has been of a definitely sociological sort, dealing objectively with the processes involved in the growth, maintenance, and decline of local parishes.

In addition to these institutions, there are many others which perform functions peculiar to our society. In other societies there have likewise existed many institutions which do not fall neatly into our traditional categories. A function which under certain conditions was performed in informal fashion may become the special function of a new institution. The modern school is an example; the trade-union is another; the numerous service clubs, trade associations, and philanthropic social agencies are others. These and other new institutions yield especially interesting information not only about the collective problems of our society, but about the nature of institutions and the processes by which they come into being.

SELECTED READINGS

Chapin, F. S. *Contemporary American Institutions.* New York: Harper & Bros., 1935. Chap. 2.

Chapin, F. S. *Experimental Designs in Sociological Research.* New York: Harper & Bros., 1947.

Hertzler, J. O. *Social Institutions.* New York: McGraw-Hill Book Co., 1929. Chap. 4.

Ogburn, W. F., and M. F. Nimkoff. *Sociology.* Boston: Houghton Mifflin Co., 1940. Part 6.

Panunzio, Constantine. *Major Social Institutions.* New York: Macmillan Co., 1939. Chap. 1 and Part 3.

CHAPTER TWENTY-SIX

INSTITUTIONS IN PROCESS

CRITICAL SITUATIONS

The Genesis of Crises. Institutions, no matter how stable and unchanging they appear, are ongoing things. They consist of the complementary activity of the participating persons. In their most stable condition, the activities are so largely routine that the attention of the individual may be relaxed. He need not concern himself too much about the part which others play in the complex of institutional life, for they will do what is expected of them. But situations occur in which the expected does not happen and the unexpected does. Such situations are crises in which—to quote W. I. Thomas—"the attention is aroused and explores the situation with a view to reconstructing modes of activity." The "cake of custom" is broken.

Rise of New Institutional Forms. In crises old institutional forms are broken up. When the crisis is severe, the livelier forms of collective behavior may take the place of ordered institutional behavior. Crowds may flourish; and it is characteristic of crowds that people swept into them forget who they are. The man who forgets who he is, and what is expected of him, is disorderly and a threat to institutions. In such situations institutions can be seen in process of disintegration and formation.

A crisis in the life of an individual is not necessarily a crisis for an institution in which he participates. Indeed, one of the most common of institutional functions is provision for crises in the lives of individuals. To the individual, his marriage, illnesses, sins, and fear of death are unique and critical. To the church these crises are recurrent, and there is a way of dealing with each. Institutions, so long as they can meet the crises of the individual, are not themselves in a critical state. When, however, some new type of situation, not provided for by the existing institutions, becomes chronic and widespread, the institutions themselves are in a parlous state.

Crises within Units of an Institution. There are, further, crises which arise in the separate units of a type of institution but which do not constitute a crisis for the type as such and do not presage any major change in it. The early death of a wage-earning father is a crisis for his family. Likewise divorce, desertion, unemployment, and delinquency of a child, fatal as they may be to a given family, are not necessarily threats to the family as the prevailing type of co-operative unit of kin. Indeed, families are constantly being broken up and new ones established. Every marriage in our society is likely to lead to the establishment of a new family. There may follow a tug-of-war between the family of the husband and that of the wife. The new unit may be subordinated to one or the other; it may also be emancipated from both.

The average life of families is short in our society. It varies from class to class, according to the character of the property and tradition which families accumulate, and their success in transmitting those possessions from generation to generation. Short as the life of a family may be, it does not mean that the family will cease to exist as the sanctioned agency in which partners and their offspring will live in relation to each other.

The Formation of New Units. Although the foundation of new units of an institution may be provided for in an orderly manner, they do not get under way without crises, and without bringing to the surface of attention many matters which ordinarily lie buried in routine and tradition.

In the Catholic church, for instance, the parish is considered more or less indestructible. New parishes are founded on new territory, or by division of existing parishes when parishioners become too numerous. Actually, there are exceptions to this practice. When Catholics of another language and nationality move into a parish, they may, by popular movement, force the establishment of a parish of their own manned by priests of their own nationality. The movement may be not unlike that of a dissenting sect. Even when a parish is set up by episcopal initiative, there are problems and crises. A lay leadership has to be developed; the parish has to find its place in the class and financial structure of the community. It has to attach to itself the loyalty which its parishioners formerly had to their native parishes, or to eliminate indifference.

In the more completely secular institutions, any group of people may, within rather wide limits, establish a new organ of co-operation on no authority but their own. The crises involved are those of an enterprise.

Conditions of Formation of New Units. A distinction must be made as to the conditions of formation of new units. In some cases, the institution is simply propagated or extended. In others each new unit represents a degree of revolt and a new attack on collective problems. In either case, the foundation of the new unit has some of the character of a social movement, but more so in the latter than in the former case. In America, and in new countries generally, the new units of old institutions are established in free and disorderly ways.

Frontiers of Settlements. In newly populated frontier communities, the entire institutional structure may be lacking. Even if the settlers are accustomed to the same institutional devices, the functionaries and material appurtenances are wanting. No one may have the manifest authority and obligation to reconstitute the whole arrangement. For want of momentum, a maximum of attention and initiative is required to develop collective action and bring it under control. Leadership is developed on the spot.

On the American trading-post and the cattle frontiers, even the family was lacking, for the population was, for a time, exclusively male. E. S. Osgood, in *Day of the Cattleman*, tells how the highly individualistic cattlemen were forced into a measure of co-operation. But conditions changed so rapidly that no stable social structure developed. The character of the frontier itself, rather than the traditions which cattlemen had in common from their past experience, determined the nature and extent of collective action. The story of other frontiers has been told in similar vein. Studies of the Canadian farming frontier show that men came first, but that the traditional institutions did not take form until women came. As the sex and age distribution approached the normal, the institutional structure became more like that of older farming communities. It is interesting to note the order in which institutions are established in such a community, and the peculiar forms they take. The Protestant churches of the Middle West still bear the marks of the revivals and camp meetings in which they originated. In the recent Peace River settlements in Canada, the school seems to come first, while the church waits for missionaries sent out by eastern headquarters of the various denominations. The first church is usually a community affair, embracing people of various denominations. Later the competition of denominational authorities and the growth of class differences in the community may lead to splitting up on traditional denominational lines. The church seems to be among the last institutions to become completely self-supporting in modern homestead frontiers.

Where a frontier is settled not by individuals, but by an organized group, the institutional crises and consequent adaptations may not be so great. If it be a culturally homogeneous group with established authorities as in sectarian communities, the crisis comes later, when strangers and worldly settlers destroy the splendid isolation.

CULTURAL FRONTIERS

The Nature of Cultural Frontiers. At various places in the world, two or more cultures are in contact. Such places are cultural frontiers. Many of them are the result of European political and commercial empire-building.

What happens in such frontiers is not simple imposition of European institutional forms. New forms are developed. The plantation, so typical of regions where native labor is exploited to produce goods for a foreign market, was not brought from Europe ready-made. It was developed on the spot. Its European founders often regarded it as repugnant to their tradition of free wage labor. The plantation is a political institution in which the employer assumes control over the general behavior and even the movements of the workers. It is foreign to the notions of laissez faire capitalism as known in Europe.[1]

Industrial Revolution. The invasion of a foreign culture may bring an industrial revolution. A new system of classes and vested interests may arise at the expense of the old one. Old institutional claims—such as those of the family, guild, tribe, etc.—may deteriorate or be violently broken. In the succeeding period of transition new institutions arise, not only at the initia-

---

1 J. H. Boeke, *The Structure of Netherlands Indian Economy* (New York: Institute of Pacific Relations, 1942).

tive of the invaders, as did the plantation, but at that of the freed, individualistic natives or marginal men.

The Religious Mission. On such frontiers is found the religious mission. The native mission church evolves, but not necessarily toward the type known in the mothering country. The relation of native converts to the missionaries has to be defined. The missionary himself is not precisely like his fellow clergy at home; he is more zealous, and perhaps more orthodox. The native adherents, too, may come from an inferior status in the local system. This may retard the turning over of the mission church to native functionaries. In general, the missionary plays a more dominant role among his flock than does a clergyman in Europe or America. Meanwhile, native religions may take over certain features of the invading missions. An indignant Christian student from Ceylon complained bitterly about the competition offered by a young men's Buddhist association which stole Y.M.C.A. tactics.

All these changes conspire to create new classes of people and new interests, and hence to disturb the whole course of the processes involved in the traditional institutions, as well as in those transplanted or established by the invaders.

Immigration. A cultural frontier more familiar to Americans is created by immigration of people of alien culture into a world which they do not dominate, but in which they seek a place. The resulting immigrant institutions are of two kinds. Some are new units designed according to old forms, to give comfort to the immigrant by furnishing a *cadre* within which he may live according to his traditions. Others are established to meet crises peculiar to the immigrant, to enhance his status, to help him get on in the new world. Foreign churches are of the first sort; mutual-aid societies, the immigrant press, and nationalist organizations are of the second sort. They have received classic treatment in Thomas and Znaniecki, *The Polish Peasant in Europe and America*, and in Park, *The Immigrant Press*.

Immigrant institutions are never quite the same in structure and function as those which they are designed to replace. The role of the layman, in bringing about the establishment of a Catholic church for people of his own nationality within the bounds of already existing parishes, gives him a new sense of his importance. A change in the balance of power between priest and people may result.

Immigrant institutions pass through phases of their life-cycle quickly, owing to the process of assimilation going on among their participants. Adaptations have to be made in the sometimes vain effort to keep the institutions alive after the cultural differ-ences in which they had their origin have dwindled to a not always proudly cultivated memory. The church, for example, starts with both clergy and laity of foreign birth and training. Later the laity is of native birth in the new country, and there arises a problem of keeping the peace between a conservative, tradition-bound clergy and a changing and impatient laity. The immigrant institution, somewhat modified, may remain as part of the established structure of the new world.

The City as Frontier of Social Control. The modern city is the point at which new elements of culture insert an entering wedge, and from which they are disseminated to surrounding regions. Its population is recruited by migration more than by generation. Internal mobility continually breaks up accustomed aggregations of people. Institutions are therefore constantly threatened by secular contingencies, such as the moving away of their clientele, or the decrease of time-distance to the next institution of the same sort, as well as by changes in belief which lead to emancipation of people from institutional claims.

As new occupations and commodities arise, the problem of controlling them by some sort of organization follows. New interest groups, organized with reference to these occupations and commodities, grow up and become a part of the working structure of city life.

CRISES IN THE CITY. The city is a place of crisis for many persons. There are enough people sharing one type of peculiarity to allow them to join together to make a cult of it. For example, a widows and widowers' club met for monthly dances during many years in a Chicago public park; the club became a sort of matrimonial bureau. The reorganization of life in the city pro-ceeds, in some measure, by the rise of peculiar institutions which resolve personal crises. Park[1] discusses these aspects of city life in an article on the city. Spengler also noted that cities breed heresies and new cults. Charles Booth, in his study of the *Life and Labour of the People of London*, described some of the new forms which institutions take in the poorer sections of a great

---

1 R. E. Park and others, *The City* (Chicago: Univ. of Chicago Press, 1925).

city. Notable among them were the Salvation Army and the settlement house. New cults burgeon in the city not because of an increase in the amount of religion, but probably because some breakup or failure of old religious institutions leaves many people running around loose with just enough religion left in them to be susceptible to a novel attack.

THE CITY AS A FOCAL POINT OF CHANGE. We may say that cities are organized to death. This assertion, however, is not a true statement of the case. The Indian people were perhaps organized to death in the caste system; its control was complete. In the city one finds hundreds of new organizations, many of them existing precariously on casual wants of normal people or on the mutually aggravated fever of multiplied queer people. The struggle of the individual to keep life organized is at its height in modern cities. At the same time, many highly rational and impersonal institutions are the peculiar products of city life. Witness the stock exchange, and the many similar marketing institutions, in which standardized symbols take the place of the real things dealt in. It is because the city is the focal point of secular change, that institutional changes occur in it. Inventions, new occupations, and commodities upset the institutional equilibrium, and often lead to the rise of new collective forms.

Emancipation. Emancipation is a feature of secular change. It may be either physical or mental. A change in industrial techniques may give some group of people a freer disposition of their time. This is physical emancipation. Many women have been physically emancipated by easier, more rapid ways of doing housework, as well as by transfer of many industrial processes from the household to outside enterprises. Restlessness, rather than contentment, is the significant and common result of physical emancipation. While it may ease life physically, it may make the sacred office of housewife of less importance. The wife's ego may be subtly injured in the course of gaining her freedom. Women's clubs and parent-teachers' associations may be a collective effort to maintain the sense of importance which the members individually have lost in their own families.

Intellectual emancipation from beliefs and moral emancipation from claims may accompany secular change. Since beliefs and claims are so important a part of institutions, emancipation affects their functioning. Every secular change is a potential moral crisis. It is notorious that an industrial revolution begets moral issues. Prophets and other agitators seek to bring about changes in the social order to meet such issues.

TYPICAL CYCLES OF INSTITUTIONALIZATION

We will now consider some of the typical processes involved in the establishment of institutions. We postulate typical life-cycles, or courses of change, by which institutions take form. Much of what is here said can be understood only by reference to the section on Collective Behavior.

From Expressive Behavior to Ritual. Some institutions have their origins in expressive behavior, as in a religious revival. Such behavior, if repeated, does not long remain purely expressive. Wesley and his aides of the Methodist Awakening soon undertook to discipline those who saw the great light. Little patience was shown those whose ecstasy of repentance was not followed by good works and methodical recourse to the means of grace. Ecstasy soon becomes interpreted as a sign of conversion, and tests are set up to determine whether the latter is genuine. At this point an element of consistency has already been introduced; consistency implies authority. Expressive behavior brought under discipline is on the way to becoming established ritual. So long as the rightness of this recurrent ritual is recognized only by the participants, and is contested by the surrounding community, it is not fully instituted. The group may be at war with the prevailing mores, and is thus sectarian. If and when it is acknowledged by the larger society, known as "the world," it becomes instituted in a fuller sense.

SOCIAL ACCEPTANCE. From this point expressive behavior, now ritual, may come to have a generally accepted moral connotation. It may become a sign of acceptance of the sacred sentiments of a society, and the person who refrains from participating in it is then suspect. Meanwhile the ritual will have been rationalized so that people do not question its relation to the accepted moral values and legitimate pursuits of the society.

By this time, regulative and even political activities are likely to have overshadowed the original elements of expressive behavior: an institution will have developed which, having vested interests in the social system, will make certain compromises with other forces. This is the familiar cycle by which religious sects become established denominations. The political sect, in like fashion, may succeed in gaining a measure of political power and become a responsible party at the cost of its original militant fervor.

A similar cycle begins in spontaneous celebration, which develops into recurrent and expected festivity led by proper functionaries and conducted in a traditional way. The second celebration of a great event is not the same as that which broke out at the time of the event itself: the second occasion may be planned, more formal, and less violent. In time, leadership of the celebrations may be monopolized by the recognized leaders of the society. It would be impertinent of a communist leader to ask for a place in a Fourth of July parade. The celebrated event itself finally is rationalized into something more than an event; it becomes a symbol—of man's salvation from sin, of the freedom of the country, or of democracy. Being so rationalized, it will be associated with the currently dominant sentiments of the society; it acquires a conventional meaning somewhat different from that attached to the original event by the people who actually participated in it. Again and again "debunking" historians have failed to shake an established festival and its conventional meaning by telling "what really happened."

From Strike to Trade-Union. In a strike, one of the classes of persons participating in an institution collectively refrains from expected routine. Strong collective discontent is a condition necessary to the beginning of a strike; morale is necessary to its maintenance, for a strike is a form of conflict. The leaders must be agitators. But the successful strike ends in negotiation; negotiation, in turn, depends upon the leaders' ability to have the terms of settlement accepted by the strikers. The development of labor unions turns about these two contradictory functions of leadership.

The cycle runs from bitter conflict led by agitators, to the armed truce of an organized group ready for conflict but refraining from it in their own interest, and then to an established organization run by administrators who may begin to fear conflict. At this point, the workers may begin to suspect their leaders of having sold out, and "outlaw unions" led by "rank-and-file" leaders may start unauthorized strikes. These may run through the same cycle. Meantime the strike, as such, has become a recognized way of gaining the ends of labor, and of having the labor union accepted as a proper institution. Any given strike and any given union may still be suspect, because of the role which conflict plays in their origin and successful maintenance, and because of their threat to the authority of employers.

To the extent that labor unions become institutions with the sanction of contracts and law, as well as the support of the workers, they bring about a constitutional change in industrial and business institutions. They provide a new body of defined rights, new classes of recognized functionaries, and new sanctioned ways of action. For the student of institutions, these changes are of more significance than the economic question of the effects of strikes and unions upon wages and production.

Reform. Another type of cycle very common in America is that which begins in a reform movement. Self-appointed enthusiasts set about to change some aspect of the mores; failing in that they may redefine their aims toward a change of law. If successful in this, the agitating collectivity may become established as an organ of enforcement of the law. Other reformers seek to stir to new fervor the attitudes nominally accepted by everyone; they make, for example, an issue of infant mortality, which everyone admits is too high. They propose some means of remedying the situation. Such a movement, although no one dares oppose the sentiment it expresses, is an attack on the institutions already operating. The mother is told she doesn't know how to feed her children. The physicians are, by implication, accused of indifference. Such a movement may lead to the establishment of a new social agency. Similar movements have led to establishment of juvenile courts, settlement houses, playground systems, and libraries. The leaders of the original agitation may become administrators with a positively sanctioned right to deal with the matter concerned.

Revolution. A revolutionary movement aims at changing the entire institutional order. Even the family is said to have undergone fundamental changes in Soviet Russia. When a revolutionary movement passes from the stage of agitation to that of administration, it becomes especially important for the student of social institutions. It is, however, doubtful whether a revolution ever destroys all the institutions of the previous order.

Voluntary Secular Co-operation. The types of life-cycles just discussed all commence in the more lively forms of collective behavior. Discontent, enthusiasm, even ecstatic crowd expression and violent mob action may be involved. The development, if it continue long enough, moves toward subjection of the wilder forms of collective behavior, toward a cooler rule of precedent and even expediency, elaboration of a rationale, increasing rigidity of structure, and an accepted place in the existing social order. Another type of cycle begins with conscious and rational co-operation, by which each participating individual hopes to gain some advantage not otherwise to be attained. The individuals experience little or no excitement, and each enters into co-operation voluntarily and critically. The collectivity, regarded as a means to an end, may be dissolved without pain to any one. A familiar example is the trade association in which the co-operating individuals are competitors in some line of business. Real-estate agents may co-operate to protect themselves against tenants who don't pay rent, landlords who don't pay commissions, and even against agents who steal clients. If such conscious co-operative collective action continues, the ends sought are given a more general statement; new common problems are discovered, some of which inhere in the social system and are therefore not capable of definitive and final solution. With respect to these problems, precedents arise and a long-time policy is elaborated. Meanwhile the co-operating members become aware that their collective body has become a recognized instrument, and they consider it as having a place in the order of things. Outsiders likewise may eventually accept it as the right and proper body to appeal to with respect to certain public problems. Eventually everyone forgets the particular purpose for which it was initiated; indeed, it becomes like other established institutions in that persons asked what its purposes are, will give a variety of general and rationalized answers in terms of accepted sentiments. In the end, loyalty and implicit claims may arise with respect to what was in the beginning conceived as a means to an immediate end.

Many recognized institutions of our society began in this way. Ours is a society of many new occupations and types of secular interest. It is also one in which there is freedom of assembly and association. These are conditions favorable to this type of collective action.

Arrested Development. Let it be emphasized that these cycles, once begun, do not necessarily run their course to full institution. They may be nipped in the bud or they may die out. The most that can be said of them is that if they continue, institutional features develop. It is also true, as we have said earlier, that every institution has had a beginning. These are typical ways in which institutions begin. There are also certain types of collective activity which, under certain conditions, never receive full sanction but which do show some of the features of established institutions.

The "racket" furnishes an example. During the prohibition era it was against the law to make and sell alcoholic liquors. It was, in many parts of the country, not against the mores to buy and drink them. It was manifestly impossible for any one to announce publicly that he proposed to engage in the business, or to organize and control the competitors engaged in it. The racketeer did these things without public announcement; no recourse to law or appeal to public opinion was possible. But a system of control grew up, unsanctioned by laws and the mores. The result was a sort of bastard institution, in which the stabilizing public recognition of the functionaries could not develop. The sect becomes institutionalized by making peace with the mores with which it was in conflict. The racket is in conflict, not with the mores but with the law. So long as legal sanction is not accorded it, the exercise of authority within it remains in a precarious state, although the activity continues and traditional modes of behavior develop. Prostitution and gambling show similar characteristics.

SELECTED READINGS

Blanshard, Paul. *American Freedom and Catholic Power.* Boston: Beacon Press, 1949.

Cooley, C. H. *Sociological Theory and Social Research.* New York: Henry Holt & Co., 1930. Chap. 10.

Dunne, George H. *Religion and American Democracy.* New York: America Press, 1949.

Havighurst, Robert J., and H. G. Morgan. *Social History of a War-Boom Community.* New York: Longmans, Green & Co., 1951.

Park, R. E., and E. W. Burgess. *Introduction to the Science of Sociology.* Chicago: Univ. of Chicago Press, 1924. Chap. 13.

Thomas, W. I., and F. Znaniecki. *The Polish Peasant in Europe and America.* New York: A. A. Knopf, 1927. Pp. 1151–1644.

Warner, W. Lloyd, and Leo Srole. *The Social Systems of American Ethnic Groups.* New Haven: Yale Univ. Press, 1945. Chaps. 4–8.

Warner, W. Lloyd, and others. *Social Class in America: A Manual of Procedure for the Measurement of Social Status.* Chicago: Science Research Associates, Inc., 1949.

Webb, Beatrice and Sidney. *History of Trade Unionism.* New York: Longmans, Green & Co., 1920. Chap. 1.

Chapter Twenty-seven

INSTITUTIONS
AND THE COMMUNITY

DISTINCTION BETWEEN COMMUNITY
AND SOCIETY

Human aggregations may be viewed either as societies or as communities. A society is described in terms of collective behavior, social usages, sanctions, status, and sentiments: a community, in terms of competition, symbiosis, and the division of labor by which it gains sustenance from its environment.[1]

RELATIONS TO THE ENVIRONMENT

A community is always considered in relation to a physical environment, to a territory. In modern communities, raw nature is buried beneath man's multiplied and stupendous artifacts. The relations of a man to the physical environment can be comprehended only by gathering and analyzing statistics of production, transportation, trade, and employment. He is part of a world-wide community of competing and co-operating individuals, most of whom are not known to him.

Environment in Primitive Communities. In primitive communities and in outlying fringes of the civilized world, the raw physical environment is closer at hand. Such communities are nevertheless sustained by co-operation within an institutional structure.

The characteristic primitive community consists of a small, clearly defined group of individuals relatively independent of other communities for the goods required by the prevailing standard of life.

---

1 See section on Human Ecology.

Synchronized Group Activities. Such a community occupies and exploits a territory. Occupation is actually a configuration of movements and activities, many of them so often repeated as to beat paths and roads into the very ground. The anthropologist describes these movements and activities as a "round of life" turning with the seasons, with the life-cycle of the individual from birth to death, and with shorter or longer cycles of the movements of game and fish, the wearing out of the soil under crops and its renewal in fallow. In Wissler's words, "We see the community as a group of individuals, male and female, children and adults, young and old, following standardized procedures, not necessarily doing the same thing at the same time, but different things more or less according to rule, so synchronized as to feed, clothe, house, control, and entertain the members of the group."[1]

Prominence of Institutions. The anthropologist sees in such communities the objective and elementary unit for observation. The lesser institutions within are harder to discover and are understood only in relation to the whole. In our world, the many institutional units stand out as objective and fiscally separate entities. It is the community which has to be discovered.

THE LOCATION OF INSTITUTIONS

The most easily seen features of many institutions are the buildings which serve as headquarters. A building has a location which may be described with reference to other things. The description has no point unless it illuminates the relations between institutions and, ultimately, the part played by them in the lives of individuals. A newspaper, one of the most characteristic of modern institutions, is usually printed in a building near the center of a city. News must be gathered and distributed quickly. Reporters gather much of it in the near-by heart of the city where happen so many of the things that make news. Reports of world events also come quickly to the city where are focussed so many means of rapid communication. The papers are distributed by screaming trucks and shouting newsboys to the masses, who crowd the near-by streets at certain hours of the day. Quick postal and express services carry papers in all directions to the more distant parts, where families receive and read

[1] Clark Wissler, *An Introduction to Social Anthropology* (1929), chap. 2, "The Community as the Anthropological Unit." Used by permission of the publishers, Henry Holt & Co., Inc., New York.

them. Much of the advertising revenue, which is so large a part of the newspaper's income, comes from department stores. The area from which local news is gathered and to which it is distributed corresponds rather closely to the area from which people come to shop in the stores near the newspaper's office. In describing the newspaper's location one would discover the functional limits of a certain kind of community.[1]

The newspaper not only illustrates what we mean by the location of an institution; it happens also to be closely associated with cities. A city is more than a place where many people live close to each other insulated from the raw physical environment; it is a focal point of the activities and movements which bind men together in their struggle for existence. In cities a great variety of activities is carried on in a grander and perhaps technically more efficient, but less personal way than in smaller communities. Institutions, functionaries, and experts multiply, and with them, a rational and impersonal spirit.

FUNCTIONS OF INSTITUTIONS IN COMMUNITIES

Basic and Service Institutions. McKenzie has divided institutions into *basic* and *service* according to their functions in communities. Basic institutions furnish the economic base of the institutional hierarchy; service institutions provide cultural services and consumption goods. Large industrial and commercial enterprises are basic, since they contribute to the wealth and income of the local population; but they are service institutions in the larger region to which they supply goods. Churches, theaters, retail enterprises, etc., are service institutions.

The distinction refers to the place of a given institution in a community. A church generally takes its character from the community, and is thus a service institution. But the shrine at Lourdes, which performs a service for the many people from all parts of the world who believe in it, is the basic institution from which the local population of Lourdes lives. The papacy, with its elaborate constellation of auxiliary institutions, gives life and character to Vatican City and even to Rome. A university is the basic institution of many a seat of learning as surely as the factory is that of a company town. In a farming community, the family-operated farms are the basic institutions for which the

---

1 R. D. McKenzie, *The Metropolitan Community* (New York: McGraw-Hill Book Co., 1933), Chap. 8, "Newspaper Circulation and Metropolitan Regions."

village centers perform the services which the population wants and can afford.

Wants Supplied by Service Institutions. A service, in the sense meant, is simply something which people of the given culture and resources want and get; groceries, medical care—whether furnished by physicians, midwives, or patent-medicine peddlers—motion pictures, sermons, schooling, prostitutes, and so on. The service institutions are the organized means of supplying these wants. Standards of living are the sum of the actual choices which people make from among the services offered, within the limits of the time, energy, interest, and money they have to spend. People whose only free evening is Sunday may spend it and a little money in a gospel hall, a theater, a roller-skating rink, or in the bosom of the family listening to the radio. They cannot do all of these things. People of given means may try to keep up with the Joneses, who live in a fine house, or with the Smiths, who send their children to college.

The Pyramid of Service Institutions. The service institutions display the economy of values of people, given their means and the techniques of their culture. As wants compete within the individual, so do institutions in the community. McKenzie has remarked that in the United States places of the same size have approximately the same number and types of service institutions. A small and isolated community usually lacks services available in larger and more accessible ones. Some institutions are found in almost all places; most American children live within walking distance of an elementary school. Churches are almost as widely distributed. Other service institutions are less frequent, either because less frequently wanted or because of the costly equipment and staff required. Facilities for removing the appendix are used by a given individual but once; it takes many potential customers to keep them going. Operatic companies are, in America, found in only a few cities. There is, then, a pyramid of service institutions; at the base are those found wherever a few people live. Higher in the pyramid and fewer in number of units are those which can survive only where accessible to a larger number of people. At the top are those highly specialized institutions found only in metropolitan cities with continents as their "hinterlands."

The Institutional Complement. The typical set of service institutions present in communities of a given type, McKenzie called its institutional *complement*, after the term used to indicate the number and kinds of men required to man a certain kind and size of ship.

FACTORS AFFECTING INSTITUTIONS IN A COMMUNITY

Population Movements. The existence of the local units of an institution depends upon the continued presence of a population which will support them. A sharp decline in rates of reproduction will, in the absence of immigration, threaten certain institutions. Decline of the basic institutions may deprive the community of the means of supporting its service institutions. In our mobile world a population of one set of economic and cultural standards is often succeeded by another. In a community where this is in course of happening, churches, societies, and lodges, perhaps even restaurants and theaters may disappear. For while the newcomers may be religious, they often do not want the religious institutions of their predecessors. They are sociable, but within the framework of their own culture. They eat and amuse themselves, but may prefer spaghetti and Verdi to roast beef and Gilbert and Sullivan. While most business institutions may adapt themselves to succession, less secular institutions often can not. Succession itself is often the result of change in basic institutions; it is, in turn, followed by change in many of the service institutions. If one were to discover which institutions do not change following such a succession of population he would have found an objective common denominator of our culture.

Ecological Factors. The ecological method of study has been most generally and thoroughly applied to business institutions. R. D. McKenzie, in his book *The Metropolitan Community*, has systematically analyzed current trends in the distribution of such institutions in the larger cities of the United States. He gave less attention to other institutions, largely because the data were not adequate. There may be other reasons for this emphasis. Since business is freer of sacred tradition than are religion, family, and politics, business institutions seem more responsive to the secular contingencies of competition. In our part of the world, at least, the basic institutions which give sustenance and character to a community are those of industry and business. Seats of learning and cathedral cities do not loom large on the American landscape, while industrial and commercial centers abound.

Recently representatives of Protestant churches have studied the problem of the survival of congregations in certain types of communities. It is generally agreed that a local church flourishes best upon a stable group of families of the same religious background and social class, living in a fairly compact area. Departure from these conditions causes churches to decline, die, or to be changed in character. In meeting the secular crises resulting from changes in their communities, churches of different denominations sometimes forget their doctrinal differences enough to co-operate or even to unite. This is not surprising in view of the finding of the Lynds, in their study of Middletown, that Protestant churches tend to vary more according to the economic class of their adherents than according to denominational lines. Sermons and church buildings are, within the limits of common religious belief, items in standards of living. Insofar as this is true, churches are in competition with one another. When districts cease to be solid residential neighborhoods and become rooming-house areas, slums, or foreign colonies the existing churches may survive by becoming missions, settlement houses, or clubhouses of the Y.M.C.A. type. In that case, they are generally supported by philanthropic gifts or by the mission funds of central bodies rather than by the people who patronize them. One may advance the hypothesis that increase in mobility and in diversity of culture and decrease in the intensity of sectarian spirit of the population of a community all tend to make the continued existence of local churches precarious.

The ecologically significant unit of family life is the household. It consists ordinarily of a married couple and their minor children, living under one roof and supported from a common fund. Where the family owns and operates a farm or other enterprise the physical equipment is considerable and tends to fix the family. Such a household may outlive several generations, if there is some scheme for transferring the land or other equipment to some one member of the succeeding generation. In rural Quebec, for instance, enough children are ordinarily born to furnish the required farm labor, but the land is regularly turned over intact to one son. In the absence of drastic changes in the method of exploiting land, such a system can exist only if there is constant emigration. If it does prevail, the number of families living in a given territory may remain the same over a long period of time. The result is a stable community.

The town or city household is ordinarily maintained by the wage-work of some one or more of its members. They earn their wages in institutions over which the family has little or no control. The location and the character of the family's house depend very largely upon the availability of work and the wages earned. Conversely, in a factory town at least, the number and kinds of households will depend upon the demand for labor. Households are, however, less mobile than individuals; certain families manage somehow to remain where they are even when there is no opportunity of earning. Many are broken up when the wage earner disappears or loses his earning power.

The household, among the mass of town and city people, endures less than a lifetime. It begins with marriage and may last until both of the couple are dead. It may, however, be broken up when the children are grown and leave home, especially if the parents have not acquired the means of providing for their old age. The present trend toward public support of the aged is probably related to changes in the survival of households. No such problem exists in a rural community where the household goes on unbroken through the generations.

Standards of living inhere in the family household living from a common fund. Studies of birth-rates indicate that such standards have a great deal to do with the number of children a woman will bear. The white-collar group, with a relatively high standard but with inflexible incomes, has notoriously small families. Laborers' and farmers' families are larger. The city family pays for its living with money; it grows no vegetables and bakes little bread. If it lives in an apartment house, its sons fire no furnace and rake no leaves. The additional cost of an extra child is relatively greater than on a farm or in a small town. If a grandparent comes to live with them, the family must move to larger quarters or some one must sleep on the sofa, which means a decline in the standard of living.

In large cities the various types of family dwellings are distributed in rather distinct areas (such as suburbs with single-family houses, apartment-house areas, rooming-house districts) and into many rental classes. Each area tends to have a distinctive age and sex distribution; the normal pyramid of numerous children and fewer adults with the sexes about equal is most closely approached where the family household is the prevailing type. It is probable that schools, churches, and the various institutions in which people find informal sociability flourish best in such a district.

The talk here is not of the mores governing family life, but of the secular conditions which affect the nature and survival of households. While most people would say that a person should support his parents and assist his brothers and sisters, the difficulties of extending such aid beyond the walls of the household are very great; and the household itself, although not fixed in space, is not very flexible as to size under modern wage-earning and cash-rent conditions. These conditions have, indeed, put a heavy strain upon the mores.

Sentiment and Secular Conditions. It is not probable that any institution could be completely understood by studying the secular conditions of its survival alone. Some institutions, such as schools, are maintained by political means. A given community may have a better school than it could or would pay for, because some central administrative body allocates support to it. Thus the school is not completely responsive to the competitive forces of the community where it operates. Certain institutions are so dominated by sentiment that they seem less directly sensitive to secular contingencies. But the units of every institution are in some fashion subject to the survival of human communities and to the economy of wants and the technical means available within a given culture and physical environment.

SELECTED READINGS

Barnes, Harry E. *Society in Transition.* New York: Prentice-Hall, 1946.

Herskovits, M. J. *Man and His Works.* New York: A. A. Knopf, 1948.

Hoebel, E. A. *Man in the Primitive World.* New York: McGraw-Hill Book Co., 1949.

Jacobs, Melville, and Bernhard J. Stern. *An Outline of General Anthropology.* New York: Barnes & Noble, Inc., 1947.

Lowie, R. H. *Social Organization.* New York: Rinehart & Co., 1948.

Slotkin, J. S. *Social Anthropology: The Science of Human Society and Culture.* New York: Macmillan Co., 1950.

CHAPTER TWENTY-EIGHT

INSTITUTIONS AND THE PERSON

INDIVIDUALS AND INSTITUTIONS

Interdependence. Institutions furnish the individual with a routine of life, patterns of expected behavior by which he will be judged, objectives and ambitions toward which he may strive. The more subtle effects of these factors upon his personality are studied by social psychologists and psychiatrists. Conversely, institutions exist in the integrated and standardized behavior of individuals.

Status. In every society there are accepted social usages, but they are not the same for all persons. Boys and girls are distinguished from birth by costume and names. They are treated differently and expected to behave differently; constant emphasis is laid upon the different roles and careers which lie before them. They do not have identical rights and duties before the law. This is a difference of *status*. Some societies recognize many kinds of status depending upon one's sex, race, family, occupation, religion, or combinations of these. Persons of each status have their own special rights and duties, sanctioned by the society.

Ours is a society of few fixed categories of status. The person finds his place in the social structure. He has many choices, subject to his own capacities and opportunities, to such limitations of status as do exist, and, finally, to the social structure itself. The few fixed status categories of our society are in contrast to its great variety of institutions and its extreme division of labor. Institutions play a great part in the process of social differentiation which the person cannot escape.

Individuals in Institutional Life. The individual meets various institutions at different periods of his life, and for longer or shorter terms. He is considered part of his family from birth, but his position in it changes as he grows older. The state and some religious institutions claim him from birth until death; in these also, rights and duties change. In infancy and childhood he has little direct connection with the state; at a certain age he passes from the status of a minor to that of majority. Child offenders are dealt with by special juvenile courts. Children of certain ages may be required to go to school; young men may be called to military service, and so on. Still other institutions are met by the person only at later ages, and his relation to them may be contingent upon his other activities and roles. If he enters a certain occupation, he may be drawn into direct participation in the activity of a whole group of institutions. This leads to the distinction between *voluntary* and *involuntary* institutions.

Voluntary and Involuntary Institutions. Voluntary institutions are those in which the person is free to participate or not, as he chooses. Others are involuntary; a person is expected or compelled to participate in them. A child is inescapably part of a family; he may later renounce or desert it although at great emotional cost. The school is involuntary for a certain period. All persons owe the state allegiance and some duties.

Some institutions are voluntary in a limited way. One is free not to participate in them, but exercise of his freedom would be socially costly. People do not have to take jobs in factories, but there may be no other way of obtaining food. No one has to become a physician; once he does so he cannot escape the instituted medical profession. A businessman is free to ignore fraternal orders, clubs, and churches, but to do so may jeopardize his standing. He may have to accept burdensome office in charitable bodies on pain of impairment of his business: a person of his standing is expected to assume these responsibilities. The exercise of freedom with respect to institutions is thus subject to many sanctions.

Right of Participation in Institutions. All persons have the right to participate in some institutions, but not in all. The right to determine who shall participate and in what capacity sometimes lies with the functionaries of the institution itself, sometimes with some or all of the participating persons, or it may be a matter of status in the society.

The Functions of Specialization. Cooley has said that a person enters into an institution only with a trained and specialized part of himself. As examples he mentioned the legal part of the lawyer, the ecclesiastical part of a church member, and the business part of a merchant.[1]

Institutions vary both in the degree of specialization demanded of persons and in the completeness of control over their lives. The lawyer may perform his professional duties satisfactorily and yet have a great deal of private life. A nun is expected to have no private life at all; even her secret meditations are expected to be pious. The saying that a woman's work is never done expresses that complete devotion to the family formerly, if not now, expected of the wife and mother.

Within the same institution, various degrees of specialization and of devotion are expected of different categories of people. In certain communities everyone is counted part of the church, but specially trained and dedicated persons, the clergy, devote their whole time and thought to the church and are expected to dress and act in a distinct way at all times.

Specialization as here conceived has two dimensions. One is that of knowledge and technique; the other, that of duties and prerogatives. The lawyer has expert knowledge: so have the priest, the businessman, and even the mother. But each of them has also prerogatives and duties by which he is distinguished from other people. Identification of one's self with one or more established sets of rights and duties is part of the process by which an individual becomes a person with a social identity.

FUNCTIONARIES

Role of Functionaries. The more specialized activities of an institution are carried on by functionaries who fulfill offices. An institutional office consists of a defined set of rights and duties vested in a person, but capable of being transferred to another person in some accepted way. This does not mean that a father, for instance, can be replaced in his family easily or completely, for personal attachment becomes too great. But when one becomes a father there is a pattern of expected conduct lying in wait for him. In other institutions, the functionaries can be changed within the individual units; at the funeral of an aged monarch the tears are not bitter and the mourners look out of the corners of their eyes at the beloved prince who will soon be happily crowned.

1 C. H. Cooley, *op. cit.*, p. 319.

Impersonal Character of an Office. An office is impersonal in two respects. First, it is older than the individual incumbent and is expected to outlive him. Second, each incumbent is expected to behave, within limits, as have his predecessors. Ritual offices are the most impersonal, for in them the incumbent speaks in set phrases which he is not free to alter. The person in an office is judged by the expectations of the office. So long as he meets them, he is free from personal criticism. The office sets the limits of his responsibilities.

Personal Aspect of an Office. An office is personal in that the fulfilling of it requires the conscious identification of one's personal role with the historic office. The office is part of his experience. Deep emotions may be associated with it. It is also personal in that the individual may change the character of the office by his manner of filling it.

OPPORTUNITY FOR INITIATIVE. Offices vary as to the opportunity they offer for personal initiative, and in the amount of responsibility of the individual to get results. The king of England enjoys great prestige, but does not make or carry out policies. The prime minister has less prestige, but is expected to get results. Some offices combine ritualistic and symbolic features with responsibility and initiative. Priests in Christian churches manage their sees and parishes as well as administer the sacraments.

ACHIEVEMENT OF RESULTS. In business institutions, officers are judged very largely by the results they achieve. They make decisions and are expected to see them carried out. Even active offices gather a certain amount of ritual, as is seen in the familiar custom of lending weight to words by having them uttered by industrial and financial figures.

Natural History of an Office. Every institutional office has a history. Sects furnish a clear example. Joseph Smith was the founder and prophet of the Mormon sect. Brigham Young succeeded him, but he was not called a prophet. The founder is regarded as unique; after he dies a formula is developed by which some of his attributes are passed on to a successor. Eventually an office evolves, with defined prerogatives and a manner of succession. A social fiction is developed whereby the successors share the prestige of the founder.

ENACTED AND CRESCIVE OFFICES. There are other typical lines of development. The presidency of the United States was defined in a written document. It was, in Sumner's terms,[1] enacted rather than crescive; but, as is generally the case, the original enactment has been modified by experience. The present office is a product of precedent as well as of written prescription. Probably no office can be fully laid down in advance.

CHANGING CHARACTER OF OFFICES. As an institution becomes established the character of offices changes, and new ones grow up. Duties and the exercise of authority are distributed among them. The relations of offices to one another and to the various classes of people who participate in the institution are its "working constitution."

DEVICES AND DISCIPLINE. As an office becomes sacred the individual who is to fill it is separated from other people by a long discipline and is finally invested with the office in a ceremonial manner. These devices intensify the person's sense of identification with the office. He may be "called," as are the clergy. In psychiatric terms, he feels compelled to dedicate himself to the office. But institutions do not rely on a person's sense of compulsion alone as evidence that he should be invested with an office; devices are set up to test the validity of his call and to discipline his unbounded enthusiasm and sense of exalted righteousness.

DEVELOPMENT OF INSTABILITY. In a stable society, persons of succeeding generations identify the meaning and purposes of their lives with the offices of existing institutions. But there are periods in which this is not so. Some persons get a sense of a special mission not provided for in the institutions. They chafe under the bonds of institutions, and become restless. Such a situation is critical both for institutions and for persons.

CHANGES IN FUNCTION. In a changing secular society there are many institutions in process whose offices are not clearly defined. The persons who fill such offices can and do show a great deal of individual initiative; in so doing they create the offices they fill. The rights and duties of the managing boards of universities and charitable organizations, as well as of their executive officers, are still in course of rapid change. Even in well-hardened institutions some offices offer opportunities for enterprise and initiative which may bring about changes in the office itself.

SELECTION OF FUNCTIONARIES. The persons who are to fill offices are selected in various ways. In business institutions free

[1] W. G. Sumner, *op. cit.*, p. 54

play is supposedly given to the abilities and achievements of the individual, to the exclusion of race, family, and religion. In the more sacred institutions, it is but natural that more attention should be given to such matters. But both secular and sacred features operate in most cases. Piety is a characteristic necessary to the priesthood; but bishops must be men of outstanding executive ability as well. Engineers must have technical knowledge, but one who was an avowed communist would hardly be chosen for a responsible position in a large corporation.

THE CLASS STRUCTURE. The selection of functionaries is related to the general class structure of society. Clergy, in America at least, apparently do not come from the most influential families of laymen. The administrative boards of universities and charitable institutions are generally composed of wealthy people. A large proportion of legislators are lawyers, and so on. Facts of this nature reflect the actual place of the institution within the social structure.

PARTICIPANTS IN INSTITUTIONS

Categories of Participants. Several categories of persons participate in an institution or at least have some occasional relations with it. The significant categories can be determined by study alone. A few examples were given in the discussion of the classification of institutions. Another significant example, characteristic of our society, follows.

PROFESSIONAL SOCIAL WORKERS. The people most actively and continuously concerned with social agencies are trained professional social workers, who may move from one agency to another. Formerly there were many volunteer workers. Managing boards and committees govern the agencies and assist in raising the necessary money; these people are chosen on the basis of their interest and their status in the community. They are generally large donors to the agency. The solvent members of the general population are contributors in a small way, but know little of the inner workings of the agency. Then there are the people, euphemistically called clients, who are looked after by the agency. There is little movement from one of these categories to another. The donors rarely become professional workers or clients; the clients almost never become donors, professional workers, or members of boards. In this case, the categories of people in the institution and the part played by each is clearly related to the general structure of society. A somewhat similar pattern is found in all institutions supported by philanthropic giving.

THE ENDOWED UNIVERSITY. The endowed university shows similar categories, with certain significant differences. The governing boards are constituted in somewhat the same way. A professional group, the professors and administrators, devote their time to the university and have their careers within it. But the students occupy a quite different position, and seldom come from the poorest classes. The students continue, as alumni, to have a sentimental interest in the university and may even have a part in forming its policies.

THE SPREAD OF PARTICIPATION. In both these cases the managing boards are persons of wealth and social position. The institution, although undoubtedly important to them, is incidental to their careers. The taking of such responsibility is expected of and urged upon them; they, too, consider it their right to act so. They are the patrons. The professional groups, social workers and faculty members, have their careers and living in it. They interpret the meaning of their lives in terms of the value of the institution to the community. They carry its main body of tradition and technique, and regard it as their right that the community should support them. In both cases a third group of persons directly receives services. Ordinarily they are in contact with the professionals, but not with the patrons. The "clients" of the social agency may have little or no sense of loyalty to the institution; it is simply a help in time of trouble. The social agency seldom has alumni. Students, however, generally remain sentimental toward their universities, for they had some of the greatest thrills of their lives on the campus, although not necessarily in the classroom. The university has also become a symbol of one's role in society as well as the means of acquiring knowledge necessary to a career. Finally, a larger interested public knows about these institutions, and thinks them necessary and worthy of support.

Changes in Personnel. A fundamental change in any one of these categories of persons would lead to change in the institution. All institutions depend upon the continued presence in the community of the various kinds of persons involved in its ongoing activities. It is doubtful whether the social agencies of today could be run entirely by volunteer workers as they once were. It is possible that the university of the future may not be so liberally supported by people of great fortune as in the past few decades. Such changes may occur without people ceasing to believe in the desirability of these institutions. A shift of enthusiasm and of a sense of responsibility is sufficient to make a difference. People may continue to "believe in" an institution long after they have ceased to regard it their special duty to devote time and effort to it.

STUDIES OF TURNOVER. Sorokin has studied the rate of turnover of personnel in various institutions. In universities, students come and go most rapidly; the teachers of lower rank more rapidly than those of higher rank. In the larger and more famous of universities studied, the turnover of staff was slower. Another student has noted that in labor unions where the turnover of members is rapid, control falls largely into the hands of the paid agents. Such studies reveal the most stable element in the institution. This knowledge should be of use in understanding the processes of control in the institution and its meaning in the lives of persons.

INSTITUTIONS AND THE LIFE OF
THE PERSON

Order. Institutions, it has been suggested, give order to the life of the individual. In early infancy and childhood his identity in the community is entirely determined by the family of which he is a member. Later he is identified with other institutions — the school, church, etc. Eventually he finds a job if he can, becomes a full-fledged adult citizen, and participates in some fashion in many institutions. Some of them influence his life without his becoming aware of it.

Self-Appraisal. From a fairly early age he develops a sense of his own identity, of the role he plays in the eyes of others and in his own eyes. He is also likely to conceive of himself in terms of his future, although it may not turn out to be what he expects. As he moves on through life he passes through a sequence of relations to other people and institutions; at each point—if he is at all introspective—he tries to square his past with the present, and to interpret the meaning of his present for his future. He sees life in a moving perspective.

Dominant Interests. Some of the institutions in which he has a part will mean much to him; others will mean little. To some persons, family life remains the sole dominating interest.

The priest must leave his family and have his being in the church, although his family may gain prestige by his action. In the secular pursuits of business and industry many people find the leading interest of their lives, and all their hopes are set upon achievements in this field. Still others plug along at some job, but find the crucial prizes of life in their families, religious institutions, fraternal orders, local politics, charities, or what not. Thus each institution is an arena in which some people seek what they most want, while for others it is merely a casual or an incidental thing. While not all personal enthusiasms and aims are directed toward institutions, many of them are. So much is this true that the life-history of most individuals would be, in considerable part, an account of their relation to institutions. Subjectively, it would be an account of how the person viewed these institutions and how he conceived himself in relation to them; objectively, it would be an account of his achieved places in them.

The Career of an Individual. In a society of rigid status categories, a person's career is largely determined by his birth. Even in ours, status limits the careers of some kinds of persons, such as Negroes and women. On the whole, we live in a relatively free society in which the individual can make his own career within broad limits.

SCHOOLING. One set of limits lies in the expected line of development of the person, which is hardened in the schools. A child is expected to learn things at certain ages and in a fixed order. If his schooling is interrupted, it is hard for him to take it up again. In some European countries the child, or his parents, must choose between divergent lines of schooling before he has reached the level of our high schools. Some provisions are made in America for those who wish education at a later age, but there is still and will probably continue to be a certain fatality in the interruption of one's formal schooling.

MATURITY. Meanwhile the person has attained the status of an adult, whether he wishes it or not. He must work for a living, unless he is of the favored few. Pride may prevent him from doing and learning the things conventionally appropriate to an earlier age. Thus when the person has reached the end of adolescence a great many things have happened to fix not only his habits, interests, and knowledge, but his social role and his probable career. The expected line of development of the individual tends to make decisions and actions irrevocable.

BUREAUCRATIC CAREERS. Careers which tend to proceed by fixed steps are called bureaucratic. In the civil service, the army, and wherever the principles of seniority and selective examination prevail, careers tend to be of this type. In such careers, Karl Mannheim has said, one receives at each step a neat package of prestige and power whose contents are known in advance. Security is at a maximum and enterprise at a minimum. Many people believe that our society is becoming increasingly bureaucratic.

A measure of the bureaucratic tendency appears in many institutions. In school systems, in railroads and other large corporations, even in universities and social agencies there are signs of it. Wherever the knowledge and function of a kind of work become standardized it is likely to appear.

EXCEPTIONS TO BUREAUCRATIC TENDENCIES. In many fields of activity career lines are not fixed. In institutions where they are fixed, some offices are filled from outside the line of expected bureaucratic advancement. When a new subject is introduced into the curricula of universities, the people who study and teach it will for a time come from irregular sources; such has been the case with sociology until recently. University presidents have likewise escaped the bureaucratic tendency. Judges of juvenile courts have not in the past been ground out of the regular legal and political mill. School superintendents and executive heads of social agencies often are not picked from those who have "faithfully served" in the lower ranks of their institutions. Although this matter has not been thoroughly studied, it appears probable that offices which require initiative and executive ability are difficult to standardize.

It may be that the careers of individuals can not be forced completely into institutional molds even in the most rigid of societies. Native abilities, extraordinary ambitions and efforts, and the contingencies of social change make for open places in the frozen structure of society. For most individuals, however, both the meaning and the course of life are closely bound to the institutional structure.

SELECTED READINGS

Bendix, Reinhard. *Higher Civil Servants in American Society*. Boulder: Univ. of Colorado Press, 1950.

Cooley, C. H. *Social Organization*. New York: Chas. Scribner's Sons, 1929. Chaps. 28, 29.

Dawson, C. A., and W. E. Gettys. *Introduction to Sociology*. Rev. ed. New York: Ronald Press, 1935. Chap. 21.

Haring, Douglas G., ed. *Personal Character and Cultural Milieu: A Collection of Readings*. Rev. ed. Syracuse: Syracuse Univ. Press, 1948.

Hertzler, J. O. "Religious Institutions," *Annals of the American Academy of Political and Social Science*. (March 1948), 256:1–13.

Hughes, E. C. "Institutional Office and the Person," *American Journal of Sociology* (1937), 42:404–413.

Niebuhr, H. R. *The Social Sources of Denominationalism*. New York: Henry Holt & Co., 1929. Chaps. 2–4.

Veblen, Thorstein. *The Higher Learning in America*. New York: B. W. Huebsch, 1918. Chaps. 2, 5.

Warner, W. L., and P. S. Lunt. *The Social Life of a Modern Community*. New Haven: Yale Univ. Press, 1941. Chaps. 6, 12–17.

Warner, W. L., R. Havighurst, and M. Loeb. *Who Shall Be Educated?* New York: Harper & Bros., 1943.

White, Leslie A. *The Science of Culture*. New York: Farrar, Straus and Co., 1949.

Chapter Twenty-nine

SOCIAL CONTROL

INFORMAL AND FORMAL SOCIAL CONTROL

In primary group life, the individual is sensitive to the actions and gestures of his intimate associates. In crowds there prevails a collective mood in which individuals lose the self-restraint of quieter moments. In both cases an informal collective control is exercised over the individual: in both appears that mutual responsiveness of human beings which is perhaps the ultimate basis of all social control.

Folkways. A new element is introduced when conventional ways of behaving develop, as they inevitably do when people live together. Sumner designates as *folkways* the common modes of behavior accepted as natural and right in any group or society.[1] Through them present behavior is controlled by that of the past. It is still a matter of individuals controlling one another, for the folkways are communicated from living persons to living persons. Each person becomes an agent of the folkways in so far as he himself adheres to them and gives his frown or his approving nod to other people depending on whether they likewise depart from or conform to the folkways.

Usages and Mores. Sumner further divides folkways into *usages* and *mores*. Usages are merely practiced, whereas mores are considered necessary to group welfare and are sacred. In the terms used by Radcliffe-Brown, the mores are *sanctioned usages*.

All social usages have behind them the authority of the society, but among them some are sanctioned and others are not. A sanction is a reaction on the part of a society or of a considerable number of its members to a mode of behavior which is thereby approved (positive sanctions) or disapproved (negative sanctions). Sanctions may further be distinguished according to whether they are diffuse or organized; the former are spon-

---

1 W. G. Sumner, *op. cit.*, p. 57.

taneous expressions of approval or disapproval by members of the community acting as individuals, while the latter are social actions carried out according to some traditional and recognized procedure.[1]

The *mores* are folkways subject to *diffuse sanctions*. Institutional control is distinguished by *organized sanctions;* it involves recognized rules, formal procedures for their application, and a structure consisting of persons acting in office. Anyone may lift his brow at a departure from accepted usage, or join with his neighbors in ostracizing someone who has violated the mores. Only the proper officers or functionaries may undertake the sanctioned procedures of an institution. None but very fanatical persons or those whose feelings have been extremely outraged interfere with a parent's way of looking after his children. Any one may suggest that the stock exchange is a den of thieves, but constituted authority alone may eject a broker from his seat.

Formal Control. The ultimate instance of institutional control is the law, as formally interpreted by courts and executed by police power. Some students have applied the term law to all social rules, whether systematically formulated or not, and whether or not subject to organized rather than merely diffuse sanctions. Roscoe Pound, however, limits law to "social control through the systematic application of the force of politically organized society." [2] So defined, law is but one form of social control among others.

Law derives from many sources, among them custom, legislation, administrative orders and decrees. But none of these constitutes law in the strict sense until courts have passed upon them. Many usages and even mores are never embodied in law. Others may be. Justice Cardozo considered that a rule or convention was a part of law when it became so established that one could predict with reasonable certainty that a court would uphold it. According to this view much of the process of lawmaking occurs without legislation and before the matter reaches court.

A sociology of law would study the evolution of social rules, the nature and development of courts and their fields of jurisdiction, and the evolution of the systems of thought used by lawyers and judges in arriving at decisions.

---

1 A. R. Radcliffe-Brown, "Social Sanction," *Encyclopaedia of the Social Sciences* (1934), 13:531–534. Used by permission of the publishers, Macmillan Co., New York.
2 See Roscoe Pound, "The Purpose of the Legal Order," *Readings in Philosophy* (New York: Barnes & Noble, 2nd ed., 1950), ch. 23.

Courts have their history and functions which are not understood without reference to other institutions. According to the anthropologist Malinowski, the binding force of the law derives from the structure of institutions in the given society. Courts adjudicate, but do not form the relationships within families, in business, or between physician and client. Even in an orderly society, only a small part of all violations of rule which might be tried in court ever are so tried. While certain types of laws are enforced at the instance of the functionaries of the state itself, with respect to others the initiative is taken by persons representing the interests of other institutions or by proponents of some reform in the mores themselves.

Any institution is subject in some measure to the common stock of mores. In addition, it will be the vehicle of conscious and formal control over some limited phase of life and, usually, over some special group of persons. Against the background of the moral consensus of society, special groups of persons work out and apply formal rules and procedures to specific activities and interests.

Some institutions, such as the church and state, tend to exert authority over a wide range of activities and over all members of society. Their functionaries often attempt to bring to explicit formulation matters that have been subject to the mores, and to apply to them the formal procedures of the institution. Insofar as functionaries successfully set themselves up as the proper persons to define and enforce the mores, the latter take on the qualities of law.

Other institutions regulate only some very narrow phase of life, such as the practice of a profession. In this case the professional group consciously formulates and attempts to enforce rules. Although it may exert some control over the occasionally affected general public, the institution is, in turn, subject to the mores and popular usage. Professional medicine, for instance, cannot escape the general mores and popular beliefs with respect to healing.

CLASSIFICATION. Every institution involves some classification of the people of the society, according to the degree and manner in which they fall into the orbit of the institution. The relations between persons within each category, and between those of different categories, are defined. Institutional rules refer typically to the obligations of persons according to status and office.

Thus, however intimate its life may be, the family remains a system of sanctioned relationships between husband, wife, children, and other kin. The obligations of each to the others are defined in usage, in the mores, and in law. A citizen is a person who enjoys certain privileges in, and owes certain obligations to a state. Employers, managers, foremen, and workers in a factory; board members, donors, social workers, and "cases" in a social agency; trustees, presidents, deans, professors, students, and alumni of colleges; judge, jury, lawyers, witnesses, defendants, and plaintiffs in a court; physician, nurse, and patient —these are a few examples of institutional classifications of persons. When we say that the law is no respecter of persons, we mean that it treats them in terms of such instituted categories as are pertinent to the case in question, to the exclusion of matters irrelevant to it. The process of developing and changing such categories, with reference to the complex current activities and interests within a society, is the very heart of the institutional process.

INSTITUTIONAL CONTROL

The Professions. The processes of institutional control are well illustrated by the professions. The members of a full-fledged profession possess a technique and a body of knowledge pertaining to it. These they apply in performing some service for other members of society. So long as their competence is recognized by society at large, the members have a common status, and interests are shared by all of the members and may be injured by any one of them.

The persons who are served by the profession are interested only occasionally in its technique and knowledge. A body of unsystematic beliefs and practices may be adhered to by the general populace and communicated informally from generation to generation. In contrast with the general populace, however, the members of the profession are constantly and consciously interested in the matter involved, such as law, medicine, or accounting. Within the limited circle of the profession, technique and knowledge are systematized and passed on by formal means and in esoteric language. The professionals claim the sole right to judge knowledge and practice in their field of activity.

A constant problem of professional control is that of determining who are members, and, therefore, colleagues. This problem is resolved into two questions. *First,* who is competent to practice the profession? *Second,* who has a right to practice it?

The question of competence can be settled only by defining what the professional technique is and what services are to be given. The physician, the druggist, the surgeon, the midwife, and the dentist all perform services relating to the health of the human body. Within the last century the lines between them have been more clearly drawn, at the same time that the relevant bodies of knowledge and techniques have been improved. The physicians and surgeons have been drawn into a single body with a common type of formal training, often followed by special training in a medical or surgical speciality. Physicians have, for the most part, ceased to operate drugstores. Obstetrics has been increasingly included in medical training, and the midwife in many places has been forced out of practice. The dentists have become a more coherent group with a recognized type of formal training and an increasing body of knowledge and technique.

At the same time, the method of learning medical technique has been made more formal. A combination of general university education, training in a recognized medical school, and a practical internship in a hospital are required of every candidate. He must pass an examination set by authorities delegated nominally by the state, but in fact by the profession. The license then granted him is at once a certificate of competence and of his legal right to practice. The individual who has such license is a colleague of other physicians. A person who learned the practice of medicine in some irregular way and had no license would not be a physician and would have none of the privileges of the profession.

CONTACTS WITH THE FOLKWAYS. The clear definition of the group of colleagues does not completely and forever settle the problem of keeping practice in their hands alone. It sometimes happens that scientists who are not physicians make discoveries which affect medical practice. If the discovered knowledge is not at once accepted by the professionals the scientist may accuse them of conservatism. Furthermore the populace persists in many beliefs and practices not approved by the profession, or may wish kinds of service which it does not give. Other persons continue to give these services. Baldness, about which the medical profession does not claim to know much, is a persistent source of profit to barbers and patent-medicine venders who claim they do know something about it. Anxiety and many diseases difficult to diagnose and cure are treated by various kinds of unlicensed practitioners, by religious cults, and at shrines. Certain medical and surgical services, notably abortion, are forbidden by law; since regular physicians will not give them, people resort to other sources. An organized profession, whether from high motives or low, has to deal with such vagaries of popular belief and usage if it is to dominate its particular field of interest. It has to reckon with the folkways.

RELATIONS TO COLLEAGUES. The relations of colleagues to one another and to their clients must be defined. The colleagues compete with one another for clients. The services offered are such that the client is not supposed to be able to judge their value with accuracy. If one buys a suit, he judges its quality by its wear. But a surgical operation or the advice given by a lawyer is not subject to lay judgment in the same degree. The patient may suffer and die under the best of treatment; a case may be lost by an expert lawyer. Each physician must, therefore, protect himself against criticism by saying that he has done all that medical science can do. His failures must be attributed to the state of technique and knowledge of the profession as a whole, not to his own shortcomings. He must allow the same defense to his colleagues, for if the impression gets abroad that some of the properly trained and licensed professionals are incompetent, the public may come to believe that none is to be trusted. The layman may then take the next step of daring to form a judgment as to matters of professional practice. Every professional must, therefore, curb the natural desire to praise his own work and to criticise that of his competitors.

From this situation proceeds the rule against advertising one's special qualifications. In some states, a physician is allowed to put on his window only his name and title. In other places, he may note his specialty. Such invidious distinctions as might be suggested by prominent naming of the school at which he studied and the hospital in which he interned are frowned upon.

The conditions under which one professional may accept a client who has formerly received the services of another, and the relations between the general physician to whom a patient comes and the specialist to whom it becomes necessary to refer his case are also problems of competition.

RELATIONS TO THE PUBLIC. Another set of problems has to do with the duties of the professional toward his client, toward certain other individuals and toward the general public. Shall the physician, asks E. A. Ross,[1] report to a man's wife that her husband suffers from communicable venereal disease? Shall the priest report to police the confession of a crime? Shall a lawyer defend a person he knows to be a criminal?

Matters such as these cannot be settled by doctrine alone. As the technique of the professions changes, new problems of control arise. Changes apparently unrelated to the profession may make existing rules unworkable. The advertising physician continues to practice probably because the anonymity of city life renders it difficult for physicians to be known personally to potential patients and for the latter to know a physician if one is suddenly wanted. Specialization may break up the coherence of the profession both as to knowledge and interests. The corporation lawyer and the criminal lawyer, for instance, may have little in common and may actually disagree about many problems. The specialist attached to a hospital and the general physician working in a poor neighborhood may likewise have little understanding of, or sympathy for one another.

The rules governing these matters amount to a code and an etiquette of the profession. Both are produced by the professional group rather than by other parts of the society. The *etiquette* is a body of ritual which grows up informally to preserve, before the clients, the common front of the profession.

The *code* consists of rules elaborated to meet recurrent problems in the relations of the professionals to one another, to their clients, and to society at large.

Professional Creed. Besides having an etiquette and a code, a profession is likely to have a *creed* which states its ideals in general terms. Thus, the medical profession exists to alleviate suffering, the legal profession to further justice, and so on. The creed, while seriously believed in, cannot be enforced by sanctions; the code can be so enforced if the profession has enough moral consensus. The ultimate penalty is expulsion from the group of colleagues. In reality, consensus is more easily maintained with reference to a creed than on the specific points of a code. There is also a tendency for the rules of a code to become matters of creed, more stoutly defended in words than by sanctions. At bottom all professional control—etiquette, creed, and

1 E. A. Ross, *Principles of Sociology* (Rev. ed.; New York: D. Appleton-Century Co., 1930), chap. 44, "Professionalization."

code—rests upon the sense of community of status and of interest, among the members; that is, upon an implicit consensus.

COMMUNICATION. The underlying consensus of a profession, as of any group, is maintained by intimate communication of its members. In a professional school much more than science and techniques is transmitted to the students. Traditional attitudes are communicated in asides by teachers who are themselves members of the profession. The students learn a lingo which expresses the fact that they are in possession of peculiar knowledge not given to laymen. In what medical laboratory is there not a little byplay to get the neophyte over his first sense of horror at seeing dismembered cadavers? Who has not observed the profound and meditative sucking of the pipe by first-year law students poring over their first examination, dealing, perhaps, with the ownership of a much-travelled and battle-scarred barrel of molasses? Who has not heard theological students cracking jokes about ridiculous errors made in performing solemn ceremonies? Professional training is, in short, an initiation into a fraternity. One learns to guard its secrets, to cherish its ideals, and to have a feeling of being one of a group apart. The personality becomes identified with the historic professional group, symbolized in medicine by the figure of Hippocrates.

Sense of Honor. It is upon such close personal identification with a historic group having a special status, that a sense of honor ultimately rests. Honor combines features of formal rule with the scruples of conscience. Every person has some scruples of his own. They are not a matter of honor, for in following them he is responsible to himself alone. Every person is also subject to certain formal rules toward which his conscience is not especially acute; he obeys them, if he does, to avoid application of formal sanctions. Honor consists of a sense of conscientious scruple with reference to rules defined by a group and applicable to all its members. The person thus becomes compelled by his own conscience to live up to rules not of his own making. The most extreme manifestation of honor is formal suicide following an unavoidable breach of the rules of one's group.

Honor operates as a means of control only when the rules are specific, when there is consensus with respect to them, and when the person accepts them into his stock of moral compulsions. Within a professional group there is likely to be an inner circle who possess sufficient consensus to be governed by honor. In general, however, changes in technique and in the conditions of practicing a profession are inimical to rule by honor. For it is not sufficient that the members be conscientious; the rules must be clearly defined. In a democratic, mobile society, with a minimum of clear status, honor is difficult to maintain in its more extreme and rigid forms.

CONFLICTING TRENDS IN PROFESSIONAL CONTROL. Professional control, according to Dawson and Gettys,[1] seems to be currently subject to two conflicting trends. One is an increase in the number of specialized techniques with their relevant bodies of theoretical knowledge. The resulting elaboration of the division of labor has been accompanied by an increase in the number of occupations which are professional in character. At the same time there has been a change in the circumstances under which professional services are performed. The traditional professional man had many clients, any one of whom he might lose without great danger to his standing or living. Many professionals now have employers, in fact, if not in name. A lawyer, for instance, may live almost entirely from the patronage of one large corporation: in his office will be a number of other lawyers who, in effect, work for him on salary. A physician may be attached to a hospital or clinic, and have little outside practice. Engineers, accountants, nurses, and many other people of professional type are employed outright. Under these conditions the professional may be so dependent upon the good will of some one outside the profession that he is not entirely free to act with his professional group. Also the profession cannot easily discipline an individual who has a job of this type. Thus, autonomous professional control becomes difficult to maintain.

POLICY AND PUBLIC OPINION

Social Sanctions. Every institution has some relations with the larger public. It has interests to defend against the world at large; the final interest being its right to exist and to perform the functions which it does perform. The institution is ultimately sanctioned in some fashion by society at large.

THE FAMILY. In the case of the family, the sanction rests in the mores. The family furnishes the undoubtedly right way for people to live together and bring up their children. No one who wishes to establish a family has to justify this way of behaving. He may have to argue his own right to do it. People may

---

1 C. A. Dawson and W. E. Gettys, *Introduction to Sociology* (Rev. ed.; New York: Ronald Press Co., 1935), pp. 101–102.

think he is too young or too old, too poor, or that the mate he has in mind is not of the proper age, social class, race, or religion. His mother may think he should devote himself to her alone. The particular circumstances may be open to question; marriage and family life as such are not.

THE SOCIAL SET. Every family has, also, to keep up a "front" and to gain acceptance within some group of families. It becomes identified with a social class, or with a "social set" in which it plays a role. This role requires effort and conscious thought on the part of some members of the family. The family income will be budgeted among various kinds of expenditure according to the conception the family has of itself and according to the role it wishes to play and the group in which it seeks a place. Although the family as a type of institution is sanctioned by the mores, each separate family has to maintain, by a conscious effort, its place among other families. It has, indeed, a policy, although it is seldom admitted or put into words.

SHARING AUTHORITY. At the same time, as society changes, the functions of the family change. In recent decades many institutions have arisen to take over control of various phases of the lives of children who are still under the guardianship of their parents. A parent is, in most places, no longer free to keep his children from school. Public authority may compel him to have his child inoculated against various diseases. Although general social doctrine still says that the parent is responsible for his children, a specific and conscious public opinion has developed with respect to education and health. Functionaries of other institutions may and do claim authority over the child, even against the will of the parent. This illustrates the manner in which an institution supported by the mores loses part of its authority to other institutions because of a change in public opinion.

Institutional Policy. Other institutions, much more than the family, are impelled to define consciously their place in society and to justify their own existence. The functionaries develop a *policy* of action toward other institutions and toward individual members of society. This policy they state in terms of the values accepted by society at large; that is, in terms of the mores, and of the current social philosophy.

The policy will relate to those matters which the functionaries believe, from their experience, to concern in critical fashion the continued functioning of the institution. They will learn to scent remote dangers, and may consequently make a great to-do about some apparently small matter which might be taken as an unfavorable precedent. Policy, in short, involves seeing the present in the perspective of past and future.

THE CATHOLIC CHURCH. The Catholic church, for instance, thinks of itself as eternal. Its essential problem is to save erring humanity. It must, however, meet the facts of life in a given age. It watches closely the slightest changes of law with respect to education, and interprets each with reference to its belief that education should be controlled by the church and by its knowledge that education under the church produces better Catholics. From time to time, the Pope issues official statements on the relation of the church to the state, on marriage, birth control, and economic problems. In all these, a fine line is drawn between the particular occasion and the general principle or doctrine.

PRECEDENT. Other institutions, although they see their problems in a shorter perspective, develop an equally sharp eye for precedent. A real-estate board may interfere with the methods used in selling a given lot, because they might endanger the whole real-estate business and the place of agents within it. One real-estate board spent a great deal of money opposing a law requiring property owners to clean the snow off sidewalks. This small item was seen as a step toward increased burdens upon real estate. Every such burden presumably decreases the desirability of real estate as an investment.

INTERDEPENDENCE OF INSTITUTIONS. In any policy lies some set of assumptions about the structure of the society in which the institution concerned has its vested place. The medical profession has an obvious interest in foundations, hospitals, medical schools, clinics, and all devices adopted or proposed for supplying medical services to the public. Even institutions which are often in conflict may depend upon one another's existence. The trade-union, which disputes some of the actions and prerogatives of employing corporations, must negotiate contracts with them. The functionaries of universities sometimes have to defend their policies against wealthy people, yet the American university has depended for support upon large gifts from just such people.

INTERNAL COHERENCE. The maintenance of a policy depends upon the inner coherence of the units of the institution. If the functionaries do not have sufficient control to be accepted as official spokesmen, there can be no policy. Even a family cannot maintain its place unless its members can be counted upon to keep up a solid front; a skeleton cannot be kept in the cupboard without discipline.

DOMINANT POINTS OF VIEW. In the case of large institutions, the policy eventuates from a political process by which a dominant and accepted line of action and point of view emerge. In business institutions control is so completely in the hands of the entrepreneurs and managers that they may make policies without much question from lesser employees. The managers are, however, held in check by the customer public. In professional groups, there develops a dominant point of view as to the interests of the profession and the proper way of pursuing them. If a considerable element of the profession refuses to accept this point of view, the policy cannot be carried out.

CURRENT EVENTS. Every institution is sensitive to some order of events with which its functionaries must keep abreast. This is particularly evident in secular institutions, such as the market. The price of a commodity, such as cotton, may be set by thousands of presumably rational judgments by buyers and sellers. Their judgments are based on news which bears on the probable supply of and demand for cotton for the season. Drought, pestilence, floods, and wars may affect supply and demand. Whatever agreements dealers make will be effective only if the agreements accord with the pertinent facts. Lloyd's, an association of insurance brokers in London, long ago developed a weather reporting service for practically the whole world, because this news was pertinent to their business of insuring ships and cargoes. These are examples of news which have no relation to the mores and the public mood; i.e., it is not political news. Other institutions are sensitive primarily to news of the political and moral state of the world. Messengers come to Rome to inform the Pope of social and political events that occur in the most obscure parts of the world. Large institutions develop research bureaus to ferret out facts pertinent to their affairs and to make predictions as to the probable effects on the institution. Whatever their doctrines, the functionaries of institutions must pay heed to the unpleasant facts of life.

THE NEWSPAPER. In this lies some of the significance of the modern newspaper. As Park points out,[1] the reporter who

---

1 R. E. Park, *op. cit.*, chap. 4, "The Natural History of the Newspaper."

gathers and reports events, rather than the editor who comments upon them, has become the important figure in the modern commercial newspaper. The newspaper gathers and publishes news on the basis of which people can act with reference to specialized interests. By what is there reported, people judge which stocks to buy, the price to pay for cotton, or whether the home team is worth betting on. Generally speaking, the actions based on published news are taken in connection with institutions.

Incidentally, the newspaper also records, in its human-interest stories, the protests of individuals against the institutional order of society. Human-interest stories give some expression to the moral pulse of society; they reveal society to itself. This is perhaps the reason why they are suppressed so severely in countries in which it is not considered proper that the general public should have a hand in the making of public policy.

Propaganda and Policy. The carrying out of a policy requires some control over public opinion. In so far as an institution is subject to public opinion, it will carry on propaganda. If an institution has a solid place in the traditions of society, and if its functionaries are accepted as having authority, they can speak dogmatically to those who believe in that authority. In our society, many institutions lack traditional authority, and even those which have it are required to meet the counterpropaganda of conflicting forces. Propaganda is, in its essence, an attempt to get people to think and act as the propagandist would like them to.

Propaganda by secular institutions is not, as a rule, designed to change the popular conceptions of social welfare. It attempts rather to establish an association between the institution and existing values. Thus in our society, propaganda will generally make use of the terms *liberty* and *democracy* and, recently, of the term *social security.*

Propaganda must, however, go much further than mere association with accepted ideas. The functionaries have policies to carry out, and they must win support for them. So they must and do attempt to define the interests of the public. For instance, when chain stores are taxed with being inimical to the interests of small businesses, they respond by telling the public that in addition to their low prices they benefit society by employing many people. Even the churches, whose association with the mores is solid enough, engage in propaganda to show the value of specific programs of action and to convey to a somewhat indifferent world the conviction that the church promotes public welfare as currently conceived.

In a world so free and changing as ours, the ultimate problem of most institutions is that of maintaining the active good will of the public. Sumner[1] went so far as to state that the aim of most modern institutions is to please the common man. In their efforts to do so, the functionaries of certain types of institutions, not too well grounded in the mores, have become expert in gauging and exploiting the mood of the public. Especially must those institutions which live by annual public appeals for funds, continually court good will. Thus, a social agency can by no means rely on a general sentiment in favor of charity; it has annually to prove to the public that the agency is the proper instrument to perform charity, that it knows how it ought to be done, and that the general obligation of persons to help the needy is specifically an obligation to give money at once to this agency. The constant and conscious effort of a great many organized forces to keep the active good will of people gives our society an air of always changing its opinions. This fact means not that we lack mores, but only that the institutions which carry on the organized life of our society are in a state of flux.

FUNDAMENTAL CONCEPTS

We may conclude this section by referring again to certain fundamental concepts relating to social control. The *folkways*, adhered to by the masses of people, are simply the ways of behaving accepted without argument as natural and right. Among these folkways the *mores* are those regarded as peculiarly sacred and necessary to social welfare. *Public opinion*, however, is more conscious, and is the result of argument and differences of opinion as to the means of achieving accepted social aims. The functionaries of institutions attempt in varying degrees, by means of propaganda, to formulate public opinion, and to control the actions of people. In institutions, active leadership and the conscious attempt to regulate human behavior play upon the folkways and popular beliefs of the masses of people.

SELECTED READINGS

Aronson, M. G. "Cardozo's Doctrine of Sociological Jurisprudence," *Journal of Social Philosophy* (1930), 4:5–44.

---

1 W. G. Sumner, *op. cit.*, p. 50.

Brady, R. A. *Business as a System of Power.* New York: Columbia Univ. Press, 1943.

Briggs, Harold E., ed. *Language . . . Man . . . Society: Readings in Communication.* New York: Rinehart & Co., 1949.

Carr-Saunders, A. M., and P. A. Wilson. *The Professions.* Oxford: Clarendon Press, 1933.

Cooley, C. H. *Social Organization.* New York: Chas. Scribner's Sons, 1929. Chaps. 12–14.

Hart, C. W. M. "Industrial Relations Research and Social Theory," *The Canadian Journal of Economics and Political Science* (1949), 15:53–73.

Hughes, H. M. "Human Interest Stories and Democracy," *Public Opinion Quarterly* (1937), 1:73–83.

Lattimore, Owen. *Ordeal by Slander.* Boston: Little, Brown & Co., 1950.

Malinowski, B. Introduction to H. I. Hogbin. *Law and Order in Polynesia.* New York: Harcourt, Brace & Co., 1934.

Park, R. E., and E. W. Burgess. *Introduction to the Science of Sociology,* Chicago: Univ. of Chicago Press, 1924. Chap. 12.

Pound, R. *Social Control through Law.* New Haven: Yale Univ. Press, 1942.

Radcliffe-Brown, A. R. "Primitive Law," *Encyclopaedia of the Social Sciences* (1933), 11:202–206.

Riggs, Fred W. *Pressures on Congress.* New York: King's Crown Press, 1950.

Timasheff, A. N. *The Sociology of Law.* Cambridge: Harvard Univ. Press, 1939.

Additional Readings on Social Institutions

Barnes, H. E. *Social Institutions in an Era of World Upheaval.* New York: Prentice-Hall, 1942.

Burgess, E. W., and H. J. Locke. *The Family, from Instituion to Companionship.* New York: American Book Co., 1945.

Douglass, H. P., and E. de S. Brunner. *The Protestant Church as a Social Institution.* New York: Harper & Bros., 1935.

Golden, C. S., and H. J. Ruttenberg. *Dynamics of Industrial Democracy.* New York: Harper & Bros., 1942.

Hobhouse, L. T., and others. *The Material Culture and Social Institutions of the Simpler Peoples.* London: Chapman & Co., 1915.

Hughes, E. C. *The Growth of an Institution: The Chicago Real Estate Board.* Chicago: Society for Social Research, 1931.

Kennedy, A. J., and others. *Social Settlements in New York City.* New York: Columbia Univ. Press, 1935.

Klapper, J. T., and C. Y. Glock. "Trial by Newspaper," *Scientific American* (1949), 180:16–21.

Lee, Alfred M. *The Daily Newspaper in America: The Evolution of a Social Instrument.* New York: Macmillan Co., 1937.

National Resources Committee. *Structure of the American Economy.* Washington: Government Printing Office, 1939.

Noyes, C. Reinold. *The Institution of Property.* New York: Longmans, Green & Co., 1936.

Warner, W. L., and J. O. Low. *The Social System of the Modern Factory.* New Haven: Yale Univ. Press, 1946.

Webb, Beatrice and Sidney. *Methods of Social Study.* New York: Longmans, Green & Co., 1932.

Young, Pauline V. *Scientific Social Surveys and Research.* New York: Prentice-Hall, 1942. Chap. 16, "A Study of a Social Institution."

Part Six

—

Socialization
of the
Individual

By

ALFRED McCLUNG LEE
Brooklyn College

PART SIX

SOCIALIZATION OF THE INDIVIDUAL
By Alfred McClung Lee

TOPICS

Chapter XXX. Individual and Environment.
"Original Nature."
Environment and Nurture.
Personality and Personality Change.

Chapter XXXI. Child and Family.
The Person in an Evolving Institution.
The Family Drama.
Childhood.
Adolescence.

Chapter XXXII. Courtship, Marriage, Divorce.
Types of Marriage.
Courtship Customs.
American Marriage Patterns.
Separation.
Desertion and Divorce.

Chapter XXXIII. Roles.
Societal Roles.
Group, Class, and Caste Roles.
Personal-External Roles.
Personal-Self Roles.
Roles in Social Movements.
Role Change and Vertical Mobility.

Chapter XXXIV. Deviants.
Types of Deviants.
The Deficient and the Deranged.
The Criminal.
The Famous.
Leaders and Social Causation.

Chapter XXXV. The Person and Social Policy.
The Undistinguished and the Unreasonable.
A Society of Free Men.
The Role of Sociology.

CHAPTER THIRTY

INDIVIDUAL AND ENVIRONMENT

Perspectives upon Society. Sociology provides two major perspectives upon society. It furnishes (1) a *societal* view of the structure, functionings, and changes in the patterns of interrelationship between men, groups, and classes in a tribe, nation, country, and the "great society." It also helps more specifically to answer the question, What about *me?* In other words, how am *I* related to society? What has society done to *me?* What can *I* do to and with society? In grappling with these questions, sociology and social psychology have begun to work out—with the help of psychology and psychiatry—(2) a more adequate *personal* orientation to society. This perspective has already demonstrated that it is much more accurate and useful than one derived solely from traditional preconceptions and personal interests.

In the preceding sections of this outline, the authors deal with the contributions of sociology to both of these perspectives, with somewhat more emphasis upon the societal. In the present section, it is proposed to concentrate upon the latter, the personal viewpoint or orientation. In so doing, a means is provided to bring together into a different synthesis strands from the earlier sections as well as to digest other sociological findings concerning the roles of the individual in society.

Individual and Society. An individual matures physically, accumulates habits that canalize his drives and help him to cope with his needs and wishes, and thus gradually comes to function in due course as an adult person, a product and a continuing illustration of the processes of socialization at work. He is, to use the terminology of Leo W. Simmons, in *Sun Chief* (1942), a *creature* of his biological descent and of his physical and human environment, and a *carrier*, a *creator*, and a *manipulator* of group and societal culture. The first four chapters of this section

(XXX–XXXIII) treat of the evolving person as a creature and a carrier of culture. Chapters XXXIV and XXXV tell of ways in which a person may become a creator of cultural elements, of societal variations, and Chapters XXXIII–XXXV also outline analyses of his potentialities as a manipulator.

Scientific Approaches to Personality. Psychologists and psychiatrists as well as sociologists study this gradual conversion of a generalized organism into an adult personality with a complex mechanism for thought and communication. The fields investigated by these specialists overlap, but their contributions provide invaluable cross-stimulation obtainable only through such overlapping from different starting points. The psychologists, in their researches, approach the socialization processes from what, for the sake of simplicity, may be called the psychic or neurological viewpoint, from within the subjects' skins, as it were. Sociologists, on the other hand, begin with the societal aggregate and stress interpersonal rather than individual aspects. Social psychologists, who may regard themselves as either sociologists or psychologists, have done much to bring together such contributions by working in the overlapping area. And psychiatrists find that their clinical needs bring them more and more to the utilization of a synthesis of both approaches.

"ORIGINAL NATURE"

The Individual. The late Russell Gordon Smith liked to remind his Columbia undergraduates that each had arrived in this world "a polymorphous-perverse little ape with a billion years of biological evolution precipitated, so to speak, in your dimpled organism." Other than such generalized equipment, with potentialities for maturation that depend in part upon the influences of physical and human environment, each had little else—no clothes, modesty, language, food tastes, or dexterities, and certainly no notions about aesthetics, morality, religion, and science. "You came with no higher desires than to have your capacious belly filled with milk and your somatic and visceral itches scratched by loving hands. . . . Think of yourself as a bawling and puking brat with your nose and bladder in perennial flux, and then look at yourself now."

The term individual as used technically is a biopsychological conception. As Charles Horton Cooley wrote in 1902 in his *Human Nature and the Social Order* (rev. ed., 1922), "A separate individual is an abstraction unknown to experience, and so likewise is society when regarded as something apart from individuals." An individual, according to E. T. Hiller in his *Principles of Sociology* (1933), is an "organism with its innate physical and mental capacities. We are individuals at birth, but we become persons when we acquire status in a group, a reputation, a role, and a conception of our place among our associates and even among our contemporaries generally."

Heredity. A socialized individual cannot be sliced up, like a cadaver, and have any great meaning for purposes of social psychological investigation. Neither can one select out factors or traits and label some products of "original nature" and some the results exclusively of "environment" or "nurture." From inception the physical environment and from birth the physical and social environment constantly interact with the individual's existing potentialities and characteristics. "The so-called hereditary factors can only be acquired in response to an environment, and likewise the so-called acquired factors can only be secured by a modification of already existing structure, which in the last analysis is hereditary structure."[1] This is not to support old wives' tales concerning the transmission of acquired characteristics and the role of "prenatal influences" in the postnatal life of a child, how little Johnnie became a physician because his mother nursed a sick aunt while carrying him.

To a sociologist, an individual's or mankind's biological background is significant in three particular ways: (1) to provide, in relationship to typical human environment, a definition of *typical psychological equipment;* (2) to elucidate the nature of *race differences;* and (3) to contribute to an understanding of *individual differences.* In all of these areas, the biologists, physical anthropologists, and psychologists have offered useful orientation to the sociologists, and the sociologists in turn have contributed substantially to our knowledge of typical psychological equipment through cross-cultural analyses and comparisons. These findings are outlined quite briefly in the following.

Typical Psychological Equipment. A variety of efforts have been made to reduce to compact proportions, to a formula that would be useful to social scientists, the salient aspects of the

---

[1] Leonard Carmichael, "Heredity and Environment: Are They Antithetical?" *Journal of Abnormal and Social Psychology* (1925), 20:257.

human being's psychic outfit. The proliferation of lists of "instincts" early in this century, stimulated by William McDougall's *Introduction to Social Psychology* (1908), brought sharp criticism and deflation from a number but most substantially from L. L. Bernard, in his *Instinct* (1924). In place of such atomizations of human motives and drives, John Dewey, George H. Mead, and Charles H. Cooley among the social psychologists and Sigmund Freud and his followers among the psychiatrists gave emphasis to a more organic or "whole" view of human urges, drives, motives, or whatever the aspects of the libido or vital force might be labeled.

PSYCHIATRIC CONCLUSIONS ON NEURAL EQUIPMENT. Recognizing the basic fact of the irritability of living matter, more recent "whole" views of drives begin with a pleasure-pain theory which may be elaborated in the manner of Freud into one of frustration and aggression. Man, like other organisms, seeks to prolong or repeat pleasure-giving stimuli and to avoid or combat painful ones. Painful stimuli make for frustrations that turn the organism toward overt aggressions or, where that is not possible or expedient, toward "boiling inwardly." With this background, Freud then related the canalizations of the individual's libido to his life-history. Through the conditioning of response mechanisms by experiences of pleasure and pain, the libido becomes canalized variously at the successive stages of maturation which he labeled as extending from the infantile (oral and anal-urethral) to the adult (heterosexual), and he ascribed colorations of motivation and personality in the adult to the "normal" (for a culture) and deviant patterns of maturational experience.

That such a theory touches upon "shameful" matters should not prevent us from understanding it. In his *Sex and Repression in Savage Society* (1927), Bronislaw Malinowski disagreed with Freud, but he praised the "open treatment of sex and of various shameful meannesses and vanities in man—the very things for which psycho-analysis is most hated and reviled." This, he said, is "of the greatest value to science, and should endear psychoanalysis, above all to the student of man; that is, if he wants to study his subject without irrelevant trappings and even without the fig leaf." As Cooley noted in his *Human Nature and the Social Order* (1922), "The human mind is indeed a cave swarming with strange forms of life, most of them unconscious and unilluminated. Unless we can understand something as to how the motives that issue from this obscurity are generated, we can hardly hope to foresee or control them."

CROSS-CULTURAL CONCLUSIONS ON DRIVES. With a pleasure-pain theory similar to that of Freud, but on the basis of cross-cultural sociological analyses rather than the consideration of psychiatric clinical data, W. G. Sumner and A. G. Keller concluded that for sociological purposes the generalized vital drive may be thought of as being canalized by maturation under environmental conditions into hunger, sex-love, ghost-fear (anxiety in the presence of the unknown), and vanity (related to Freud's narcissism), as they indicate in their *Science of Society* (1927).

OTHER DRIVE AND WISH THEORIES. The somewhat more extensive classification of Gardner and Lois B. Murphy and T. M. Newcomb, in their *Experimental Social Psychology* (1937), is based upon physiological, cross-cultural, and social psychological materials. It includes visceral drives (hunger, thirst, air-getting, temperature regulation, sexual drives, etc.), activity drives (exercise, rest, perseveration, rhythm, novelty, exploration, etc.), aesthetic drives (color, tone, specific qualities of taste, smell, and touch, rhythm, etc.), emotions (fear, rage, disgust, shame, etc.), and social drives (need for companionship and affection, need to give attention and affection to others, quest for status and prestige, etc.). Of a somewhat more derived sort is W. I. Thomas's list of four wishes, set forth in Jennings, Watson, Meyer, and Thomas, *Suggestions of Modern Science concerning Education* (1917). His four wishes are: (1) for new experience, (2) for security, (3) for recognition, and (4) for response. But in using any list, as the Murphys and Newcomb note, one must recognize that the labels "merely indicate convenient abstractions from the infinitely complex flux of life activity," from an indivisible whole.

Race Differences. As Humphrey and Reuter indicate in Chapters V and XV of this outline, the teachings of scientists concerning psychological differences among men of diverse racial stocks are useful chiefly in deflating popular allegations of differences. Such claims are based upon *ethnocentrism* (ego-gratification through overevaluating the qualities of one's own people). *Existing evidence points to no significant inborn neurological differences, either in character or capacities, among the racial stocks of mankind.*

Individual Differences. The fact that individual men and women in all tribes, peoples, and nations range, for reasons of "original nature" and nurture, between rather wide extremes in terms of any set of psychological criteria, has considerable sociological significance. In capacities of one sort or another, in interests, in normality, the large bulk of a group usually falls into an "average" category, and small numbers of superior and inferior deviants or deviants in a number of directions can then be observed.

The causes of such variation are deeply imbedded in the nature-nurture problem. More gifted children may be found in the homes of professionals than of unskilled laborers. Why is this? Extreme eugenists claim that it is due to the superior hereditary endowment of the professional families and to the "poor human stock" of the unskilled. Without becoming environmental extremists, sociologists point to the home, economic, and social advantages and opportunities of the children of professionals. In this, too, the roles of "contacts" and of the encouragement provided by successful and familiar models should not be overlooked. A similar analysis can be made of the fact that more juvenile delinquents *become a matter of police record* from slum homes than from homes in the better neighborhoods. Not only should the deprivation of advantageous home, economic, and social factors be mentioned in this connection, but it also is pertinent that the "better" families are more likely to be given the opportunity to keep their delinquencies out of police records. In both these illustrations, above all, both nature and nurture make contributions. As Edward C. Jandy notes, in his book on Cooley (1942), "The idea that mind is social, that it arises out of the social process in its genesis and extends into that process as far as the individual's experience reaches, makes mind something more than the functional aspect of the nervous system."

Sociologists are interested in individual variations in capacity and character because such deviations figure in theories of leadership, genius, agitation, group and class structure, mental defects and abnormalities, crime, criminals, and other antisocial activity. Humphrey deals with the latter as social problems in the first part of this outline. These matters are related to the socialization of the individual in Chapters XXXIII and XXXIV below.

ENVIRONMENT AND NURTURE

Environmental Conditioning. From inception, as it is noted above, the human being is subject to influences other than those carried within its cell walls. These influences are at first physical and chemical and then, after birth, come to include in addition geographical (climate, fauna, and flora), interpersonal, and cultural factors. Studies of feral folk and of identical twins, of psychopathic cases and of diverse tribes and cultures have shed more and more light upon these postnatal environmental influences, even though, as Mark A. May so well says, you can't "drive a fence through the individual" and segregate the results of such influences from those called biological.

FERAL FOLK—"wolf children" and other "wild" and isolated boys and girls and even men and women—are human beings who have grown in isolation, with animals, or with few socializing influences. They dramatize the tremendous role of culture and interpersonal relationships in human behavior and especially in the growth and definition of personality. The feral folk, when found, behave like animals or, as in the case of the isolated girl studied by Kingsley Davis, appear to be deaf and dumb, "immobile, indifferent to those around her, and completely apathetic." Understanding human contacts have usually brought about striking changes.

IDENTICAL TWINS, especially those reared under dissimilar conditions or conditions dissimilar in well-indicated respects, provide examples of the manner in which biologically similar beings react to disparate environmental influences. "In all probability," Otto Klineberg observes in his *Social Psychology* (1940) on the basis of data on identical twins, "intelligence is to a certain degree inherited along family lines, although there is no doubt that social and environmental factors exercise a constant and important influence."

RECONSTRUCTIONS OF THE LIFE-HISTORIES OF PSYCHOPATHIC CASES, neurotics and psychotics, especially when such reconstructions can be verified at significant points, indicate much of help in understanding "normal" or average people through providing descriptions of biologically and/or environmentally stimulated deviations from the "normal." They are not only more available than similar details concerning the rest of the population, but their deviations help to highlight characteristics of "normal" people.

CROSS-CULTURAL INVESTIGATIONS have yielded, from observations of many and diverse tribes, conclusions regarding psychological and sociological elements entering (1) into all cultures known or (2) into cultures existing under given geographical and historical conditions, and (3) knowledge of the ranges of variability in patterned feeling and behavior. Some such conclusions have been touched upon, and others will enter into subsequent discussions.

Personal-Social Conditioning. Hughes, in the preceding section, Chapter XXVIII, has related one aspect of culture— social institutions—to the person, the socialized individual. When culture's impact upon personality development is viewed in more detail, with the addition of what else is implied in Kimball Young's term, *personal-social conditioning*, the full significance of the notion of the person as a creature and a carrier of culture traits becomes the more clear. Russell Gordon Smith put it this way in his *Fugitive Papers* (1930): "nine-tenths of all you do or say or think or feel from the time you get up in the morning until the time you go to bed at night is done and said and thought and felt, not in independent self-expression, but in uncritical, unconscious conformity with rules, regulations, group habits, standards, codes, styles, and sanctions that were in existence long before you were born." The "nine-tenths" is of course a rough guess; the fraction might be larger.

Let us define briefly terms for some of the aspects of culture and personal behavior that are to be used in the balance of this section. Some of these terms have been used before in other sections of this outline, but it will be well to bring them into the present perspective.

Conventions, Folkways, and Practices. W. I. Thomas, in his *Source Book for Social Origins* (1909), defines culture as "that complex whole which includes knowledge, belief, art, morals, law, custom, and other capabilities and habits acquired by man as a member of society." In Chapter I of this outline, Humphrey relates culture to theories of social problems, and in Chapter XVII, Reuter defines and outlines the characteristics of culture, chiefly from a societal or general point of view. To relate culture more specifically to the socialization of the individual, it can also be treated segmentally and defined in terms of its personal and group aspects.

When culture is viewed in terms of separate traits or segments, it is well to bear in mind that each such trait is an integral part of larger patterns or complexes, patterns of personal behavior (roles) and of social structure (institutions and associations, classes and groups). With this in mind, the terms conventions, folkways, and practices are defined as respectively the societal, group and class, and personal versions of culture patterns that are related to similar interests, wishes, needs.

Conventions are traditional abstractions of similar behavior patterns (verbal and other) exhibited by members of various groups or at least presumed to be esteemed and adhered to by various groups in a society. Conventions, in turn, provide norms for group folkways and individual practices. The general language of a country, the "dictionary language" of a small abridged dictionary, not including colloquialisms and other special words and terms, is a large section of a society's conventions.

Folkways are group typifications based upon the relatively similar behavior group members exhibit in the presence of similar stimuli. They are patterns of behavior, more or less modeled after the conventions, which have become common and customary in a group or class. Group versions of a common language, whether dialects, trade jargons, professionalisms, or other group mannerisms, emphasize differences between the linguistic segment of our conventions and folkways.

Practices are socially exemplified behavior patterns as adapted and taken on by individuals. They are the personal counterparts of folkways and conventions plus the results of peculiar individual experiences and somewhat unique or variant inferences and interpretations. They are more or less permanent elements of personality. The similarities and differences between "dictionary language," a given group's ways of saying things, and a given person's mannerisms of speech illustrate the relationships of practices to conventions and folkways.

Morals, Mores, and Habits. To certain of the three types of trait patterns—conventions, folkways, and practices—society, social groups, and persons attach a greater degree of compulsion. These more imperative societal, group and class, and personal patterns are named respectively morals, mores, and habits.

Morals are conventions to which have been given a judgment of societal welfare. They are traditional generalities concerning right, wrong, duties, rights, and taboos handed down in a society and frequently formalized into sets of commandments, codes of ethics, or canons of ethical principles. They contain large elements of asceticism, humanitarianism, and formalism or ritualism. They dominate the teachings of societal surrogates

—parents, ministers, teachers—even though they are frequently at odds with the group mores of such surrogates and of the groups served by them: "Do as I say, not as I do!" Morals represent crystallizations of a society's traditional aspirations as vaguely defined and somewhat colored by dominant group and class mores, but with significant rationalistic concessions to the dominated. They are chiefly useful in shaping the superegos of the young and in providing the main staples for propagandists —glittering generalities and name-calling symbols, righteous justifications and condemnations, suitably and variously interpreted, for social institutions, functionaries, roles, and courses of action. Morals have no necessary congruity with mores of constituent groups or with habits of individuals. Such subjects as theology, ethics, and traditional—but not scientific—social science concern themselves to a great measure with working out rationalizations between morals and group mores.

Mores are folkways that have had added to them, as Sumner stated in *Folkways* (1907), "a judgment that they are conducive to societal welfare." R. E. Park and E. W. Burgess, in their *Introduction to the Science of Sociology* (1924), note that "Under the influence of the mores men act typically, and so representatively, not as individuals but as members of a group." Folkways and especially mores define the characteristics of social roles and institutions as they are acted out. They are crystallizations of the expediencies of group experience. Conventions and morals provide façades for social institutions and cloaks for social roles, about as influential "internally" as façades and cloaks usually are.

Habits are practices the taking on of which has been accomplished by some form of real or fancied, actual or potential, societal and group compulsion. They are the personalized counterparts of mores and morals, the corresponding group and societal patterns. They include the results of peculiar individual experiences and somewhat unique or variant inferences.

The motto, "Honesty is the best policy," is a useful illustration of these three terms. As stated, it is a part of the morals of our society. Modified to "Honesty is the best policy, but business is business" or to "Honesty is the best policy, but labor has to look out for labor," one has a *mos* (singular of *mores*), an example of group adaptation of a moral. Further modifications in either mos formula through the addition of such words as these, "but in *this* case I've got a higher loyalty to myself," supplies a habit pattern that might be interpreted by others in any given instance as shrewd, expected, peculiar, or criminal.[1]

COMPARED WITH LINTON'S CLASSIFICATION. Ralph Linton, in his *Study of Man* (1936), without relating culture adequately to social structure and to the socialization of the individual, advances a theory that culture in a society consists of "universals," "alternatives," and "specialties." His "universals" are roughly equivalent to societal morals, as used here, but his "alternatives" suggest far too great a range of choice when contrasted with social realities. His "specialties" resemble certain group folkways, but his conception overlooks the variant versions of similar cultural elements existing on the societal, group and class, and personal levels.

PERSONALITY AND PERSONALITY CHANGE

Personality. Kimball Young, in his *Social Psychology* (1944), defines personality "as the more or less integrated body of habits, attitudes, traits, and ideas of an individual as these are organized externally into specific and general roles and statuses and internally around self-consciousness and the concept of the self, and around the ideas, values, and purposes which are related to motives, roles, and status." Young summarizes by saying that personality has two aspects, "role and status with respect to behavior affecting others, and selfhood, ego, or life organization with regard to internal motivation, goals, and ways of viewing one's own and others' behavior." In the terms used here, the external aspect of personality is defined by practices and habits which represent personalized versions of folkways and mores, conventions and morals. Depending upon our degree of intimacy with a person, the man-as-he-seems may be known in terms of his roles as defined by conventions-morals, folkways-mores, or practices-habits. The number of roles taken on by a person depends upon the number of statuses he holds in various groups and in society generally.

Self. As Young points out, self is the internal aspect of personality. Cooley noted that the self is always a social self, a "looking-glass self," and in his *Human Nature and the Social Order* (1922) he assigned it "three principal elements: the imagination of our appearance to the other persons; the imagination

---

1 Digested from A. M. Lee, "Levels of Culture as Levels of Social Generalization," *American Sociological Review* (1945), 10:485–495.

of his judgment of that appearance; and some sort of self-feeling, such as pride or mortification." George H. Mead, in his *Mind, Self & Society* (1934), concluded that self-consciousness arises through "taking the role of the other" and related the social compulsions behind morals and mores to the psychological role of a "generalized other," a conception resembling somewhat Freud's superego. Freud perceived three phases of self which he called superego, ego, and id. The *superego* is roughly equivalent to that which is ordinarily labeled conscience, formed especially through early training in the morals. The superego is partly conscious, partly sunk in the subconscious. The *ego* is the conscious phase of self, the part of the self which attempts to understand and cope with external and internal realities and phantasms. The *id* is the subconscious, that to which Cooley chiefly referred when he spoke of "a cave swarming with strange forms of life, most of them unconscious and unilluminated." Here are elements of the superego, past experiences, old fears, submerged temporarily or permanently beneath the level of consciousness but still operative in motivation.

How Do Personalities Change?   John Dollard [1] believes that there are "at least five situations in which the habits of individuals may change." He mentions "(1) the situation of culture change in the society, (2) life dilemmas in social group, (3) the psychiatric learning situation, (4) the psychoanalytic learning situation, (5) the situation of the clinical group." Of these five situations, the first two might well be elaborated here. It should be understood (*a*) that culture change in a society may affect certain groups and classes more than others, (*b*) that the form of the conventions and morals—especially their symbolic portrayals in words and otherwise—may give every appearance of permanence while the "content" or the functioning folkways and mores of constituent groups may have changed, and (*c*) "life dilemmas in social group" should be thought of as including the personality adaptations necessitated during any typical life-history as the person leaves and enters groups or statuses in groups. As such changes take place in a personality's externalities, concomitant internal changes in the self may be anticipated.

---

1 "The Acquisition of New Social Habits," in Ralph Linton, ed., *The Science of Man in the World Crisis* (New York: Columbia Univ. Press, 1945), pp. 442–64, pp. 442–3 quoted.

SELECTED READINGS

Alexander, Franz. *Fundamentals of Psychoanalysis.* New York: W. W. Norton Co., 1948.

Allport, Gordon W. *Personality: A Psychological Interpretation.* New York: Henry Holt & Co., 1937. Chaps. 4–5, 7.

Bogardus, Emory S. *Fundamentals of Social Psychology.* 4th ed. New York: Appleton-Century-Crofts, 1950.

Bossard, James H. S., and Eleanor S. Boll. *Ritual in Family Living.* Philadelphia: Univ. of Pennsylvania Press, 1950.

Britt, Stewart H. *Social Psychology of Modern Life.* Rev. ed. New York: Rinehart & Co., 1949.

Child, C. M. *Physiological Foundations of Behavior.* New York: Henry Holt & Co., 1924.

Cooley, Charles H. *Human Nature and the Social Order.* Rev. ed. New York: Chas. Scribner's Sons, 1922.

Coutu, Walter. *Emergent Human Nature: A Symbolic Field Interpretation.* New York: A. A. Knopf, 1949.

Davis, Kingsley. "A Case of Extreme Social Isolation of a Child," *American Journal of Sociology* (1940), 45:554–565.

Dewey, John. *Human Nature and Conduct.* New York: Henry Holt & Co., 1922.

Dollard, John. *Criteria for the Life History.* New Haven: Yale Univ. Press, 1935.

Dollard, John, and Neal E. Miller. *Personality and Psychotherapy.* New York: McGraw-Hill Book Co., 1950.

DuBois, Cora. *The People of Alor.* Minneapolis, Minn.: Univ. of Minnesota Press, 1944.

Dunlap, Knight. *Habits: Their Making and Unmaking.* New York: Liveright, 1932. Chaps. 1–2, 5, 9.

Faris, Ellsworth. *The Nature of Human Nature.* New York: McGraw-Hill Book Co., 1937.

Freud, Sigmund. *New Introductory Lectures on Psycho-Analysis.* Trans. by W. J. H. Sprott. New York: W. W. Norton & Co., 1933.

Gesell, Arnold. "Growth Potentials of the Human Infant," *The Scientific Monthly* (1949), 68:252–256.

Hilgard, E. R., and D. G. Marquis. *Conditioning and Learning.* New York: D. Appleton-Century Co., 1940. Chap. 12.

Horney, Karen. *New Ways in Psychoanalysis.* New York: W. W. Norton & Co., 1939. Esp. chaps., 10, 13.

Horney, Karen. *Our Inner Conflicts.* New York: W. W. Norton & Co., 1945.

James, William. *Habit.* New York: Henry Holt & Co., 1914.

Jennings, H. S. *The Biological Basis of Human Nature.* New York: W. W. Norton & Co., 1930.

Kluckhohn, C., and H. A. Murray, eds. *Personality in Nature, Society, and Culture.* New York: A. A. Knopf, 1948.

Linton, Ralph. *The Cultural Background of Personality.* New York: Appleton-Century-Crofts, Inc., 1945.

Maguinness, O. D. *Environment and Heredity.* New York: T. Nelson & Sons, 1940.

Mead, George H. *Mind, Self & Society.* Ed. by Charles W. Morris. Chicago: Univ. of Chicago Press, 1934. Part 3.

Mead, Margaret. *Sex and Temperament in Three Primitive Societies.* New York: Wm. Morrow & Co., 1935.

Menninger, Karl A. *The Human Mind.* 3rd ed. New York: A. A. Knopf, 1945.

Miller, Neal E., and John Dollard. *Social Learning and Imitation.* New Haven: Yale Univ. Press, 1941. Chaps. 8–13.

Newcomb, T. M., and W. W. Charters, Jr. *Social Psychology.* New York: Dryden Press, 1950.

Newcomb, T. M., E. L. Hartley, and others, eds. *Readings in Social Psychology.* New York: Henry Holt & Co., 1947.

Park, Robert E., and E. W. Burgess. *Introduction to the Science of Sociology.* 2nd ed. Chicago: Univ. of Chicago Press, 1924. Esp. chaps. 2, 4–6.

Rosett, Joshua. *The Mechanism of Thought, Imagery, and Hallucination.* New York: Columbia Univ. Press, 1939.

Sherif, M. *Outline of Social Psychology.* New York: Harper & Bros., 1948.

Smith, Russell Gordon. *Fugitive Papers.* New York: Columbia Univ. Press, 1930. Pp. 3–39.

Stern, Bernhard J. "Concerning the Distinction between the Social and the Cultural," *Social Forces* (1929), 8:264–271.

Vaughan, W. F. *Social Psychology.* New York: Odyssey Press, 1948.

Wechsler, David. *The Range of Human Capacities.* Baltimore: William & Wilkins Co., 1935.

Woodard, James W. "The Role of Fictions in Cultural Organization," *Transactions of the New York Academy of Sciences* (1944), 6:311–344.

Woodworth, R. S. *Heredity and Environment: A Critical Survey of Recently Published Material on Twins and Foster Children.* New York: Social Science Research Council, 1941.

Young, Kimball. *Social Psychology.* 2nd ed. New York: Appleton-Century-Crofts, Inc., 1944.

CHAPTER THIRTY-ONE

CHILD AND FAMILY

The Family in Socialization. The socialization of the individual typically begins in the family, as that institution may be defined by a given culture, and it continues largely under family domination during the individual's most impressionable years. Mother, father, and siblings, or substitutes for any or all of them, provide the most decisive mold for the individual's personality, the consequences of which persist throughout life. Family members accomplish this (1) through exemplifying customary interaction patterns (culture, in this sense viewed as defining the "family drama") and carrying on their spontaneous interactions with each other in situations as they arise; (2) through furnishing the "looking glasses" out of which the "looking-glass self" develops; (3) through establishing the "right" models for generalized and specific group and societal roles; and (4) through serving as surrogates of society and of various groups and classes in making the new person a unit in the complex of culture series represented by the family's members.

Since the cultural definition of the family drama differs from society to society and through time in a given society, it will be useful to touch briefly first upon the nature of the family as a social institution, an elaboration in terms of socialization of points made by Hughes in Chapter XXV. The discussion will then turn to the functioning of the family and the significance of the family drama, then to sociological aspects of childhood and adolescence. This chapter emphasizes the person as the *creature* of society through the mechanism chiefly of the family, of what W. Lloyd Warner calls the "family of orientation" (one's parents, siblings, and self). The next chapter, taking up courtship, marriage, and divorce, deals more with the person as the *carrier* of culture through the family medium, through what Warner calls the "family of procreation" (one's spouse, children, and self).

THE PERSON IN AN EVOLVING INSTITUTION

Rate of Change. Society's basic life-conditions change, and its institutions adjust to them with more or less delay, after more or less painful and pleasant lack of adjustment. Elements more closely related to individual existence—matters of sustenance and domination—change most immediately to meet the tests of efficiency and workability in terms of new conditions of social contact, invention, and physical environment. Religious elements, on the other hand, come down to us with comparatively gradual modification from a remote past. The family as procreator and orientor has a rate of change somewhere between the extremes of economics and religion, with both of which it is interrelated. Rates of cultural evolution or adaptation differ, too, for various classes and groups in a society, and for the moral and moretic versions of culture.

Consanguine and Conjugal Family Organization. The historical foundations of the American family institution may be found in the folk culture of western Europe and its antecedents. The tribes Julius Caesar found and the more recent peasantry from whom Americans more directly have sprung emphasized patriarchal controls, childbearing, and child rearing. In addition, their family organization performed important economic, educational, religious, recreational, and more broadly societal functions. When Christianity succeeded earlier forms of worship, it at first continued to stress a strong moral-religious interpretation of the family's role, and this included doctrines of otherworldliness, sexual sin, and low status for women. Under such conditions, the consanguine family organization played a highly important part in locating the conjugal unit (parents and children) in the social structure and in assuring it some degree of stability.

As better methods of transportation and agriculture developed, the consanguine family changed in character and began to diminish in cohesiveness and extensiveness. The conjugal family became the predominant and characteristic unit, with increasingly important economic, political, religious, and other social ties outside consanguine limits.

The Modern Family. With the rise of industrialism, urbanism, and gadgetism, even more drastic changes in family organization appeared. The husband's work locus moved away from the family home or farm, sometimes many miles away to a factory or office building. The extensive primary group controls of the ancient consanguine family and of the more recent farm modifications thereof gave way to urban anonymity, to new types of less immediate and compulsive social relationships. Hollingshead has outlined the ecological nature of these changes in Chapter XI.

RISE OF COMPETING INSTITUTIONS. Educational, religious. recreational, and other social functions drifted rapidly into the hands of specialists, carried on to a great extent or exclusively outside of the home. Even births and deaths were arranged to take place, when possible, in hospitals, with burials from "funeral homes." With the appearance of modern birth control techniques and a rise in the proportionate cost per child for delivery, care, and rearing, the conjugal family unit has continued to decrease in size. Only some one-half of modern urban families in the United States have children living at home, and the average is much smaller than a generation or more ago. As a result of family size and the delay of marriage due to economic and status considerations, the affectional elements in family relationships have been emphasized to the extreme, and the status of women has risen rapidly. The latter has also been aided by the increasing ability of women to obtain remunerative employment.

PERSONALITY-FORMING FUNCTIONS STILL SIGNIFICANT. Even though much of the educational function has been shifted from the family, W. F. Ogburn and M. F. Nimkoff note in *Sociology* (1940) that "the personality functions of the modern family are among its most important ones." In the smaller families, children spend more time during their most impressionable years with parents and less with siblings and playmates, and the responsibility thus placed on the parents has become very great.

In the family institution, as it has evolved, its member persons have gradually gotten somewhat different personalities from it. The clashes between grandmother's and mother's ideas on raising the baby dramatize somewhat, among other considerations, the rate of change, as well as the greater susceptibility of youth to the modifying influences of changed life-conditions.

THE FAMILY DRAMA

Range of Variations. In view of the wide range of conditions of family organization to be found in the United States between rural, suburban, and urban areas and among Americans of various ethnic and racial backgrounds, it is difficult to generalize about the patterning of the family drama. And when one takes into consideration the even greater differences in other parts of the world, the difficulty becomes extreme. Even in the United States, examples of the patriarchal father and the matriarchal mother, of the closely integrated consanguine family group and of tiny two- and three-member conjugal units may be found. In an outline way, however, some tenable generalizations may be offered about socialization processes in the human family and concerning its examples in the United States.

Family Member Roles. As a child grows up in a family, he sees his mother and father and to a less extent his siblings, or their substitutes, as stock players in a drama. The mother and father, as he understands them, furnish basic conceptions of woman and man, wife and husband. Typically both mother and father in our society attempt to give the child an idealistic moral rather than a moretic picture of their roles. The interaction patterns that they follow day after day sink into the child's mind, with all their pleasures and frustrations, anxieties and opportunities for expression, and these patterns of affection and struggle, co-operation, competition, and conflict come to characterize his thinking about interpersonal relationships. Extra-familial characters may also figure in these mental formulations. In later life, the person has a tendency to place new associates into old family drama roles and then to attempt to carry out old and familiar interaction patterns with them, more or less adapted, modified, and rationalized for the occasion. If such a new associate as a wife does not perform the role "properly," her failures may become a source of friction, the causes for which may be quite mysterious to her.

Roles of Family Members in Other Institutions. To change the metaphor slightly, the members of the family "stock company" present themselves upon the family "stage" in roles of other institutions and groups as well as in their basic ones as family members. These roles are largely defined for their wearer in terms of group folkways and mores, but the father or mother or sibling usually attempts to present them to the other group members as they are defined by conventions and morals, in terms of the societal cloaks of the roles. A specific mother, therefore, may exemplify *the* clubwoman, artist, community or church leader, professional woman. A specific father may illustrate *the* postage stamp collector, bricklayer, boxer, professional man, lodge potentate, soldier, political leader, church dignitary. These models aid in the moral training of the child's superego, the direction of ambition, and the assurance of a degree of invidious distinction and thus something of what passes for psychological security.

Societal Surrogates. Especially in their ambivalent attitudes toward their social roles, parents serve automatically to make themselves societal surrogates, instructional representatives of society. The contrasts between moral and moretic roles, outlined more fully in Chapter XXXIII, arouse sufficiently the guilt feelings of parents (based upon their own morals-dominated superegos) to make them want to present their roles and many other ideas about society in moral terms. It has been as a part of this whole moralistic (ascetic and idealistic) situation that parents in our society so long disliked to tell their children facts of sex, even of sex hygiene. Such revelations went behind and, they apparently thought, tended to debase the societal façade or moral cloak of the roles of motherhood and fatherhood.

Group Surrogates. Children gradually mature, and facts present themselves to them that demand explanation, facts the morals do not recognize. Thus mothers eventually find themselves compelled to "have a heart-to-heart talk with daughter." Fathers eventually find it wise to pass along to their sons bits of expedient wisdom, the folkways and mores of masculine groups, of their trade or profession, of political and social life. In such efforts to usher the child from the moral absolutes of childhood into group mores, parents are acting as group surrogates, educational representatives of groups to which they belong. Because of the social distance morals may interpose in certain areas between parents and children, group surrogates may be persons other than parents or even other than professional teachers. The latter, except in trade and professional schools, are likely to perform chiefly as societal surrogates.

From the foregoing, it is not to be inferred that children learn little but idealized patterns from their parents, but what they do learn is presented to them in a moral context. The Murphys and Newcomb, in their *Experimental Social Psychology* (1937), conclude that the "child takes over the patterns of behavior of those whom he loves, sometimes those whose strength he envies." This, they say, is a "*major clue to the process of becoming like one's parents and other associates, and of taking over the culture of the group.*" This taking on of culture may be in the sense of preparing a predisposition, not in all cases of a complete assimilation of a pattern; it constitutes many times an emotional conditioning rather than the acceptance of cultural detail as such. The cultural detail fits into the general configuration later. The Murphys and Newcomb illustrate the point by saying, "Deep as the American's respect for the flag may be, the roots of the respect have to be laid in attitudes toward the family and the neighborhood group with whom one first takes part in patriotic exercises."

CHILDHOOD

Feeding and Cleanliness Training. Through cross-cultural comparisons, anthropologists have learned from their data what psychiatrists suggested from theirs: Differences in the feeding and cleanliness training given children are powerful determinants of intercultural differences in personality formation. Customs concerning breast feeding and weaning, regarding the control of defecation and urination vary widely. Some apparently stimulate tendencies toward dependence, revolt against maternal or paternal authority, competitiveness, co-operativeness, self-expression in accumulative or oral activity, etc.

In our own society, the casualness with which many responsible medical practitioners ignore the personality consequences of early child training is rather shocking at times. *Time* (July 9, 1945) reports a rare attack on hospital deliveries by a physician, Dr. Harry Bakwin of the New York University College of Medicine, thus: "Separating the baby from its mother at birth, instead of allowing it to be cuddled and breastfed, is a bad beginning. . . . The crime is compounded when the baby is put on a clock-ruled feeding schedule." Here, as in so many other places in our society, institutional and professional convenience rather than personality consequences becomes the factor controlling policy.

Growth. The psychological growth of a child may be regarded as a long process of learning through imitation and rejection and of ego-reinforcement or psychological weaning, of gradually achieving independence from mother and father. "Wise parents keep several jumps ahead of the child, welcome the changes in him, and help him discover the more mature satisfactions of each successive stage. These changes come with such rapidity and complexity, especially in the early years, that even the best parents feel their capacities of adjustment to be inadequate."[1]

The Course of Personality Development, like that of the physical organism, is never a straight line. There are spurts, plateaus, and even regressions. A. L. Gesell, in his *First Five Years of Life* (1940), concludes, "even in the prodigiously complicated field of personality formation, growth factors are primarily determining. . . . Growth is a key concept." Kurt Lewin and others, on the other hand, have demonstrated the effects of frustration in retarding and even lowering the level of a child's achievements, and they have also attested to the value of favorable stimuli. At any rate, the basic training period (oral and anal-urethral), the family drama, and the fact of growth join with the emotional experiences of certain transitional periods ("little adolescence" and adolescence) as crucial aspects of the person's life-history.

Sequence of Age-Roles. Between the ages of two and four, the child begins to get around more freely, to function more independently. His critical abilities develop more rapidly than his dexterities, and a certain degree of floundering and frustration results. This is the age of the "little adolescence," as it has been called, the period of transition from the child's first role, that of being a baby, to a role labeled enticingly by parents as that of "big girl" or "big boy." Unless parents have great patience and understanding, this is a period of considerable strain for the child.

As children mature, they proceed through a series of ill-defined roles, roles that identify them with children of a similar age level and sex and that provide them with invidious distinctions from the age-roles now behind them. This sequence of roles, this quest and struggle for greater maturational status, plays a significant part in sibling rivalry and in the formation of play groups, gangs, and friendships. Jessie Bernard, in her *American Family Behavior* (1942), comments thus on the consequences of such sibling rivalry: "One man's whole life is spent in achieving goals which his sister unconsciously set for him

---

1 Katharine W. Taylor, "Parent-Child Interaction," chap. 20 in R. Hill and H. Becker, eds. *Marriage and the Family* (Boston: D. C. Heath & Co., 1942), p. 454.

years ago; he must prove to her that he can do it. One woman's life is shattered because of her ambivalent attitude of hatred and love for a brother who dominated her childhood."

ADOLESCENCE

Nurture and Adolescence. Margaret Mead, in her *Coming of Age in Samoa* (1928), and other investigators do not find in certain primitive societies the tensions and strains, the sharp contrasts between childhood and maturity, which characterize adolescence in our society. Because of the morals-mores contrasts in our culture, coupled with our competitiveness and emphasis upon individuality and personality, the transitional period known as adolescence is indeed a difficult one among us.

Problems of Adolescence. In our society, the social distance between the generations and the moralistic rather than moretic preparation for adulthood leave children nearing sexual maturity to work out many problems alone or with inadequate or damaging guidance. Symptoms of the period are a boy's regressive unkemptness and crude manners, a girl's similar silliness and irresponsibility, contrasted sharply with periodic efforts at mature appearance and behavior. Major developments towards which such evolving personalities strive are: emotional emancipation from parents; initiation into the mores of adult groups; and satisfactory heterosexual adjustment.

SELECTED READINGS

Anshen, Ruth N., ed. *The Family: Its Function and Destiny.* New York: Harper & Bros., 1949.

Brown, F. J. *Educational Sociology.* New York: Prentice-Hall, 1947.

Calhoun, A. W. *A Social History of the American Family.* New York: Barnes & Noble, 1945. Re-issue of 3 vols., 1917–1919, in 1 vol. Vol. 2, chaps. 6, 8, 9; vol. 3, chaps. 4–6, 8.

Deutsch, Helene. *The Psychology of Women.* New York: Grune & Stratton. Vol. 1, "Girlhood," 1944.

Elmer, Manuel C. *Sociology of the Family.* Boston: Ginn & Co., 1945.

"The Family," *American Sociological Review* (1937), 2:591–778.

Folsom, Joseph K. *Family and Democratic Society.* New York: John Wiley & Sons, 1943.

Frazier, E. Franklin. *The Negro in the United States.* New York: Macmillan Co., 1949.

Gesell, Arnold, and others. *The Child from Five to Ten.* New York: Harper & Bros., 1946.

Goodsell, Willystine. *A History of Marriage and the Family.* Rev. ed. New York: Macmillan Co., 1934. Chaps. 9, 11.

Groves, Ernest R. *The Contemporary Family*. Philadelphia: J. B. Lippincott Co., 1947.

Groves, Ernest R., and others. *The Family and Its Relationships*. Philadelphia: J. B. Lippincott Co., 1949.

Hill, Reuben, and Howard Becker, eds. *Family, Marriage, and Parenthood*. Boston: D. C. Heath & Co., 1948.

Isaacs, Susan. *Social Development in Young Children*. London: G. Routledge & Sons, 1933. Part 1, chap. 3.

Klein, H. R., H. W. Potter, and Ruth B. Dyk. *Anxiety, Pregnancy, and Child-birth*. New York: Paul B. Hoeber, 1950.

Kluckhohn, Clyde, and Henry A. Murray, eds. *Personality in Nature, Society, and Culture*. New York: A. A. Knopf, 1948.

Landis, P. H., and J. T. Landis. *Social Living*. Boston: Ginn & Co., 1949.

Lumpkin, Katharine D. *The Family: A Study of Member Roles*. Chapel Hill: Univ. of North Carolina Press, 1933.

Murdock, G. P. *Social Structure*. New York: Macmillan Co., 1949.

Murray, H. A., and others. *Explorations in Personality*. New York: Oxford Univ. Press, 1938. Chap. 5.

Nimkoff, M. F. *The Child*. Chicago: J. B. Lippincott Co., 1934.

Partridge, E. D. *Social Psychology of Adolescence*. New York: Prentice-Hall, 1938. Chaps. 6–7.

Piaget, Jean. *The Moral Judgment of the Child*. Trans. by Marjorie Gabain. London: K. Paul, Trench, Trubner & Co., 1932. Chap. 4.

Sears, Robert R. *Survey of Objective Studies of Psychoanalytic Concepts*. New York: Social Science Research Council, 1943.

Shirley, Mary M. *The First Two Years*. Minneapolis: Univ. of Minnesota Press, Vol. 1, 1931. Vols. 2 and 3, 1933.

Stern, Bernhard J., ed. *The Family: Past and Present*. New York: D. Appleton-Century Co., 1938. Chap. 13.

Sumner, W. G., and A. G. Keller. *The Science of Society*. New Haven: Yale Univ. Press, 1927. Vol. 3, part 5.

Thomas, W. I., and Dorothy Swain Thomas. *The Child in America*. New York: Alfred A. Knopf, 1928.

Thomas, W. I., and Florian Znaniecki. *The Polish Peasant in Europe and America*. 2nd ed. New York: Alfred A. Knopf, 1927. 2 vols.

Truxal, A. G., and F. E. Merrill. *The Family in American Culture*. New York: Prentice-Hall, 1947.

Van Waters, Miriam. "Adolescence, *Encyclopaedia of the Social Sciences* (1930), 1:455–459.

Waller, Willard. *The Family: A Dynamic Interpretation*. New York: Dryden Press, 1938. Chaps. 1–6, 22.

Warner, W. Lloyd, and Leo Srole. *The Social Systems of American Ethnic Groups*. New Haven: Yale Univ. Press, 1945. Chap. 6.

Westermarck, Edward. *History of Human Marriage*. New York: Macmillan Co., 1921. 3 vols.

Williams, Frankwood. *Adolescence*. New York: Farrar & Rinehart, 1930.

Zachry, Caroline. *Emotion and Conduct in Adolescence*. New York: D. Appleton-Century, 1940.

CHAPTER THIRTY-TWO

COURTSHIP, MARRIAGE, DIVORCE

Marriage Defined. Marriage is the public joining together, under socially specified regulations, of a man and a woman as husband and wife. It may or may not initiate cohabitation. It gives social recognition to the formation of a new family of procreation, to use W. Lloyd Warner's term, but this conjugal unit may take its place within a large and cohesive consanguineal family organization.

The marriage ceremony may be a very simple act or the occasion for elaborate celebrations lasting for many days, but throughout the world its essential characteristic is that it is a public agreement. Premarital and extramarital sexual arrangements are not to be confused with marriage, a morally and moretically defined social institution.

TYPES OF MARRIAGE

Most Common Types. At the time of Christ, the most common type of marriage specified by societal morals was the *monogynous* (one husband, one status or ranking wife, and one or more non-status or assistant wives or socially recognized concubines). The most common type of marriage actually practiced then, for numerical and economic reasons, was monogamy. At the present time, the morals most commonly specify *monogamy* (one husband and one wife at a time).

Other Types. But the world's tribes have sanctioned many other arrangements. In fact, all mathematical possibilities in formalizing relationships between men and women have been tried in the world's multiplicity of cultures. Other types of marriage have included *monandry* (one husband, not necessarily permanent, does not exclude polygyny), *polyandry* (one wife and two or more husbands who are usually brothers), *polygyny* (one husband and two or more full-status wives), and *group marriage* (two or more husbands, two or more wives).

All of these forms are far from comparable in prevalence and persistence to the two major types, monogyny and monogamy. All except monogamy are properly referred to as forms of *polygamy* (many marriages in force at once).

Multiple wives (especially monogyny and polygyny) are associated with economic conditions under which they perform valuable functions, or they are a means to obtain or demonstrate heightened status and prestige. *Multiple husbands* (polyandry, group marriage) may be an adjustment to female infanticide or to arduous economic conditions. Examples of polyandry are found among the Todas of southern India, the northern Tibetan tribes, and occasionally elsewhere; of group marriage, among the Todas, the Chukchee of eastern Siberia, and the experimental Oneida Community established in 1848 in New York State.

Significance of Marriage Types. The mere fact that "everything has been tried" in marriage forms is not an argument for claiming that "everything" might well be attempted in our society. Each of the marriage forms mentioned is or has been a part of the culture of a number of tribes. Each was taken seriously, believed in, and lived by. Any notion that they have been or should be treated casually is without supporting evidence of an adequate sort.

Endogamy and Exogamy. Groups and classes in all societies define, with more or less precision, the groups and classes from which their young people may obtain or into which they may be taken as spouses. Groups, classes, castes, and tribes are thus said to be exogamic (to practice "out-marriage") with respect to a certain in-group of variable extent, and to be endogamic (to practice "in-marriage") within a certain wider or different group. Examples in our society are the moral and legal prohibitions on marriage between close relations and the social pressure brought to bear upon a person to make a "suitable" marriage, that is to say a marriage with someone within certain prescribed groups, determined ethnically, racially, economically, religiously, and educationally.

Sociologically, endogamy and exogamy have greatest significance in terms of cultural borrowing and stimulation or cultural isolation. Regardless of whatever might be true physiologically, too close inbreeding in a class, caste, or society makes for *cultural* sterility. Exogamy, within broad limits, especially between spouses with diverse ethnic backgrounds, makes for cultural stimulation through the intimate assimilation of new practices.

COURTSHIP CUSTOMS

Variability. Courtship customs vary throughout the world at least as much as do marriage customs. They include conventions ranging from the use of force, music, dancing, and exchange of presents to periods of trial sexual intercourse, "bundling," and other more or less controlled ways of "keeping company." The highly romantic coloration of courtship and even the kissing in our culture are far from universal. Whatever the customs may be, however, they are geared to family interests, marriage morals, and the provision of care for the resulting offspring. Exceptions are not morally sanctioned, even though they may occur and may even have the moretic sanction of a group or groups in a society.

In the United States. J. L. and J. P. Gillin, in their *Introduction to Sociology* (1942), list four objectives of American courtship, as follows: (1) *selection*, an opportunity to assess the qualifications of potential mates; (2) *accommodation*, apprenticeship in the business of getting along on intimate terms with one of the other sex; (3) *maturation*, the development of a sense of personal and social responsibility; and (4) *sexual stimulation*. The first three objectives, to the extent that they are functionally operative, represent group and societal interests given effect by mores and morals; the fourth point provides the dynamic.

GETTING ACQUAINTED. The means through which the sexes may become acquainted differ in terms of social classes and such class attributes as education, organizational resources, family connections, money, social prestige, and definition of the purposes of various kinds of "dates," not all of which anticipate marriage as a possible outcome. The methods vary from meetings in carefully sponsored organizations and parties to "blind dates" and "pickups," any of which might and sometimes actually does lead to marriage.

TYPICAL STEPS IN COURTSHIP. The sequence of steps to be followed during a complete courtship is described in current terms and with appropriate modifications to suit a range of needs in the popular magazines, comic strips, motion pictures, and gossip. After the initial meeting, the steps may include a period of "dating," with progressively more intimate "necking" and "petting," the exchange of gifts to suggest seriousness, finally the "heart-to-heart talk," then "steady dating," the proposal, and the announcement of the engagement.

COURTSHIP PROBLEMS. While some nine of ten American adults eventually marry, courtship problems include the difficulty with which educated women in certain professional groups meet potentially suitable males. Various dating bureau schemes have been tried, as supplements to existing facilities, but there remain a number of apparently unwilling and eligible isolates. The World War II situation further aggravated this problem by removing so many men from the United States for periods of years, some of whom married in other countries.

AMERICAN MARRIAGE PATTERNS

Ethnic and Racial Minorities. The colorful marriage customs and ceremonials in some of our urban minority sections suggest that other Americans might eventually be tempted to adapt some of them to their own uses. But in discussing family patterns in their *Social Systems of American Ethnic Groups* (1945), W. Lloyd Warner and Leo Srole comment, "The American social system is not, strictly speaking, a 'melting pot' which fuses its diverse ethnic elements into a new amalgam, as was once popularly believed, but is rather a system which performs the transmutation of diverse ethnic elements into elements almost homogeneous with its own." Backgrounds are forgotten or rejected; even names are changed. The personalities of American-born children of Irish descent, for example, "in a complete sense, are American Catholic." More and more, marriage patterns deviate along class and class-religious lines.

The American Ideal. Ideally, monogamy is not only the rule, but the theory is that Americans should be joined together "until death," some say "forever." This implies premarital chastity, postmarital fidelity, and a single standard of morality. While a delay in childbearing has greater moral sanction now than formerly, marriage morals call for the establishment of a home and the procreation and proper care of children as primary objectives of marriage.

Changing Marriage Mores. Even though marriage morals change but slowly and more in interpretation than in form, group mores defining marriage practices may be at considerable variance with them and may even exhibit striking sensitivity to changing climates of opinion. For example, as a result of the backwash of World War I and of the business boom of the 1920's, social compulsion developed in the younger set for its members to "go as far as they dare." The sobering effects of the depressed 1930's and of World War II apparently diminished this compulsion toward sexual looseness among the unmarried, and the war stimulated early marriages. It is likely that another wave of sexual laxity among the young will follow the second war.

Working Wives. Time was when women worked outside their conjugal homes only when they *had to.* Husband, children, and house were primary considerations. With the rise of gadgetry, bakeries, laundries, corner restaurants, nursery schools, and school restaurants, not to mention modern contraception techniques, in certain groups it is now a matter of whether or not wives can get outside employment. They dislike the routine of small homes, the anonymity of urban living or the "goldfish bowl" existence of the suburbanite, and want to get out and meet new situations. In 1900, one in eighteen married women was gainfully employed; in 1940, one in less than five. World War II further stimulated this trend, and as after World War I, women are not likely to give up all of their gains toward this type of independence. Such working and also prolonged education are frequently associated, but not necessarily, with delayed childbearing and the fact that the United States has almost as many "criminal" abortions as live births.

Increasing "Marriedness." Working in particular is more significantly correlated with such facts as the increasing "marriedness" of the American population. In 1890, 55 per cent of those fifteen years of age and over were married; in 1940, a little more than 61 per cent were. Modern conditions of shared responsibilities, the spacing of births in a wise and hygienic manner, and better educational opportunities for both man and wife have encouraged and permitted more of the population to be married. If we achieve an increasingly rational view of sex and sex hygiene and of the roles of motherhood, fatherhood, and family life, and if we obtain more adequate opportunities for employment and for the enjoyment of life, the "criminal" abortion rate will drop sharply.

SEPARATION

Marriages may be temporarily broken by war, migration, hospitalization, imprisonment, or employment conditions, or permanently broken by desertion, divorce, hospitalization, imprisonment, or death. If the separation is more than a brief one, it can create far-reaching problems.

War Separations. War becomes a great major premise in private discussions and arguments, a reason or a rationalization for many private courses of action. It stimulates the abbreviation of courtship. It provides a way for husband or wife to solve temporarily an irritating family situation by enlisting or, in the case of the husband, more plausibly, by being drafted. It is a heart-rending period of anxiety for wives who got on well with their husbands and who want and need them back. The breaking up of a crystallized relationship, the working out by each party of new wartime adjustments which may come to appear more desirable than the old, the need for making new postwar adaptations between spouses with somewhat changed personalities— these are crucial problems for husbands and wives to face in wartime separations. Children may have to confront, possibly during their most formative years, the consequences of the absence of father or mother, of makeshift living conditions, of a broken home with all that that implies.

Other Temporary Separations. The migrant husband, with newly gained sophistication, may be shocked by th\ extent to which he has "grown away" from his family. He ma⸳ also anticipate this, not send for them to come to the new home, and "disappear." Long-term hospitalization raises humanitarian and sentimental considerations that may make the sacrifices entailed much easier to bear than in other cases. But the shame of imprisonment makes a permanent break the more likely.

Bereavement. One-fourth of American marriages, according to M. F. Nimkoff, are currently widowed at any time, and four-fifths of these broken marriages are husbandless. To meet the shock here and also in the case of divorce, routines are invaluable during the time needed for a reintegration of the survivors' perspectives and relationships. Some cultures prohibit remarriage of a widow and others make remarriage for widow or widower difficult, but in our society an intelligent attitude by associates can prevent handicaps.

DESERTION AND DIVORCE

Desertion. Thomas D. Eliot estimates that there are at least 50,000 desertions a year in the United States, more during depressions. Desertion differs from separation in that separation involves some arrangement or understanding, some "agreement to disagree." The separation arrangement may be voluntary or compulsory, and it usually includes provision for support. In both desertion and separation, as Eliot observes, "there may be hope or fear of return on either side." Desertion, most often by the husband, results chiefly from emotional, even neurotic problems. It is a way out for those who cannot bring themselves to use more regular procedures and who lack the imagination, resources, or luck to engineer an "unavoidable" separation.

Types of Desertion. Because of the social pressures of associates, legal recourses available to the deserted, and need for the severance of professional and other status ties, desertion is relatively rare among middle- and upper-class families, more common among low-wage-earning groups, both skilled and semiskilled, and among such underprivileged people as the Northern urban Negroes. Earle E. Eubank, in his *Study of Family Desertion* (1916), lists these five types of deserters: (1) the *spurious*, interested in dodging or in helping his family dodge some financial responsibility; (2) the *gradual*, an outgrowth of enforced absences from home, found especially among immigrants and discharged soldiers; (3) the *intermittent*, chronic but temporary deserter; (4) the *ill-advised-marriage*, also called the "poor man's annulment"; and (5) the *last-resort*, flight from what appears to be a family situation with no other solution, the "poor man's divorce."

Divorce in the Light of Culture Comparisons. As Mabel A. Elliott and Francis E. Merrill note, in their *Social Disorganization* (1950), "Since marriage is often a leap in the dark, many unforeseen situations arise which make continued sharing of a common life impossible. Hence legal provision for release from the bonds of matrimony is as inevitable as legal wedlock." Most cultures provide, therefore, some method or methods for handling marital frauds, misunderstandings, and errors. Methods range from the return of a bride price or dowry with some form of public renunciation or cancellation of vows to legal proceedings looking toward annulment or divorce. Causes depend upon the character of marriage standards and upon the status of women. They may be restricted to one or a few, such as barrenness, disloyalty, and disabling mental and physical diseases, or they may include such broad categories as "incompatibility."

Divorce in Our Culture. St. Paul and other early church fathers had little enthusiasm for marriage and less for divorce. In I Corinthians, St. Paul advised, "If they cannot contain, let them marry. For it is better to marry than to burn." He was strongly opposed to divorce. "Let not the wife depart from her husband," he wrote, "but and if she depart, let her remain unmarried, or be reconciled to her husband and let not the husband put away his wife." Jesus, according to St. Matthew, recognized fornication as a basis for a man putting away his wife, with the stipulation that anyone marrying such a woman committed adultery. As a result of these positions and of revolts against them in personal behavior and in the mores, a constant struggle between Christian fundamentalists and advocates of a more socialized doctrine covering marital relationships has been in progress for many generations.

Divorce in the United States. Divorce—like marriage—laws differ in the states of the United States, as well as from country to country in what we are pleased to call our Western Civilization. But the variations in divorce law create striking problems, because a person may be married to one spouse in terms of the law of one state, to none in another, and to several in a third. Acceptable causes range widely, but actual causes probably have much more in common. Actual causes are irritations and tensions, misunderstandings and incompatibilities, that drive husband and wife apart. Because of the artificialities of the law, the causes stated and argued in court may have little in common with the actual psychological ones, which as a matter of fact the principals might not even recognize themselves. Current morals demand that the wife should sue for divorce and that the husband, regardless of the situation unless the wife is too notorious, should provide proper and tenable legal grounds for divorce. In other words, collusion to mitigate the harshness of the divorce morals is relatively common. Wives initiate three in four divorce suits.

Adultery is accepted throughout the United States as a ground for divorce. Bigamy has similar status with respect to annulment, and it may be grounds for divorce in one-fourth of the states. Most states also recognize conviction of a crime,

cruelty, desertion, fraud, impotency, insanity, and nonsupport
as justifiable grounds for divorce action.

Two major types of divorce exist: (1) *absolute*, which returns
the parties to the status of single persons; and (2) *partial*, or legal
separation of "bed and board." Decrees *nisi* may provide the
latter type for a trial period, perhaps a year, before the divorce
is declared "absolute." Alimony, usually payable to the wife
but occasionally as in Illinois to a needy husband, is provided
for in all states. It is intended as a way of effecting equitable
adjustments in financial arrangements, especially to cover the
costs of child-care.

Is More Divorce More Family Disorganization? Just short
of a quarter-million divorces are granted in the United States
each year. Even though the people of this country have tended
to be more and more married, the rising tide of divorces has
brought talk about marriage being an "outmoded institution."
Children of divorced parents suffer psychological damages such
as one expects from broken homes, but the children of incom-
patible parents who are "fighting it out" may suffer even greater
psychological wear and tear. Some say that it "builds character"
to face a marital maladjustment judiciously and continue to
live and work it out. In general, however, taking into consideration as many handicaps and problems as possible, the weight
of evidence seems to indicate that the frank and wise use of
divorce as an instrument of social adjustment has made of
marriage a more workable human institution.

SELECTED READINGS

Baber, Ray E. *Marriage and the Family*. New York: McGraw-Hill Book Co.,
1939. Chaps. 6–9, 14, 15.

Bernard, Jessie. *American Family Behavior*. New York: Harper & Bros., 1942.
Chaps. 15–20.

Bowman, Henry A. *Marriage for Moderns*. New York: McGraw-Hill Book
Co., 1942.

Bromley, Dorothy D., and Florence H. Britten. *Youth and Sex*. New York:
Harper & Bros., 1938.

Burgess, E. W., and Leonard S. Cottrell, Jr. *Predicting Success or Failure in
Marriage*. New York: Prentice-Hall, 1939.

Burgess, E. W., and H. J. Locke. *The Family*. New York: American Book
Co., 1945.

de Rougemont, Denis. *Love in the Western World*. New York: Harcourt,
Brace & Co., 1940.

Deutsch, Helene. *Psychology of Women*. New York: Grune & Stratton. Vol. 2,
"Motherhood," 1945.

Drake, St. Clair, and H. R. Cayton. *Black Metropolis*. New York: Harcourt, Brace & Co., 1945. Chaps. 19, 20.

Eliot, Thomas D. "Family Crises and Ways of Meeting Them," chap. 22 in R. Hill and H. Becker, eds. *Family, Marriage, and Parenthood*. Boston: D. C. Heath & Co., 1948.

Elliott, Mabel A., and Francis E. Merrill. *Social Disorganization*. 3rd ed. New York: Harper & Bros., 1950.

Elmer, M. C. *The Sociology of the Family*. Boston: Ginn & Co., 1945.

Folsom, Joseph K., ed. *Plan for Marriage*. New York: Harper & Bros., 1938.

Foster, Robert G. *Marriage and Family Relationships*. New York: Macmillan Co., 1944.

Goldstein, S. E. *Marriage and Family Counseling*. New York: McGraw-Hill Book Co., 1945.

Groves, Ernest R., and G. H. Groves. *The Contemporary American Family*. Philadelphia: J. B. Lippincott Co., 1947.

Groves, Ernest R., and others. *The Family and Its Relationships*. Rev. ed. Philadelphia: J. B. Lippincott Co., 1949.

Harper, Robert A. *Marriage*. New York: Appleton-Century-Crofts, 1949.

Hart, Hornell, and E. B. Hart. *Personality and the Family*. Boston: D. C. Heath & Co., 1935.

Jennings, Helen Hall. *Leadership and Isolation*. 2nd ed. New York: Longmans, Green & Co., 1950.

Levy, J., and R. Munroe. *The Happy Family*. New York: A. A. Knopf, 1938.

Lichtenberger, James P. *Divorce*. New York: McGraw-Hill Book Co., 1931. Chaps. 4, 5, 10, 14.

Lindsey, B. B. *The Companionate Marriage*. New York: Boni & Liveright, 1927.

Merrill, Francis E. *Courtship and Marriage*. New York: William Sloan Associates, 1949.

Mowrer, Ernest R. *Family Disorganization*. Chicago: Univ. of Chicago Press, 1939.

Mowrer, Harriet R. *Personality Adjustment and Domestic Discord*. New York: American Book Co., 1935.

Nimkoff, M. F. *The Family*. Boston: Houghton Mifflin Co., 1934. Chaps. 10, 11.

Smith, Russell G. *Fugitive Papers*. New York: Columbia Univ. Press, 1930. Pp. 40–59.

Terman, L. M., and others. *Psychological Factors in Marital Happiness*. New York: McGraw-Hill Book Co., 1938. Esp. chaps. 8–10.

Truxal, A. G., and F. E. Merrill. *The Family in American Culture*. New York: Prentice-Hall, 1947.

Vernier, Chester G., and others. *American Family Laws*. Palo Alto: Stanford Univ. Press, 1931–1938. 5 vols. Esp. vol. 2.

Waller, Willard. *The Family: A Dynamic Interpretation*. New York: Dryden Press, 1938. Esp. pp. 173–304.

Waller, Willard. *The Old Love and the New*. New York: Boni & Liveright, 1930.

Williams, P. H. *South Italian Folkways in Europe and America*. New Haven: Yale Univ. Press, 1938. Chap. 6.

CHAPTER THIRTY-THREE

ROLES

We each have numbers of more or less related roles that we assume and put off, store in our minds for future use, revise, or permit to retire into our subconscious, perhaps to be brought forth again. As the preceding chapters suggest, these roles are of four major types: societal; group, class, and caste; personal-external; and personal-self.

SOCIETAL ROLES

Definition. Societal roles are prescribed by the conventions and morals of a society. Just as societal institutions represent configurations of conventions and morals in terms of broadly felt needs, interests, and wishes, so societal roles are configurations of morals in terms of the man-as-he-should-be in some area of social life, to take another term from W. G. Sumner's *Folkways* (1907). Such roles include those for bride and groom, mother and father, and various age levels of sons and daughters, to mention only the chief ones touched upon in the two preceding chapters. They also include functionary and member roles in other societal institutions. Hughes discusses such roles and their personal significance in relation to institutions in Chapter XXVIII.

Societal roles, like the morals giving them substance, tend to be absolute in statement or form, albeit vague and open to interpretation and rationalization. They contain large elements of promise and aspiration, asceticism and humanitarianism. To the extent that societal functionary roles are believed in popularly, such roles provide valuable crystallizations of status and power for those publicly granted to possess them, for example government officials, physicians, ministers, teachers.

Ambivalent Attitudes toward Functionaries. The roles of societal functionaries of considerable prestige arouse ambivalent sentiments in the minds of their publics, the groups with which they are in contact. A mother or father, as a societal surrogate, is both loved and hated by his or her offspring. Individuals who have reached the intimate and trusted status achieved by the medical profession are similarly subject, personally and as members of a group, to feelings both of gratitude and high expectation on the one hand and of distrust and rejection on the other. Illustrations of such attitudes toward governmental officials readily come to mind.

In a Changing Society. Especially as society changes, human beings can seldom measure up to the idealizations current concerning how they as societal functionaries should behave. Regardless of the brightness and shininess of their tunics, the creatures within them are forced to reveal themselves, at least to those who prod, as what they are, human beings with feet of clay. But supported as they are in their necessary shortcomings by their group's mores, societal functionaries in a changing culture do what they can to combat efforts to undermine their prestige by frantic or noble efforts to re-establish popular acceptance of the weakened moral patterns. A part of this is frequently the drafting and promulgation of codes of ethics.

Although it may be far from fair, the public which helps to create impossible idealizations also seldom excuses its idols for failing to appear to live up to these idealizations. News stories or unprinted rumors of fee-splitting by physicians, of the unfairness of "company" doctors to employees, founded or unfounded gossip concerning irresponsibility by practitioners in times of private crisis, even misrepresentations of a physician's natural weariness at the end of a hard day as callousness—all these are very real problems to the medical profession.[1] And in our changing culture, other societal functionaries have similar problems more or less as pressing.

Member Roles. Societal roles prescribe both how the man-as-he-should-be behaves as a functionary in places of responsibility, prestige, or leadership, and also how he acts as a member, a part of the rank-and-file of institutions and associations. Such societal member roles define what the citizen, the consumer, the soldier, the businessman, the trade-unionist, the parent ought to be like. They are useful in social control and, like uniforms, in giving otherwise insecure persons the security that comes

---

[1] See A. M. Lee, "The Social Dynamics of the Physician's Status," *Psychiatry* (1944), 7:371–377.

through a sense of identification with something much larger than themselves.

GROUP, CLASS, AND CASTE ROLES

Definition. Group and class roles are prescribed in the folkways and mores of the groups and classes of a society. Where there is a caste system, as the Negro-white one in this country and the more elaborate one in India, one effect is to slice the society's groups and classes along caste lines. Group and class mores are similar on either side of the caste line, except for the pervasive influence of the fact of segregation expressed in terms of conventions and morals and of modifications in folkways and mores.

Group Roles. A group role represents an integration of a group's traditional experiences and expediencies, its folkways and mores, to set the *intragroup* pattern of the man-as-he-has-to-be in the area of social interaction of concern to the group. This is a type which usually contrasts in many respects with the *intergroup* or societal pattern, the moral man-as-he-should-be prescribed by the corresponding societal role. Social distance obscures such contrasts to outsiders, and appropriate rationalizations make them tenable to insiders. A group (an association, a clique, or whatever) is brought into being, of course, to satisfy one or more common interests, needs, or wishes of its membership. It may be an association, a class, a caste, or one of the more dynamic types mentioned by Blumer in Part IV of this outline. The child, marriage, and family roles mentioned in the two preceding chapters illustrate what is meant by group roles as well as by societal roles.

Class Roles. A class role is a role prescribed for a member of one of those larger and rather inclusive groups called social classes. W. Lloyd Warner and Paul S. Lunt, in *The Social Life of a Modern Community* (1941), define a social class as one of "two or more orders of people who are believed to be, and are accordingly ranked by the members of the community, in socially superior and inferior positions. Members of a class tend to marry within their own order, but the values of the society permit marriage up and down. A class system also provides that children are born into the same status as their parents. A class society distributes rights and privileges, duties and obligations, unequally among its inferior and superior grades." Warner and his associates found six social classes among the whites in "Yankee City," as follows: (1) *upper-upper*, "old families" born to their position; (2) *lower-upper*, "new families" or newly rich; (3) *upper-middle*, the successful men and women who are the "pillars of society," the skilled managers and professionals who see that things "get done"; (4) *lower-middle*, the small tradesmen, skilled workers, and white-collar workers "who cling to the virtues of the 'protestant ethic,' despite the fact that many are members of other religions"; (5) *upper-lower*, "the poor and respectable workers, who hope and strive to do better than they are doing, but who worry for fear of falling into the class below them"; and (6) *lower-lower*, the "shiftless Yankees" and the "ignorant immigrants." Negroes, where they are sufficiently numerous, have a somewhat similar class hierarchy. The first three classes, according to Warner and Srole, *The Social Systems of American Ethnic Groups* (1945), comprise less than 15 per cent of the population but are "the big people" who regard themselves as "above the common run of men."

Each of these classes, or however the class system may be defined in a given community or society, tends to orient the whole pattern of thinking, striving, and behaving of its members for whom it prescribes roles. Group, class, and caste roles have powerful influences upon the formation of the personalities of their members.

Caste Roles. A caste role is a role or coloration of other roles set in a larger sense by conventions and morals and more specifically by caste folkways and mores for all parties involved in the caste system. Castes differ from classes in being quite strictly endogamous, with sanctions brought to bear against both in-groupers and out-groupers who break the taboo. In analyzing an extreme caste expression by whites, a lynching, Neal E. Miller and John Dollard, in *Social Learning and Imitation* (1941), attribute the drive behind a lynching to "three closely allied but separable forms" of fear: "fear of economic rivalry, fear of sexual assault on white women, and fear of bodily attack to white men or women." Norman D. Humphrey and the author concluded in their *Race Riot* (1943) that such Negro expressions as the Harlem Uprising of 1943 have similar motivations. Because the Negro caste is the submerged one, these motivations take the forms of frustration in the face of economic exploitation (including too-successful rivalry), dread of sexual exploitation of Negro women, and insecurity occasioned by white domination of police and government and their own political ineffectuality.

Caste roles, even more than class roles, are characterized by the fostering of centripetal sentiments of caste ethnocentrism. These take the form of overevaluation of a given caste, caste justification, and stressing caste identifications such as color as inescapable labels.

PERSONAL–EXTERNAL ROLES

The personalized aspects of societal and group roles that are socially performed are prescribed for individuals by their practices and habits, terms related to group and societal trait patterns in Chapter XXX. Except for permissible mannerisms, as for example personal variants in speech, personal-external roles resemble quite closely the group and societal role types the supposed audience supposedly anticipates.

The number of short stories and novels written about the theme of the tyranny of social roles, especially by unadjusted writers in such periods of flux as that following World War I in the 1920's, testifies to a fact not usually bothersome or even recognized, viz., the tyranny of social roles over our behavior. It takes a maladjusted or unadjusted person to detect this tyranny, and it takes an unadjusted period to give his writings a vogue.

Lincoln Steffens sums up the popular attitude toward the deviation of group and personal-external roles from those of the societal man-as-he-should-be in a passage in his *Autobiography* (1931). "I have told how," he notes, "as the boy chum of a page in the Legislature of California, I had seen from below the machinery and bribery of politics; as a New York reporter I had seen police, political, legislative, and judicial corruption; but I did with these observations what other people do with such disturbing knowledge: I put them off in a separate compartment of the brain. I did not let them alter my conception of life." It was for this reason, he says, that for many years he was an acceptable newspaper reporter and editor. "You may beat the public to the news, not to the truth." As much can also be said of personal-external role deviants in other ways (see Chapter XXXIV). Most men, even under a yoke as bitter as Nazism must have been to the sensitive, forego opportunities for heroic social service to protect themselves and their families with the "protective coloration" at least of adhering to societal role patterns.

PERSONAL–SELF ROLES

The self is the internal aspect of personality. It is usually analyzed further into its subjective constituent, the ego or "I," and its objective constituent, the superego or "me." The subjective self is what consciously reacts to stimuli. It is the integration of the person's consciousness. It is the element of the self which the person looks to see reacting in its "looking glasses," in the responses of other people, to use Cooley's conception. To use Mead's terms, what the "I" is doing is patterned by the "me," directly or indirectly, positively or negatively. The "I," as Mead puts it in *Mind, Self & Society* (1934), is "the response of the organism to the attitudes of the others; the 'me' is the organized set of attitudes of others which one himself assumes." The "me" or objective self is the sum of social experiences with others, an extended conception of the conscience. It includes an awareness of the behavior traits of others, both specifically (practices) and in generalized forms (folkways and conventions).

Personal-self roles are roles of the "I" taken on from the "me" and from fantasies as reactions to internal and external events. They are self-dramatizations for the benefit of self, either kept in the realm of fantasy or permitted to color the person's social behavior. To give the "I" some stability and security in the face of the frustrations and uncertainties of life, the "I" dramatizes itself in terms of various roles which are accurate or distorted counterparts of the roles performed by admired, envied, or detested people plus those recounted in historical and imaginative writings. Genealogies, lodge rituals, religious personages and roles, cults, and imagination all aid in the substantiation and proliferation of such self or "I" roles.

ROLES IN SOCIAL MOVEMENTS

Social movements, as Blumer says in Chapter XXII of this outline, "can be viewed as collective enterprises to establish a new order of life." Member roles in such movements in part derive from the role types prescribed by societal and group culture and in part represent novel and experimental modifications in such types. The roles of functionaries in movements, however, include certain well-recognized types.

Types of Roles in Social Movements include (1) agitators, (2) professional promoters, (3) "fronts," (4) bureaucrats, (5) "heelers," (6) "just members," and (7) "fellow travelers." These are not mutually exclusive categories. They are rough role types. Naturally, too, these like other more or less specialized roles draw different emotional and intellectual types to them depending upon the types to which they appeal.

Agitators usually partake of what Max Weber has called the charismatic. They have been given some special grace. They have a mission. Whether paid or volunteer, they furnish the emotional drive, the personal symbolism, the unflinching zeal, the really dogmatic and uncompromising fanaticism that serves as the spearhead of a movement's campaigns and program.

Professional promoters differ from agitators chiefly in these two ways: (1) their motivation is primarily "professional," i.e., monetary, service, artistic, security-giving, or status-giving; and (2) they sell their services upon the basis of professional competence in one or more areas necessary to the movement. Tending to have an objectivity unmixed with super-emotionalism, they help to stabilize and direct a movement towards realizable goals.

"Fronts" are non- or slightly-participating people possessed of statuses of prestige, some of which prestige they presumably transfer to the movement through accepting a tenuous identification with it.

Bureaucrats trail behind the agitators and professional promoters in any movement. They are those with small talents and narrow aspirations who see opportunities for jobs as such and little more. They know the arts of memo-passing, protective coloration, and self-preservation and care for little else than the comparative security thus provided.

"Heelers" and *"just members"* are the great rank-and-file of any movement. Heelers are the more faithful and helpful soldiers of the army. Just members are the casual contributors of funds, the members of audiences, the bulk of mailing lists of "interested people," the persons who "think it's a good thing" and "want to be identified with it."

"Fellow travelers" are those who perform the role of carrying a movement's message without being identified with the move-

ment's organizations and perhaps without even knowing of their role in the movement.[1]

From the foregoing, it is apparent that professional promoters and all the rest except agitators derive their value to a movement chiefly from their roles in other connections as defined societally and in more stable groups, including classes and castes. The agitator role represents a tentative new integration of aspirations which may have characterized the morals for many generations, but in addition the agitator portrays other roles (class, caste, ethnic, vocational, religious, or whatever), possibly exaggerated, which bring him into relation with other people.

ROLE CHANGE AND VERTICAL MOBILITY

To go from one social class to another, either up or down in the prestige scale, requires the acquisition of a new class role, a decided shift in personality. As Miller and Dollard point out, in their *Social Learning and Imitation* (1941), "Persons subordinated in a hierarchy have great difficulty in fully approximating the behavioral symbols of those above them. It requires a long period of specific training to change social habits completely, and most people, even those who are most mobile, rarely find themselves in a really adequate learning situation." (See last part of Chapter XXX above.) Even the entering of a new intraclass or interclass group, whether of age or interest and in which no class change is necessary, as we have seen, presents problems. But these problems are rendered less difficult in such cases by initiation arrangements of a formal and informal nature. But to "pass," to go from one caste to another, granted skin color suitable for the purpose, requires decided and rather fundamental adjustments.

The circulation of individuals from class to class or from caste to caste is referred to as *vertical mobility*. Anti-circulation forces include both the centripetal ones that build class and caste solidarity and also centrifugal ones that work against those who attempt to invade the group without adequate identification. Both groups of forces are aided in the United States by the fact that immigrant ethnic and racial groups are usually forced to "start at the bottom and work up." The price for being permitted to "work up" frequently becomes that of assimilation, loss of ethnic minority and racial identity.

1 Adapted from A. M. Lee, "Techniques of Social Reform: An Analysis of the New Prohibition Drive," *American Sociological Review* (1944), 9:65–77, esp. 73–74.

SELECTED READINGS

Britt, S. H. *Social Psychology of Modern Life*. Rev. ed. New York: Rinehart & Co., 1949.

Cooley, Charles H. *Human Nature and the Social Order*. Rev. ed. New York: Chas. Scribner's Sons, 1922.

Davis, Allison, and John Dollard. *Children of Bondage*. Washington: American Council on Education, 1940. Part 2.

Dollard, John. *Caste and Class in a Southern Town*. New Haven: Yale Univ. Press, 1937.

Dollard, John. *Personality and Psychotherapy*. New York: McGraw-Hill Book Co., 1950.

Hartman, G. W., and T. M. Newcomb, eds. *Industrial Conflict*. New York: Dryden Press, 1939.

Hartshorne, Hugh, and Mark A. May. *Studies in the Nature of Character*. New York: Macmillan Co., 1928–1930. 3 vols.

Jennings, H. H. *Leadership and Isolation*. New York: Longmans, Green & Co., 1943.

Johnson, Charles S. *Patterns of Negro Segregation*. New York: Harper & Bros., 1943. Chaps. 11–15.

Kluckhohn, C., and H. A. Murray, eds. *Personality in Nature, Society, and Culture*. New York: A. A. Knopf, 1948. Part 2.

LaPiere, R. T., and P. R. Farnsworth. *Social Psychology*. 3rd ed. New York: McGraw-Hill Book Co., 1949.

Lindesmith, A. R., and A. L. Straus. *Social Psychology*. New York: Dryden Press, 1949.

Mead, George H. *Mind, Self & Society*. Ed. by Charles W. Morris. Chicago: Univ. of Chicago Press, 1934. Part 4.

Murphy, Gardner. *Personality: A Biosocial Approach to Origins and Structures*. New York: Harper & Bros., 1947.

Newcomb, T. M., and E. L. Hartley, eds. *Readings in Social Psychology*. New York: Henry Holt & Co., 1947.

Parsons, Talcott. *The Structure of Social Action*. Glencoe, Ill.: The Free Press, 1949.

Sherif, Muzafer. *Outline of Social Psychology*. New York: Harper & Bros., 1948.

Simmons, Leo W. *Sun Chief*. New Haven: Yale Univ. Press, 1942.

Veblen, Thorstein B. *The Theory of the Leisure Class*. New York: Modern Library, 1934.

Warner, W. Lloyd, and others. *Social Class in America*. Chicago: Science Research Associates, Inc., 1949.

Weber, Max. *The Protestant Ethic and the Spirit of Capitalism*. Trans. by T. Parsons. London: G. Allen & Unwin, 1930.

Young, Kimball. *Social Psychology*. 2nd ed. Appleton-Century-Crofts, Inc., 1944.

CHAPTER THIRTY-FOUR

DEVIANTS

Deviants and the Processes of Socialization. A society has within it tremendous forces making for uniformity, for the persistence of trait, personality, and institution types, for the preservation of the *status quo*. Its rewards and punishments stimulate overwhelming drives toward accepting and adhering to its norms of behavior and toward finding self-expression in terms of them. At the same time, in society—as throughout the known universe—is the pervasive and disturbing fact of change. Conditions change and help to select societal variations that adapt somewhat to them. The pressure for change, especially when resisted, may bring breaks in established structures, and such breaks in societal structures may assume the proportions of a revolution or of annihilation.

Individual deviations along "innate" lines and personal, group, and societal deviations along cultural lines are constantly appearing in human society. Some personal deviants become symbols or spearheads of social change. Others have limited utility for a time and then yield to social pressure. Many others fail, and society ignores them or places them in institutions for the segregative care of criminals and mental patients.

Social deviants as social problems are treated by Humphrey in Part I of this outline. In the present chapter, the salient phenomena of social deviation are interpreted in terms of the socialization of the individual.

TYPES OF DEVIANTS

Definition. Deviants are taken to be persons who, for any given complex of causes, do not conform to social norms sufficiently to keep from being regarded as different, queer, superior, inferior, unusually virtuous, or unusually evil. Because of their social significance, famous or notorious deviants individually and problem deviants considered as groups are of more interest to sociologists than minor deviations.

Causation. The outline of nature-nurture influences in Chapter XXX applies here as well as elsewhere. In his book on the type of deviation known as genius, a noted investigator[1] characterizes the causation situation for famous and notorious deviants in general by saying that that type of deviation depends upon "nothing absolute" and consists of "not a being but a working." Genius, he goes on to say, may result from "a favourable concatenation of circumstances"; "the concentration of fame upon one individual instead of upon the real multiplicity of producers"; "the might of psychopathological illusion"; or "the outcome of supreme talent." And he adds, "Almost everywhere, and especially in the subjective fields of imaginative writing, religion, and music, gifted 'insanity' gains the victory over simple, healthy talent."

Studies of inventors, political and business leaders, scientists, artists, and criminals come to similar conclusions. To become famous or notorious, such persons must have been (1) born at the right time and place or precipitated in some other way into the right combination of circumstances, (2) given credit due as well to many others, (3) fortunate in the psychic delusion that drives them, or (4), probably not nearly as often as one might expect or wish, except in combination with the others, possessed of a "supreme talent." Most commonly, one finds combinations of all such factors have been at work.

Cross-cultural studies indicate that a type of mental deviant that is outcast, hospitalized, exploited, or imprisoned in one society may be accorded special status, honor, and authority in another. Whether or not a deviant is a social problem, a social asset, or just another person depends upon the whole cultural situation, group, class, caste, and societal. Here as elsewhere in society the principle of societal or cultural relativity has application. Every person and every cultural element depends for what it is upon the other persons and cultural elements in the society and upon the society's general configurations.

Types. For the purposes of this outline, deviants are treated under these headings: (1) the deficient and the deranged, (2) the criminal, and (3) the famous.

---

[1] Wilhelm Lange-Eichbaum, *The Problem of Genius* (trans. by E. and C. Paul. New York: Macmillan Co., 1932), pp. 28, 140, 159.

THE DEFICIENT AND THE DERANGED

Feeble-mindedness. In *The Inheritance of Mental Diseases* (1925), Abraham Myerson notes that feeble-mindedness, "as a symptom, is a congenital or early acquired lack of mental ability, manifested by an incapacity or diminished capacity to remember, to learn, to carry out the functions of mind in the degree we recognize as normal." It may be caused by malformation, malnutrition, injury, disease, or a combination of two or more of these afflictions. Some, not as amented as others, are called subnormals or borderline defectives. In terms of the Stanford Revision of the Binet-Simon test, the definitely feeble-minded have intelligence quotients (I.Q.'s) below 70; the dull or borderline, 70–80; the very superior, 120–140; and "near" genius or genius, 140 and more. Regarded as more satisfactory now are the various measurements of mental "profiles" which test aptitudes, talents, dexterities, and potentialities along a number of different lines. They are called "profile" tests because the scores are not averaged but given separately for each aspect, and a person's series of scores may then be compared with available norms.

Because of the hereditary and intra-uterine factors in feeble-mindedness, various sterilization plans have been advanced to help decrease the problem. Fortunately, in view of the fact that a large share of feeble-mindedness is not hereditary but caused or augmented by other factors, the states of the United States have approached the matter with extreme caution. Situational therapy, special educational techniques, and kindly understanding are said to yield useful results here, and the encouragement of reproduction by the mentally superior is likely to do more to offset inferior biological and cultural parentage than sterilization of a radical sort.

The Mentally Deranged. Because of the strangeness of mental derangements, the demented have often been treated throughout history with the extremes of superstition and brutality. Dementia may be functional or organic; it may be a neurosis or a psychosis. But no such broad, general division of the field is too satisfactory, because of controversies over definition. The 1934 classification adopted by the American Psychiatric Association includes lists of psychoses due to infection; intoxication; trauma; disturbances of metabolism, growth, nutrition, or endocrine function; new growth; and "unknown or hereditary causes, but associated with organic changes." It also sets forth lists of "disorders of psychogenic origin or without clearly defined tangible cause or structural change," prominent in which are psychoneuroses and psychasthenia or compulsive states.

The account by Clifford W. Beers of his own experiences as a mental patient, *The Mind That Found Itself* (1908), did much to stimulate the scientific study and prevention of mental disease. Another more recent book, *Alcoholics Anonymous* (1937), and the organization of the same name, a co-operative movement of alcoholics who know they are mentally ill and who seek to aid themselves and others, have done much to broaden the group interested in a more scientific and humane approach to the problems of psychotics and neurotics in general.

The Deranged as Failures in Socialization. Except for those incurably deranged at birth, derangement represents either a failure of the processes of socialization in which the person has taken part, a maturation of innate deranging elements in the person's make-up, or an accident, a deficiency, or a disease. Some such failures in socialization were mentioned in the discussion of feral boys and girls in Chapter XXX. Others may result, not from the deprivation of ordinary social and cultural contacts, but from aberrations in them either continually or at certain critical life-history periods. The latter may be situational or linked more specifically to what are called traumatic experiences. One of the great problems in environmentally initiated or nurtured derangements is the lack of understanding of the person by others, the frequent failure of others to accept the fact that the deranged person is mentally ill. Experts in psychic abnormalities agree that popular education could do much to diminish the extent of mental disease in this country.

Therapies for the Deranged. The therapeutic techniques used to cope with mental diseases vary widely. Medical psychiatrists use a range of drugs, shock treatments, sedatives, rest, occupational procedures, music, hypnosis, situational modifications, etc. Psychoanalysts try to help their patients make the facts of their life-histories conscious for the purpose of re-examining, "re-living," and thus understanding and adjusting to them. This is done to allay old anxieties and fantasms, to enable the patient to live more sensibly with his subconscious self and superego. J. L. Moreno, through his psychodrama, encourages his patients to re-enact traumatic and other possibly significant incidents in a theater-like setting with the help of "auxiliary egos" who take the parts of others in incidents. Others, for example Fritz Redl, have developed what are known as clinical group-work techniques in which carefully designed interacting groups, with appropriate activities, are used for therapeutic purposes. Such group work has been used especially with delinquent and deranged juveniles. Unfortunately, the techniques available for curing or readjusting the deranged are expensive, and trained workers are few in number.

Under the impact of high-speed modern life, with our cultural elements in a flux that confuses many, with strains that make for growing anxieties, figures for the mentally ill continue to mount, especially in urban areas. Great strides have been made in World War II in effecting practical adjustments for patients, in educating them in classes and with publications and other visual materials, and in instructing their families and the American public as a whole in the nature of psychoneurotic discharges from the armed forces and of mental illnesses in general. In this, certain regular commercial motion pictures have probably been the most helpful. The improvement and broadening of such efforts can do much to promote human mental health.

THE CRIMINAL

Definition. As ordinarily conceived, a criminal is a person who has broken a criminal law, has been caught, and has been convicted. Some might increase the scope of the definition; they might say that a criminal is a person whose conduct has been adjudged antisocial in a respect covered by the criminal laws.

But such crystallizations of societal morals leave many sociological questions of significance unanswered. In his startling 1939 presidential address before the American Sociological Society, Edwin H. Sutherland pointed to the narrowness of such definitions in an analysis of white-collar criminality. He pointed out that relatively few so-called criminals are members of the dominant upper and upper middle classes, that crime and criminology are defined in terms of lower-class convictions, but that even those investment swindlers, stock waterers, unpatriotic cartel manipulators, and others who are caught cost society far more than all lower-class criminals combined.

What Sutherland pointed to is this broad sociological and human situation: Convicted criminals are a sample drawn by a social mechanism ;from a much larger group of people who have violated criminal statutes. Even that much larger group is, in turn, a segment of a still larger group who have committed anti-social´acts. What an antisocial act might be at a given time and place is, of course, a function of the society's evolving morals and of the class interests dominant in its moral structure.

What makes people violate criminal statutes? What makes people engage in antisocial behavior? How are criminals selected at any given time and place?

John Steinbeck suggests the pervasiveness of such questions in his novel, *Cannery Row* (1945). He makes a lovable character say to a friend, "It has always seemed strange to me. . . . The things we admire in men, kindness and generosity, openness, honesty, understanding and feeling are the concomitants of failure in our system. And those traits we detest, sharpness, greed, acquisitiveness, meanness, egotism and self-interest are the traits of success. And while men admire the quality of the first they love the produce of the second." It is perhaps an over-simplification, but it is a probing suggestion, and it is not some-thing to be found only in our own culture.

Criminals and Socialization Processes. Generally speaking, antisocial persons are products of (1) individual deviation, (2) group deviation, or, most commonly, (3) a mixture of both. Juvenile sexual perverts are usually more of the first type. Juvenile thieves and gangsters are frequently quite "normal" members of groups whose folkways and mores are regarded by "society" as delinquent. Since individual deviants tend to find and join deviant groups and are thus stimulated in their devia-tion, mixtures of both rather than "pure types" are usually found.

From a causal standpoint, this is a highly significant typifi-cation. In the first group are persons who are psychologically maladjusted, mentally ill, and should be treated as such. Upon them, for personal, family, and other reasons, the ordinary proc-esses of socialization failed to produce the usual degree of uni-formity. A deviant family drama, traumatic experiences at critical periods in life-history, or some physiological problem may have initiated the situation. In the second group, the group deviants, are persons who took on the membership characteristics or roles of social groups whose folkways and mores specified behavior regarded by "society" as criminal. Here one has a problem of adjusting the person to new group cultures and of changing group cultures that make for lower-class or white-collar criminality. Such students of man and law as Judge Ben Lindsey, Clarence Darrow, and Lincoln Steffens took the position that, in many criminal cases, society might well be convicted of permitting such group culture and conditions to persist but that the person in custody only did what might have been anticipated.

THE FAMOUS

Problems of Eminence. In *The Way of All Flesh* (1903), Samuel Butler differentiates the ordinarily successful man from other deviants by saying, "The successful man will see just so much more than his neighbors, as they will be able to see too when it is shown them, but not enough to puzzle them. It is far safer to know too little than too much. People will condemn the one, though they will resent being called upon to exert themselves to follow the other." It is because of social pressure toward uniformity that it takes an unusually aggressive, persistent, heedless, or fortunate person to scale the heights of popular acclaim or esteem that are labeled eminence or fame. It is thus little wonder that in so many cases, as it is mentioned at the outset, "gifted 'insanity' gains the victory over simple, healthy talent."

Factors Making for Fame. After investigating the life-histories of 628 eminent American women, Elizabeth Briant Lee in her *Eminent Women* (1937) concludes that her subjects achieved fame, on the whole, because of (1) need, especially economic need frequently precipitated by the death of the male breadwinner, (2) a combination of social and cultural factors, and (3), but not nearly as frequently or importantly as the two preceding, superior mental endowment. Subjects "were found whose capacities appear not to have been especially extraordinary yet who chanced through a fortunate combination of circumstances ultimately to have become famous." She listed the following social and cultural factors as being especially propitious, granted the drive furnished by need: (1) born into a small family; (2) a high standard of living but not too great wealth, enough to provide formal schooling and other means to develop abilities but not enough to prevent the growth of self-reliance and economic independence; (3) childhood in or very near a large urban center; (4) a professional father and an active mother who share their lives and interests with their few offspring; (5) familiar early association with outstanding characters, either as relatives or family friends; (6) liberal religious training; (7) available educational opportunities; and (8) available economic or career opportunities. With so many different careers represented by the 628 women, this is naturally a very generalized summary.

The situation for men requires only a few obvious modifications. Need, in the form of economic need, is more prevalent, and the need can probably be satisfied more readily by men than by women. This is where extra drive, opportunity, or luck plays its part. Liberal religious training, point (6) above, probably has more significance for women than for men because of the taboos on female deviation in many fundamentalist beliefs. The last two points may be broadened and illustrated with some "as ifs." If Charles Darwin had become as an infant a member of the primitive Todas of southern India, he might have been something of a leader, but he would not have been enshrined in biology textbooks and Westminster Abbey. Similarly transferred at birth, Abraham Lincoln would not have become President of the United States or even of India, and he would not have been likely to free any slaves.

LEADERS AND SOCIAL CAUSATION

Leadership Defined. A leader is a person (1) who occupies a leadership status, a culturally set position of dominance or control, in a group or society, (2) who is the symbol of a movement and understands its personnel well enough to be its internal and external spokesman, or (3) who has few or no immediate followers but who charts courses later taken up and followed. Illustrations are respectively (1) a hereditary kingship, (2) the headship of a new trade-union, and (3) a writer "ahead of his time."

What Can a Leader Do? Extreme answers to this question are common. With a contempt for the common man that led him into pro-Nazi sympathies, Alexis Carrel in his *Man the Unknown* (1935) asserted, "Humanity has never gained anything from the efforts of the crowd. It is driven onward by the passion of a few abnormal individuals, by the flame of their intelligence, by their ideal of science, of charity, and of beauty." A far more measured conclusion is that of A. G. Keller, in his *Societal Evolution* (1931), when he says, "The great man is the product of his time and place, and his greatness consists in his insight, or luck, in producing a variation—in anticipating some massive movement that is about to take place anyhow. He is the protagonist in adjustment to existing . . . and to altered life-conditions of society, not the dictator or challenger of either. This is no derogation from his greatness. . . . But the determining social cause is something very different from the human agency; the latter is always secondary and relatively incidental, and wholly ineffective by itself. . . . The effective cause lies in the unpremeditated movement of the masses of men. The great man interprets them to themselves."

SELECTED READINGS

Anastasi, A., and J. P. Foley. *Differential Psychology*. New York: Macmillan Co., 1949.

Barnes, H. E., and N. K. Teeters. *New Horizons in Criminology*. Rev. ed. New York: Prentice-Hall, 1947.

Blumer, Herbert, and P. M. Hauser. *Motion Pictures, Delinquency, and Crime*. Chicago: Univ. of Chicago Press, 1933.

Bogardus, Emory S. *Leaders and Leadership*. New York: D. Appleton-Century Co., 1934.

Burrow, Trigant. *The Neurosis of Man*. New York: Harcourt, Brace & Co., 1949.

Cantor, N. F. *Crime and Society*. New York: Henry Holt & Co., 1939.

Carr, L. J. *Delinquency Control*. Rev. ed. New York: Harper & Bros., 1950.

Cavan, Ruth Shoule. *Criminology*. New York: Thomas Y. Crowell Co., 1948.

Cooley, Charles H. "Genius, Fame, and the Comparison of Races," *Annals of the American Academy of Political and Social Science* (May 1897), 9:317–358.

Cox, Catharine M., and others. *The Early Mental Traits of Three Hundred Geniuses* (L. M. Terman and others, *Genetic Studies of Genius*, vol. 2). Stanford Univ. Press, 1926.

Davies, Stanley P. *Social Control of the Mentally Deficient*. New York: T. Y. Crowell Co., 1930.

Elliott, Mabel A., and Francis E. Merrill. *Social Disorganization*. 3rd ed. New York: Harper & Bros., 1950.

Ellis, Robert S. *The Psychology of Individual Differences*. New York: D. Appleton-Century Co., 1928.

Faris, Robert E. L., and H. Warren Dunham. *Mental Disorders in Urban Areas*. Chicago: Univ. of Chicago Press, 1939. Esp. chaps. 2, 10, 11.

Fülöp-Miller, René. *Leaders, Dreamers, and Rebels*. New York: Viking Press, 1935.

Glueck, S. S. and E. T. *Criminal Careers in Retrospect*. New York: Commonwealth Fund, 1943.

Horney, Karen. *Neurosis and Human Growth*. New York: W. W. Norton Co., 1950.

Keller, A. G. *Societal Evolution*. Rev. ed. New York: Macmillan Co., 1931. Chap. 4.

Klineberg, Otto. "Genius," *Encyclopaedia of the Social Sciences* (1931), 6:612–615.

Lasswell, Harold D. *Psychopathology and Politics*. Chicago: Univ. of Chicago Press, 1930.

Lee, Elizabeth Briant. *Eminent Women: A Cultural Study*. MS. Ph.D. dissertation. New Haven: Yale Univ. Library, 1937.

Lee, Alfred M., and Elizabeth Briant Lee. *Social Problems in America*. New York: Henry Holt & Co., 1949.

Leuba, James H. "Religious Beliefs of American Scientists," *Harper's* (1934), 169:291–300.

Lindner, Robert M. *Rebel without Cause*. New York: Grune & Stratton, 1944.

Mowrer, Ernest R. *Disorganization: Personal and Social*. Chicago: J. B. Lippincott, 1942. Chaps. 3–7.

Pigors, Paul J. W. *Leadership or Domination*. Boston: Houghton Mifflin Co., 1935.

Pollack, O. *The Criminality of Women*. Philadelphia: Univ. of Pennsylvania, 1950.

Reckless, W. C. *The Crime Problem*. New York: Appleton-Century-Crofts, 1950.

Reckless, W. C. *Etiology of Delinquent and Criminal Behavior*. New York: Social Science Research Council, 1943.

Redl, Fritz. "Group, Emotion and Leadership," *Psychiatry* (1942), 5:573–584.

Schmidt, Richard. "Leadership," *Encyclopaedia of the Social Sciences* (1933), 9:282–287.

Smith, Mapheus. "Occupations of Eminent Men," *Scientific Monthly* (1943), 57:52–62.

Sutherland, E. H. *Principles of Criminology*. 3rd ed. Chicago: J. B. Lippincott Co., 1939.

Sutherland, E. H. *White Collar Crime*. New York: Dryden Press, 1949.

Taft, D. R. *Criminology*. Rev. ed. New York: Macmillan Co., 1950.

Tannenbaum, F. *Crime and the Community*. Boston: Ginn & Co., 1938.

Tappan, P. W. *Juvenile Delinquency*. New York: McGraw-Hill Book Co., 1949.

Thomas, W. I. *The Unadjusted Girl*. Boston: Little, Brown & Co., 1923.

Thorpe, Louis P. *The Psychology of Mental Health*. New York: Ronald Press, 1950.

Von Hentig, H. *Crime: Causes and Conditions*. New York: McGraw-Hill Book Co., 1947.

White, R. W. *The Abnormal Personality*. New York: Ronald Press, 1948.

Wood, A. E., and J. B. Waite. *Crime and Its Treatment*. New York: American Book Co., 1941.

Chapter Thirty-five

THE PERSON AND SOCIAL POLICY

Society is pictured to us popularly in many guises. Some are terrifying and are calculated to encourage us to depend for security upon some great and good source of authority. Others give the person a challenge and self-reliance.

Society as a Super-Monster. To some, society is a monster crashing its way down through the forests of time. Each of us, like a cell in the monster's body, has his day in the huge functioning organism and then disappears. Management—the definition and execution of social policy—is an automatic affair dictated by the nature of the beast and of other beasts (societies) and the exigencies of the jungle. That is a caricature of the nineteenth-century perspective of such social philosophers as Herbert Spencer. It still has adherents from among those whose cells are well placed and who thus believe that change might be disastrous to the lumbering superorganism.

Society as a Mechanism Guided by Wise Men. To others, society is or should be like the mechanism of a huge corporation or of a gigantic governmental bureaucracy. Each person works or should work in an office or plant at understood tasks and had best leave problems of policy to the wise men at the helm, the financiers, skilled management technicians, and possibly labor union leaders of a "responsible" sort. The degree to which the "wise men" are left alone depends upon the extent to which the society has relatively a loose or a definite class system. The more definite and accepted the class system may be, the greater will be the power of rationalizations that the "wise men" know what is "best" for the rest of us. The basis for this "wisdom" may be divine revelation, personal age, hereditary status, conquest, or scholarship. But whatever the basis, so long as popular compulsion upon those in control is lacking, it is an aristocratic or pseudoaristocratic conception, with all the limitations that that implies.

Society as All of Us. To still others, society consists of and depends upon the activities, experiences, and thoughts of all of us. This conception is well illustrated by the way in which scientific advancements take place. Such advancements result, with rare if any exceptions, not from sweeping "flashes of genius" by occasional "great men." They come from the gradual accumulations of bits of knowledge by thousands of small men, the "hod carriers" and "bricklayers" of science. Even in the arts, the outstanding practitioners show their heads and shoulders *among* their fellows in a movement. So, too, changes in social policy frequently come, not because the wise men at the helm want them and plan for them, but because of the gradually accumulating experience and conviction of thousands and millions of people. Despite tremendous opposition, "open-shop" cities and industries have become unionized, sometimes by unions with meager resources of a financial sort. Despite tremendous vested power, too, outworn governments have crashed before the onward sweep of new and popular political movements.

THE UNDISTINGUISHED AND THE UNREASONABLE

Sociologists tend to favor the latter view of society, society as all of us. They know the utility of leaders and great men as symbols, as crystallizers of sentiment. They know that leaders can sense the direction being taken and can rush out ahead and say, "Follow me!" And this may at times save some wear and tear on the body politic by facilitating social change. But sociologists are even more aware of the contributions to social policy and social change by the rest of us, *the undistinguished*, and those who goad us, *the unreasonable*.

Tolerating "the Unreasonable." In this whole situation, the chief problem sociologists see is this: When there is orderly and gradual change, the fewest people are hurt by change, the most gain by it, and society remains most healthy. The prevention of well-indicated changes stores up periods of tension and suffering. But the way-breakers for social change, whether gradual or drastic, are social deviants. They are those sufficiently aggressive and heedless to defy the overwhelming social forces making for uniformity and the maintenance of the *status quo*. They are the social manipulators of change just as the successful dominators of society are the social manipulators of stability or against change. And the chief characteristic of such manipulators or agitators of change is that they are—to established and satisfied members of society—unreasonable.

In his *Free Speech in the United States* (1941), Zechariah Chafee, Jr., presents quite clearly the social need for tolerating the "unreasonable." He cogently observes, "Too often we assume that such persistent trouble-makers are the only persons injured by a censorship or a sedition law, and conclude from the indiscreet and unreasonable qualities of their speech and writing that after all the loss to the world of thought has been very slight. Too often we forget the multitude of cautious and sensitive men, men with wives and children dependent upon them, men who abhor publicity, who prefer to keep silent in the hope of better days. We cannot know what is lost through the effect upon them of repression, for it is simply left unsaid." And he adds that the "agitator's effort is made on behalf of those thoughtful men as well as for his own sake; and if he wins, the gain to truth comes, not perhaps from his ideas, but from theirs."

A SOCIETY OF FREE MEN

The problem of encouraging the undistinguished through tolerating the unreasonable poses, stated otherwise, the problem of stimulating freedom, of maintaining a constantly rejuvenating society through making it a society of free men.

What Is a Free Man? In a novel of Italian life under the Fascist dictatorship, *Bread and Wine* (1937), Ignazio Silone has an anti-Fascist give his impression of what it means to be a free man. "Liberty isn't a thing you are given as a present," the man asserts. "You can be a free man under a dictatorship. It is sufficient if you struggle against it. He who thinks with his own head is a free man. He who struggles for what he believes to be right is a free man. Even if you live in the freest country in the world and are lazy, callous, apathetic, irresolute, you are not free but a slave, though there be no coercion and no oppression. Liberty is something you have to take for yourself. It's no use begging it from others." But the hero of Sinclair Lewis's *Gideon Planish* (1943) had a more typical reaction. "All the rest of his life, in crises, Gideon Planish was to say, 'But this isn't the time for it,'" relates Lewis. "It is the slogan of discreet Liberalism."

Now vs. Not Now. All are not freedom-loving deviants like Silone's anti-Fascist who suffer and die for human privileges. All are not self-centered puppets like Lewis's Planish who do nothing and do it in a valiant and dramatic fashion. The problem is to maintain sufficient freedom of discussion, sufficient access to the facts, and sufficient means of translating opinions into expressions of social policy for all significant minorities to make their actual impression upon social policy without recourse to extreme measures. As Marshall Field concludes, in his *Freedom Is More than a Word* (1945), "The greatest good can only be arrived at by discussion, conflict of opinion, and group decision. It cannot be planned nor can it be imposed from above. Anyone who labors under the delusion that it can is either a prospective tyrant or is in danger of throwing away his freedom to a demagogue. Discipline, yes—the survival of democracy depends on discipline. But it must be a self-discipline imposed by ourselves and for objectives we mutually decide upon. It must never be a discipline imposed from above by any person or group."

THE ROLE OF SOCIOLOGY

The struggle to keep our society reasonably in adjustment to changing life-conditions, reasonably rejuvenated, Robert E. Park said should take the form of a "revolution absolute," a continual rather than a spasmodic series of adaptations. And he regarded as the essential element in that "revolutionary" process, the acquiring and disseminating of accurate knowledge about society, both accurate facts and accurate theoretical formulations. The critics and guides in this process are the general social scientists, the sociologists, and their fellows in the segments of social science, especially the economists and political scientists.

From sociology, as Franklin H. Giddings put it, the practical man wants to know the range of possible choices or lines of activity, and the scientist furnishes such a conception by portraying as precisely as he can the nature of social order. "To the scientific mind the universe is order; to the practical mind it is possibility," Giddings observed in his *Studies in the Theory of Human Society* (1922). "Both minds, however, know that order and possibility are compatible; it is only the mind that is neither practical nor scientific which imagines that they are not."

As our scientific knowledge of sociology increases, practical men will have more confidence in it and come to base their decisions perforce more and more upon it. Within the framework of order and possibility thus described, the "undistinguished" multitudes—goaded by "unreasonable" deviants—will exert their pressures toward social change under their selected leaders. It is the duty of sociologists to make their facts more accurate, their theories more tenable, and thus their impartial guidance of social policy—in the society of "all of us"—the more sure and useful.

SELECTED READINGS

Allport, Gordon W. "The Psychology of Participation," *Psychological Review* (1945), 53:117–132.

Britt, S. H., ed. *Selected Readings in Social Psychology.* New York: Rinehart & Co., 1950.

Bury, J. B. *The Idea of Progress: An Inquiry into Its Origin and Growth.* London: Macmillan & Co., 1920.

Chapin, F. S. *Experimental Designs in Sociological Research.* New York: Harper & Bros., 1947.

Edwards, L. P. *The Natural History of Revolution.* Chicago: Univ. of Chicago Press, 1927.

Forbes, R. J. *Man the Maker.* New York: Henry Schuman, 1950.

Freud, Sigmund. *Civilization and Its Discontents.* Trans. by Joan Riviere. New York: J. Cape & H. Smith, 1930.

Gee, Wilson. *Social Science Research Methods.* New York: Appleton-Century-Crofts, 1950.

Giddings, Franklin H. *Civilization and Society.* Arr. and ed. by Howard W. Odum. New York: Henry Holt & Co., 1932.

Gouldner, Alvin W., ed. *Studies in Leadership.* New York: Harper & Bros., 1950.

Horney, Karen. *Neurosis and Human Growth.* New York: W. W. Norton Co., 1950.

Lundberg, George A. *Can Science Save Us?* New York: Longmans, Green & Co., 1947.

Lynd, Robert S. *Knowledge for What? The Place of Social Science in American Culture.* Princeton: Princeton Univ. Press, 1939.

Mannheim, Karl. *Diagnosis of Our Time.* New York: Oxford Univ. Press, 1944.

Odum, Howard W. *American Sociology.* New York: Longmans, Green & Co., 1951.

Ogburn, William Fielding. *Social Change: With Respect to Culture and Original Nature.* New York: Viking Press, 1922.

Parsons, Talcott. *The Structure of Social Action: A Study in Social Theory.* Glencoe, Ill.: The Free Press, 1949.

Renier, G. J. *History: Its Purpose and Method.* Boston: Beacon Press, 1950.

Sorokin, P. A. *Society, Culture, and Personality.* New York: Harper & Bros., 1947.

Sumner, William Graham. *Folkways.* Boston: Ginn & Co., 1907. Chaps. 19, 20.

INDEX